THE HISTORY
OF THE
OMEGA PSI PHI
FRATERNITY INC.

A BROTHERHOOD OF EXCEPTIONAL MEN OF LIKE ATTAINMENTS

AN UPDATE FOR THE PERIOD 1960 TO 2008

THIS UPDATE WAS WRITTEN AND ORGANIZED
BY
VERNON STEVE WEAKLEY

PUBLISHED BY ZWORLDNET PUBLISHING INC.
ISBN 0-9712310-5-2

THE HISTORY OF

A FEW WORDS FROM THE CHIEF AUTHOR

As Omega Psi Phi Fraternity celebrates its 100th year anniversary and many other glorious years beyond this historic date, it will be extremely crucial to its continued success for its members to know and clearly understand where we came from and how we got here. Armed with this valuable historical knowledge and wisdom, we will be able to soar to even greater heights and insure not only Omega's very existence but attain consistent levels of excellence long into the future. We pray that this effort in providing this long over due Omega History Book update, will accomplish this task. **Be it publicly known that this book is not commissioned, sanctioned or authorized by Omega Psi Phi fraternity Inc. It is an independent effort by Zworldnet Publishing.** *Purchasers be also advised that this book is subject to future revision and/or update after the 100th year anniversary and long into the future as necessary.* **Long Live Omega Psi Phi Fraternity Inc.!**

<<>>

Copyright 2012 by Zworldnet Publishing
This is a re-vision of the originally published version
ALL RIGHTS RESERVED

THE OMEGA PSI PHI FRATERNITY INC.

A GREAT OMEGA MAN ONCE SAID, "EVERYTHING RISES AND FALLS ON LEADERSHIP."

And with this opening statement, I give you our beloved Founders whose extraordinary vision and leadership we so humbly follow, have transformed the world.

THE FOUNDERS OF THE OMEGA PSI PHI FRATERNITY INC.

DR. ERNEST E. JUST

(1890-1941)

PROFESSOR FRANK COLEMAN

(1890-1967)

DR. OSCAR J. COOPER

(1888-1972)

BISHOP EDGAR A. LOVE

(1891-1974)

LONG LIVE OMEGA PSI PHI FRATERNITY INC. AND WITH IT THE DREAM OF ITS BELOVED FOUNDERS!

THE HISTORY OF

~ DEDICATION ~

First and foremost, this book is dedicated TO ALL MEN Of OMEGA PSI PHI FRATERNITY INC. This new update of the Omega History Book, (1960-2008) is also an extraordinary testament to the greatness of our courageous leaders past and present and the many, many hours that they have had to toil, sacrifice and spend away from their love ones and families to make certain the work of Omega was accomplished in excellent fashion. **Thank you, thank you, thank you, proud men of Omega.**

A great former Grand Basileus by the name of Burnel E. Coulon once shared with me how painful it was for him to be away from his family during the many years he labored for Omega in a leadership role. He went on to say that even though this excruciating pain, (constantly being away from his love ones, facing the dangerous lonely highways alone on many occasions, struggling ever forward even in times when he was not feeling well and often traveling in extreme bad weather) was almost unbearable at times, he knew that Omega deserved his all and with that he freely gave of this tremendous sacrifice so that the work of Omega Psi Phi Fraternity, Inc. could go on to lift his brothers, the Black community with them and the entire world as well. **There is no greater love than this my brothers!**

All of our leaders, at all levels of our fraternity, from our great Founders down to our local officers and committee chairmen deserve the utmost praise and the undying gratitude and respect from us all for their many sacrifices, extraordinary dedication and hard work. Further**, it is my honor to also officially proclaim that ALL MEN of Omega** are deserving of historical note and our everlasting love and utmost respect for their role in perpetuating this great organization. **It is to the gallant men of Omega Psi Phi Fraternity Inc. that we dedicate this new historical update of our beloved Omega Psi Phi Fraternity.**

As an additional special tribute, this labor of love is also dedicated to four now deceased great **Omega men.** They are Grant Reynolds, the 21st Grand Basileus of Omega Psi Phi Fraternity entering Omega chapter July 09, 1999; Herbert E. Tucker Jr., the 23rd Grand Basileus of Omega Psi Phi Fraternity, entering Omega chapter March 1st, 2007; Richard "Dick" Smith, who served Omega diligently at headquarters until his retirement and death, entering Omega chapter November 5th, 2006 and brother Eddie H. Taylor, who had the distinction of being the longest living Omega man for many years. He entered Omega chapter September 07, 2007 at the age of 98. All four were extraordinary men who helped Omega's brilliant light to shine and light the way for the world. They were tireless workers and fearless Bridge Builders who are missed tremendously. They are gone, yes. But, they will never be forgotten by **the loyal men of Omega Psi Phi Fraternity.**

~ INTRODUCTION ~

Greetings! This is Vernon Steve Weakley, a loyal, dedicated and loving son of Omega Psi Phi Fraternity Inc., I greet you in the Holy name of the Supreme Basileus of the Universe, the Holy Spirit and my Lord and personal savior Jesus Christ. This literary work is an update of the History of Omega Psi Phi Fraternity Inc. for the period 1960 to 2008. This book humbly takes up where brothers Herman Dreer's, Robert L. Gill's and their outstanding committees' published history books stopped. Be it publicly known by all that this new update is published independent of Omega Psi Phi fraternity Inc.. It has been published by Zworldnet Publishing for the historical enlightenment of the members of Omega Psi Phi fraternity and the general public.

Be clearly advised my brothers of Omega Psi Phi fraternity Inc., that **no fraternity secrets or sacred ritualistic information are contained in this publication.** Just as the previous historical updates by both Dreer and Gill were public information, this new update is published for the same purpose. Be advised that this book is an unauthorized publication. Be also clearly advised that no money came from Omega Psi Phi fraternity to produce this book. All funds to create this new version of this re-release/book as well as the initial release were independently provided by Zworldnet Publishing and/or Vernon Steve Weakley.

This Omega History Book project will provide a clear and accurate history of Omega Psi Phi Fraternity and its impact on America and African Americans in particular for the period 1960 to 2008. This new History update will serve to clearly demonstrate how Omega Psi Phi Fraternity Inc. has, not only made a significant positive difference in the lives of Black people, but the entire world. It is this author's **fervent** hope that this update will not only enlighten, be a beacon and shed light on our illustrious history but will also be an inspiration to young people, the general public at large and all Omega Men, past, present and future.

This new update involved the comprehensive gathering of historical data on Omega Psi Phi Fraternity Inc. from all across America and internationally for the period 1960 to the 2008. **It** endeavored to encompass all significant contributions, all noteworthy efforts and the resulting factual recordation of Omega Psi Phi Fraternity and all Omega men who have had pertinent impact on America and Omega Dear during this period. This project was massive and took over six years to complete. The resulting final product will be an enlightening, inspiring, uplifting literary work for many years to come.

Be clearly advised readers that this is an update of the previous history books written by the honorable Herman Dreer, Robert L. Gill and their committees. This book, with the exception of containing some basic historical information to enlighten a person who has no knowledge of Omega Psi Phi Fraternity, **will not routinely cover past historical information shown in the great works of Dreer and Gill occurring prior to this update period.** Additionally, please be advised that the quality of some of the pictures in this book are not good, given the years involved and their state when we found them. Rather than omit them, we elected to include them for historical purposes. **This is the nature of historical documents/files/pictures/books going back many years.**

The history rich period for this update has provided many interesting challenges for Omega and its members. The Founders of Omega Psi Phi Fraternity did not shrink from the task, nor did they pity themselves for being given the tremendous challenge to uplift the African American race. W.E.B. DuBois' talented tenth assertion must be our rallying cry in that it crystallizes the fact that Omega men must be in the forefront in lifting the Black community to higher heights.

Omega men are indeed the cream of the crop endowed with the divine gift of greatness. And, our great history and our individual and unified deeds bare witness to this fact and with that our readiness to step to the fore. Omega Psi Phi Fraternity Inc. is filled with many great Omega men who have had significant positive impact on America during this update period. There are undeniable facts, inspiring legends, and exceptional Omega men who have accomplished great things in their districts and at the international level, as well as in their personal lives and in their gallant exploits/professions across the nation. It is time that the world knows of Omega Psi Phi Fraternity's extraordinary contributions to the greatest country on earth and our proud race.

Information to produce this history book was obtained from many sources. Its historical content came from the official records of Omega Psi Phi Fraternity (the international office, Districts and local chapters) along with the Oracle, Clarion Call, the Grand Basileus Sword and Shield publication, the Omega Bulletins for the period, "Others Thought I Could Lead" by 28th Grand Basileus James S. Avery, interviews with significant internal parties such as all living Grand Basilei, and Dr. John S. Epps (the distinguished and highly regarded former Executive Director of Omega Psi Phi Fraternity for many years), from official Supreme Council minutes, Grand and District officer reports, Undergraduate Summit reports, the Grand Basileus joint and individual video interviews, The Omega Men of Distinction Booklet, various other history books and factual records on African Americans, Omega web sites containing factual historical data etc., Conclave and Leadership Conference minutes, the Omega Psi Phi Fraternity 2000 and 2001 Historical Calendar, Supreme Council minutes, the Clarion call, etc.

The author did not try to re-create the wheel where basic known history facts are concerned and/or were available. **Omega men please do not be offended because the history in this book came from many sources rather than exclusively from the independent creative efforts of the author.** This is the nature of historical facts, documents and its recordation. My mission was to gather and organize what was available from many sources, tie it together with our God given talents and from there, attempt to present it in an enthralling fashion. Omega's published history and the extraordinary men who have made it will be its own great reward to its membership, the world and most especially to its future members.

It is the author's hope **that Omega men will temper their judgment with the fact that the last sanctioned published history of Omega Psi Phi Fraternity was done in 1961.** The writing of an Omega History book is not an easy task. This new update is long over due and many men and/or committees going back to the seventies have tried but failed to get it done. Additionally, it is recommended by this committee that future historical updates at a minimum be performed and published at least every ten years. The latter will alleviate the problems associated with allowing so much history to accumulate. The latter created tremendous recordation and retrieval challenges that were encountered by this committee.

Additionally, it is also important to note that this is a **living document** that can be added to as necessary. I make this comment to make the point that while we painstakingly attempted to find every piece, be it microscopic or other wise and/or every hint of applicable Omega history so that we could include it in this update, we found that charge impossible given the sheer volume of information and the fact that much of the historical recordation are lost or not retrievable due to damage, poor storage conditions etc. We will continue to diligently search for, retrieve, repair and publish more applicable history, as we find it. The latter is also significant in that as Omega's glorious history continues to unfold, it will be necessary to record and continue to update this information. Please feel free to provide any verifiable corrections to the information in the book, additions or future historical information to Vernon (Bop Swalos) Weakley at Zworldnet@aol.com. Please put "Omega History Book Update 60-08" in the subject line.

As the author of this labor intensive work, I make the recommendation that in the future that Omega's historical recordation efforts be on going rather than stop and start or be non-existence as it was many of the last forty-eight years. The design of this particular project will allow for future historical inclusions for not only the future but also the past as it is found and retrieved. For the most part, I believe we have done a good job of compiling an enormous amount of Omega's pertinent history. I do understand the danger in the latter comment where the word pertinent is concerned. I ask that the membership have faith and trust that we (the committee) gave an extraordinary try to include all and accomplish the mission and the spirit of the objective.

Further, be advised that while it was the author's hope to be able to add all historical information of the great men of Omega Psi Phi Fraternity from the local, districts and international level, alas, it was not humanly feasible. **The history of Omega and the thousands of great men who call it their own is so great and vast, that it would cause this book to be over a thousand pages long, thereby placing it well outside of reason and the cost market for Omega as well as the buying consumer.** The point to be made and to remember is that Omega men or indeed on the move and are doing great things in all fields and areas in America. **WE ARE AN EXTRAORDINARY POSITIVE FORCE IN THIS COUNTRY INDEED** who have made an undeniable great mark! This is a testament to the greatness of Omega Psi Phi Fraternity Inc.. For this, our beloved Founders, I am certain in us, would be well pleased.

We have numerous Omega heroes who are doing fantastic things in their communities. While we, (this committee) cannot and will not diminish these great efforts, once we started to include them all, we found them simply to numerous to record. It was necessary to elect to reflect those major historical international, district and local level impact contributions rather than for example, who received a local honor in a particular chapter or other local level chapter accolades. We applaud these local efforts and publicly state that their work is indeed note worthy, but given the sheer volume, it did not make it feasible to do so in this book. This circumstance while unfortunate is in a sense a great thing if we are able to look to the silver lining because it says that **Omega Psi Phi Fraternity, having so, so many contributions, has truly done its part in, "Making A Difference In the Lives of Black People" and the World.**

For example, we have **had a nationally mourned hero come from our ranks. Dr. RONALD E. McNAIR, the famous tragically deceased Astronaut who lost his life in the 1986 Challenger space ship disaster, was a very active member of Rho Beta Beta chapter of Omega Psi Phi Fraternity Inc. at the time of his death.** This great and heroic Omega Man lost his life in an effort to advance the cause of mankind.

It is said that lightning rarely strikes in the same place twice. I dispute this theory where Omega Psi Phi fraternity is concerned and offer undeniable evidence of the greatness of the members of Omega Psi Phi Fraternity and this talent rich, God blessed organization. To provide additional examples of Omega's incredible contributions to America in a specific area, in addition to Dr. Ronald E. McNair, **I also proudly submit astronauts Robert H. Lawrence Jr., Major Frederick Drew Gregory, and Commander Charles F. Bolden Jr.**. These extraordinary men and legendary space pioneers are all Omega men. In fact, the first four African Americans to enter the training program and/or to actual become astronauts and fly in space are Omega men.

NASA Space Shuttle Commander **Charles F. Bolden** Jr. is a Hall of Fame, U.S. Astronaut who not only was the first African American Commander of a U.S. Space Shuttle but was also at one point, the highest ranking African American officer in the U.S military, serving as Major General in the Marine Corps. ***UPDATE- On May 28th 2009, newly elected president Barack Obama nominated Omega man Charlie F. Bolden to head NASA.** After confirmation hearings, Omega man, Charles F. Bolden became the first African American head of NASA. This is an extraordinary honor and accomplishment. The latter achievement again makes my point. Excellence is indeed our standard. Omega men always strive to rise to the top of their field, regardless of the challenges set before them. Omega man, Robert Henry Lawrence Jr., who earned a Ph.D. Degree in chemistry at Ohio State University was the first Black man selected to the United States astronaut program in 1966. He was tragically killed in 1967 in a training exercise in the infancy of the space program before having an opportunity to go into space. The latter fact is not something that is taught in American class rooms or is very well known. **Nevertheless, Robert H. Lawrence's gigantic foot print in the pages of history, will not be denied or left out as long as Omega Psi Phi Fraternity remains on this earth.** His courage, name and contributions will live on forever. The accomplishments of these great men will forever be known in the annals of American history. This is no coincidence.

Omega men have constantly been in the forefront of human advancement and made significant contributions in all areas in America. As an organization, Omega prides itself on this fact.

[1]

---

[1] Design by Jam All Night/ from the Rho Beta Beta website Jamal D. Williams Sr.

The men shown in the preceding pictorial collage are just a few of many extraordinary Omega men who have made profound and lasting contributions in their professions, to America and the African American race. Many African Americans who have distinguished themselves so clearly in numerous other areas are members of Omega Psi Phi Fraternity. **This is no accident. Omega Psi Phi fraternity routinely attracts greatness and men of extraordinary high quality and attainments endowed with what the Founders of Omega called the "Germ of Greatness." The Founders expressed hope was that Omega Psi Phi Fraternity, by way of its great men and their great deeds, and goodness, would infect the Black race in a very positive way and in doing so uplift the entire world.** The latter undeniably has been the case.

There are many great Omega men recognized as leaders in their organizations, communities, academics, the arts, science, military, athletics, business, in entertainment, civil rights, education, and government at the local, national and international levels just to name a few areas. You will be reading about their accomplishments in a chronological manner for this update period as this book unfolds. Some of these men include former Executive Directors of the NAACP Roy Wilkins, and Benjamin Hooks, former President of the National Urban League, Vernon Jordan, the Omega Psi Phi Fraternity Grand Basilei for the period and their Supreme Councils, Dr. Charles Drew the perfector of blood plasma, James A. Elam, successful business man and entrepreneur, President & CEO of the Rainbow/PUSH Coalition Jesse Jackson Entertainer Producer Bill Cosby and Judge H. Carl Moultrie I, just to name a few. In addition, two former governors William H. Hastie (U.S. Virgin Islands) and L. Douglas Wilder (Virginia), numerous presidents of historically Black colleges and universities; Earl Graves, Publisher of Black Enterprise Magazine, great politicians such as U.S. Rep. James E. Clyburn, Tony Grant, Banking genius and one of America's highest ranking business executives and many other extremely successful men in America are members of Omega Psi Phi Fraternity, Inc. Omega Psi Phi Fraternity Inc. applaud these men for their great work.

As humble as we Omega men may be, it is now time for our legendary deeds, outstanding attributes, contributions to our country and good work during this period to be told to the world. **More importantly, it is crucial to our future success for our**

membership to know and understand where we came from so that armed with this knowledge; we can soar to even greater heights. I pray that this new Omega History Book update accomplishes this task.

It is the author's expressed hope that this historical project will serve to lift Omega Psi Phi Fraternity to even higher greatness for many years to come. It is my expressed aim to energize, enthrall, excite, enlighten, and inspire our membership to even greater heights with the heightened awareness of and pride in Omega Psi Phi Fraternity's glorious history, exciting Omega heroes and its numerous past contributions and accomplishments during this history rich period (1960 to 2008) where men took steps on the moon and boldly walked into a new un-chartered millennium. And, with these great strides and accomplishments for mankind, came **undeniable Herculean efforts by Omega Psi Phi Fraternity and the many great Omega men who played key roles in improving our country, and in doing so, making a difference in the lives of Black people.**

Vernon (Bop Swalos) Weakley
Chief Author

<<>>

And now, an UPLIFTING, parting quote from the great MOSES C. NORMAN Sr., the 33rd Grand Basileus of Omega Psi Phi Fraternity, Inc. (Term 1984-1990)

"The Lamp is aflame, the candles are lit, the pearls are aglow, and our hearts are warm and filled with the love of brotherhood. Let us capture the moment for Omega."

<<>>

OMEGA MEN, PLEASE OPEN YOUR HEARTS AND MINDS AND RECEIVE THIS HISTORICAL KNOWLEDGE!

TABLE OF CONTENTS

PAGE

INTRODUCTION..a

PREFACE..1

Chapter I – **ABOUT THE FOUNDERS**..............................21

Chapter II – 1960-1969 - **THE TURBULENT AND RACIALLY CHARGED SIXTIES AND ITS IMPACT ON OMEGA**..................37

Chapter III – 1970-1979 - **OMEGA REACHES OUT TO SAVE THE BLACK COMMUNITY**..65

Chapter IV – 1970-79, Continuation - **A PERIOD OF UPHEAVAL IN AMERICA AND ITS IMPACT ON OMEGA**..................................94

Chapter V – 1980-1989, **ORDER IS DEMANDED BY OMEGA**..........106

Chapter VI – 1980-89, Continuation – **SOME PLEDGE PROGRAMS CALLED A DISGRACE TO OMEGA, OMEGA FLEXES ITS POLITICAL MUSCLES, & THE DOG IMAGE OUTLAWED**.................................117

Chapter VII –1990-1999–**FRATERNAL EVANGELISM INTRODUCED & PLEDGING IS ABOLISHED**..129

Chapter VIII-1990-1999, Continuation - **OMEGA, LED BY A MAN OF VISION, TAKES A DARING LEAP OF FAITH TO THE UNKNOWN**....149

Chapter IX-1990-1999 Continuation-**OMEGA'S MOVE TO GEORGIA FROM WASHINGTON D.C. & THE GROWING DIVIDE BETWEEN GRADUATE & UNDER GRADUATE OMEGA MEN**.......................159

Chapter X– **OMEGA FACES DESTRUCTION FROM LEGAL BATTLES DUE TO HAZING ALLEGATIONS**..173

Chapter XI-2000-**A NEW MILLENNIUM: AN ERA OF STRONG ECONOMIC RESURGENCE FOR OMEGA**................................187

Chapter XII-**OMEGA: TODAY, TOMORROW & FOREVER**.............207

APPENDICES..243

A. 75th Grand Conclave Supreme Council Members..................243
B. Districts, Chapters of Omega Psi Phi Fraternity & Charter Dates, etc., Omega Psi Phi Federal Credit Union....................262
C. Grand Basilei of Omega Psi Phi Fraternity........................297
D. First Vice Grand Basilei of Omega Psi Phi Fraternity..........298
E. Second Vice Grand Basilei of Omega Psi Phi...................299
F. Grand Conclaves of Omega Psi Phi 1960 forward..............301
G. 75, 70, 60, 50, 40, 25 Year Men of the 75th Grand Conclaves..302-305
H. 70 Year Men of the 74th Grand Conclaves......................306
I. 60 & 50 Year Men of the 74th Grand Conclaves................306
J. 40 Year Men of the 74th Grand Conclaves.......................307
K. 25 Year Men of the 74th Grand Conclaves......................308
L. Books Written by Omega Men.....................................309
M. Omega Men Honored on Postage Stamps........................315
N. Omega Men Recipients of the Spingarn Award..................316
O. List of District Representatives of Omega........................317
P. Highlights of Omega Psi Phi Fraternity 1911-1960.............332
Q. Oracles of Omega Psi Phi Fraternity..............................334
R. Omega Bulletins of Omega Psi Phi Fraternity....................344
S. List of Clarion Call..345
T. The Sword & Shield..346
U. Famous Omega Men of Omega Psi Phi Fraternity..............347
V. Distinguished Omega Men of Omega Psi Phi Fraternity.......356
W. Mandated Programs of Omega Psi Phi Fraternity..............374
X. Budget Sanitized 75th & 74th Grand Conclave Minutes........376
Y. The Omega Youth Leadership Program..........................420
Z. An interview with Founder Love on the History of Omega Psi Phi Fraternity-The beginning & a 1973 interview of Edgar A. Love by Josua M. Hyman...424

INDEX...437

<<>>

ILLUSTRATIONS

                                                                PAGE

THE GREAT SHIELD OF OMEGA PSI PHI FRATERNITY INC...................*i*
THE FOUR FOUNDERS OF OMEGA PSI PHI FRATERNTIY INC............*iii*
THE SHIELD OF OMEGA...*a*

THE OMEGA PSI PHI FRATERNITY INC.   k

COLLAGE PICTURE OF FAMOUS OMEGA MEN..................................*f*
THE GREAT SHIELD OF OMEGA PSI PHI FRATERNITY INC..............*1*
PICTURE OF FOUR FOUNDERS WITH SHIELD........................*5*
THIRKIELD HALL...*8*
ALPHA CHAPTER 1912..*11*
PICTURE OF 1946 ALPHA CHAPTER LAMPS..........................*18*
FOUNDER BISHOP A. LOVE...*21*
FOUNDER ERNEST E. JUST..*24*
FOUNDERS FRANK COLEMAN..*28*
FOUNDER OSCAR J. COOPER...*30*
SOMBER PICTURE OF FOUR FOUNDERS WITH SHIELD...............*33*
GRAVE SITE OF FOUNDER EDGAR A. LOVE............................*33*
GRAVE SITE OF ERNEST E. JUST..*34*
GRAVE SITE OF FRANK COLEMAN..*34*
GRAVESITE OF OSCAR J. COOPER..*35*
PI CHAPTER PICTURE WITH MALCOM X................................*37*
JESSE L. JACKSON IN PICTURE WITH MARTIN LUTHER KING.........*40*
JESSE L. JACKSON WITH AFRO GIVING SPEECH IN HIS YOUTH......*41*
JESSE L. JACKSON AS PRESIDENTIAL CANDIDATE....................*42*
GRAND BASILEUS   I. GREGORY NEWTON............................*42*
GRAND BASILEUS NEWTON & HIS SUPREME COUNCIL..................*43*
GRAND BASILEUS CARY D. JACOBS......................................*48*
GRAND BASILEUS GEORGE E. MEARES..................................*52*
ALPHA CHAPTER ABEL'S 27 LINE IN 1967..............................*53*
GRAND BASILEUS ELLIS F. CORBERT....................................*57*
OMEGA PSI PHI BETA CHAPTER LINCOLN UNIV 1969..................*58*
FALL 69 LAMPS OF YE CHAPTER JACKSON STATE UNIVERSITY......*63*
FALL 72 PICTURE OF OMEGA MEN YE CHAPTER........................*64*
PICTURE OF GRAND BASILEUS JAMES S. AVERY.......................*65*
OMEGA'S @ INDIANA UNIV. 1971..*70*
FOUNDERS LOVE AND COOPER AT 54TH GRAND CONCLAVE............*71*
GRAND BASILEUS AVERY WITH ROY WILKINS AND BROTHERS---*72*
PSI PHI CHAPTER'S LAMPADOS CLUB PROBATE SHOW 1971............*73*
GRAND BASILEUS AVERY WITH FOUNDERS LOVE & COOPER.........*74*
WALTER "CROW" RIDDICK..*77*
GRAND BASILEUS MARION GARNETT.....................................*79*
GRAND BASILEUS MARION GARNETT & AVERY.........................*80*
GRAND BASILEUS AVERY TESTIFYING AT MOULTRIE HEARING...*81*
UPSILON EPSILON OMEGA MEN JUST BEFORE JSU KILLINGS....*86*
PICTURE OF OMEGA MARCHING BOOTS.................................*88*
PICTURE OF EXECUTIVE SECRETARY, CARL H. MOULTRIE.........*91*
GRAND BASILEUS EDWARD BRAYNON..................................*94*
GRAND BASILEUS BURNEL E. COULON...................................*103*
GRAND BASILEUS BURNEL E. COULON...................................*106*
GAMMA EPSILON CHAPTER PICTURE.....................................*107*
GRAND BASILEUS. BENJAMIN LIVINGSTON..............................*117*
PICTURE OF CANINE IMAGE..*124*
JESSE L. JACKSON..*128*
GRAND BASILEUS MOSES C. NORMAN..................................*129*
BENJAMIN L. HOOKS...*131*

THE HISTORY OF

JOHN S. EPPS, OMEGA'S FORMER EXECUTIVE DIRECTOR..............134
DR. RONALD E. MCNAIR...138
HALL OF FAME ASTRONAUT CHARLES F. BOLDEN JR.......................148
GRAND BASILEUS C. TYRONE GILMORE...149
OMEGA WORLD CENTER HEADQUARTERS..151
GRAND BASILEUS DORSEY C. MILLER JR..159
PICTURE OF FORMER VICE GRAND BASILEUS ADAM MCKEE.........167
THE MIGHTY PI CHAPTER..168
OMEGA FRIENDSHIP FOUNDATION...170
THE JAMES A. ELAM AUDITORIUM...171
GRAND BASILEUS LLOYD J. JORDAN, ESQ.......................................173
GRAND BASILEUS JORDAN & BROTHERS IN ANTI HAZING PSA.....178
PICTURE OF EXECUTIVE DIRECTOR SYLVESTER EARL WILSON....182
PICTURES OF BASKETBALL GREAT MICHAEL J. JORDAN...............185
PICTURE OF MAJOR GENERAL CHARLES F. BOLDEN JR..................186
GRAND BASILEUS GEORGE H. GRACE..187
HALL OF FAME ASTRONAUT, CHARLES F. BOLDEN..........................204
OMEGA'S SURGEON GENERAL CHARLES A. CHRISTOPHER............205
WARREN G. LEE, THE 38TH GRAND BASILEUS.................................207
THE 74TH GRAND CONCLAVE ELECTED GRAND OFFICERS..............209
PICTURE OF CHARLES JOHNSON OF THETA ALPHA CHAPTER......212
JOHN H. WILLIAMS, OMEGA'S INTERNATIONAL PHOTOGRAPHER 216
GRAND BASILEI JOINT INTERVIEW PICTURE...................................218
GRAND BASILEI INTERVIEW COLLAGE..219
FIRST VICE GRAND BASILEUS CARL A. BLUNT..............................220
BRIAN S. GUNDY, FORMER SECOND VICE GRAND BASILEUS........222
PICTURE OF 2007 UNDERGRADUATE SUMMIT................................223
PICTURE OF 2007 UNDERGRAD SUMMIT LEADERSHIP...................223
PICTURE RICKY SMILEY...225
PICTURE RICHARD (DICK) SMITH...229
GRAND BASILEUS HERBERT E. TUCKER...231
PICTURE OF KENNETH L. HALE AT AWARD CEREMONY.................232
PICTURE OF EDDIE H. TAYLOR...233
GENERAL KIP WARD..235
U.S. CONGRESSMAN JAMES E. CLYBURN...237
PICTURE OF PRESIDENT ELECT BARACK OF OBAMA......................240
PICTURE OF GRAND BASILEUS WARREN G. LEE..............................240
PICTURE OF FOUR FOUNDERS...242
PICTURES OF ALL 08 DISTRICT REPRESENTATIVES..............248 & 249
PICTURES OF EDGAR A LOVE FROM RECORDED INTERVIEWS......426
PICTURE OF CHIEF AUTHOR, VERNON (BOP SWALOS) WEAKLEY..449
THE GREAT SHIELD OF OMEGA – THE END......................................451

~ PREFACE ~

We Omega Men must assume that the Heavenly Father, the Supreme Basileus of the Universe, placed us here on earth at this special time and place for a divine purpose given the wondrous brotherhood we have encountered in our journey as Omega men and the many worthy tasks he has set before us. Clearly, we have been chosen to lift our race and therefore provide the continuing spark and the resulting perpetual motion that will insure its very survival. We must be ever mindful of this fact and yet be sorely burdened as a direct result of the consequences of our failure. Therefore my brothers, failure is not an option. Although this challenge be perilous and fraught with disaster at every turn, we must surge ever forward with courage and resolve to SEE IT THROUGH as our beloved Founders would want us to!

There is no greater love than Omega love and there is no earthly force that can withstand the unlimited strength of these unified men of like attainment set on their journey to seize their destiny. Omega men hear me and heed the call to step forward and lift the entire Black community, America and even the world on your mighty arms. We have indeed been called by almighty God to endure; to struggle, suffer and yes die if need be in accepting this holy quest. Armed with Manhood, Scholarship, Perseverance and Uplift and the many secret pearls of wisdom that our beloved Founders in their infinite vision have given us, we are confident that our Holy quest can and will be achieved. Praise be to all mighty God for loving us and leading us to our beloved Omega Dear!

<<>>

Omega Psi Phi Fraternity Inc. during this update period (1960 to 2008) and the many great men who call it their own have stood the test of time and has been an intricate part of the fabric of America. This golden period in world history has seen many great accomplishments and as a result has provided many potential distractions for young men who would seek out Omega Psi Phi

Fraternity Inc. But nevertheless, in spite of the challenges, thousands of men (young and old) have continued to come and take the sacred oath of Omega. And with them, came new ideas and an unbridled spirit that has caused this great organization to flourish during this magical period and be a brilliantly burning light that has guided the way for the world to follow.

Could the Founders of Omega Psi Phi Fraternity, *(OSCAR J. COOPER, EDGAR A. LOVE, FRANK COLEMAN AND ERNEST E. JUST)* have predicted such growth and the extraordinary impact that their beloved Omega Dear would achieve? I dare say they not only knew this but also have seen far beyond where we are today in time. Black America, as the Founders knew then, is rising and is on a destiny that must be fed by its brightest and best. It will desperately need its sons, the talented tenth, and the mighty men of Omega Psi Phi Fraternity Inc. to uplift and save her. And from there, take her on to greatness long into the future. It is with this charge we must provide the fuel to accomplish this end. This update of the Omega History Book I pray will, in even some small way, help accomplish this task.

Bolstered by the four cardinal principles of Omega Psi Phi Fraternity, everlasting brotherhood, friendship and unity we can conquer all. Our Founders in providing these tools purposely wove these concepts into the life lesson and experience that every man hoping to enter the sacred halls of Omega had to learn before ultimately becoming an Omega man. Are these noble concepts worth dying for? And, even more importantly, are they worth living for, which we all know is much harder than dying when the future holds only continued torment and seemingly insurmountable obstacles. Thus is the plight of the Black man in America. And so, we must cherish the tools given to us by our beloved Founders and hold them tightly to our bosom and from there use them as a model for our lives.

The great Founders of Omega Psi Phi Fraternity in their infinite wisdom knew that the African American race would need all of these crucial values and concepts to pull themselves up from the institutionalized racism that has been cleverly designed as a perpetual stumbling block and an invisible weight that had acted as a detriment to advancement.

African American unity, given the unjust racial conditions that were prevalent in 1911 and it could be argued even till this very day, will need to be at its strongest to even have a slim chance of breaking free of the invisible chains that bind African Americans, not only in America, but around the globe. Is this objective out of reach and therefore forever unattainable? I believe the Founders of Omega Psi Phi Fraternity would say it is worthy, attainable and that nothing worth truly having comes easy.

The true depths of brotherhood, friendship, unity and love come from pain, suffering and the sincere desire to willingly sacrifice yourself for the good of yourself or another. Nothing good and long lasting should come easy. Jesus Christ gave this opulent principle and unselfish example to the world when he gave his life on the cross at Calvary so that the sins of mankind could forever be forgiven. This concept has also soundly demonstrated itself through the shining examples of good parents and love ones in sacrificing their all to save and/or raise their children. And now, having set the stage for Omega Psi Phi fraternity's birth, all that was needed for Black men to climb was an avenue that would not lead to a public lynching for their audacity to gather and wish to improve themselves.

At the turn of the 20th century, American colleges and universities began to admit more and more students of African descent. In addition, colleges and universities established solely to support the education of the so called "Negro" began to expand physically, and interests in other non-scholarly endeavors started to emerge among students. Prior to this period, a well known social order called the "fraternity" was established in the 18th century at the College of William & Mary in Williamsburg, Virginia. The members of this fraternity named it Phi Beta Kappa and for 50 years it proliferated as a secret social organization. During that time, other fraternities were established at other colleges, each taking on a 3 letter Greek designation and in some cases 2 Greek letters were used as was the case with Kappa Alpha. All of these organizations thrived and became social havens for the elite college man. **Be clearly advised readers that at this point in American history, these all white fraternities were not open to membership for African descendents.**

The exclusion of the African American student from the traditionally white fraternities did not satisfy many who longed to fellowship and socialize in a fraternal organization. Because of the fears of many white Americans about the establishment of secret social orders for African Americans, fraternities and sororities were not favorable avenues or options. This trend was challenged however in 1906 with the establishment of the Alpha Phi Alpha Fraternity at Cornell University in Ithaca, New York. Shortly thereafter, Alpha Kappa Alpha was formed on the campus of Howard University but remained a local organization until incorporation and expansion became an issue later in the decade. Kappa Alpha Psi Fraternity Inc., was formed in Indiana in February of 1911.

Not satisfied with the offerings of Alpha Phi Alpha and Kappa Alpha Psi, Oscar Cooper, Frank Coleman, and Edgar Love consulted with Professor Ernest E. Just to establish a new fraternity at the campus of Howard University in our nation's capital. Working with Professor Just and against the wishes of several unnamed faculty members on campus I might add, they established the Omega Psi Phi Fraternity on November 17, 1911, at 9PM in Thirkield Hall, then a building dedicated to the sciences. Omega Psi Phi Fraternity credits Professor Just as a Founder as well and together with the three undergraduate students, Love, Cooper, and Coleman, founded Omega Psi Phi fraternity.

For those reading this update who are not familiar with brother Herman Dreer's and Robert L. Gill's previous books on the History Of Omega Psi Phi Fraternity, or who have little or no knowledge of Omega Psi Phi Fraternity Inc, I will provide a history of the organization and the events that sparked this literary project. **Readers, please do not make the mistake of thinking that the upcoming history on the birth of Omega in this chapter was just taken from the latter two History Book update**s. Additional research was done to find any heretofore unknown subtle nuances and/or behind the scene facts and/or occurrences that would enhance the powerful, positive message contained in the birth of Omega story line.

Omega man Herman Dreer (a renowned minister, highly successful teacher and prolific writer) chaired a committee to write the history of Omega Psi Phi Fraternity. He was the primary writer on the project. His book, "The History of Omega Psi Phi Fraternity" was copyrighted by Omega Psi Phi fraternity and published in 1940.[2] It covered all significant history of Omega Psi Phi fraternity from its beginning in 1911 to 1939.

Another great Omega man, Robert L. Gill, PhD, along with his committee wrote, "The Omega Psi Phi Fraternity and the Men Who Made Its History".[3] This book was copyrighted by Omega Psi Phi fraternity and published in 1963. Dr. Gill's book covered from 1911 to 1961.

In 2006, a committee chaired by Vernon Steve Weakley was commissioned by the 38th Grand Basileus, Warren G. Lee, to do an official update of the Omega History Book for the period 1960 to 2008. This completed book is the product of that sanctioned request.

<<>>

And now, without any further delay, on to the initial history of Omega Psi Phi Fraternity.

[4]

[5] In 1911, shortly after they had returned to begin their junior year at Howard University, Edgar A. Love and Oscar J. Cooper made a survey on their campus. They stood on the steps of the main building at Howard and looked West, North and East. They observed Clarke Hall, Miner, the new Hall of Manual Arts, the Science Hall and Carnegie Library. They then, being caught up in the conversation of how to uplift the Negro race, left the main building and walked towards Rankin Memorial Chapel. The view from that vantage point allowed them to see the Washington,

---

[2] Omega Psi Phi fraternity official website /2 The History Of Omega Psi Phi Fraternity by Herman Dreer

[3] . "The Omega Psi Phi Fraternity and the Men Who Made Its History" by Dr. Robert L. Gill

[4] Image from the 5th District Web site, http://www.omega5d.us/fhistory.php

[5] Omega Psi Phi fraternity official website /2 The History Of Omega Psi Phi Fraternity by Herman Dreer

District of Columbia, and the majestic skyward reaching domes of the Capitol and the Library of Congress. Love and Cooper were very inspired by the view.

As they walked to the quadrangle of Howard's campus, they passed many new students. Some were discussing their studies; others were speaking of more social subjects such as athletics and of getting ready to defeat Lincoln in football on Thanksgiving Day. These conversations were fairly typical of any college scene in America at that day in time. Love and Cooper pondered the various activities in which the students' engaged and wondered about the effect of them upon the students' development. After speaking with many of the new students, they found that some were in college because they were sent; others had come to college to get married; some had come as a sort of fashion. But the majority was there, it seemed, to prepare for places of leadership that they would assume in their respective communities. **The latter fact was particularly note worthy in that it spoke highly of their character and desire to be a positive uplifting force in their race.** This sparked the interest of Love and Cooper even further. In the last group they saw some whom they believed to be more capable of leadership than others and who appeared willing to give to something greater than themselves. The combination of these two sterling qualities was extremely intriguing for Cooper and Love.

The two friends were not long in concluding, **after a few observations that the prospective dynamic leaders would increase their vision and their willingness to serve, if they could be united with like ideals and vow to give themselves to the execution of these ideals.** They believed that they should be united for creative action to perpetuate the brotherhood of the college man. **They also believed that college men united in this way, planning for each other and living for each other, had something to give mutually that the university could not give.** The university might inspire them; but this they believed only college youth could give to each other. Adults, as they knew, always seemed to have a message for youth; which had to be counted as fair, given the valuable wisdom acquired in their life journey. But, they believed also that youth had his own message for themselves. Especially did they believe that Negro youth needed their own ideas and progressive vehicles to make themselves more ready for the journey of Black life and its many obstacles. Having come to this profound premise. They now asked themselves, "What form should their idea take?" A Greek-letter fraternity came immediately to their collective thoughts.

Love and Cooper believed that the students should be united not just at Howard, but united as college men wherever they might go. Such an organization, national in scope and universal in its ideals, had never been started on the Howard campus. **Such an organization created by Negroes in a Negro college environment could be extremely effective and blaze the trail for a common attack upon the discriminations and injustices that are barriers to human progress.** Some day these young people would leave Howard and settle in various states and cities. If these young people would be self motivated and think out side of the box and create some of their own ideals and by sacred vows guide their lives in college accordingly, Brother Love and Cooper thought that they would more nearly follow those ideals than ones that might be set up for them by adult writers of books. Thus, could thousands through the years become one in aim, one in thought, and one in loyalty? As they were men of action it was natural for Love and Cooper to continue this thought process and develop their idea.

After discussing the matter further, Brothers Love and Cooper thought of their friend, Frank Coleman. He was their confidant and they would do nothing important without him. The friendship of students Love, Cooper and Coleman gained notoriety on campus. People would see them together constantly. It was obvious that there was a special devotion and bond between these three young men. They were known on campus as the three musketeers based on the legendary literary story by Alexander Dumas.

When they (Love and Cooper) talked with Frank Coleman about the wisdom of organizing a national fraternity at Howard, he said he had been thinking along that line as well and believed it to be an honor for a national Negro fraternity to be born at their Alma Mater that would go on to inspire Negro youth throughout the Nation. The three friends discussed the matter many times and as a result concluded that they should have some guidance. Cooper immediately suggested Professor Ernest E. Just, who seemed to him to have a keen appreciation for the problems of young people. The next day after class was out, while working in the laboratory, Cooper discussed the matter with the young professor, who readily consented to serve as an advisor.

During his earlier career at Howard University, professor Just often spent his social hours with students, going on field trips, playing tennis and swimming. He had also acquired the reputation as a very intelligent, but open minded and sagacious personable counselor and friend to all students on campus, always willing to offer advice and reliable guidance to the students. Professor Just was trusted and was well liked by all the students at Howard.

Thus, as history would record, the three Liberal Arts students boldly walked into Ernest E. Just's office on November 17, 1911. It was a dark and stormy night with blast of thunder loud as the roaring sea.

SCIENCE HALL, HOWARD UNIVERSITY
Where the Founders of Omega Psi Phi Fraternity met and organized Omega Psi Phi Fraternity. This building is now known as Thirkield Hall.

These young men were resolute in their interest in forming the first Black Fraternity founded on a Historical Black College or University.[6]

Ernest E. Just, if he was a man lacking courage or one who shirked hard work, could have easily turned a blind ear to these young excited students and said no given the fact that this idea,

---

[6] Omega Xi chapter website

although profound, brilliant and filled with hope for a downtrodden race, was also fraught with the possibility of serious negative consequences/blowback for his own career. Would he lose his job, be black balled and made to suffer for encouraging radicalism on campus if this venture failed or caused trouble? He, given the weight and sheer magnitude of the idea would be a crucial encouraging part of such a forward thinking idea? Weighing the consequences, professor Just chose to take the road less traveled. Without fear and hesitation he said yes and quickly consented to serve as their advisor. Truth be known, he was not only extremely impressed with this incredible idea, but was amazed even more so at the wisdom and vision of the three (soaking wet from the rain that was pouring outside that they had just come in from)) outstanding young men who stood before him with such a ground breaking idea for their campus and the world.

Apprehensive of a secret organization, at the outset, the faculty and the administration which was composed of mostly Caucasians opposed the whole idea. The idea when first publicly presented was rebuked by the then President of the University, Dr. Wilbur P. Thirkield, who was also Caucasian. Professor Just and these young men however did not back down. They stood their ground and with the persuasive oratory skills of an Alexander Dumas lawyer type extraordinaire, the young idealistic students made their case. Professor Just also played a major role in bringing the administration around. He worked behind the scene in lobbying the faculty as well as along side of the students when necessary of this long running debate. As a result of his tenacity, outstanding communication skills, diplomacy and persuasiveness in enlightening the opposition as to why this new bold idea (Omega Psi Phi fraternity) by the three young students was a good one, the name of Ernest E. Just is venerated by all Omega men who love it and call it their own. Often, youth is not supported by older people in their radical and far-reaching ideas. But in this case, these three bright eyed young men had found a true hero, **a real man** and a courageous champion.

It is also extremely important to note that the three students played a major role as well in making their case. Do not make the mistake of thinking that they just let Professor Just (The adult Founder) carry the ball for them. No, no, no, no, no! These three young students were out front and running full blast. They did their home work and were well prepared when their turn came to present their case to President Thirkield and the reviewing faculty committee. Although initially it did not appear that the committee would approve their request to start a fraternity, the three students went about their preparations as if they would receive approval anyway, even to the point of deciding on and creating the four now famous cardinal principles, selecting a name, motto, pin, and escutcheon prior to actually gaining approval. **Be advised reader, the time line here is very important.** The first meeting occurred on November 17, 1911. Several other productive meetings occurred there after which was prior to ultimate approval by the University. Little did the Founders know that the road to success would be an extremely difficult one laced with embarrassment and long nights of hard work to achieve their ultimate victory.

With the assistance of their faculty adviser Ernest E. Just, three brave college students gave birth to the **Omega Psi Phi Fraternity**. This event occurred in the office of biology Professor Ernest E. Just, the faculty adviser, in the Science Hall (now known as Thirkield Hall). The three liberal arts students were Edgar A. Love, Oscar J. Cooper and Frank Coleman. Once word of the this action of the three students and advisor got around on campus, many fellow students openly praised Cooper, Love, and Coleman for showing great courage and taking such a bold step. Their fellow students publicly praised and applauded them for trying to do something that had never been done before on any Black campus in America.

From the initials of the Greek phrase meaning "friendship is essential to the soul," the name Omega Psi Phi was derived. The phrase was selected as the motto. Manhood, scholarship, perseverance and uplift were adopted as cardinal principles. A decision was made regarding the design for the pin and emblem, and thus ended the first meeting of the Omega Psi Phi Fraternity.

To prepare for the coming second meeting, the three students began to study the student body carefully. Each placed in a notebook, the names of prospective candidates. Men who were considered high quality and worthy from the point of view of scholarship, ability to fraternize, courage and the other crucial cardinal principles already agreed on, were to be approached as to their willingness to cooperate in this new bold idea. Prior to the meeting, Love Cooper and Coleman had a secret assignment to "feel these potential candidates out diplomatically in their subtle but probing discussions and make a detailed report on each at their next meeting. The student Founders, even after placing the candidates through their most critical intellectual scrutiny to insure they had the cream of the crop, found that there was a number of capable, courageous and interested men who would be indeed worthy of Omega.

The second meeting of Omega Psi Phi Fraternity was conducted on November 23, 1911. Edgar Love became the first Grand Basileus (National President). Cooper and Coleman were selected Grand Keeper of the Records (National Secretary) and Grand Keeper of Seals (National Treasurer), respectively. Eleven Howard University undergraduate men were selected as charter members. **Again, keep in mind that at this point in time, the proposed fraternity (Omega Psi Phi Fraternity) was only wishful thinking and had not yet gotten approval by the university to even be on campus.** A committee, nevertheless, consisting of the three student Founders were appointed to move forward any way and draw up a constitution and the ritual.

Alpha Chapter was organized with fourteen charter members on December 15, 1911.

ALPHA CHAPTER - 1912

Love, Cooper and Coleman were elected the chapter's first Basileus, Keeper of Records, and Keeper of Seals, respectively.
The development of the constitution was critically important to the ultimate success of getting approval, given the faculty's indication of a negative final approval and the fact this document would be submitted first to President Thirkield for faculty approval. It had been obvious that President Thirkield was not in their corner. Therefore, this document had to demonstrate their high intellect,

far reaching vision and be as close to perfect as possible, to even have a chance of acceptance. After countless hours of hard work, intense research with included soliciting the thoughts/input of other faculty members, presidents and deans of other colleges and even getting the thoughts of many students on the subject, a constitution was developed. Each chapter member signed the original document that was to be submitted to President Thirkield.

They had worked very hard to prepare the document, sitting up sometimes until two and three o'clock in the morning. They knew they had to give it all they had to win approval from president Thirkield and the already leaning against them faculty committee. **This was the age old battle of young vs. old.** The District of Columbia was still strictly southern holding many of their Christian views, values and set in stone judgments. College fraternities to date were thought by older faculty members, some of them who were white and who were in large number on the committee, to be subversive of good southern morals and just plain out of bounds for young Negroes.

The expressed open thoughts by many of the older Faculty members were that it was also very dangerous to trust young Negro men with a secret society. It was not uncommon for Negroes to be lynched in America at that point in time for just the thought they may be organizers trying to shatter the racial status quo. Although the students who had signed the constitution were among the best citizens and the brightest on campus, the faculty committee elected to delay a decision and hold over the approval. One could speculate that this was a strategic never ending delay tactic with the hope the students would eventually get the message and just go away. But, no, no no! Our heroes pushed ever forward.

As faculty approval seemed to the young members of the newly proposed fraternity to be coming too slowly, the Founders and proposed members decided to take a unified bold action. They got up early one morning, long before breakfast and placed on trees, bulletin boards, fences and in various other conspicuous places, small signs about three and a half by six inches in size, which announced the existence of the Omega Psi Phi Fraternity. The signs listed the names of all Founders and the new chapter members. The campus was all excited about what the young brave students had done. Given the extreme positive reactions from their follow students, the men of this new, now highly publicized, but not yet approved organization, felt that their approval would now be a fore gone conclusion. **Anyone reading this story at this point in the book probably have already guessed that our young heroes were in big, big trouble with the school administration, and most especially President Thirkield.**

The very next day during chapel service, President Thirkield publicly discussed what had been done by the students and declared that at Howard there was no such organization as the Omega Psi Phi Fraternity. **You could cut the tension in the air with a knife as those words thundered off President's Thirkield's lips.** For a few seconds, there was a nauseating dead silence. Then, as you may expect from youth, many of the other students began to laugh at the circumstance. Not so were the men of Omega. This was no laughing matter to them. They were stone faced and silent.

They were not embarrassed as many of the laughing students thought that they would be, or should be. **In stead, this circumstance made the men of Omega even more determined to convince President Thirkield that Omega Psi Phi Fraternity was indeed worthy of approval.** One not so convinced in his position, given President's Thirkield's temperament when he made the public announcement and the obvious error they had made in jumping the gun to force the administration's hand, would have not pursued this heated circumstance further. **That moment in time could have easily been it and the death blow for the hopes of Omega.** But, this was not the case with these young men. They soundly demonstrated perseverance and raw courage. That day, after President Thirkield action, the young Founders had lunch together and discussed what had occurred, which included the reactions of their fellow students. After setting up an informal meeting with President Thirkield, who quickly received the young Founders, together they discussed the matter at length freely and frankly in his office.

President Thirkield began by scolding the students for their impetuous actions. He told them they would have to wait, whether they liked it or not, until a final ruling was rendered by the committee. They inquired as to when the decision would be made. But he would give no time line to the students as to when that approval may come. It was obvious this "The You Will Wait" point was being driven home to the student. Although it had gotten pretty heated in the room, to his credit it must be stated, President Thirkield after scolding the young men and calming down, gave them a chance to speak. Given his authority and the rashness of what they had done, he could have easily put them out of his office without allowing them not even one word. Almighty God, the Supreme Basileus of the Universe, was watching over them no doubt and was indeed in that room with our Founders at that very moment.

What came next in my opinion, was the greatest testament to the unbreakable spirit of youth, intelligence and the raw courage to stand up for what you believe in, **IN SPEAKING TRUTH TO POWER** in spite of the terrible consequences that can ever be given. Showing maturity and putting away the opportunity to lash back at President Thirkield for scolding them and publicly embarrassing them in front of their fellow students, the three Founders laid out a calm and rationale argument that set the stage for not only the eventual approval of Omega but the rationale as to why youth, and in particular, young Black men who have proven themselves academically worthy, should be given great responsibility and authority. A brief general outline of the premise of their historic argument is as follows:

1. They deserved to be trusted with the building of the Omega Psi Phi Fraternity on the basis of their past academic records. These three students as well as the men who had been selected to be a part of the organization were the top students on campus. The latter was beyond reproach and was a known fact throughout the university and the District of Columbia.

2. More training for leadership within and beyond the halls of Howard would arise in the Fraternity, because it was an organization of the student's creation and one that they would guide without faculty domination.

3. Manhood is developed by placing responsibility and responsibility was placed in a fraternity as it could not be placed in other school organizations.

4. If at any time the Omega Psi Phi Fraternity would show immoral tendencies, the faculty would have power to destroy it, while also having the opportunity to gauge its positive progress and success.

5. The fraternity is a desirable organization to have on a campus and that the faculty should be willing to guide it.

6. The faculty should think it an honor for Howard to be the first Negro institution of higher learning to have a national Negro fraternity organized on its campus.

* *A word to the wise from the author*-Some of the arguments above are very relevant and powerful and thus valid for use even today in worthy applicable circumstances by undergraduate brothers etc. who face difficult and/or unjust administrations on their college/university campuses. There are some colleges/universities even today that fail or simply refuse to see the value of Greek organizations on their campus. The, "Just give us any reason to boot you off campus" attitude unfortunately is a reality that must be faced.

After carefully listening to this powerful argument by the Founders of Omega Psi Phi fraternity, President Thirkield softened his position significantly and advised them that he would give the matter more consideration and even deeper thought. In the interim he asked that the students remove all the signs they had prematurely put up announcing the existence of the Omega Psi Phi Fraternity. The men of Omega showed respect to President Thirkield and promptly obeyed his request. Despite all that happened up until this point, most especially the hardy laughs that had occurred at the young men's expense, the general student body was still openly supportive of the new organization. They felt that a new uplifting powerful force had now finally come upon the campus that was not afraid to put it on the line and fight for justice not only for themselves but to significantly improve student rights for all, and set an even higher standard of academics for all to aspire to. The Founders of Omega and it proposed chapter members continued to submit its constitution and other necessary paper work for consideration to the committee.

On March 8, 1912, the previously submitted fraternity constitution was rejected by the Howard University Faculty Council. The Faculty Council proposed to accept the fraternity as a local but not a national organization. The fraternity initially refused acceptance as a strictly local organization. **This point again could have been a stopping point for the life of Omega**. It could be said that a great victory had been won, even with only gaining approval of being just a local chapter. But again, the young men of Omega chose to continue to fight for national status for their fraternity. After several meetings and head to head discussions by both the faculty committee and the men of Omega, finally, the Omega Psi Phi Fraternity won approval of the faculty committee as a national organization. This victory was vital and was a catalyst that enabled Omega Psi Phi fraternity to become the great organization it is today.

When the news circulated around the campus, the entire student body was in a positive uproar in total support for the members of Omega Psi Phi Fraternity. **Oh what a great day and victory for these young students. The men of Omega Psi Phi Fraternity celebrated openly in hardy fashion. They shook hands, threw up their hats and some even cut capers and danced.** It was indeed a day of great rejoicing.

Perseverance is that quality that causes one to steadfastly pursue an objective until success is achieved. There is a tremendous lesson to be learned here. Perseverance played a major role in the launching of the Omega Psi Phi Fraternity Inc. as an organization. The Founders were confronted with obstacle after obstacle as orchestrated by the administration of Howard University. But praise God; because of the Founders' perseverance they were able to overcome their adversities.[7]

OSCAR COOPER became the fraternity's second Grand Basileus in 1912. **Cooper** authorized the investigation of a proposed second chapter at **Lincoln University**, Pennsylvania. **Edgar Love** was elected as the third Grand Basileus in 1912 and served until 1915. In 1914, **Howard University** withdrew its opposition, and the **Omega Psi Phi Fraternity** was incorporated under the laws of the **District of Columbia** on October 28, 1914. **Beta Chapter** at **Lincoln University** was chartered in February, 1914.

GEORGE E. HALL, the fourth Grand Basileus, had been initiated at Alpha Chapter in 1914. Grand Basileus Hall authorized the establishment of **Gamma Chapter** in Boston, Massachusetts.

---

[7] The Spring 1988 Oracle, from Article Perseverance: Overcoming Adversity to Achieve Success" Speech by Dr. Edward J. Braynon

However, the chapter was eventually established during the administration of the fifth Grand Basileus, **JAMES C. MCMORRIES. Omega Psi Phi Fraternity was incorporated into a national organization in December of 1914.** An Amendment to Certificate of Incorporation was done June 21, 1951.[8]

Beta Chapter was formed at the home of Sister Lottie B. Wilson for students of Lincoln University. In March of 1917, **Gamma Chapter** was organized for students in the Boston, Massachusetts area. In January of 1919, **Delta Chapter** was chartered for students at Fisk University and Meharry Medical College. George E. Hall, the fourth Grand Basileus, had been initiated at Alpha Chapter in 1914. Grand Basileus Hall authorized the establishment of Gamma Chapter in Boston, Massachusetts. However, the chapter was eventually established during the administration of the fifth Grand Basileus, James C. McMorries.

During the administration of the sixth Grand Basileus, **CLARENCE F. HOLMES**, the fraternity's first official hymn, "Omega Men Draw Nigh", was written by **OTTO BOHANNON**. **RAYMOND G. ROBINSON**, the seventh Grand Basileus, established **Delta Chapter** in Nashville, Tennessee in 1919. Robinson left office in 1920 with a total of ten chapters in operation.

STANLEY DOUGLAS served as Editor of the first Oracle published in the spring of 1919. **HAROLD K. THOMAS,** the eighth Grand Basileus, was elected at the 1920 Nashville Grand Conclave. It was at this Conclave that **CARTER G. WOODSON** inspired the establishment of National Achievement Week to promote the study of Negro life and history. The 1921 Atlanta Grand Conclave brought to an end the first decade of the **Omega Psi Phi Fraternity**.

In 1922, Grand Basileus **J. ALSTON ATKINS** appointed the first District Representatives. Today, as of this writing, there are eleven such officers who are elected annually by the district conferences/meetings. **In 1922, the office of Vice Grand Basileus was created.** The Grand Keeper of Records became the Grand Keeper of the Records and Seal. The first Omega Bulletin was published in 1928. Campbell C. Johnson was the Editor. "Omega Dear" was adopted as the official hymn in 1931. Two

---

[8] An Amendment to Certificate of Incorporation was done June 21, 1951.

faculty members from Howard University, **CHARLES R. DREW**, Professor of Surgery, and Mercer Cook, Professor of Languages, were the composers. Cook wrote the music and first stanza; Drew wrote the last two stanzas.

From its inception, the fraternity has worked to build a strong and effective force of men dedicated to its Cardinal Principles of Manhood, Scholarship, Perseverance, Uplift, and capable of giving expression to the hopes and aspirations of an un-free people in the land of the free. In 1927, at the urging of fraternity member Carter G. Woodson, the Fraternity made National Negro Achievement Week an annual observance, and it continues today as Black History Month.

The Omega "Sweetheart Song", with words and music by **DON Q. PULLEN**, was adopted as the official sweetheart song by the 1940 Nashville Grand Conclave. Founder Ernest E. Just entered Omega Chapter in 1941. In 1941, Dr. Charles Drew perfected the use of blood plasma as a life saving tool. **WILLIAM HASTIE** resigned as Civilian Aide to the Secretary of War in protest against discrimination in the Armed Forces. He was later appointed Governor of the Virgin Islands by President Truman.

1946 Alpha Chapter Lamps on display [9]

In 1949, the first National Headquarters Building at 107 Rhode Island Avenue, N.W., Washington, D.C. was purchased. **H. Carl Moultrie**, I was selected to serve as the first National Executive

---

[9] Alpha Chapter Web site/Photo Gallery

Secretary. In 1949, the scholarship fund was renamed the Charles R. Drew Memorial Scholarship Fund. Since 1945, the fraternity has undertaken a National Social Action Program to meet the needs of African Americans in the areas of health, housing, civil rights, and education. Omega Psi Phi has been a patron of the United Negro College Fund (UNCF) since 1955, provides an annual gift of $50,000 to the UNCF, and is a National Pan-Hellenic Council (NPHC) member.

During the fifties, the thrust was social change. Thousands of Omega men in every area of the country were actively involved in the fight to eliminate racial discrimination. An entire book could be written about this phase of Omega activities. The 1955 Los Angeles Grand Conclave initiated a program whereby each graduate chapter would purchase a Life Membership from the NAACP. Between 1955 and 1959, chapters contributed nearly $40,000 to the NAACP. **In the fifties, Omega Psi Phi took an official position against hazing as a fraternity activity.** This anti-hazing position remains in effect today, and the policy banning hazing has been strengthened.

Today, Omega Psi Phi has over 700 chapters throughout the United States, Bermuda, Bahamas, U.S. Virgin Islands, Korea, Japan, Liberia, Germany, and Kuwait. **Omega continues to flourish, largely because Founders Love, Cooper, Coleman and Just were men of the very highest ideals and intellect. The Founders selected and attracted men of similar ideals and characteristics**. It is not by accident that many of America's great Black men are/were Omega Men. To this date, there are very few Americans whose lives have not been touched by a member of the Omega Psi Phi Fraternity.

[10]

<<>>

THE HISTORY
OF THE
OMEGA PSI PHI
FRATERNITY INC.

A BROTHERHOOD OF EXCEPTIONAL MEN OF LIKE ATTAINMENTS

MANHOOD   SCHOLARSHIP

PERSEVERANCE   UPLIFT

AN UPDATE FOR THE PERIOD
1960 TO 2008

MAY GOD BLESS OMEGA PSI PHI FRATERNITY INC.
◇◇◇◇

CHAPTER I

ABOUT THE FOUNDERS OF OMEGA PSI PHI FRATERNITY, INC.

FOR THOSE WHO TRULY SEEK KNOWLEDGE AND DIVINE INSPIRATION, I GIVE YOU ENLIGHTENING FACTS ABOUT OUR BELOVED FOUNDERS

<><>

BISHOP EDGAR AMOS LOVE

(1891-1974)

Bishop Edgar A. Love, the son to the late Rev. Julius C. Love and Mrs. Susie C. Love, was born in Harrisburg, Virginia, September 10, 1891. He was the son of Methodist ministers. His father was an honored member of the Washington Annual Conference of the Methodist Episcopal Church until his death in 1927. His mother was also a licensed minister in her own right. She was also the first woman graduate of Morgan College.[11] Edgar Love received his early training in the public schools of Virginia and Maryland. In 1909, he graduated from the Academy of Morgan College, in 1913. Edgar Love believed and openly demonstrated to all he came in contact with, that with Love, Faith, Friendship, Commitment, Hard Work, Unity and God's grace, no

---

[11] The Oracle, Spring, 1974, Vol.57,No.1 /Last of Surviving Founders enters Omega Chapter//The Omega Xi website and International Office website

obstacle will be undefeated. This premise was ingrained in his heart and was his rock of success in his life. He wanted to share this information with other Black men, and bring men with the same ideals together into a fraternal fold that would serve to liberate and uplift his race. The times he lived in, (the late 1800s and early 1900s) was a dark, unjust and dangerous period for all people of color. Black people were still being openly lynched in many areas in America for just the perception of stepping out of their so called place and/or for being organizers of their own kind.

On November 17, 1911, Bishop Love along with two colleagues, Oscar Cooper and Frank Coleman, joined Dr. Ernest Everett Just in discussing the formation of a fraternity. This fraternity would be the first to be formed at a Black institution. This was a courageous step for men of color, given the extremely dangerous times they lived in, Nevertheless, they boldly proceeded ever forward in spite of the possible deadly consequences. They decided that this new Fraternity's motto would be "Friendship is Essential to the Soul." This would be their shield of unity that they would carry before them for the rest of their lives.

The Founders of Omega Psi Phi Fraternity were men of vision and knew full well that their new creation fueled with this divine universal truth, "Friendship is Essential to the Soul," would be a brilliantly shining guiding light for the world to follow. This haunting motto would take the world by storm, endure for many years and live in the hearts of thousands of African American men around the world. It has been the foundation for achieving success and a source of strength for countless loyal and dedicated men that have served to uplift the African American race.

Edgar A. Love graduated from Howard University with the honor Cum Laude and the degree of Bachelor of Arts. In 1916 after three years of additional hard work, he received from Howard University the degree of Bachelor of Divinity. To intensify his training further, he entered Boston University, from which he received in 1918 the degree of Bachelor of Sacred Theology. Later he spent two sessions in graduate work at the University of Chicago. Because of his distinguished work in religion as a teacher, pastor and inspired civic worker for the advancement of all humanity, in June, 1935 Morgan College conferred upon him the honorary degree of Doctor of divinity.

Reverend Love pastored for fifteen months at Fairmount, Maryland, for four years at Washington, D.C., for three years at Annapolis, Maryland, for three years in Wheeling, West Virginia, and for two years at Baltimore Maryland, directing the great John Wesley M.C. Church. As a pastor, Reverend Love, inspiring and efficient, made the Church, wherever he was, function as a community center for the people of the neighborhood, as well as a temple of worship for the Most High God.

When the call of the United States came for our youth to do service in France, our hero Edgar A. Love promptly entered the Officers' Training Camp at Des Moines, Iowa and was commissioned as a First Lieutenant. He was assigned as Chaplain to the 368 Infantry, with which unit he saw service in the Vosges Mountains, and in the Argonne Forest, spending eight days in the great offensive, where, even though he was gassed in this struggle, was still able to inspire the men he ministered to press on in this grave battle. While in the army he had supervision over 3,000 men.

Aside from administering to the spiritual needs of the soldiers, he also taught in the army school. He helped to organize a school for illiterates in the 809th Pioneer Infantry, which was developed into a regular school system. The school included in its curriculum subjects ranging from reading and writing to motor mechanics and philosophy. Fourteen teachers were drafted from the ranks and constituted the faculty. In 1919, Edgar A. Love was honorably discharged from the army with the rank of Captain.

Containing the divine germ of Omega and with that the God given ability to infect others with his greatness and vision, **Edgar A. Love will forever be loved by all men of Omega Psi Phi Fraternity. Without a doubt, he served his church, his country, his race and his beloved Omega Dear nobly. Omega man, Edgar A. Love entered Omega chapter on May 1st, 1974.**

DR. ERNEST E. JUST

(1883-1941)

Ernest Everett Just, an eminent marine biologist, was born in Charleston, South Carolina. The son of a wharf builder and a school teacher, he rose from very humble beginnings to become the foremost Black American Biologist of his time. As Ernest E. Just was clearly marked for greatness, his rise was inevitable. Seeking a substantial education, he attended the Industrial School of State College, Orangeburg, South Carolina; Kimball Academy at Meriden, New Hampshire; and Dartmouth College. He graduated magna cum laude from Dartmouth College in 1907. Each school he attended was proud to have him because of his kindly demeanor and his extraordinary ability as a scholar.

[12] His father – Charles Fraser Just – was comely, "light-skinned and curly-haired." Genetically, these physical characteristics were transmitted to Ernest. "His forehead, like his father's slanted back ever so slightly, high lighting his dark, recessed eyes, which were shaded by heavy but unobtrusive brown eyes. Always stern, his countenance revealed the same aura of dignity, perhaps even a tad bit of arrogance," so symbolic of his father's profile. His parents had been short and stocky while he in great contrast to them was tall, slender and witty. His hair resembled a bronze toupee; coarse

---

[12] The Fall 1988 Oracle- Article by H. Leon Prather Sr., Ph.D an adaptation of Black Apollo of Science: The Life of Ernest E. Just by Kenneth R. Manning

and well groomed, with a part down the middle, it glowed against his light tan skin. By conventional standards he was strikingly handsome, carrying the racial mix well.

Earnest E. Just was born in impoverished Charleston, S.C., to a philandering father, whose excessive alcoholism caught up with him and claimed his life before Ernest was even four years old. **But his mother (Mary Matthews Just) is the gem in this story. Without the assistance of a husband, she vowed to move heaven and earth if need be to see her son succeed in life. She worked numerous jobs for long hours so that her son could at least have an opportunity that was denied many other poor Black kids**.

In that day and time most Black children never saw the in side of a school. They worked full time in the field and or other manual labor jobs or did continuing income generating chores for their families and had no hope of ever getting an education. Mrs. Just simply would not entertain this fate for her son. By today's standards, she perhaps could have been called one of those "stubborn mamas." She worked her fingers to the bone to make certain that her son's education was not interrupted. It was through Mrs. Mary Just's stern resolve to see him do well in life that she provided him with his entire early education: then sent him to the Colored Normal Industrial, Agricultural and Mechanical College at Orangeburg. One story is told of how Mary Just, with no funds, contacted the principal of the Kimball Union Academy in Meriden, New Hampshire, "asking if her son, Ernest E. Just, could come anyway."

Symbolic of Booker T. Washington, Ernest Just worked at odd jobs along the way in the hope of earning enough money to attend the Kimball Union Academy, eventually arriving at the Academy. Not having all of the funds necessary and required, the principal, feeling the weight, desperation and sheer pain in his mother's earlier letter, accepted his application and assigned him work in the kitchen as cook and helper. After receiving a premonition that something was wrong at home, Ernest E. Just left the Academy briefly to return to his home town to sadly find that his mother, who he loved so dearly, had died.

With no parent now to guide him, Ernest E. Just, if he would have chosen this defeatist route, had a perfect alibi not to continue his education. He never really knew his father since he had died when he was so young. She (his mother Mary Just) was his rock! In great contrast to his father, his mother had been many things to him. These included her dedication to cleanliness, education and the will to forge ahead against the odds. These traits remained a dominant part of Ernest E. Just's character and life. They also served him well in the formation of Omega Psi Phi Fraternity. After returning to the Academy after his mother's death, he become deeply involved in all school activities, including those after school as well. He joined the debating society and worked on the school paper-The Kimball Vision, of which he was elected editor in chief during his senior year. In 1903 he completed the vigorous four year classical courses in three years. Ernest E. Just was such an outstanding student that he won the rare honor of delivering one of the few speeches before a crowd of students, parents and alumni.

Ernest E. Just, that fall enrolled at Dartmouth College, located at Hanover, N.H., just fifteen miles away from Meriden. This would give him the opportunity to "return to Kimball to visit old teachers and friends from time to time. This link proved to be a plus for all concerned. It allowed him to retain access to the wisdom of his teachers, the run of the research hall and allowed him to mentor many of the students who needed assistance. Ernest E. Just went on to have an impressive record at Dartmouth College. His academic accomplishments ranked him as the Rufus Choate Scholar for two consecutive years. He would go on to graduate Magna Cum Laude." at Dartmouth. At Dartmouth, Ernest E. Just also won the Phi Beta Kappa Key, the highest scholastic award to be given to a student in an undergraduate college. Upon graduating from Dartmouth he became a teacher in the M Street High School of Washington, D.C., now the Dunbar.

Soon he answered the call of Howard University to become an instructor in Biology, his major field. It was here he fascinated the hearts of Negro youth, inspired them and made them ambitious. Here he met Oscar J. Cooper, who told him of the fraternal dream of a collegiate empire in his mind and in the minds of his bosom friends, Edgar A. Love and Frank Coleman, all members of the Howard University class of 1913. He listened to their fancies and their dreams, helped them become realities, and thereby became with them a beloved Founder of Omega Psi Phi Fraternity.

In 1915, after displaying unusual brilliancy in research, the National Association for the Advancement of Colored People conferred upon him the Spingarn Medal, which each year is given to a Negro who has been most outstanding in achievement. The following year he obtained the degree of Doctor of Philosophy from the University of Chicago. Ernest E. Just did his work so well, that he was selected as guest investigator, to engage in research at the Kaiser Wilhelm Institute for Biology. In 1919, he spent six months in Biological Research at Naples, Italy. He had also at his disposal the private laboratories of several of the crowned heads of Europe.

For twenty years, Ernest E. Just did research work at the Marine Biology Laboratory at Woods Hole, Massachusetts. A gift from the Rosenwald Fund of about $80,000.00 a year for several years made it possible for Dr. Just to be relieved of his undergraduate teaching assignment and devote all his time to research and the teaching of graduate students.

Although Dr. Just was considered a leader and authority for his work with cell development, as an African American, he was a victim of racism and prejudice. For this reason, Dr. Just decided to continue his research in Europe in 1930. It was in Europe that he published his second book, The Biology of the Cell Surface. While in Europe in 1938 he published a number of papers and lectured on the topic of cell cytoplasm. Ernest E. Just was a member of the National Research Council, editor of the international Council, editor of the international Journal, "Protoplasma." He was a member of the American Society of Zoologists, the American Naturalists, and a corresponding member of La Society des Science Naturelles et Mathematiques de France. Dr. Just was selected by leading biologists of Germany as the best fitted among world scholars to write treaties on fertilization.

If Ernest E. Just' achievements in science are to be judged by those standards set up by men of science, it can be said that Dr. Just was a brilliant accomplished internationally known and respected Biologist who had no equal... If he is judged according to his value to Negro education, it can be said that he demonstrated the utmost possibility of human achievement regardless of race or color. Ernest E. Just was named the first recipient of the Spingarn Medal from the NAACP in 1915 for his extraordinary contributions to science and for his advancement of the cause of Black Americans by improving standards at Negro medical schools.

Our hero, Dr. Ernest E. Just, died October 27, 1941 in Washington D.C.

<<>>

PROFESSOR FRANK COLEMAN

(1890-1967)

On July 11, 1890, the birth of a son made joyous a progressive home in the Washington, District of Columbia. Frank Coleman, the most reserved of the three student Founders of Omega Psi Phi Fraternity was a serious minded philosopher in childhood. He expressed a desire to not let life pass him by without his keen investigative involvement. He wanted to know the reason why things happened, plain and simple and he tenaciously went about the business to find out why without depending on others. This proclivity naturally led him into the field of science. This unbridled inquisitiveness combined with the sea of unknowns that are common to the field of science was a marriage made in heaven for this young man. Frank Coleman was also a very strong, charismatic and worthy leader in all levels of his schooling. The latter factor caused his school mates to gravitate to him and eagerly cooperate with and follow him. As a young man it could be said, that he had a Pied Piper effect on his peers.

With distinction, Frank Coleman completed the work required in the elementary schools of Washington and then went to the M Street High School, now called the Dunbar. His extra-curricular activity centered on being a high school cadet. He received very high honors, notice and respect in this area. Early in high school he also became keenly interested in physics and conducted numerous original and innovative experiments, well beyond his age group, with the hope of uncovering some new secret of nature. Regarding what he had learned as only a modicum of what nature had to teach of her mysteries, he decided early to make physics his specialty in college. Frank Coleman went on to graduate from M. Street High School with very high honors.

Immediately after finishing high school Frank Coleman entered Howard University, from which he obtained his Bachelor of Science degree. His undergraduate record there was so outstanding that upon graduation he was appointed as an instructor in Physics. Frank Coleman later earned his Master of Science degree from the University of Chicago. He did subsequent graduate work at the University of Pennsylvania and met all requirements for his Doctorate except completion of his thesis.

When America entered the World War, Frank Coleman joined the army and as a result of his extremely high intelligence and leadership abilities, was selected to go to the Officers Training Camp at Des Moines, Iowa. The latter was a rarity at this point in time given the racist state of the military for men of color. The overwhelming majority of Black men could only even hope to be no more than cooks or servants in carrying out their military duties. Frank Coleman rose through the ranks in spite of the many racial barriers he encountered. It was not long that his outstanding work ethics, extremely high intelligence, and leadership abilities became noticed, and as a result, he was commissioned as a First Lieutenant, and from there went on to serve his country honorably overseas.

Aside from carrying on his regular work in the field of physics, Brother Coleman was a member of the Boys' Committee of YMCA, a Mason, an American Legionnaire and a Congregationalist. In the latter capacities, Frank Coleman sought to encourage patriotism and a love for God in others and to teach the principles of the brotherhood of man. Frank Coleman's work and the everlasting value of his achievements in science and the military have stood the test of time. Frank Coleman was truly a pioneer who rose to greatness, in spite of the racial barriers set before him. **Founder Frank Coleman entered Omega Chapter February 24, 1967.**

<<>>

DR. OSCAR JAMES COOPER

(1888-1972)

Into the home of two God fearing and ambitious parents on May 20, 1890 was born a bouncing baby boy named Oscar J. Cooper. His parents resolved not to spoil the energetic and precocious infant but to guide him and discipline him by strenuous tasks to become a strong man. They also stressed that their son develop self control as a necessary virtue of a democratic leader. They taught their son Oscar Cooper to master the fine art of being a gentleman. Accordingly, they taught him to be neat and punctilious in his dress and distinctly chivalrous in his manners, never flashy or ostentatious, but always fashionable, prim and precise. These ideas stayed with Oscar J. Cooper and became the foundation for the development of the habits of order and system that gave birth to his scientific mind.

Where his grades were concerned, in both grade school and high school, Oscar Cooper received the affection of his teachers for he was in many ways the knight without fear and without reproach. **Oscar Cooper was of high moral character and never hesitated to do what was right. This was especially true when it came to telling the truth and reaching out to help others.** Oscar Cooper never complained of hard work, as many of his classmates did. He took on all assignments with eagerness and with great initiative and independence. He completed his work in excellent fashion and then reached out to help his fellow class mates who needed assistance. Upon finishing the elementary schools of Washington, Oscar Cooper entered Howard University, where he obtained his baccalaureate degree and his Doctor of Medicine degree. Some of the academic subjects proved little interest for him; for his all-absorbing interest in college was Biology. His aptness and proficiency along this line drew him to Professor Just, who was teaching Biology at Howard at the time. So accomplished was Oscar J. Cooper in this subject that he was made a laboratory assistant in Biology.

Oscar J. Cooper was the crucial link between the other Founders, all Juniors, in the fall of 1911, and Professor Just, the eminent, young, associate professor, who advised the three young pioneers; Love, Cooper and Coleman. Oscar J. Cooper early on showed that he believed both in hard work and in pleasure. He liked to work; to work hard for the achievement of great ends, but he also liked to socialize. Accordingly in the founding of Omega, Oscar J. Cooper worked unsparingly along with the other Founders many a night until late in the morning. Oscar Cooper, it could be said, was the glue that connected all of the necessary parts (social and academic) that led to this ever lasting friendship and eventual brain trust that gave birth to and has continued to perpetuate Omega Psi Phi Fraternity Inc. God's master plan led them all to each other of course. But it was Oscar Cooper who

God used like a fine surgical instrument in getting these four incredible men together.

Upon completing his medical studies, Brother Cooper settled in Philadelphia and worked untiringly and persistently until he built up one of the most lucrative practices to be found among the physicians of Philadelphia. Brother Cooper was ever discovering new techniques in the field of Biology and efficiently applying them. He maintained an excellent general library and medical library. It was often said by his peers that it was a real inspiration to tour his libraries and through his office. He was a head of the curve and often devised highly innovative methods and procedures to accomplish his daily work. As a result of his extraordinary accomplishments, innovation and unique dedication in his field, He is recognized internationally as a trail blazer in the field of Biology that has continued to inspire many young up in coming scientist to greatness, even to this very day. **Omega Psi Phi Fraternity Founder, Dr. Oscar James Cooper, entered Omega chapter on October 09, 1972.**

[13] **The first book of the Old Testament** of the Holy Bible gives an account of the formation of the planet earth. For example, **" And then there was light,"** does not just suggest the sun, but something new. Have you ever felt "enlightened" when a new idea comes to you? As the excitement grows, you give your new idea life by putting your thought/idea into action! The latter process, although critical to the ultimate success of the idea, is not all that is needed. In order for your idea to take flight and truly have lasting impact, it must have love/passion to endure the obstacles that are sure to come **This is how our beloved Founders felt about organizing and creating their beloved Omega Psi Phi fraternity**. First there was the idea, second the substance, and third the time/dedication, and unconditional LOVE we have all given it for many years. This crucial intangible is what has served as the foundation for its longevity and sets Omega Psi Phi fraternity head and shoulders above all others.

---

[13] From the Omega Xi web site Founders section

~ GONE BUT NOT FORGOTTEN ~

ALL GOOD AND TRUE OMEGA MEN,
AT LEAST ONCE DURING THE COURSE OF THEIR LIFE TIME, SHOULD
JOURNEY TO THE SACRED BURIAL SITES OF OUR BELOVED FOUNDERS
TO PAY THEIR RESPECT TO THESE GREAT MEN. AND BROTHERS, WE
MUST ALSO KEEP THESE SACRED SITES WELL TENDED/IMMACULATE
TO THE END OF ALL TIME.

◇◇◇◇

~ THE RESTING PLACES OF OUR FOUNDERS ~

BISHOP EDGAR A. LOVE

FOUNDER EDGAR A. LOVE entered Omega chapter on May, 1, 1974.
His body is interred at the Mt Auburn Cemetery, Baltimore, MD. His grave site is located off Saint Rest Road at lot 1020.

~~~~

DR. ERNEST E. JUST

FOUNDER ERNEST E. JUST entered Omega chapter October 27, 1941. He is interred at Lincoln Memorial Cemetery 4001 Suitland, Maryland. Section 1 plot #226, site #2. It is overlooking a hillside. His grave is a granite monument simply marked with his last name, "JUST."

~~~~

DR. FRANK COLEMAN

FOUNDER FRANK COLEMAN entered Omega Chapter February 24, 1967. He is interred at Lincoln Memorial cemetery at 4001 Suitland Maryland, Section K, plot #199, site 4. Founder Coleman lies next to his darling wife. His tombstone is a simple bronze nameplate stating: Frank Coleman, District of Columbia, 1st Lieutenant 368 Infantry, World War I, July 11, 1889-February 24, 1967.

~~~~

DR. OSCAR J. COOPER

Founder Oscar J. Cooper entered Omega Chapter October 09, 1972. He is interred at White Marsh Memorial Park, Ambler, PA, Section P, plot #223, Site #1

~~~~

THE SUPREME BASILEUS OF THE UNIVERSE SPEAKS

I am the Creator and Architect of the Universe.
I am the Alpha and Omega, the Beginning and the Ending of all things..." (Rev. 1:8)

You may think that I am far, far away my Omega Men, looking down on you. No! I am in your heart, mind and soul. I am with you each and every day. You are my Holy Temple. I am within you. I can help you Omega to become an even greater shining light for others to follow.

***Know that I am the Supreme Basileus of the Universe!
And know that your beloved Founders are with me in Heaven/Omega Chapter.***

I was with your beloved Omega Founders on Friday evening, November 17, 1911. *I searched their hearts, was deeply touched and therefore judged them worthy of my special love and wisdom. I gave them the Four Cardinal Principles to give to you to live by. If you have personally fallen short, know that all things work to the glory of God! Draw near to the UPLIFT in the four Cardinal Principles, the pearls of wisdom and unwritten laws that your Founders and I gave you to guide you? Cling to these sacred things and keep them ever with you. Always keep me first in Omega and I will be your refuge.* **Trust and follow your chosen Leadership,** *for I have* ordained, hand picked them and anointed them with my own hand. **Always stay active in Omega** and know that only with your continuing active help, can Omega be the worthy, great uplifting force for your race that I and your Founders intended it to be.

I have seen the seeds of division by some in your ranks. This saddens your Founders and me very much. Remember, Satan is a liar, is very jealous of your love for me and is always there to test, try to divide and mislead my children. Also, be ye ever mindful of the fact that, "The glory of young men is their strength, eagerness and newly born burning fire, of old men, their wisdom, good judgment and experience." Be wise Omega men and do not fall into Satan's divisive tricks! Look deep inside yourselves. Let your love for ME AND Omega Dear guide and unite you and turn these things (seemingly divisive stumbling blocks) into positives. For what Satan means for bad, I can easily turn into good. Embrace ye one another (new school and old school), rather than repulse and separate from each other. And, therein will you find my deeper blessings.

Be true to your great brotherhood, friendship, secret pearls, poems and your four Cardinal Principles and they will see you through. New school, respect those older than you, because with their blood, sweat, eternal love, hard work and tears, they faithfully maintained and held the torch of Omega **high so that its brilliant light captured your heart and eye**. This did not have to be so! Old school, respect, nurture, cherish, understand and yes protect your young and newer brothers, for you, whether you will admit it or not, were once them. Remember, respect begets respect. They are not your little children. Your beloved Founders and I have called them forward. Therefore, they are indeed worthy. Embrace them and do not resent or be jealous of them for enjoying life and feeling their way through their youth. Eagerly be the instrument and guiding light to shape them to be what your Founders and I would want them to be.

Bind yourself even closer in your unity and brotherly love and openly **live by my words men of Omega** and no earthly force will be able to stop you. "Stop listening to Satan's voice that contradicts what you know in your heart to be right." (Proverbs 19:27) Arm yourself with truth and seek only my face and with my help, he will get behind thee. I repeat for your benefit a part of your Omega Hymn. "Live nobly as all real men do...with faith in God and heart and mind." In times of trials and doubt, "Search your hearts Omega Men" and there you will find your Founders and me. We Love you and will forever protect and guide you, if you let us. **And lo, we (Cooper, Just, Love, Coleman and I, the Supreme Basileus of the Universe) will be with you always, EVEN TO THE END OF THE WORLD.** [14]
PRAISE BE TO ALMIGHTY GOD, THE SUPREME BASILEUS OF THE UNIVERSE!

---

[14] The 1988 Oracle, Vol. 71, No.1* Poem by unknown writer "the Supreme Basilue Speaks" served as bases/blue print. Modified by the Author/Vernon Steve Weakley

CHAPTER II

1960-1969

THE TURBULENT AND RACIALLY CHARGED SIXTIES AND ITS IMPACT ON OMEGA

Pi Chapter located at Morgan State College in Baltimore, Maryland. The chapter was supporting a public forum featuring Minister Malcolm X.

The struggle for social justice shifted into high gear during the turbulent sixties. Brothers were active participants in the "sit-ins" and other demonstrations designed to call attention to the plight of Black Americans. Undergraduate Omega brothers especially were involved in the demonstrative aspect of the civil rights struggle. Blacks could not eat at white establishments, could not even use the same bath room as whites or drink at the same water fountain as whites in the south prior to and into the sixties. Further, Black Americans were not given equal rights, particularly in the critically important area of education, were openly beaten and many were lynched in the dark of night if they spoke up and tried to correct their circumstance in any form or fashion. Clearly injustice ruled the day where Black Americans were concerned.

Martin Luther King Jr. was a champion of peace and with that he called for a non-violent solution to the blatant civil right's injustices oppressing Black Americans. Medgar Evers, a NAACP Field Secretary of Mississippi, who had tried this same approach a few years before him, was cut violently down (assassinated) at 37 in the prime of his life by a white man in June 1963, who boldly strolled into his neighborhood with a 30/30 rifle. Black people at that time in America's history were marching for freedom and injustice all across the nation. Many were met with vicious German Shepard dogs, beaten severely with billy clubs, had high powered water hoses put on them and often had to endure the indignities of humiliating public arrests by brutal, racist police. These embarrassing indignities were shown over and over again on television stations all across the world, adding to the belittling stigma of black people.

In an obvious contrast to the teachings of Martin Luther King Jr., other voices such as Malcolm X, H. Rap Brown, and the Black Panthers advocated harsher methods such as fighting fire with fire with extreme violence to force America's hand in correcting its injustice on black people. **Which method would the men of Omega choose?** Time would tell! The untimely and surprising death of President John F. Kennedy in 1963 proved to be a stumbling block to all of Black America. He had given a glimpse of hope for a better day in America for people of color with his positive stance and advocacy. But in spite of this great set back, Black Americans moved forward to the dawn of a new era in the civil rights movement.

Omega Psi Phi Fraternity attempted to go on about its business even though America was slowly turning into a constantly growing, rumbling powder keg around it. In 1961, the Washington, D.C. Grand Conclave did an excellent job of highlighting the fifty years of accomplishments by Omega Psi Phi Fraternity Inc. Brothers attended the 1961 Golden Anniversary Conclave in record numbers. Founders Love, Cooper, and Coleman were present. Thirteen of twenty-three former Grand Basilei were also in attendance. **Young brothers had the once-in-a-life-time opportunity to mingle with some of the greatest Black men that America had produced.**

The Golden Anniversary Conclave authorized $140,000-$150,000 for the construction of a new National Headquarters

Building in Washington, D.C. In 1964, the new National Headquarters was dedicated. The building was a dream come true and **was the first building of its type to be built by a black fraternity.** Founders Love, Cooper and Coleman participated in the ceremonies. The name was later changed to the International Headquarters. It was located at 2714 Georgia Avenue, N.W., Washington, D.C. 20001. The 1968 Charlotte Grand Conclave mandated a Constitutional Convention for the revision of the Constitution and By-Laws as well as the Ritual.

<<>>

Founder FRANK COLEMAN enters Omega Chapter FEBRUARY 24TH, 1967. He had been a steady rock in our midst that we simply were not ready to be apart from. The death of our beloved Ernest E. Just many years previous had battered, severely bruised and tested us but did not prepare us for what we knew was sure to come. Founder Frank Coleman's death shook us all to the core and made Omega face the stark reality that **the Angel of Death had now come to steal Omega Psi Phi Fraternity's pride and joy, our beloved remaining Founders.** Our unified prayers soared even higher in an effort to hold back the inevitable.

<<>>

Martin Luther King Jr. was, without a doubt, the leading champion of the Negro cause in civil rights in America at that time. **BAYARD RUSTIN, an Omega man initiated into Omega in Upsilon Chapter, Wilberforce University in 1932**, was credited by Martin Luther King himself in the early stages of the civil rights movement with counseling him and the movement on the theory and technique of non-violence. Bayard Rustin was the key behind the scene player and organizer of the 1963 March on Washington. He also was a youth organizer for the 1941 march on Washington as well. The significant contributions of Omega man Rustin are often over looked in American history books.

On April 4th, 1968, Martin Luther King Jr. the noted civil rights leader was assassinated in Memphis Tennessee at the Loraine Hotel. He was mourned by the world in addition to all members of Omega Psi Fraternity. Although not a member of Omega Psi Phi fraternity, his tragic death had significant impact on Omega as it did on all of America. And, as if this wasn't enough, in the same year Robert Kennedy, leading candidate for the U.S. presidency, was also assassinated. He had reached out and showed enormous public displays of love to black America, prior to his death in many national settings as if to continue and even improve on the love affair his previously assassinated brother (President John F. Kennedy) had initiated.

    The deaths of these two great men in the same year were the straws that broke the camel's back. Black America was in an uproar. Many of our cities, particularly our black communities, were burning to the ground from intense rioting in the streets. People both black and white were losing their lives. Millions upon millions of dollars of property was being destroyed and going up in smoke. America appeared to be on the verge of coming apart at the seams.

    Out of the ashes of our tears, sorrow and dark despair came a young, courageous Omega champion named **JESSE JACKSON** to lead Black America. He would go on to become the 2nd Vice Grand Basileus of Omega Psi Phi fraternity, Inc.

15

    Jesse Jackson was at Martin Luther King's side as he lay dying on the balcony of the Loraine Hotel. This event and the many experiences that led him to it propelled Jesse Jackson as well as many other Omega men to the fore front of the national civil right's movement. **Omega Psi Phi Fraternity, Inc. had taken a side. It chose the road of peace as set before us by Martin**

---

[15] Live search.com/Jesse Jackson 3 images on on this and preceding three pages

Luther King and a big afro wearing young man named Jesse Jackson. An odd sort of calm slowly crept its way across America that prevented its path to destruction.

Jesse L. Jackson, Omega Psi Phi Fraternity's strong young lion, would leap to the fore and go on to be president of Operation PUSH, found the Rainbow Coalition, and be the first Black man to run for the office of the president of the United States. He ran for this prestigious office in 1984 and 1988. This is just one of many great accomplishments in the area of civil rights for Jesse Jackson. It could be said that, "**What the Devil meant for bad, a loving and merciful God turned into good.** I am sure that the evil men who plotted to take Martin Luther King's life calculated that his death would strike sheer terror in the hearts of decent, peaceful, law abiding Black people and thus surely be the end of the Negro civil right's movement in America, given his vital role. This was not the case. Jesse Jackson boldly took up where Martin Luther King ended and has continued to the writing of this book to be a major civil rights force in America.

This bold talking, often rhyming charismatic Omega man has also played major roles on the international scene in the release of many American hostages both military and civilian. This fact is not so widely publicized but his courage and well known integrity and unique diplomacy approach succeeded in many instances, when the U.S. government could not even get an audience with the warring country. Jesse Jackson also showed extraordinary courage in moving forward to advance the cause, given the murder of Martin Luther King in this blood soaked period of American history. His outstanding efforts during this period made a significant positive difference in the lives of BLACK PEOPLE.

Jesse L. Jackson, with the great work that he did in this era, has indeed made all of his brothers in Omega Psi Phi Fraternity proud. He is and has always been an openly proud member of Omega. Psi Phi Fraternity.

The I. Gregory Newton, (the 24th Grand Basileus of Omega Psi Phi Fraternity) era begins: (Term 1958-1961)

THE OMEGA PSI PHI FRATERNITY INC. 43

Elected officers[16]

I. GREGORY NEWTON – Grand Basileus; Cary D. Jacobs-Vice Grand Basileus; James L. Felder-Second Vice Grand Basileus; Walter H. Riddick-Keeper Of Records and Seal; Jesse B. Blayton-Grand Keeper Of Finance; Ellis F. Corbett-Editor-In-Chief of Oracle; Carl A. Earles-Grand Counselor; William D. Martin-Grand Marshal; H. Carl Moultrie, I-National Executive Secretary

Grand Basileus Newton was initiated into Omega Psi Phi Fraternity in Beta Phi chapter. At the Golden Anniversary Conclave Grand Basileus Newton elaborated on the state of the fraternity and its role in uplifting America and the Negro Race. He stated, "We should pause to reflect upon the growth and development of our association of men nurtured by Founders who possessed foresight and judgment. We are bold to assert that we are better men today than we were yesterday because we are part of a human grouping which is far better today than it was yesterday. The second half of our fraternal century brothers will present challenges we must be prepared to meet. To that end, that brothers must prepare themselves for progress within the latter half of the century, we should rededicate ourselves to fulfill the four cardinal principles of our Dear Omega-manhood, scholarship, perseverance and uplift."

---

[16] I. Gregory Newton & elected officer information and picture reference from the Beta Phi web site http://www.betaphi.com/ignewton.htm

The Annual Report of the National Executive Secretary to the Supreme Council for the Conclave Year, 1960 substantiated that for the first time since 1955, the number of initiations reported exceeded the preceding year; the active roster reflected an increase over 1959; total chapters equaled 265 and total income represented a substantial increase over 1959. Omega was growing.

Additionally, the administration felt that it detected in some areas a slight increase in academic awareness. If this is true Grand Basileus Newton stated, "we have managed to scratch a surface which up to now appeared to have the resistance feature of "Indestructible Formica." It is felt that the only way we can realize any consistent success in developing academic awareness and intellectual progress is to pursue the subject constantly and relentlessly. Those of us in academic pursuits have been made to realize more and more that the salvation of our youths is to be found in the extent to which they are prepared to compete successfully with any other person or group." Grand Basileus Newton decided it was time to invest in and pay more attention to the progress of Omega's under-graduate brothers.

Major recommendations made by the Newton Supreme Council were:

1. That the Supreme Council be authorized to employ an assistant to the National Executive Secretary when ever it is of the opinion that the financial status of the fraternity may permit. One of the responsibilities of this officer will be to work very closely with the undergraduate program.

2. Compulsory Grand Conclave Attendance. Chapter 3, Article 1, Section 1 of the By-laws; Section 1A-stated, official representation from each chapter to the Grand Conclave is required. Any chapter not officially represented at the Grand Conclave at least once within a sequence of two Conclaves shall be devoid of the right to conduct initiations and be suspended from performing any activities. This legislation shall become effective as of the 1964 Grand Conclave.

<<>>

Omega men honored at the 50 Anniversary Conclave were:

Omega Man of the Year – **GEORGE L. P. WEAVER**

Outstanding Citizen Of The year – **ROBERT C. WEAVER**

Special Scholarship Citation – **ARTHUR P. DAVIS**

<<>>

The following are "Golden Words" from the remaining three living Founders at the 50th Anniversary Conclave in Washington D.C. in 1961. A rare public lighter side of these great men was shown to the delight of the large audience.

~ FOUNDER FRANK COLEMAN ~

Mr. Grand Basileus, Master of ceremonies, Distinguished Public Officials, the New Grand Basileus, My Colleagues of 50, 40, 30 and on down to one year, My Brothers and friends:

What can one say in an occasion of this kind? I'm sure I don't know. I can assure you of one thing. I'll not bore you. I'll not tire you. I can take a hint. I would say as a matter of fact, that I am very glad that I have a very short time, because I wouldn't know what to say, realizing the very small part that I played in the development of this tremendous benevolent and powerful organization.

I might rumble and reminisce, but I doubt if it would mean a great deal. We were and are friends. We have been friends. We will be friends. We can say about anything we want to each other. Nobody gets angry. Because we're very certain that the other one of us that said it simply hasn't very much intellect.

But, whatever strength and continuity existed in those early times was based on the thing called friendship among a group of men that stuck together. And, as I looked over this great audience, even before Moultrie said it, I visualized small groups around the tables containing personal friends or comprised at least of personal friends. They say of personal friendship that it spreads and spreads and spreads. I simply want to salute you, congratulate you, and to name Oscar Cooper as one of those boys who shared in this particular friendship and I now present him to you.

~ OSCAR J. COOPER ~

Brother Cooper: Brother Grand Basileus, Co-Founders Coleman and Love, Members of the Supreme Council, Forty-year Men, Brothers and Friends,

What are you supposed to do when a man hands you a period and asks you to be brief? This fraternity in its growth has stepped over its original concept of a Founders' Day celebration. We were told that Founders day was a day of which we could run loose and say anything we wanted to as long as we wanted to. Consequently, not being an extemporaneous speaker, I have always prepared a paper. But for the last several Conclaves I have written my paper and put it in my pocket and carried it back home with me, because I have been told to be brief.

Tonight, as I said, we were given a period, so I don't know what to do. However, I think of the words of Browning when I think of the growth of this fraternity and what it has meant, when he said:

"Grow Old along with me! The best is yet to be, the last of life, for which the first was made. Our times are in his hand. Who saith, A whole I planned, Youth shows but half; trust God; see all, nor be afraid!"

Now, just another word. If it were possible for you all to stretch your imagination and look back upon time when a little conversation in the early part of 1911 has developed into a gigantic organization with unlimited power for good as we see here tonight, you could think of the saying that from a little acorn a mighty oak was developed.

We have got that just a thousand times-from a little conversation a wonderful organization which has been a powerful force not only for themselves but for all humanity, for everybody with whom they come in contact.

And, using my period, I'll simply say here that as the men of Omega look upon themselves they will ask themselves, in words used by our great president Kennedy when he was being sworn in, in his inaugural address: **Ask not what the fraternity has done for you but what as loyal members you have done for the Omega Psi Phi Fraternity.** I thank you.

I have another period. There is another young man among us, who, though older than I, had a great deal of respect for my leadership as a student. A young man whose notes I had to read to him before his examination which were too cold for him to read. Our illustrious, Bishop, Edgar A. Love.

~ FOUNDER EDGAR A. LOVE ~

Brother Love: Brother Grand Basileus, Brother Toastmaster, Brothers in Omega and Friends;

I had more than a period handed to me. When I came in I was asked how many watches did I need. And I brought one, and he asked me did I need another one.

This is a glorious occasion. I know each one of us would like to say a lot of things tonight. This happens only once in 50 years. But it's a good thing we can't say it all.

But let me say one thing to start with. I don't think any three men have been closer together than Frank Coleman, Oscar Cooper and I though all these 50 years. A reporter asked me today how Omega started and I told him it started with three young men, particularly before we consulted Ernest Just, who wanted to cement their friendship in the college and then to make sure that the friendship carried on through the years, and then bring other men in to cement a friendship in college that would be carried on into the years beyond. And you here tonight, every one of you is an expression of that desire, because you are all friends.

There is an organization in America called the Society of Friends. I think it has the most beautiful name of any organization I know. We call them the Quakers, but their name is the Society of Friends. That what I like to think Omega is as well. It's a society of friends (applause)

I wish I knew every one of you. I wish I could know you as intimately as I know these two men. I do know so many of you. I love people. I think everybody in Omega is a person who loves people. And, I wish I could know you. There's so much you could add to me. I wouldn't give much to you but there's so much to add to me. These sessions we have been having year after year have kept us young. Frank Coleman, Oscar Cooper and I, we stay out where life is flowing. And if you get out where life isn't flowing, it's going to pass you by. You'd better stay out where life is. That's what we're trying to do. Thank you very much. And we'll be with you on the 75th anniversary and also on the 100th anniversary.

<<>>

The Cary D. Jacobs, (the 25th Grand Basileus of Omega Psi Phi Fraternity, Inc.) era begins: (Term 1961-1964)

Elected Officers at the 48th Grand Conclave held in Washington D.C. (The Golden Anniversary for Omega Psi Phi Fraternity)

CARY D. JACOBS – Grand Basileus; George E. Meares First Vice Grand Basileus; Robert H. Tucker- Second Vice Grand Basileus; Walter H. Riddick- Grand Keeper of Records and Seal; J.B. Blayton-Grand Keeper Of Finance; Ellis F. Corbett-Editor of Oracle; Jeff Greenup, Grand Counselor; Harry L. Pettrie, Grand Marshal; and H. Carl Moultrie, I-National Executive Secretary.

The administration above was elected at the 1961 50th anniversary Grand Conclave in Washington D.C.

<<>>

A nation-wide voter registration drive was the significant focus of this administration. It was widely held by Omega's leadership that the American Negro would need political clot to change his circumstance. To this end, Omega Psi Phi Fraternity, Inc. openly encouraged its membership to not only register to vote themselves, but also get out and vigorously campaign publicly for others to do so as well. This Omega initiative was successful in significantly swelling the voting rolls of Negroes across America.

Under Grand Basileus Jacobs' administration at the 1962 Indianapolis Conclave, the Social Action committee chaired by attorney **HERBERT E. TUCKER**, an assistant District Attorney for the Commonwealth of Massachusetts presented a rousing report about the Negro plight that made many black papers across America. An example is shown below from the Indianapolis Recorder, December 29, 1962 issue. The committee lashed out at the people of the United States "who would stand in the way of making America the arsenal of democracy."

THE REPORT SAID that "acts such as those perpetrated by Mississippi Governor Ross Barnett and Arkansas Governor Orval Faubus (who both were nationally known racist bent of stopping the progress of integration in America) hinder this nation in continuing to be the chief custodian of the democratic heritage of the free world." The report went on to say that in many instances America was "missing the boat" in its nuclear race, by not using all available man power, because of petty jealousies and bigotry. The human race was greatly endangered by discrimination and segregations. The report went on to enlist the support of all its members (Omega Psi Phi Fraternity) to support the NAACP.

It was pointed out in the report that many Omega chapters had taken life memberships in the NAACP and that there were some chapters still paying on memberships. It also scolded chapters for not starting to get on board with getting their chapter memberships. The report set out that no devoted American citizen should rest on his laurels until every vintage of second class citizenship was erased from this nation. The report was also cognizant of the fact that the Negro must be prepared to perform efficiently, when the opportunity presented itself.

Grand Basileus Cary D. Jacobs's administration's second term began in 1962. One historical point of note and change in his administration was at 2nd Vice Grand Basileus. **JESSE L. JACKSON**, a relatively unknown college student at this point in time in history, was elected and served Omega well in this position.

Under Grand Basileus Cary D. Jacobs leadership and courage, Omega Psi Phi Fraternity, Inc. took a bold step and went on public record in backing the famous march on Washington. This act clearly demonstrated to the world that Omega Psi Phi Fraternity, if no other organizations would, dig in its heals and take a public stand against violence and injustice in all forms against the Negro in America. The Supreme Council of the fraternity as a part of its social action program boldly endorsed the nation wide civil rights demonstration for the march on Washington scheduled for August 28, 1963. Omega Psi Phi Fraternity, Inc. called for all chapters to have representation in Washington on that day.

An Article in the Carolinian, (North Carolina's leading weekly) in Raleigh N.C. on Saturday May 4, 1963, read:

"Frat Head Warns Negro of Plight in Present Order"

Vice Grand Basileus George E. Meares echoed his administration's and Omega Psi Phi Fraternity's sentiments to members at Hayes-Taylor, YMCA, Sunday morning. He firmly stated that, "the failure of the Negro to preserve his traditions was hindering his fight to achieve first class citizenship."

Omega Psi Phi Fraternity's Vice Grand Basileus, Meares was extremely critical of any educational system that tended to **only educate the head and not the hand**. To provide an example of the times, he told how the Negro was once in control of bricklaying industry in America. "In the old days the job paid about $10.00 per day and a worker had to lay 3000 bricks. Today the job pays about $40.00 per day and one cannot lay but 300 bricks. The Negro left the job after pioneering it and now does not enjoy the money being paid, said Meares. He was also much concerned about the story going around about Negro consumer power. He felt that the Negro should be interested in production. He also attacked the fact that Negroes are buying Cadillacs and parking them beside rented houses. He warned that if the Negro is going to be a power in the economic world, he must stop buying what he wants and be satisfied with getting only what he needs.

Grand Basileus Meares tore into the Negro's participation in politics as well. He was fearful that too many Negroes voted the politician slate and not one studied and appraised by himself. He also pointed out that Negroes should stop asking what will I get out of politics but what can I do to strengthen the political system so that vice and corruption can be taken out. He was mindful that Negroes did not make contributions to political parties, but rather begged for dinner tickets and other favors, in exchange for their participation. He further stressed the fact that Negroes who graduated from school and colleges are too prone to forget the school after they have gone. "Many of us leave a school and if some one asks us to make a contribution or endow the school, we become insulted," he said.

He further stated, "Our gratitude should extend beyond graduation day and we should remember that someone made it possible for us and we should make it possible for someone else." Grand Basileus Meares closed with a resounding note on credit buying. He admonished the fraternity that long range credit buying was a noose and in many instances required one having two jobs. The latter lent itself to nervous tension and much embarrassment. He pointed to the fact that economics was the prime factor in taking the first step toward integration. Financial stability should be the goal, not financial liability."

<◇>

Medgar Evers, nationally known NAACP Field Secretary was slain by an assassin's bullet on June 19, 1963. This event represented a sharp turning point in the civil rights movement propelling it to national attention. Dignitaries both black and white from all across the nation attended his funeral and vowed to resolve the historical injustice toward Negroes in America. Omega Psi Phi Fraternity was there!

The GEORGE E. MEARES, (the 26th Grand Basileus of Omega Psi Phi Fraternity) era begins: (Term 1964-1967)

Ellis F. Corbett – First Vice-Grand Basileus; Second Vice-Grand-Dorsey C. Miller; Grand Keeper of Records and Seal-Walter H. Riddick; Grand Keeper of Finance-Jesse B. Blayton, Sr.; Editor in Chief of Oracle-Audrey Pruitt; Grand Counselor-Marion W. Garnett; Former Grand Basileus-Cary D. Jacobs; Nation Executive Secretary H. Carl Moultrie, I.

Brother George E. Meares was a Supreme Council member for more than a decade. He provided extremely valuable leadership and hands on experience to incoming future Grand Basilei and various other Supreme Council members that enabled Omega Psi Phi Fraternity to continue to ascend to a high level of performance for its membership for many years long after he left the scene. Grand Basileus Meares was initiated in Epsilon Chapter in 1938. He served Omega in many capacities throughout his life. A criminal justice scholarship for deserving students was established in his name that continues even till this day.

1967 - ABEL'S FABULOUS 27 – Alpha Chapter

*In 1967, while still under out going Grand Basileus George E. Meares, an incident occurred where Negro military men and members of the fraternity were not given rental housing in The Boston surrounding area. The NAACP made a special appeal to Omega Psi Phi Fraternity at the Conclave to assist them in their protest on the matter of the segregated hotels etc. . After being called to Order, Ground Basileus Meares immediately made an emergency motion regarding this matter.

Sunday, August 13, 1967

A motion was made that a Special Committee be appointed on the hotel matter. Brother **HAROLD D. THOMPSON**, **ROBERT MCDANIELS** and **FLOYD FRANKLIN** were appointed to the committee.

---

[17] Howard University, Alpha chaptet web site

As a means of simplifying and making quite understandable Omega Psi Phi Fraternity's position on this serious matter, a letter was written in as a direct response to a request of the National Association for the Advancement of Colored People. As a loyal, many year supporter of the NAACP, a letter addressed to the President of the United States in the name of the Omega Psi Phi Fraternity was deemed necessary. This action, given the racially unjust times for the American Negro, was yet another bold and potentially dangerous step for Omega. **The latter is evidence that Omega Psi Phi Fraternity, no matter the cost, would not just live within itself. It would reach outward as a strong unified force into its community and make a difference in the lives of black people**.

Omega Psi Phi Fraternity Inc. protested to the president of the United States who was at that time Lyndon B. Johnson and successfully won a major success for all Negroes in America.

Below is the content of the letter from Omega Psi Phi Fraternity and the response from the president of the United States office.

AUGUST 14, 1967

President Lyndon B. Johnson
The White House
Washington, D.C.

Dear Mr. President

We, the fifty-six year old Omega Psi Phi Fraternity, Inc. assembled in National Conclave in Boston, Mass., where 197 years ago America's first "Freedom Fighters" – Chrispus Attucks and four compatriots fell - do this day most profoundly thank you for the administrative action of June 23, 1967 whereby all apartments and trailer camps near military bases in the "Free State" of Maryland refusing to accommodate Negro service men were decreed off-limits for all personnel.

Because this sanction so effectively ends one of the racial segregations phases undermining the American principles for which the flower of her manhood dies, we respectfully implore and urge you to issue a like directive —sanction against all segregating units inn the vicinity of every military base in the land.

Because the most of our members are of the blood of Attucks and of the 300,000 Negro service men inconvenienced and humiliated by racial segregation, we see a connection. Our common heritage of Boston Commons were effort in a common cause transcended race, 'ere our nation was born, we know... We know equally well the neutralizing effect of racial segregation on the hearts and minds of these, our men, in uniform. We, therefore, unhesitatingly attest the need to vouchsafe this historic oneness of spirit to our day-equally in peace as in war.

Mr. President, an administrative decree that military housing be open for all or for none would express again, most forcibly in this additional area, the sincere intent of the Executive Branch of our government to be guided in spirit as well as in letter by the decisions of the Supreme Court of the United States. Our letter is the applause and the appeal of 30,000 college and university trained men, organized into 298 chapters, located in 36 states and the District of Columbia.

For your understanding consideration, we are forever grateful.

Respectfully,

The Omega Psi Phi Fraternity, Inc.

George E. Meares

Grand Basileus

Response Letter from President Lyndon Johnson's office:

23, AUG, 1967

Mr. George E. Meares
Grand Basileus
Omega Psi Phi Fraternity, Inc.
2714 Georgia Avenue, N. W.
Washington, D.C. 20001

Dear Mr. Meares:

President Johnson has asked that I reply to your letter of 14, August 1967 in support of the recent action of the Department of Defense aimed at eliminating off-base housing which discriminates against Negro military personnel.

I am enclosing for your information a copy of the memorandum which Secretary McNamara issued on 22 June 1967 pertaining to Andrews Air Force base. This memorandum restricts new entails by servicemen in multi-unit dwellings to those where racial discrimination is not practiced against uniformed personnel.

The actions subsequently taken at other Maryland installations have been substantially similar to the actions at Andres. We are now engaged in vigorous efforts at major installations in the United States to obtain equal opportunity in housing for all military families.

We thank you for the encouragement and welcome your continued interest and support.

Sincerely,

Thomas D. Morris

<<>>

The ELLIS F. CORBERT, (the 27th Grand Basileus of Omega Psi Phi Fraternity) era begins: (Term 1967-1970)

E. F. CORBETT

Elected officers in the administration with Grand Basileus Corbett:

GRAND BASILEUS ELLIS F. CORBETT, First Vice Grand Basileus, James S. Avery Sr.; Lincoln C. Scott, 2nd Vice Grand Basileus; Walter H. Riddick, Grand Keeper of Records and Seal; J.B. Blayton Sr. Grand Keeper of Finance; Audrey Pruitt, Editor of the Oracle; Marion Garnett, Grand Counselor; Gerson L. Stroud, Grand Marshal; H. Albiob Ferrell, Grand Chaplain; George Meares, Immediate Past Grand Basileus; H. Carl Moultrie, National Executive Secretary; Finus C. Winkler, Assistant Executive Secretary.

Grand Basileus Corbett was a highly respected jovial, pleasant man who had been the Editor of the Oracle, (our fraternity's communication organ) for many years (seventeen) prior to his move upward to Grand Basileus. Corbett had strong ideas about what was right for Omega. He recognized long before it became a universally accepted theme that the talents of educated Black men-especially those in organizations like Omega Psi Phi Fraternity could be the necessary force to break the will of the strong segregationist forces in America at that time. He felt Omega should be put to the test of relevancy where its role and impact in the Black community was concerned. Additionally, Grand Basileus Corbett was also a publicist in his nine to five life in Greensboro, North Carolina. He was on the staff of North

Carolina A&T University. This valuable experience served him well in enabling him to effectively communicate his ideals to the membership of Omega Psi Phi Fraternity. Brothers had known Grand Basileus Corbett from his great work as the Oracle Editor and trusted him for his straight forwardness and easy going nature.

Two very significant accomplishments of Grand Basileus Corbett were establishing a senior high rise for senior citizens by Omega Psi Phi's National Housing Authority and nationwide Diabetes testing. Omega received national acclaim from Negro organizations such as the NAACP and also from the major Negro media sources of the day for these highly innovative national outreach efforts.

Another major challenge for Grand Basileus Corbett during his administration came from a movement by some of the members to lower the grade point average for in coming under graduate members which would have represented a move to 2.5 under the 4.0 system and a move to 1.5 under a 3.0 system. Grand Basileus and his administration stood their ground even to the point of asking those who insisted on lowering the standards of Omega to leave and form their own new fraternity. This stanch position by Grand Basileus Corbett ruled the day and in doing so, enabled Omega to keep the very high scholastic standards its Founders stood for and established.

~ A REFLECTION IN TIME ~

Members of Beta Chapter Lincoln University 1969

PERTINENT EVENTS AND/OR OMEGA ACCOMPLISHMENTS DURING THIS PERIOD

18th **Grand Basileus Z. ALEXANDER LOOBY**, famous civil rights attorney, home is bombed on **April 19, 1960.**

<<>>

THETA RHO Chapter, Frankfurt, Germany takes 1st action to acquire a chapter on **June 20, 1962.**

<<>>

Omega man, **WILLIAM O. WALKER**, became the first African American State Cabinet member in Ohio on **January 14, 1963**

<<>>

The former National Headquarters at 2714 Georgia Avenue, N.W. dedication ceremony was conducted on **November 28, 1964**

<<>>

Omega man, **ROY WILKINS** elected Executive Director of the NAACP on **July 08, 1965**

<<>>

Omega man, **ROBERT C. WEAVER** became the first African American U.S. Cabinet member on **January 17, 1966.**

<<>>

Omega man, **Lt. Col. NORMAN A. McDANIEL**, awarded the Silver Star for his courage while a POW in Vietnam on **July 20, 1966**

<<>>

Founder, Professor **FRANK COLEMAN** entered Omega Chapter on **February 24, 1967**

<<>>

Omega man, the great **LANGSTON HUGHES**, internationally renowned Poet, writer enters Omega Chapter on **May, 22, 1967**

<<>>

Omega man, Dr. **WILLIAM ""BILL" COSBY, famous actor, comedian and author** receives an Emmy Award for the TV series "I SPY" on **June 4, 1967."**

<<>>

Omega man, **ROBERT H. LAWRENCE** (in 1966) was selected as the first Black to serve in the United States Astronaut Program. Lawrence earned a Ph.D. Degree in chemistry at Ohio State He was killed in a tragic training exercise in 1967 on December 08th.

FAMOUS OMEGA MEN WITH ACCOMPLISHMENTS OF SPECIAL NOTE DURING THIS PERIOD ARE AS FOLLOWS.[18]

Langston Hughes
1902 - 1967
Xi Phi Chapter-1926
POET, AUTHOR EXTRAORDINAIRE

Born in Joplin, MO. Graduated from high school in Cleveland, Ohio. Graduated from Lincoln University in 1929. He began his career as a full time writer in 1930. Hughes learned a great deal as a young man from his extensive travels in Mexico, Europe and Africa. Langston Hughes published ten volumes of poetry and sixty-odd short stories. He also produced dramas, operas, and anthologies, in addition to his humorous books and two autobiographies. He was **awarded the Spingarn Medal in 1960 as "Poet Laureate"** of the

---

[18] Omega Men of Distinction/4th printing

Negro Race.

<<>>

William "Bill" Cosby
Born in 1937, was initiated in
Beta Alpha Alpha Chapter in 1988.
Entertainer, Educator, Actor, Philanthropist, Comedian

He was born in Germantown, a district of North Philadelphia. He attended Temple University on an athletic scholarship, but withdrew to follow his comedy career. **He rose from a life of poverty to become the first African-American to obtain a starring role in a weekly television series (1965).** Bill Cosby has earned recognition as an American Entertainment Megastar. He wrote his own material and developed a style of humor that became his internationally known trademark.

<<>>

Robert C. Weaver
was born in 1907
Initiated in Kappa Omicron Chapter-1926
Presidential Cabinet Member

Omega man Robert C. Weaver was the first African-American to be appointed as a United States presidential Cabinet Member. Born in Washington, D.C. Educated at Harvard, he earned his BS in 1921, MA in 1929 and his Ph.D. in 1934. He served in the [19]Roosevelt New Deal Program. He also taught at Northwestern, Columbia and NYU. The John Hay Whitney Foundation appointed Weaver to administer its Fellowship Program. Robert Weaver **served as advisor to John F. Kennedy in 1960, who later appointed him administrator of the Housing and Home Finance Agency. In 1966 President Lyndon B. Johnson nominated Robert Clifton Weaver to the newly created Cabinet Post of Secretary of Housing and Urban**

Development.

<<>>

Earl G. Graves
Born 1935
Initiated into Omega at Pi Chapter-1954
Publisher, Magazine Editor

Born in Brooklyn, New York. Omega man, Earl G. Graves received his B.A. from Morgan State College. He was a **staff member of Senator Robert F. Kennedy. (1965 - 1968)** He later established a number of successful enterprises. The best known is Black Enterprise Magazine. This highly successful a magazine became accepted as an authority on the progress of minorities in business, advocating social activation and responsibility to its readership in the black middle class.

<<>>

Benjamin E. Mays
1894 - 1984
Initiated in Omega at Gamma Chapter-1919
College President, Minister, Role Model for Leaders

Benjamin E. Mays was born in Epworth, Sc. His parents were slaves. He received his BA at Bates College in Maine in 1920. MA, at University of Chicago in 1925, and his Ph.D. in 1935. He published works in 1933, Dean of School of Religion at Howard University in 1934. Omega man Mays was a central figure in the National Urban League, NAACP, and World Council of Churches. Mays influenced Martin Luther King Jr., worked with Mahatma Ghandi, served at Howard in 1940, and was the **President of Morehouse until retirement in 1967.** He also was a **k**ey figure in the United Nations Children's Fund and International Youth Organizations. He wrote his highly regarded autobiography in 1971.

<<>>

1968 was a tough year not only for Omega, but all America as well. The M.L. King assassination, The Bobby Kennedy assassination and the fiasco at the Democratic National Convention in Chicago all occurred during this ill fated year.

Additionally, on **February 8th, 1968** the killings and shootings at S.C. State also occurred. Three students (two college and one high school student) were killed and many others were seriously wounded on February 8th in this terrible event. A protest occurred the day before at the local bowling alley which students were attempting to integrate. Cleveland Sellers was a student leader. The NAACP field director at that time was **Rev. J. HERBERT NELSON, SR.**, the pastor of St. Luke Presbyterian Church. He was a member of Omega Psi Phi fraternity in the Orangeburg graduate chapter and an advisor to the undergrad chapter at Lambda Sigma (Claflin U). He was very much involved with the civil rights movement in Orangeburg and the surrounding area. Cleveland Sellers, a student activist/organizer and an Omega man, was an up close and personal eye witness to history in this water mark event. As of the writing of this book, Cleveland Sellers is the president of Voorhees College at Denmark, South Carolina.

<<>>

~ A REFLECTION IN TIME ~
FROM SCARED LITTLE LAMPS TO OMEGA MEN

FALL 1969 LAMPS OF UPSILON EPSILON (YE) CHAPTER, JACKSON STATE UNIVERSITY

64 THE HISTORY OF

Lee Benard
Charles Barnes
James Gibson
Overtee Garnicle
Charles Darden
Dee Denard
Robert L. Grant

Lee Hampton
Kenneth Hamilton
Sylvester Hall
Lee Jackson
Arthur Kinnard
Charles Larry
Ernest Largo

Bruno Moreland
Ray Munson
George Myers
Joe Neely
Larry Otis
Dewey Reeves
James Staples

Troy Smith
Vernon Winkley

1972 Group Photo / YE CHAPTER MEMBERS, JACKSON STATE UNIVERSITY

CHAPTER III

AMERICA'S DECADE OF PAIN
1970-1979
(Omega Reaches Out To Save The Black Community)

The James S. Avery, (the 28th Grand Basileus of Omega Psi Phi Fraternity) era begins: (Term 1970-1973)

Grand Basileus Avery was initiated in Omega in 1957 at Omicron Chi Chapter. He is still a member there at the time of this writing. The civil rights movement was in full blast during his era. Omega men would not miss or be found standing on the side line during a good fight under his leadership. Omega Psi Phi Fraternity became more visible and active and had significant impact in uplifting the Black community not only in the mandated areas but also in other meaningful areas as well. Yes, Omega was eagerly doing its mandated program. But the world cried out for more from Omega. Particularly in regards to playing a more out front role in countering the painful effects of the drug problem in America.

---

[20] Reginald E. Vance, Donald Ray Hornbuckle and Michael Lyles are contributing writers on this chapter

JAMES S. AVERY was elected at the 53rd Grand Conclave in Pittsburgh,

The Supreme Council Officers elected at the 53rd Grand Conclave were:

Marion W. Garnett, 1st Vice Grand Basileus, Grand KRS C.D. Henry, Grand K.F. John H. Moore, 2nd Vice Grand Basileus Richard L. Taylor, Chaplain H. Albion Ferrell; Grand Counselor J. Franklin Spruill; Grand Marshal Alvin West.

As Omega Psi Phi, Fraternity Inc. embarked upon a new decade, the end of an era had passed with the death of Martin Luther King, Jr., notably the greatest civil rights icon of the twentieth century. Camelot gave way to a jaded American citizen. Vietnam sucked the life blood out of many poor black communities, drugs made their way more prevalently into the lives of America's cities and crime, welfare and jobs were forefront in Omega's line of sight.

The chaotic events of the 60's including war and social change seemed destined to continue in the 70's. Major new trends included a growing disillusionment and dissatisfaction with government, advances in civil rights, increased influence of women, a growing and organized concern for the environment and increased space exploration were the topic of the day for one and all.

Many of the radical ideas of the sixties gained broad acceptance in American culture. Amid war, social strife, presidential impeachment proceedings, America still found a way to flourish. Indeed, the events of the times were reflected in and became inspiration for much of what Omega Psi Phi became in its traditions, administration and fashion. Omegas' in many photos of the time sported Afros, bell bottoms, Apple hats and black power symbols, along with the "shield" of course.

The chaos, riots and protests of the late sixties consumed much of the urban "ghettos" of the north and the college campuses north and south. This gloom and doom atmosphere spirited away the hopes of many Black people who were desperately waiting for [21] deliverance from the social ills which confronted them. During this time, Omega as a product of the achievements and failures of [22] Black American society searched its soul. Omega and Omega men not far removed from the troubles of their day, sought throughout the seventies more than anything to be relevant to themselves, their communities and to the lives of black people all over the world. The seventies more so than any other decade of Omega, saw a noted shift in its programs and philosophy of aid to Black People.

Social movements were particularly prevalent during the 1970's. The anti war movement went into high gear and was very visible on college campuses. The Kent State massacre was a terrible reflection of the times. Four students were gunned down by Ohio National Guardsmen attempting to control the demonstration. Ten days after Kent State, two black college students at Jackson State University were shot and killed by rogue members of the Mississippi Highway Patrol and many others were wounded in this historic event. This protest epidemic had now made its way to Black college campuses. Court ordered desegregation, the tough answer to the slow progress of Brown v. Board of education's mandate, led to Court-ordered desegregation plans and "Forced" busing of School children in Northern cities, which often led to additional violence.

Many books published during this decade manifested the general theme of man's alienation from his spiritual roots. Authors like Toni Morrison examined the Black American experience as never before. Omega men also searching for this lost spirituality questioned their own mandates and posed serious questions about how to get along with each other and with God. Achievement Week and Conclave themes echoed this mood throughout the early seventies especially.

This chapter explores through the conclaves, district meetings and major events shaping the life of the fraternity in the seventies just how Omega adjusted to new times and sought to remain relevant to the lives of black people everywhere, especially in the urban north.

The major thrust of Omega programming laid out by Grand Basileus Avery for his administration is best detailed in his message to the Fraternity where he discusses Omega's emphasis on "purposeful educational development, building self-dignity, race pride, motivating our young people, parenting counseling, providing housing for the needy, solving community health problems, and helping [the] indigent and less fortunate."[23]

Grand Basileus Avery made it known immediately after coming into office via this message in one of his first communications to the membership that he thought Omega was not doing enough to make effective use of its members talents in helping to ameliorate and solve some of the civic and social concerns of the black community. He noticed that social action programs by Omega were being carried out spottily on the local level but they were not unified national ones.[24] He made it crystal clear to his Omega membership that given the fact that Omega men were part of the educated black population; why shouldn't Omega men be out front leaders in getting involved and utilizing its collective skills and abilities to uplift others? To accomplish this Omega membership would have to be more unified and organized from the local level up and from there its top leadership would need to be in lock step with one another on the same page.

One of the first things that Grand Basileus Avery did when he got into office was to reorganize the Supreme Council, the ruling body of the fraternity and put in place a system of accountability. Specifically, he put several committees under the leadership of Brother Garnett, committees such as Fraternity Programs, Personnel Administration, Community Housing, and Communications. Other committees were placed under the leadership of Brother **RICHARD TAYLOR**, committees such as Initiation and Procedures, Budget and Finance, Social Welfare, and Awards and Honors. Along this same line of thinking, the men that Grand Basileus Avery picked for the various national committees were handpicked men, not chose as had frequently been the case in the past with political concerns but with the intent to pick exceptional men who he felt were most able and dedicated.[25]

---

[23] The Oracle, Summer 1971 Edition, Volume 55 Number 1, p. 1.

[24] "Others Thought I Could Lead by James S. Avery

Before appointing each man, Grand Basileus Avery visited with each giving them **the eyeball to eyeball test**. That is to say, he looked them in the eye, man to man and from there clearly explained what he expected of them and most especially he meticulously explained the objectives of his administration. He publicly made it known to all that he wanted his administration to be the best of all administrations to ever come through Omega. Standing on the shoulders of all the great Omega men who had come before him and with its memberships and God's help, he knew that this was possible. Omega Psi Phi Fraternity Inc. deserved only the very best from him and his members he proclaimed throughout the organization.

As a result of their astuteness, clarity of thought and focus Grand Basileus Avery and his administration are known for their outstanding work in leading Omega Psi Phi fraternity in community outreach. His administration had several major programs where Omega Psi Phi Fraternity received national acclaim, particularly with the Black press for their extraordinary Uplift in the Black Community. Grand Basileus Avery aggressively pushed to focus Omega Psi Phi Fraternity's national strength on areas where it could make visible impact.

A very clear example of Grand Basileus Avery's leadership in this area was Project Uplift, a national drug education program in which all national chapters could participate in a coordinated and strategic manner. Grand Basileus Avery had the national office, distribute thousands of bumper stickers to local chapters that read: "Omega says Stamp out Dope." This initiative had merit and was effective. These bumper stickers were on automobiles and in store windows all across America.

Omega Psi Phi Fraternity also gave out booklets, speech data and little handouts that helped parents, guardians and others to identify the systems of drug use. Coordinated by Omega's national Social Action Committee, it proved to be an excellent project that identified Omega Psi Phi Fraternity with fighting an extremely critical national issue. It is no doubt that the beloved Founders of Omega, in us, would have been well pleased.

The newly revised Constitution and By-Laws and the Ritual became effective at the close of the 1970 Pittsburgh Grand Conclave.

~ A REFLECTION IN TIME ~

Omegas @ Indiana Univ. 1971

The 54th Grand Conclave in December of 1971 was held in Houston Texas. During this conclave the issue of relevance of Omega was discussed and debated often. (James S. Avery the 28th Grand Basileus posited that Omega men and Black Greek letter organizations special ness was being tested or even crashing down due to a lack of relevancy in Fraternity programming. [26] As of December 31, 1969 there were 8,594 (3,315 Undergraduate/ Intermediate and 5,279 Graduate) active members in 322 chapters in the Fraternity, according to the report Annual Report of the National Executive Secretary to the Supreme Council presented February 1970.

Grand Basileus Avery, in order to uplift the Omega membership, is quoted as saying, "The real Omega Man does not accept commonplace. He does not weaken to practices that are negative, substandard and demeaning. The real omega Man sets the pace and leads the way in his manhood, his Scholarship and his civic commitment. When our Founders created the Omega Psi

---

[26] The Oracle, Summer 1971 Edition, Volume 55 Number 1, p. 1.

Phi Fraternity, Inc. in 1911, they had a vision a vision for an organization that would be a strong, socially effective Brotherhood, bound together with a Friendship that would stand any test of human consequence. This vision is self evident in the preamble of our Fraternal Constitution.[27] Omega men must live up to these high standards set by the Founders of Omega Psi Phi Fraternity, Inc." This was his strong rallying cry to the organization.

~ A GOLDEN REFLECTION IN TIME ~

Founders Love and Cooper at the 54th Grand Conclave in Houston Texas.

The 54th Grand Conclave was held as the 60th anniversary of the Fraternity in Houston Texas. Omega selected Bro. **JOHN L. CASHIN** as National Omega Man of the Year at the 54th Grand Conclave.

The 1971 Supreme Council officers elected at the Houston Grand Conclave were as follows:

---

[27] James S. Avery as taken from the The Challenge of Living the Vision Article in the Summer 2002 Oracle.

JAMES S. AVERY - Grand Basileus

Marion W. Garnett-First Vice Grand Basileus; Samuel W. Johnson, 2nd Vice Grand Basileus; Charles D. Henry, Grand KRS; John H. Moore, Grand KF; J, Franklin Spruill, Grand Counselor; Alvin West, Grand Marshall; Larry D. Walls; Carroll G. Boswell Will McCain, III, Undergraduate Representatives; H. Albion Ferrell, Grand Chaplain; Otto McClarrin, Editor to the Oracle; H. Carl Moultrie, National Executive Secretary Emeritus; Harold J. Cook, National Executive Secretary;

District Representatives

Clifton Moore – 1st District; Milton Johnson - 2nd District; Melvin Washington – 3rd District; Floydel H. Anderson – 4th District
Albert G. Berry – 5th District; Zoel Hargrave, Jr.; 6th District
Edward Braynon – 7th District; Edgar A. Burnett – 8th District
C. D. Henry – 9th District; Frederick Birth – 10th District
Thomas McPhatter – 12th District

Grand Basileus Avery boldly moved Omega Psi Phi Fraternity into the mainstream of life on all fronts...its programming, its communication mechanisms, the deep commitment of those who worked with him and the overall relationships with the world around Omega.

Grand Basileus Avery with Roy Wilkins, Lloyd Bell and Harold Cook (NES)

The major thrust of Omega programming laid out by Brother Avery for his administration is best detailed in his message to the Fraternity where he discusses Omega's emphasis on "purposeful educational development, building self-dignity, and race pride, motivating our young people, parenting counseling, providing housing for the needy, solving community health problems, helping [the] indigent and less fortunate."[28]

Project ASPIRATION was initiated by Grand Basileus James Avery and his fine Supreme Council. This program was conducted under the auspices of the Charles Drew Memorial Scholarship Commission and served to move young men and boys particularly to stay in school and to improve their scholastic achievement.[29]

The Fraternity also initiated the HEALTH-O-RAMA program to combat inadequate health information in the Black community and was conducted as a pilot program at Meharry Medical College under the auspices of the National Social Action Committee and under the direct leadership of Brother Dr. **HENRY MOSES**.

<<>>

27th Grand Basileus, **ELLIS FRANKLIN CORBETT**, entered Omega chapter on **March 3, 1971.**

<<>>

Among Grand Basileus Avery's most powerful emotional memories in being Grand Basileus is the fact that he was at Founder Oscar J. Cooper's bedside until almost the last few minutes of his death. He said this parting will forever be in his heart. Grand Basileus Avery was also the person who gave the official Omega resolution at the funeral of Bishop Edgar A. Love. These tender loving memories, Brother Avery stated, will forever be with him.

<<>>

---

[28] The Oracle, Summer 1971 Edition, Volume 55 Number 1, p. 1.

[29] The Oracle, Summer 1973 Volume 56 Number 2, p. 27.

Grand Basileus Avery and Executive Secretary H. Carl Moultrie presenting plaques to Founders Love and Cooper at the 1971 Houston Conclave

<<>>

FOUNDER, DR. OSCAR JAMES COOPER enters Omega Chapter on **October 09, 1972.**

It was as if a dark sorrowful shroud came over Omega. Every Omega man felt the pain of Founder Cooper's passing. After losing Founder Frank Coleman just five short years earlier, it was as if the very seam of Omega was starting to slowly unravel. These great men had led long and glorious lives. They had been there at each turn, every up and down, and twist and scary bend in the road for Omega. They had guided us as good Shepards do and kept us out of trouble. Our selfishness to hold them close to our bosom and be in their presence forever, alas, could not be. The members rallied and aggressively hurled themselves so as to be with and protect the remaining Founder Love, at every opportunity as if to hold back Death itself from our precious, last remaining jewel. It was he, (Edgar A Love) like a strong Moses like father figure, who calmed our fears and soothed our pain with the very thing he had always taught us for so many years and cherished the most about living life. He consoled us with his faith in God and the fact that his good friend Cooper, although now away from us who we all loved so dearly, was now in an even better place, in the sweet, sweet bosom of the Lord.

(A personal reflection from the author, Vernon Steve Weakley)

THE OMEGA PSI PHI FRATERNITY INC. 75

<<>>

The Achievement Week theme for 1972-73 was "Better Community Relations Through the 3R's: Role, Respect and Responsibility"[30] The numbers of participants showed steady decline from 1969-70 with 511 contestants to 1972-73 with 233 contestants, despite increased publicity. Even though there was no study or ethic breakdown for participants the fraternity yet discussed how to engage more black children to take part in the essay contests. The Achievement Week Committee selected **DR. HOWARD THURMAN** of San Francisco California, Chaplain Emeritus of Marsh Chapel of Boston University and Director of the Howard Thurman Trust, esteemed theologian and organizer of the Church for the Fellowship of All People.

<<>>

Although difficult, Omega moved ever forward. The goals of the Fraternity changed little from 1972 to 1973 as Omegas sought to place greater emphasis on all matter of social importance to Black people in the U.S., including civil rights, political involvement, access to healthcare and better housing and education.

The first organized Conclave sanctioned step/march competition was held at the 55th Grand Conclave in St. Louis Missouri.

<<>>

Brother **MATTHEW WALKER**, M.D. was elected Omega Man of the year at the St. Louis, Missouri Grand Conclave. He was cited and applauded by all members of Omega for his unselfish and dedicated service to Omega, to his country and to mankind. He was born in Waterproof Louisiana in 1906. He was a brilliant surgeon, medical Educator and Humanitarian. He first received public recognition in 1956 when he performed surgery and radioactive gold treatment for cancer in the national program, "Medical Horizons." In 1973, Brother Walker was honored by the American College of Surgeons when a documentary film was

---

[30] 55th Grand Conclave Transcript of Proceedings Vol. II, p. 507.

prepared on his surgical procedures for cancer of the stomach. Brother Walker was initiated into Omega Psi Phi fraternity at New Orleans University and was also associated with Delta chapter, Meharry Medical College and Gamma Phi chapter in Nashville Tennessee.[31]

<<>>

Summer of 1973: Omega man, **Z. ALEXANDER LOOBY** Passes. His life was celebrated and remembered in the Summer Oracle of 1973. The Urban Leagues Executive Director Bro. **VERNON L. JORDAN** is selected as the National Omega Man of the Year.) **Lambda Rho Chapter** of Waterbury Connecticut and its Omega Housing Development Corporation secured $1.6 Million with the backing of the Federal Housing Authority to build a seven story apartment complex for the elderly called the Lambda Rho Apartments, which was dedicated in the summer of 1973.

<<>>

Bro. **CLARENCE E. LIGHTNER** was elected the first Black mayor of Raleigh North Carolina. Lightner was among the first African-Americans elected to political office following passage of the Voting Rights Act in 1965. He was already well-established as a business and community leader in the city. His leadership stature won him election to the Raleigh City Council, where he served from 1967 until 1973, until he was elected as mayor. He defeated G. Wesley Williams in the mayoral campaign. Lightner served as a charter member of the Southern Conference of Black Mayors, the parent organization of the National Conference of Black Mayors. After serving as mayor, Lightner was appointed by Governor Jim Hunt in 1977 to replace State Senator John Winters, who had resigned. Lightner served the remainder of Winters' term until 1978.

---

[31] Matthew Walker, Omega man of Year 1973/Oracle/Spring 1974,vol57,No1

THE LIFE MEMBERSHIP STORY

Bro. Walter "Crow" Riddick
(A very critical part of its lasting success)

The Life Membership Program was the brainchild of National Secretary Emeritus, the late Judge H. Carl Moultrie. It was voted into law by the Grand Conclave of 1958 in Cleveland, Ohio. Past Grand Basileus, Cary D. Jacobs, (1961-1964) was Life member number one. Judge Moultrie was designated as Life member number two. For some unstated reason, there was the fear by the general membership that such a program would destroy the local chapters and as a result, the activities relating to life membership lay virtually dormant. Over the years, this proved to be false. This program was revived and it can be said saved by the forward thinking of Grand Basileus, James S. Avery and the hard work of Walter "Crow" Riddick.

During the 54th Grand Conclave in Houston, Texas, in 1971, Grand Basileus James S. Avery appointed Brother Walter "Crowe" Riddick, Grand Keeper of Records and Seal Emeritus, as chairman of the Life Membership Program. Brother Avery gave him specific instructions in carrying out this very challenging but yet an extremely important mission for the Life Membership Program and [32] with it, Omega Psi Phi fraternity. He directed him to revive this program and create an endowment for Omega. The total paid and partially paid members at that time numbered only 47. The original goal was set for 1,000 members. Brother

---

[32] James S. Avery, "Others Thought I Could Lead" & Life Membership web site & Oracle/summer1979 61 - Life Membership story

Riddick took on this daunting and seemingly impossible task with an intense commitment to see it through. He had understood the extreme importance of this program, as laid out to him by Grand Basileus Avery. Brother Riddick vowed to reach that goal during his tenure as Life Membership Chairman.

Brother Riddick appeared before the Supreme Court at the Phoenix Conclave to present an update progress report on the Life Membership Program. His hard work and the efforts of Grand Basileus Avery in taking this bold step to remove it from the shelf where it had been lying for a number of years since its creation and was slowly dying.

As all great stories where hard working men of courage and vision insert themselves, this famous little known Omega story will also have its happy ending. The magic number of 1,000 was reached about the time that Brother Walter "Crowe" Riddick entered Omega Chapter, July 23, 1977. Out of respect for his inspirational leadership and outstanding success, the 58th Grand Conclave mandated that Life Membership number 1,000 be retired as a perpetual memorial to Chairman Emeritus, Brother Walter Riddick. At each successive Grand Conclave, a Life Membership Fellowship will be held.

A revived Life Membership Program resulted in a very large number of new Life Members. Today, there are over 5000 life members and the program continues to attract more Men of Omega every year. Long Live Omega Psi Phi fraternity and this outstanding program.[33]

Before Grand Basileus Avery and his Supreme Council's administration were over, they had made a profound positive impact On Omega Psi Phi Fraternity's. Growth and the black community via their highly innovative and effective out reach efforts and policies. Sixty-seven new undergraduate chapters, twenty-eight graduate chapters and three intermediate chapters

---

[33] From James S. Avery's book, Others Thought I Could Lead."and the Life membership seb site.

were chartered during this administration. Additionally, chapter strength increased by thirty-three percent during this three year period. It is no doubt that this was indeed a positive moment in time for Omega Psi Phi Fraternity.

Many great pearls of wisdom have been sent down through Omega leaders that are attributed to Grand Basileus Avery. One of special note was his views on leadership. Brother Avery talked about leadership as being a way of life that did not put you first but rather in a position to make leadership a realization at all levels of the organization. Unfortunately, some of our fraternal leaders have not sought to see it that way.

To quote brother Avery, " In each instance, where I was given a responsibility of some kind, to be of service in some way, I always felt from the time of my youth that I had a corollary responsibility to do everything possible to do that job better than it had been done before. Leadership to me involves a lot of things such as having integrity, honor and a strong desire to serve in ways that brings benefit to others. And, its not a matter of having power, just because a person is in a position of power does mot make him a leader. It is the matter in which the power is used. And, once again, the leader is not always necessarily the person out front. Leadership involves having a vision and having what it takes to help enable others to find their place in that vision."

"There are to many instances where leadership is sought for all the wrong reasons...for selfish, personal aggrandizement, for the benefit of special interest, for a myriad of reasons that have no relationship to improving things for the good of all concerned. Instead, let us take the unselfish way, let us strive for excellence in giving service to the common good, seeking to invest our participation in life with a wide and enduring significance." These powerful pearls of wisdom have enhanced this author's life and I feel they will continue to echo through time and enrich new Omega leaders and its members for many, many years to come. Long Live Omega Psi Phi Fraternity Inc.

Other notable events of this period were:

Bro. **JOHN W. CROMWELL, JR.**, the first Black Certified Public Accountant entered Omega Chapter. Bro. **RICHARD TAYLOR**, Second Vice Grand Basileus in 1970-71 and Scholar of the year award recipient became a Rhodes Scholar.

Trends: Dues for undergraduates in 1971-73 were $7.50 and Graduate dues were $20.00. The 55th Grand Conclave was slated to be held in St. Louis in August 1973.

<<>>

The MARION W. GARNETT, (the 29th Grand Basileus of Omega Psi Phi Fraternity, Inc.) era begins; (Term 1973 to 1976)

Elected officers at the 55th Grand Conclave in St. Louis Missouri were:

MARION W. GARNETT – The 29th Grand Basileus
Edward Braynon, 1st Vice Grand Basileus; Christopher Dixon 2nd Vice Grand Basileus; C.D. Henry, Grand KRS; John H. Moore, Grand KF; James Felder, Grand Counselor; Walter J. Tilford, Grand Marshal; Richard Taylor, Oscar Turner, and Warren Lee were the Undergraduate Intermediate Representatives to the Supreme Council; Corneal Davis, Chaplain; Sam Shepard Editor to the Oracle.

DISTRICT REPRESENTATIVES

Albert Maule - 1st District: James Grant – 2nd District
Melvin Washington – 3rd District; William L. Hunter – 4th District;
Robert R. Jefferson – 5th District; Charles Brooks – 6th District;
Moses C. Norman – 7th District; Edgar Burnett – 8th District;
Warren M. Berry – 9th District; Burnel Coulon – 10th District;
Hayves Streeter – 12th District

Change In Command

The primary initiative of Grand Basileus Marion Garnett and his Supreme Council was in the area of Sickle Cell Anemia. The fraternity pledged to support eradication of this deadly disease, which affected people of African descent primarily. Quality education for Black children was also a key issue in this administration in the early seventies. Grand Basileus Garnett and his administration also resolved to mandate that Chapters and Districts address the aforementioned issues in their communities. Other items on Omega's agenda were Prison Reform, Political Action to include voter registration and running of candidates and political education drives; "stamping' out illegal drugs and Housing Programs.

Grand Basileus Garnett was a strong force in improving the administration of Omega's Life Membership Program, particularly relating to the board's functions as well as the way the funds were transferred from the fraternity to OLMF.. He also set up a committee to straighten out our financial condition after the Jesse Blayton (Grand Keeper of Finance) embezzlement was discovered. Brother **CAMERON WADE,** chaired that special committee.

By the 55th Grand Conclave Omega Psi Phi had grown to 340 active chapters. At the **55th Grand Conclave** the Founders were present to lend their support and to help guide the business of the organization.

The Achievement Week Theme voted on for the 1973-74 year at the 55th Conclave was Good Human Relations: the Keys to Love, Compassion and Understanding. The Conclave Theme was Reassessment of Goals for Black Americans in a Democracy.

A significant historical event of this year was H. Carl Moultrie the first and most notable National Executive Secretary retiring after nearly forty years of service to Omega to accept a presidential appointment from President Richard M. Nixon to serve as an associate judge in the Superior Court of the District of Columbia in 1974.

Grand Basileus Avery (far right standing at microphone) testifying at H. Carl Moultrie's investiture hearing before the Panel of Judges before his appointment. Omega man Moultrie is seated far right.

The 1974, 56th Grand Conclave in Phoenix Arizona
Theme for the Conclave: The Law Economics and You.

Supreme Council members elected:

Officers: **MARION GARNETT**, Grand Basileus (29th); Edward Braynon, 1st Vice Grand Basileus; **Warren G. Lee**, 2nd Vice

Grand Basileus; C.D. Henry, Grand KRS; Clifton Moore, Grand KF; James Felder, Grand Counselor; Ralph Long, Sr., Grand Marshal; Gregory Miller, Larry B. Boyd, Melvin Rice, Undergraduate Intermediate Representatives to the Supreme Council; Corneal Davis, Chaplain; Sam Shepard Editor to the Oracle and Harold Cook, NES.

Major Events: The 1974 Scholar of the year was **LOUIS CHARLES ROACH** of Rho Theta Chapter at Prairie View A&M University. The Conclave approved all District Representatives to be Members of the Supreme Council by constitutional Amendment, thereby increasing the representation of D.R.'s from 4 to 11 on the Supreme Council. Prior to this, only selected rotating District Representatives could sit on the council and have voting authority. It was thought that this approach prevented the districts from banding together to circumvent the will of the top executive officers and their leadership of Omega.

Grand Basileus Garnett was initiated into Omega in Iota chapter in 1950.[34] Accomplishments of Grand Basileus Garnett and his administration were: Omega Head Start Child Development Center established by Phi Iota Chapter in Phoenix Arizona and the celebration of the establishment of the Omega Foundation. These initiatives were highlight of the Conclave that year.

Financially the Fraternity was in an uproar because of a scandal involving a Brother who had allegedly embezzled funds from the organization in 1974. Grand Basileus Marion Garnett in his report to the Supreme Council sought to console the brotherhood and assuage any fears that we were failing administratively. He said "Today there is no panic, and I pray no bitterness. We have, as we always must, used this harrowing experience for the betterment of Omega. We are updating and improving our fiscal policies; we are persistently and carefully pursuing our legal remedies, with the probability of some success..."

Actual receipts for the 1972-73 budget year totaled $296, 875.48. The major portion of those receipts coming from dues

---

[34] Spring 84 Oracle/Iota chapter Alumni honorees

payments. Graduate dues received were $123,938.50 and undergraduate dues were $21, 455. In the 1973-74 budget years Omega collected $242, 497.46 of which $120,570 was collected in Graduate dues and $17,400 collected from undergraduates—signaling a decrease in membership year after year'[35]

The active membership of the fraternity as detailed in the Budget Committee's report during the 56th Grand Conclave was 9,884 members (3,433 U/I and 6,451 Grad). The fraternity posted gains in membership from 1950 through 1971 and then an era of declining membership took hold. There were 1,693 initiations conducted in 1970, which slowed to 1,496 by 1974, although over the same period many new chapters were established. 38 graduate and undergraduate chapters in 1973 alone and 10 totals in 1974. The number of chapters total however only increased by one from 1973 to 1974 from 460 in '73 to 461 in '74.[36]

The undergraduates and intermediate brothers working through their representatives to the Supreme Council held two workshops during 1974 with many recommendations coming out of those workshops developed several innovative ideas, many of which have found their way into the normal course of chapter functioning in the years since.

The Workshop among other resolutions adopted: District awards for the proper implementation of designated programs of the District; That the Undergraduate Chapters make full use of the Lampados Manual (the pledge manual); That the Second District Representative be able to officiate at an initiation; That non-financial visiting brothers be barred from participating in pledge activities; that all Lampados have physical examinations prior to the beginning of pledge activities; that all pledges complete a nationally standard written application, That the 2nd Vice DR. have his expenses paid for by the District similar to the D.R.'s expense reimbursement.

The 1975 Achievement Week Theme was "How to Treat Three Major Problems of the 70's: Dishonesty, Immorality and the Use of Dope." The committee was chaired by Brother DR. **WILLIAM MCMILLAN**, President of Rust College. Brother **SAM SHEPARD** was appointed the Assistant National Executive Secretary (NES).

---

[35] Report of the Budget Committee 56th Grand Conclave Dec. 1974
[36] Id.

Major Events 1974-75:

FOUNDER BISHOP EDGAR AMOS LOVE,
the last remaining Omega Psi Phi Founder, enters Omega chapter on **May 01, 1974.**

**(A personal reflection from the author,
Vernon <Bop Swalos> Weakley)**

This was indeed a very dark day for all of Omega Psi Phi fraternity. My God... Dear God... Oh merciful God take this searing pain and crippling sadness away from us. Let us escape this bleak and numbing reality. For I cannot bear it. Let me wake from and better yet be spared this terrible nightmare. But, alas, it was not a dream I was in. This was real life (good or bad) as only almighty God had intended it to be!!!

Tears flowed freely from my face as the words dribbled, as if in slow motion, from the lips of the brother bringing the news. As the words slowly sunk in deeper and moved from my ears into my brain, I froze in place and became completely rigid. For a few intense moments, I was loss in time, stranded in deep thought. Those not consumed themselves by the terrible news who observed me, must have thought me mad. As I began to regain control physically, all of a sudden, a second shock wave hit. This time, it was just too much! It was if the whole world stopped turning. I fought hard to contain myself to keep from crying out loud. As I stole away from the crowd of Omega men I happened to be with on that overcast day to try and regain control, **I could not help to think that it was the end of our great organization**, given the fact that **EDGAR A. LOVE** was now the last Founder to leave us.

Time of course has proven me wrong. Being relatively new in Omega at the time, (I was initiated at Jackson State Upsilon Epsilon chapter (YE) in 1969) I simply was not aware of the enduring impenetrable metal of our international leadership, organization and the sheer strength of the remaining men of Omega at the time. Our Founders had prepared us well. Not only would Omega Psi Phi Fraternity Inc. go on, but it would quicken its pace, prosper at an incredible rate and be an even greater force in the Black community, given the trying civil rights times that lay before it. I am so grateful that Omega Psi Phi fraternity, although a great light had went out with the passing of our last Founder, regained its balance after suffering this painful blow and continued on to become the great organization it is today.

<<>>

The following is an official resolution from Omega Psi Phi Fraternity read on May 07, 1974, by then Immediate Past Grand Basileus, **JAMES S. AVERY**, the 28th Grand Basileus of Omega Psi Phi Fraternity Inc. at the public funeral of Founder Love. Grand Basileus Avery's great words were a fitting tribute to this great man and they will have lasting value for us all.[37] The resolution he read is as follows:

Whereas the right Reverend Edgar A. Love, retired Bishop of the Methodist Church and Co-Founder of the Omega Psi Phi Fraternity, Inc. departed this life on May 01, 1974, and
Whereas from a quiet young man attending Howard University in the early 1900s he had indicated then that his life would be touched by sparks of greatness, and
Whereas in 1911, together with Dr. Ernest E. Just, Frank Coleman, and Oscar J. Cooper, he gave birth to the Omega Psi Phi Fraternity, Inc. and has since that time
Been a brilliant leader, a constant inspiration and a faithful Shepard to the thousands of men who have sought the life of Omega.
And Whereas, in spite of whatever else his obligations may have been, he has found the time to give to his fraternity and
Whereas his counsel and deep expression of love both in word and practice will be sorely missed throughout The fraternity.
Now, therefore, let it be resolved that the Right Reverend Edgar A. Love will live in everlasting memory of all Omega Men And be it further resolved that in this solemn hour we commend his soul to Almighty God and be it further resolved that we here and now dedicate ourselves to the principals that he so firmly espoused.

---

[37] Excerpt from James S. Avery's book, "Others Thought That I Could Lead"

Done this day, May 07, 1974, in the City of Baltimore, Maryland, by the authority of the Omega Psi Phi Fraternity, Inc.

<><>

The 56th Grand Conclave elected Brother **EARL GRAVES**, publisher and CEO of Black Enterprise Magazine as Citizen of the Year and Past Grand Basileus (1917) Brother **CLARENCE F. HOLMES** as Omega Man of the Year. Brother **LOUIS ROACH** of Rho Theta Chapter at Prairie view A&M University was elected as the National Scholar of the Year.

ADDITIONAL HISTORICAL EVENTS THAT OCCURRED DURING THIS PERIOD

JSU University/YE chapter/ Vernon (Bop Swalos) Weakley (front right) was one of seventy eight JSU students shot in this event. (A day before the JSU killings)[38]

May 14th, 1970 College students at predominately Black Jackson State University were shot and killed by the Mississippi Highway Patrol ten days after the college shootings and murders at predominately white Kent State University. Omega brothers were shot and seriously wounded in this incident. Both incidents are considered watershed historical events in American history.

<><>

---

[38] Vernon Steve Weakley's Book, "Standing At The Edge of Madness" chapter, "Saved by the Light of Omega."

On January 29, 1974 an Omega man by the name of **ED "TOO TALL" JONES** became the first player from a predominately black school to be named the No. 1 choice in the National Football League. Omega man, **ED JONES** hails from Tennessee State University. He was selected by the Dallas Cowboys.

<<>>

Omega Man, Brigadier General **WILLIAM E. BROWN JR.** assumed his position of Commander of the Air defense Weapons Center, Tyndall Air Force base, Fla.

<<>>

The Seventies brought more unpleasant news for Omega. **Founder Oscar J. Cooper entered Omega Chapter in 1972. On May 1, 1974, Edgar A.** Love, the only surviving founder, entered Omega Chapter.

<<>>

Pertinent Events and/or Accomplishments by Omega that occurred during this period: [39]

<<>>

Omega man, **JOHN SPENCER TRENT**, is the first graduate in the Polymer Science program at Pennsylvania State University on **March 09, 1974.**

<<>>

Omega Man, Dr. **CHARLES D. HENRY** joined the Big Ten Conference on June 1, 1974, becoming the first African-American assistant commissioner of any conference office. Until his death in 1982, Henry was a committed man with foresight, who helped usher in the era of women's athletics in the conference, while also dedicated to easing the transition for African-American student-athletes on all Big Ten campuses.

<<>>

Omega man, **CHARLES E. HARRY**, 1st Tenth District Representative entered Omega chapter on **August 20, 1974.**

<<>>

GEORGE E. MEARES, the 26th Grand Basileus, enters Omega chapter February 6, 1975 at the age of 65.

<<>>

World renowned scientist, research chemist and humanitarian Brother **DR. PERCY JULIAN** enters Omega chapter on **April 1975** at the age of 76. His research made possible mass production of many drugs formerly unavailable. He was featured in the March 1950 edition of the Oracle.[40]

<<>>

The March Down competition comes of age and is so successful as an undergraduate event that it becomes a permanent part of the Grand Conclave Activities. The event is mentioned prominently in the Winter Oracle of 1975.[41]

<<>>

Brother **LEROY T. WALKER** of North Carolina Central University was named the Coach of the U.S. Olympic Track and

---

[40] Oracle Spring-Summer Edition 1975 Volume 60 Number 2 and 3, p.70.
[41] Oracle Winter 1975 Edition Volume 60 Number 1. p. 14.

Field Team to take part in the summer Olympics, Montreal Canada 1976.

Omega man, **Hon. JOSEPH WOODROW HATCHETT, is named the** 1st African-American, State Supreme Court Judge in the State of Florida on **September 02, 1975.**

The 12th Grand Basileus, JULIUS SCOTLAND MCCLAIN entered Omega chapter on October 08, 1975.

Omega man, OTIS BRYANT was inducted November 1, 1975 to the Ohio University Athletic Hall of Fame. He was called one of the most outstanding quarterbacks in the Mid–America Conference. He was an initiate of Sigma Psi Chapter, Athens, Ohio.

On November 16, 1975, Omega men made a pilgrimage to Washington to dedicate a newly constructed granite Monument to the Founders on the campus of Howard University. The Omega plot within the shadows of Thirkield Science Hall memorializes the founders and the Fraternity in stone.

Patrick Henry H.S. Roanoke, VA dedicates Penn Hall in memory of 19th, Grand Basileus **HARRY T. PENN on 12, 03, 1975.**

20th Grand Basileus **MILO CRAVATH MURRAY** entered omega chapter on **March 10, 1976**.

Omega man, Hon, **WILLIAM H. HASTIE**, 1st African-American, Governor of the U.S. Virgin Islands entered Omega chapter on **April 14, 1976.**

The 1976 Atlanta Grand Conclave was the largest in the history of the fraternity up to that point in time.

<<>>

Omega man, **BENJAMIN LAWSON HOOKS,** 71st SPINGARN MEDAL recipient, elected Executive Director of the NAACP on **November 06, 1976.**

<<>>

Omega man, **ROLAND HAYES,** world famous tenor, entered Omega chapter on **December 31, 1976.**

<<>>

Omega man, **STANLEY M. DOUGLASS,** 1st Editor to the Oracle enters Omega Chapter on **January 20th, 1977.**

<<>>

Omega man, **CLIFFORD ALEXANDER** becomes the first African American Secretary of the Army. He served in this position in the Jimmy Carter Administration from February 14, 1977 to January 20, 1981.

<<>>

LAMBDA XI Chapter chartered in Korea on February 22, 1977.

<<>>

PI XI Chapter, Nassau, Bahamas receives charter on **August 22, 1977.**

<<>>

6th Grand Basileus, Dr. **CLARENCE F. HOLMES,** entered Omega chapter on **March 09, 1978**.

<<>>

Omega man, Capt. JOHN HENRY PURNELL, pioneer of Omega, entered Omega chapter on **August 22, 1979**.

<<>>

Omega man, the Hon. H. CARL MOULTRIE appointed Chief judge, Superior Court, and District of Columbia **on June 22, 1978**.

H. CARL MOULTRIE I, Omega's only National Executive Secretary to this point, (tenure 1949 to 1972), was appointed as a judge to the Superior Court of Washington, D.C., in 1972. Moultrie's resignation was accepted with regrets. Omega conferred upon Moultrie the title of National Executive Secretary Emeritus which was later changed to Executive Secretary Emeritus.

<<>>

Honored at Conclave

OMEGA CITIZEN – **BENJAMIN L. HOOKS**

OMEGA MAN OF THE YEAR – **CHARLES D. CHAMBLISS JR.** from the third District

Many new undergraduate chapters were chartered, because of the increased enrollment of black students at previously all-white colleges and universities. **"Operation Big Vote"** was successful in getting thousands of black people to vote in the 1976 election. Many Omegas were active participants.

The 1979 Denver Grand Conclave (Omega) made a commitment to contribute a minimum of **250,000 dollars to the United Negro College Fund** over the next five years.

Benjamin Hooks
Born 1924
Initiated in Omega via Epsilon Phi Chapter-1942
Civil Rights Leader

Omega man Benjamin Hooks was Born in Memphis, Tennessee. He attended LeMoyne College, Howard University and earned his JD from DePaul in 1948. A World War II Army veteran, Hooks was also ordained to the ministry of the Baptist Church in 1956. Hooks served as Pastor of Middle Baptist Church and as a local Judge in Memphis. Known as a persuasive speaker, he was a highly successful Director of the National Association for the Advancement of Colored People from 1977 until retirement. Benjamin Hooks was **appointed by President Richard Nixon, in April 1972, as the first African American to serve on the Federal Communications Commission**. During his 7 year term in this position, he concerned himself with Equal Employment opportunities in the Broadcasting field. Omega man Benjamin Hooks was awarded the prestigious Spingarn Medal in 1986.

<<>>

*This is an update to this book. **Brother James S. Avery, Sr.,** the beloved 28th Grand Basileus of Omega psi Phi Fraternity, Inc. died/entered OMEGA Chapter on May 3, 2011 at his home in Rossmoor, Monroe Twp. He was 88 years old. His book, "Others Thought I Could Lead," will be a lasting guide to live by for all Omega men to the end of all time.
42

CHAPTER IV

THE DECADE OF THE 70's CONTINUED
(A Period of Social Upheaval in America, Impacting Omega)

The Edward J. Braynon Jr. (the 30th Grand Basileus of Omega Psi Phi Fraternity Inc.) era begins: (Term 1976 to 1979)

Grand Basileus Edward Braynon was initiated into Omega Psi Phi Fraternity in 1945 at Fisk University, Eta Psi Chapter. His phenomenal rise in Omega is highlighted by the fact that of the total twenty one offices he successfully ran for in Omega, he was unopposed for all but one. He was recognized early as a person of high character, intelligence and leadership who would make a difference to any organization wise enough to win his heart/love, loyalty and seek his commitment. It was indeed a great day for Omega Psi Phi Fraternity, Inc. when Grand Basileus Braynon became its leader.

The seventies were a time of vast social change in America. The Fraternity and its members were a part of that change as well as changing itself to meet the demands of a new more global world. Women and blacks expanded their involvement in politics and women surpassed men in college enrollment in 1979. The rising divorce rate left an increasing number of women as sole

---

[42] Reginald E. Vance, Donald Ray Hornbuckle and Michael Lyles are contributing writers on this chapter.

breadwinners and forced more of them into poverty. This trend had a direct affect on Omega Programs and its social action thinking.[43]

During the seventies the United States underwent profound social upheaval. First a president and vice president (Richard M. Nixon and Spiro T. Agnew) resigned under threatened impeachment. The Vietnam War continued to divide the county even after the Paris Peace Accords of 1974 put an end to the U.S. military participation in the war. Roe v. Wade legalized abortion, Crime increased despite Nixon's law and order mantra. Black people became even more involved in politics assuming mayorship of large urban cities, like Atlanta, Detroit, Los Angeles, and Newark.

President Jimmy Carter was elected President of the United States in 1976 and appointed more Blacks to influential federal government positions than any president before him. He seemed to have a deep personal commitment to racial equality. However, the economic situation deteriorated under his presidency. The Congressional Black Caucus labeled Carter's federal budget favoring military spending over domestic funding for social relief programs, "an unmitigated disaster" for Black people. Black unemployment had remained in double digits since the mid 1970's, twice that for whites.

Omega Psi Phi Fraternity did not shrink from recognizing its responsibility to Black people during the 1970's and sought in a somewhat non-cohesive manner to adjust to the new demands with vigor. Financial and administrative stumbles within however kept the organization from accomplishing many objectives and reaching the many goals it laid out for itself. Accomplishments of individual Omega's all over the country from political gains to scientific endeavors seemed to assuage general concerns by the brotherhood that the Fraternity had lost focus.

Elected Supreme Council Officers at the Atlanta Ga. 57th Grand Conclave were:

EDWARD J. BRAYNON, Jr. Grand Basileus; Burnel Coulon, First Vice Grand Basileus, K. Earl Ferguson, 2nd Vice Grand Bas;

Robert H. Hester, GKRS; Clifton Moore, Grand KF; Melvin Washington, Grand Counselor; Marshall Grady, Grand Marshall; Undergraduate and Intermediate Representatives, Maurice Huntley, Lloyd Jordan and Michael Parham; Corneal Davis, Grand Chaplain, Marion W. Garnett Immediate Past Grand Basileus. H. Carl Moultrie, I Executive Secretary Emeritus, Harold J. Cook; nation Executive Secretary; Samuel R. Sheppard, assistant National Executive Secretary

DISTRICT REPRESENTATIVES

Theodore F. Hogan, Jr. – 1st District; Theodore N. Greer – 2nd District; Charles Chambliss, Jr. – 3rd District; R. Charles Byers – 4th District; Frank W. Bowden, Jr. – 5th District; Mitchell E. Gadsden – 6th District; Moses C. Norman - 7th District; Lynn Beckwith – 8th District; Samuel Prince – 9th District; Owseley G. Spiller – 10th District; L. Benjamin Livingston – 12th District

In August 1976 Omega Psi Phi convened its 57th Grand Conclave in Atlanta Georgia. America was also celebrating its 200th year of birth—the Bicentennial. **The Conclave was the largest in Omega History and was hosted by Eta Omega Chapter.** [44] Bicentennial celebrations dotted the American landscape the entire year. America's involvement in Vietnam had been over for nearly three years but the scars left behind in the minds, bodies and communities of Black veterans were just beginning to show itself in American cities and poor black neighborhoods. The Conclave theme was "Omega and America in Perspective, 1776-1911-1976. Which was a fitting tribute and a scathing report of America's failed promises and Omega's unfinished work for and on behalf of its members and black people around the world.

Initiatives:

The 1976 National Achievement Week Theme: Manhood, Scholarship, Perseverance and Uplift: Essential Principles for a Successful Life. The Conclave resolved to support Operation Big

---

[44] The Oracle, Winter 1976/Spring 1977 Edition Vol. 61 No. 4 and Vol.62 No.1

Vote, Support of the Resolution of the National Black Caucus regarding reassessment of the U.S. Foreign policy with regard to third world Nations independence and for majority rule in South Africa and Support for legislation which would establish a National Museum of Afro-American History and Culture in Ohio.

<><>

Omega man, **BENJAMIN L. HOOKS,** then member of the Federal Communications Commission, was elected Citizen of the Year. Brother **CHARLES CHAMBLISS** of the Third District was elected the Omega Man of the year for 1976. Omega Scholar of the year was **GERALD L. BURTON** of Livingston College.

<><>

Major events during this period

The honorable. WILLIAM H. HASTIE, Omega man, dies April 14, 1976.

<><>

Four of the six jurists receiving the first Charles Hamilton Houston Award of Merit by the Washington Bar Association on April 30 1975, were Omega men, D.C. Circuit Court Judge **SPOTTSWOOD ROBINSON**, D.C. Superior Court Judges **JAMES NABRIT** and **OLIVER HILL** and the late U.S. Court of Appeal judge **WILLIAM H. HASTIE** (posthumously).

<><>

Benjamin E. Mays
was named advisor to President Jimmy Carter in 1977.
Initiated in Gamma Chapter 1919

<><>

58th Grand Conclave held in New Orleans Louisiana December 1977. The theme of the Conclave was "Pursuit of Excellence as a Means to Black Survival."

Conclave Accomplishments: 2400 registered Omega men at the conclave;

<<>>

58th Grand Conclave Initiatives: Formal Chapter workshops on Constitutions and by-laws and ritual of the Fraternity. Lack of knowledge of these documents was a major problem. The Fraternity sought to increase the level of participation by Brothers which had trailed off at the District level. Brothers were not wearing the Fraternity pin in the required manner. Reclamation was also a big program of Grand Basileus Braynon.

<<>>

August 22, 1977 Grand Basileus Braynon presents charter to Bahamas chapter Xi Pi in Nassau.

<<>>

On November 1, 1977, **WILLIE J. WRIGHT** (initiated at Bethune Cookman College) was appointed the New Omega Psi Phi Fraternity National Executive Secretary after a six month search.

Dr. L. BENJAMIN LIVINGSTON, of 12th District Riverside, California is named the National omega man of the Year

The **58th Grand Conclave** approved a new emphasis on Black History and resolved to establish a relationship with the Association for the Study of Afro American Life and History (ASALH) organization founded by Bro. DR. **CARTER G. WOODSON**. The Omega Chapters were encouraged to initiate joint projects with the Association's branches especially during Black History Month. A central committee was appointed by the Grand Basileus to coordinate this effort. All chapters were encouraged to purchase a sustaining membership.

Statement of financial position published for 1975 current and fixed assets of the Fraternity totaled $551,134. As of October 31, 1976 Assets totaled $556,605.

In 1978, an Open Letter from Grand Basileus Braynon listed the needs and priorities of the fraternity as he perceived them. They were 1: constitution and Rituals, where each chapter was urged to conduct workshops for the express purpose of familiarizing the brotherhood with these important documents. Grand Basileus Braynon thought that the prevailing lack of knowledge was inexcusable; 2. Memorial Day was mandated to be celebrated by each chapter with an appropriate program and ceremony; 3. Better involvement of brothers in District Meetings; 4. The proper use and wearing of the fraternity pin; 5. Brothers were encouraged to be more active in the "indoctrination" of new members and urged that brothers who violate the fraternity's rules in this regard be eliminated from the organization's ranks; 6. Emphasis on reclamation was made, urging that each brother reclaim two brothers.[45]

Members were appointed to the new committee established at the 58th grand Conclave. It was the Committee for Cooperation with the Association for the Study of Afro-American Life and History. First members were Dr. **WALTER N. RIDLEY**, Chairman, Dr. **SAMUEL DUBOIS COOK**, Dr. **DANIEL B. NUESOM, SAMUEL SHEPARD,** and **CARLTON A. FUNN**.

Observance of Black History Month mandated by the 58th Grand Conclave in New Orleans begins its annual observance by Chapters in 1978.

Major Event of Note: **The First Three letter** chapter in the Fraternity, Alpha Alpha Alpha is in Shepherdstown WV (4th District) is established by the Supreme Council on September 16, 1978.

<<>>

Esteemed jurist Brother JUDGE LEON HIGGINBOTHAM, U.S. Circuit Court Judge for the Third Circuit in Philadelphia, Pennsylvania, published his first book: "In the matter of Color" a study of the racial laws in six of the American Colonies before the Revolution.

<<>>

---

[45] Omega Bulletin Vol. X No. 1 Jan-Mar. 1978 p. 1

Judge **H. CARL MOULTRIE I**, was honored as a Washingtonian of 1977. On June 7th 1978, Judge H. Carl Moultrie I, was named the new Chief Judge of the 44-member D.C. Superior Court by the D.C. Judicial Nomination Commission. Brother Moultrie was appointed to the court in 1972.

<<>>

BROTHER MATTHEW WALKER, Sr. 1906-1978 passed. He was lauded as one of the great teachers, surgeons and medical leaders in the nation. He entered Omega chapter in Nashville Tenn. He was chairman of the Department of Surgery at Meharry Medical College for 30 years and had served as Provost for External Affairs since 1973. Dr. Lloyd C. Elam, President of Meharry, summed up Walker's contribution best: "There are certain people in this country who have made a difference in the quality of life for others. Dr. Walker was one of these individuals. The poor, the sick, the disadvantaged—these were the people that experienced the good of Matthew Walker's work. His concern for raising the standard of health care for all people brought him to a leadership role in developing the concept of comprehensive health care centers for medically underserved areas.[46]

<<>>

The esteemed Brother **CLARENCE F. HOLMES** passes. He was the 5th **Grand Basileus** of Omega Psi Phi Fraternity Inc. for the period, 1917-1918. He entered Omega Chapter March 9, 1978. He was the first member to be awarded the fifty year pin when it was established in 1974 at the 56th Grand Conclave in Phoenix, Arizona.[47]

<<>>

The National Aeronautics Space Administration (NASA) announced the appointment of 35 new candidates for the space shuttle program. Brothers **RONALD E. MCNAIR, Ph.D. a civilian Physicist and Major FREDERICK DREW**

---
[46] Id.
[47] The Oracle, Summer 1978 Vol. 62 No. 2 p. 71

GREGORY, a veteran Air Force Pilot were the two Omega men selected. Up to that time only four blacks had ever been selected, the first being an Omega man, Major **ROBERT H. LAWRENCE, JR.** of Epsilon Chapter who dies in 1967 as a result of a training accident before completing his training. The first four Black men to actual become astronauts are all members of Omega Psi Phi Fraternity[48] This is a tremendous historical accomplishment that all members of Omega Psi Phi Fraternity should be proud of.

1978 Achievement Week and Essay Contest Theme: Accountability: a Continuous Process"

Grand Basileus Braynon soundly demonstrated his love for Omega before his tenure was over by humbly **leading by example, from the front**. This posture worked well for him throughout his time as Grand Basileus. As a result, a long sterling career of extraordinary Service to Omega is the hallmark that all of Omega has come to know him by. Grand Basileus Braynon is also recognized as the writer of the Omega Psi Phi Fraternity History briefs for the decades. His historical depictions are routinely used on web sites etc. even to the day of this writing to provide pertinent information on Omega's progress from its beginning to the 1990's.

<<>>

59th Grand Conclave Denver, Colorado August 1979

Presiding Supreme Council:

Edward Braynon, Grand Basileus, Burnel Coulon, First Vice Grand Basileus: Darnell Smith, Second Vice Grand Basileus; Robert Hester, Grand Keeper of Records and Seal; Clifton Moore, Grand Keeper of Finance; Charles D. Chambliss, Jr. Grand Counselor; U/I Reps: T. Maurice Huntley, Lloyd Jordan, Bennie McMorries, Jr.; Corneal Davis, Chaplain.

---

[48] Id at p.8.

ROBERT "PETE" REEDER was chosen Assistant National Executive Secretary (NES). Reeder was initiated in 1952 and worked on District and Chapter levels for many years in North Carolina. He also was highly recognized in the field of Education and public school administration. The position of National Executive Secretary (NAS) remains open during this period and a national search began. The Fraternity began to phase out the $300 life membership adding new requirements before life membership could be purchased, such as been financial with the District and a Chapter prior to life membership.[49] Pete Reeder unexpectedly, a short period after becoming assistant, was promoted to Executive Director, according to Grand Basileus Coulon, because Willie Wright decided he would just quit one day. This circumstance put a lot of undue stress on Pete Reeder and the organization. Pete Reeder, to his credit, as stated by Grand Basileus Coulon, "came through like gang busters and did an extraordinary job of filling in, although he only had a few days of training.

The Theme of the Conclave was **"Omega focuses on the Family: Keystone of our Society"**

At this Conclave Two Omega Astronauts Brother **RONALD E. MCNAIR AND BROTHER FREDRICK DREW GREGORY** were honored along with the Honorable **WALTER E. FAUNTROY**, delegate to Congress from the District of Columbia.

The Achievement Week Theme for the 1979 Conclave was "Restating our Priorities: A Commitment to Uplift"

The National Omega Man of the Year was **JAMES ALFRED PRIEST, M.D.,** a Baltimore physician, who was the family physician and confidant to the last surviving Omega Founder, Bishop Edgar A. Love. A graduate of Morgan State and Howard University School of Medicine, he was active in Omega affairs at the Chapter and National level. He was also a distinguished physician and was recognized as such by his peers and received the national Medical Association's service award for contributions to Minority Pre-Medical students.

---

[49] Omega Bulletin Spring 1979 Vol. XI No. 1

The Buzz: Alpha Chapter pledges line of "Lamps" (Lampados Club) 24 men were made Lamps after a three year period of suspension and inactivity. The Chapter membership reached fifty members with that line.

The Fraternity elects new leaders at the 59th Grand Conclave in Denver. 31st Grand Basileus, **BURNEL ELTON COULON** (only member to serve as Grand Basileus and Grand Marshal) installed as Grand Basileus **August 10, 1979.**

The Burnel E. Coulon, (the 31st Grand Basileus of Omega Psi Phi Fraternity) era begins: (Term 1979 to 1982)

Grand Basileus Coulon was initiated into Omega Psi Phi Fraternity, Inc at Tuskegee Institute, Lambda Epsilon Chapter in 1950.

Brother Coulon is on the far left side of this picture leading his Lampados Club line.

He was a four term District Representative in the 10th District prior to ascending to the top executive officer position. He was also a First Vice District Representative in the 7th District. He credits the experience of being a District Representative for so many years and having great mentors such as **JAMES MULLIN** in helping him to develop his leadership skills and his ability to get along with people. Burnel Coulon changed the Conclave format in that he brought in outside speakers such as Ernie Green, members of the Little Rock 9, Jesse Jackson Jr., Benjamin Hooks to enlighten the Omega membership. He was the first Grand Basileus to do this. He also was the first to bring in outside entertainers for concerts at the Conclave. He brought in mega acts at that time like the Fifth Dimensions. Brother Coulon credits his administrations' extraordinary success to the outstanding members of his Council. He is proud of the fact that all of his Supremem Council members (District Representatives and offices) went on to be very successful Omega leaders. His people, according to brother Coulon reads like the whose who of Omega.

BURNEL E. COULON elected as Grand Basileus.
L. Benjamin Livingston-First Vice Grand Basileus; Leon Franks-Second Vice Grand Basileus; Moses C. Norman-Grand Keeper of Records and Seal: Kenneth M. Taylor-Grand Keeper of Finance; Charles D. Chambliss, Jr.-Grand Counselor; T. Maurice Huntley-Grand Chaplain; Charles Fields-Grand Marshal; Larry A. Brown, Lloyd J. Jordan, Bennie McMorris-U/I Representatives

It can be said that Grand Basileus Coulon brought order to Omega Psi Phi Fraternity, Inc. and made it more efficient. It was he and his administration, through his tenacious leadership and vision that **brought the first certified audit to Omega Psi Phi Fraternity.** This was a big deal in light of the historic problems that were present where record keeping and finances were concerned. He and his administration successfully implemented numerous other procedures; particularly in the Washington headquarters office that had dramatic immediate improvement on Omega's over-all efficiency. Brother Coulon credits Ken Taylor, his Keeper of Finance, as doing a particularly good job in carrying out his duties.

Grand Basileus Coulon's administration found its activities concerned with financial stability and organization. Coulon's election signaled an attempt by the Fraternity to address the mistakes of its past. Grand Basileus Avery had been among those who had discovered the financial improprieties on the part of Brother **JESSE B. BLAYTON** (A long time Grand Keeper of Finance) and sought his removal. This very serious embezzlement issue will be explored in more detail in the next chapter. Rumors of its revelation reverberated throughout Omega and resulted in the membership calling for a harsh reckoning and stiff retribution for this un-brotherly situation, if it was determined to be true. An investigation was initiated when the appearance of impropriety was found to determine the validity of the rumor and determine how much damage had been done.

Under Grand Basileus Coulon's leadership Omega Psi Phi Fraternity also initiated its nation-wide campaign to contribute $260,000 to the United Negro College Fund or UNCF. Brother Dr. **WILLIAM A. MCMILLAN,** President of t Rust College was selected by Grand Basileus Coulon to head the six member committee to plan, direct and implement the national campaign. Delegates to the 59th Grand Conclave set the goal, to keenly be aware of the financial plight of these schools and their traditional role in producing and educating proportionately more black professionals than any other type of institution of higher learning. The fraternity began a major campaign to get Blacks registered with the Census coming in 1980.

The oldest living Omega Man, at this point in time, ROBERT WASHINGTON GADSDEN, who was 105 years old and a prominent retired Savannah educator and charter member of Mu Phi Chapter, dies June 22, 1979. As an undergraduate he participated in the first intercollegiate football game between two Black colleges, Tuskegee and Atlanta University.

<<>>

Brother **EMORY LEWI LEVERETTE**, A forty-two year plus member of Omega Psi Phi at this point in time was the first Black person to have a city school named in his honor in Toledo Ohio. He was an assistant superintendent of administration in Toledo.

CHAPTER V

THE DECADE OF THE 1980's
(1980-1989)
(ORDER IS DEMANDED BY THE OMEGA MEMBERSHIP)

The Burnel E. Coulon, (the 31st Grand Basileus of Omega Psi Phi Fraternity) era continues: (Term 1979 to 1982)

The conclave decade of the Eighties begins with the **60th Grand Conclave in San Francisco, California, December 26-30, 1980.** The Official theme of the Conclave was: **"The Decade is the '80's, but Black Problems Are the Same: WHAT NOW?"**

WHAT NOW?

Ebony Magazine in 1980 recognized fifteen Omega men in varying fields who it considered the most influential Black Americans. **Omega and its men throughout the 1980 continued to impact the lives of not only Black people but the entire**

---

[50] Reginald E. Vance, Donald Ray Hornbuckle and Michael Lyles are contributing writers on this chapter.

American citizenry. However, for Omega, the decade of the 1980's is probably recognized more so for 1.) The initiatives [51] Aimed at addressing internal reform within Omega, 2.) finding the resources to devote to these initiative and 3) addressing the aching administrative defects that plagued the organization since its beginnings. This chapter's theme is taken partly from the theme of that year's Grand Conclave and the fall 1980 Oracle that preceded it. Both were entitled "What Now?"

The Eighties ushered in great change in the world. Sometimes called "the Reagan Years" because of the two term influence of Republican President Ronald Reagan, Omega Psi Phi Fraternity, its chapters and individual members continued their tradition of activism and social involvement.

Pictured: (Lampados Club Pledge Line, Spring 1980 Gamma Epsilon Chapter at Hampton University)

This Chapter will serve as a broad review of the major projects, themes, successes, and failures of the Fraternity during these years of change. This Decade spans the administrations of the following Grand Basilei -- Burnel E. Coulon, L. Benjamin Livingston and Moses C. Norman, Sr. However, given his long tenure as Grand Basileus, this decade is imprinted primarily with the successes and failures of Moses C. Norman, Sr., whose tenure lasted for six years. Norman's term lasted from 1984, the 64th Grand Conclave in Louisville, Kentucky until the 66th Grand Conclave in 1990 in Detroit Michigan.

Norman's three-term tenure as Grand Basileus was unprecedented in modern times. He was the first Grand Basileus to preside over Omega during the era of bi-annual Conclaves, where Grand Officer terms had been expanded from 18 months to two years. He would however, because of a constitutional change, be the last Grand Officer to serve three consecutive terms in the penultimate office of the Fraternity.

The Decade's Trends:

By way of reference, a list of trends and items of interest are provided to aid in giving some sense of the economic and social environment in which the Fraternity and its members lived during this time.

U.S. President	Jimmy Carter
Cost of New House	$68,714.00
Average U.S. Annual Income	$19,173.00
Average Monthly Rent	$300.00
Average New Car	$7,201.00
Cost of Movie Ticket	$2.25
Gasoline (gal)	$1.15
Av. Life Expectancy	73.70 years

At the end of this council's term Grand Basileus Coulon spoke of the highlights and struggles of his administration. He said that the genesis of his administration was concerned with financial stability and organization. **This concentration, of course, coming upon the heels of the financial misdeed of a renowned (now infamous) Brother Jesse B. Blayton, the long-serving Grand Keeper of Finance, who during his tenure allegedly managed to siphon off untold hundreds of thousands of dollars from Omega's meager funds over a period of three decades.** His self-dealing was not uncovered and finally dealt with in an open forum until the early 1970's, when the Fraternity finally voted him out of office and sought through a series of audits and legal actions to determine amounts stolen and to recover as much as possible, even after his death.

Omega vowed to never allow this type of corruption to occur again. Eternal vigilance via the phrase," when it comes to money being brotherly doesn't mean blindly trusting was the watch words of the day. More on the Jesse B. Blayton debacle will unfold later in this chapter.

The Supreme Council members that opened the Eighties, many serving a second term, and elected to answer the question of "What Now?" were:

Grand Basileus - BURNEL E. COULON 1st Vice Grand Basileus - L. Benjamin Livingston 2nd Vice Grand Basileus - Leon Franks; Grand Keeper of Records and Seal - Moses C. Norman, Sr.; Grand Keeper of Finance - Kenneth M. Taylor; Grand Counselor - Charles D. Chambliss, Jr.; Charles Fields – Grand Marshal; T. Maurice Hunley – Grand Chaplain; Larry A. Brown – Undergraduate; Bennie McMorris –Undergraduate; Lloyd J. Jordan – Undergraduate; Bennie McMorris – Undergraduate; Edward J. Braynon, Jr. – Immediate Past Grand Basileus; Robert P. Reeder, Assistant NES, H. Carl Moultrie, I NES Emeritus; Samuel R. Shepard, Editor of the Oracle

DISTRICT REPRESENTATIVES

Bernard Gilliam – 1st District; Walter G. Amprey – 2nd District; Kenneth Brown – 3rd District; Richard E. Jenkins – 4th District; Willie A. Smith – 5th District; S.P. Woodard – 6th District; David Beckley 7th District; Walter Littlejohn – 9th District; Al Reynolds – 10th District; Edgar Bridges – 12th District

Supreme Council Officers elected were:

GRAND BASILEUS – BURNEL E. COULON
First Vice Grand Basileus – L. Benjamin Livingston, Grand Keeper of Records and Seal –Moses C. Norman; Grand Keeper of Finance – Kenneth m. Taylor; Grand Chaplain – T. Maurice Huntley; New Officers chosen without opposition Grand Counselor-Elbert A. Walton, Jr.; Second Vice Grand Basileus Lee Grantlin Willis Grand Marshall Ulysses G. Horner, Jr.

Personalities, Initiatives and Events:
There were many events of significance and importance to the Fraternity and the United States in the 1980's. **On October 10, 1980, Brother OSCAR W. ADAMS was the first Black person**

to be appointed to the highest State Court in Alabama, in the Alabama State Supreme Court. This was a stellar achievement given the fact that Alabama's well known segregationist past was just barely toppled some 16 years prior with the passage of the Civil Rights Act of 1964 and the Voting Rights Act of 1965.

Omega's Social Environment in the early 1980's

The Black community in the early 1980's was not without major challenges on the social level. In 1981, a disease known as Acquired Immune Deficiency Syndrome (AIDS) was discovered and its ravaging affect on black communities began. The personal computer is invented by IBM and changes the way the fraternity communicates.

<<>>

The Jesse B. Blayton (Former Grand Keeper of Finance) circumstance will now unfold further:

Unbeknownst to the Fraternity, Jesse B. Blayton, the long time Grand keeper of Finance with Omega Psi Phi Fraternity Inc. was believed to have shifted/embezzled nearly $250,000 of Fraternity funds to his personal use over his long career as Grand Keeper of Finance. Because of his experience in banking, his detailed knowledge of the fraternity and his social importance to many Omega Men nationally, he served in the Grand Keeper of Finance position virtually unquestioned about his financial dealings for more than 35 years (from 1932 until 1969). The majority of his personal financial issues and problems involved unauthorized use of fraternity money and property.

Jesse Blayton's ability to avoid detection and scrutiny was in large measure due to his financial facility as well as the poor record keeping at the national level. He owned a bank and had many years of banking and finance experience. He also handled the investment funds of the Fraternity and was so self-assured and arrogant that he was rarely questioned about the Fraternity's funds or his failure to produce reports year after year. Jesse Blayton's misappropriation of funds was discovered during the administration of **Grand Basileus MARION W. GARNETT**

(1973 - 1976, but it was not totally sorted out until the Livingston Administration (1982-1984). There might never be a full and accurate accounting of the amount of funds he misappropriated or embezzled during his tenure.

Much of the Fraternity consternation regarding Blayton's self dealing involved the fraternity's initial laxed attitude to investigate and discipline Blayton and recover the funds. For some years after the Blayton debacle was uncovered, the Fraternity implemented more stringent financial procedures nationally and locally to ensure that this potentially crippling magnitude of embezzlement did not occur in the future. The event and the way it was handled threatened to split the Fraternity. Absent legal documents in state courts of Virginia, Georgia and the District of Columbia, there is a dearth of official Fraternity records of the fiasco and its conclusion.

Many discussions and business meetings related to the legal actions taken were never recorded. It can only be speculated that the Fraternity being more concerned with its image than dealing with the issue head-on kept the vast majority of members in the dark, and with the exception of a few leaders over the years, the Fraternity has generally restrained from publicizing the story beyond the organization or its members.

Because of the sting caused by the Jesse B. Blayton fiasco and the drain on Omega's funds, the Fraternity instituted major changes in administration, such as yearly audits at the chapter and national level and term limits on the Keeper of Finance and other Grand Officers.

Grand Basileus Coulon in his Conclave address in 1982 referenced the sad chapter in Omega's history saying " the past experiences were important and necessitated that the posture of Omega's financial status change and that it should take on a new image" While no conclave report addressed these "past experiences" all brothers in attendance knew what he meant. For years after, the fraternity's leaders still found it hard to discuss the whole affair. Internal pressure, anger and shame probably caused much of the information about the financial problems to remain unknown to the brotherhood generally. According to Grand Basileus Coulon, the San Francisco and Miami Conclaves provided the first repeat clean audits of the Fraternity in 20 years of his close involvement. To date, there is no accurate accounting of all the money stolen from the Fraternity by Blayton and even after his death his estate was indebted to the Fraternity to the tune of a quarter of a million dollars. Almost immediately, Grand Basileus Coulon and his successors stressed the need for the International office to make great strides at strengthening its accounting procedures and increased its ability to share with the members the organization's financial position.

Grand Basileus, Coulon, Marion Garnett and First Vice Grand Basileus L. Benjamin Livingston, was recognized as saviors for Omega in this circumstance in that they demonstrated extraordinary courage and leadership in tackling this very tough situation. Their unmasking of the guilty resulted in much needed light and corrective procedures being brought to bear to correct these serious destabilizing problems. Similar problems of this magnitude have toppled many organizations. Additionally, it was the strength courage, regained trust and faith of the men of Omega that saw the organization through these tough times. These men, (Grand Basileus Coulon, Garnett, and Livingston) along with many other good men took the bull by the horns, so to speak and clearly demonstrated the four Cardinal Principles of Manhood, Scholarship, Perseverance and Uplift in achieving success for Omega.

Omega men serving in Grand Basileus Coulon's administration garnered many accolades and achievements. Brother Burnel E. Coulon's administrative team was invited to the White House by President Ronald Reagan. **L. BENJAMIN LIVINGSTON** served as the Chair of the Democratic Fundraising Committee in the California Governor's race and the 2nd Vice Grand Basileus addressed the National AKA Collaboration Workshop and the National Equal Opportunity Conference.

The then supreme council took every opportunity during its time to increase Omega's exposure to the nation and the world and to present the experiences of Omega men in the most positive image possible. Coulon also argued that the committee system needed improvement, if not a full time staff person at the headquarters to keep committees focused on mission. Distance and cost kept many committees from meeting their objectives. This was a problem that would have to be solved if Omega was to realize its potential.

Grand Basileus Coulon re-asserted the Fraternity's financial and material support to the Black Colleges and Universities. Omega committed itself to the United Negro College Fund. **A very tense moment arose at the 61st Grand Conclave, in response to the question from some brothers who had graduated from white colleges: "Why should we support UNCF schools,"** Coulon responded that "... the Black private college is an institution and an advocator of Black thought. These schools have been the cradle of freedom and the cathedral of learning for the Black man in times when the state refused to provide education facilities. They are Black institutions controlled by us and for us, and if "us" do not support them, who will?"[52] His comments rung true, soared and cut through the air like roaring thunder. His comment was met with thunderous and extended applause from the brotherhood assembled. Grand Basileus Coulon's wisdom and tenacity had once again carried the day in this awkward circumstance.

Pledge period problems with hazing at both the graduate as well as the undergraduate level, as usual, consumed much of Omega life, business and policy during this period. Practices at individual chapters had not caught up with National Fraternity Policy, which had leapt forward since the 70's, seeking to eliminate physical and psychological brutality, strengthen the academic progress of Lampados Club[53] members and instilled social action and leadership development. Expulsions at the Miami Conclave followed abuses of Fraternity secrets and the "making" of Omegas with no National recognition-"local ques/rogues."

This administration also listed as a hallmark of its tenure, the revision of the Conclave meeting format to stress and encourage workshops to make the Conclave a learning experience and not a political background. The Conclave they contended must become cost-effective and affordable to all members focusing on pre-registration rather than on-site registration in an effort to facilitate and encourage better pre-

---

[53] The Lampados Club was the official name of Omgea Psi Phi Fraternity, Inc. Pledge Club.

planning and programming.[54]

<<>>

FREDERICK S. WEAVER, long time editor of the Oracle and great-grandson of Frederick Douglass enters Omega Chapter in **April 1982.**

<<>>

Grand Basileus Coulon and his administration were able to save Omega a lot of money as he improved its efficiency and procedures. He credits John Epps, Lloyd Jordan (who divised innovative computer systems as undergraduate assistant), Daryl Stoutamier and Pete Reeder as standout performers in delivering on his push for dramatically improved efficency in Omega. To provide examples of items his administration changed that, although simple, generated tons of goodwill with the membership, would be, 1. They made a decision to buy Omega pins in bulk without a specific name on them. In past years each pin was specifically purchased with the intended person's name engraved on it. This method was very expensive and also added significant time to processing. Changing the latter method led to great savings as well as significantly cut down on the turn around time for members to get this precious item. This area, the lengthy time it took to obtain customized fraternity pins, had been a gigantic sore spot in the organization that had led to tremendous frustration, outward demonstrated anger leveled at leadership and headquarters and low morale throughout the organization. Making a decision to remove name engraving was not without danger however. Some brothers insisted this personalized feature was too must to give up. Grand Basileus Coulon was able to reason with the membership and get them to buy into this major change.

Similar improvements were seen and made in the area of Life Membership plaques. It took, as if forever it seemed, to get the latter item to the membership prior to Brother Coulon's Administration. He changed this and significantly improved turn around time. The processing of money was also a slow and tedious process at the headquarters prior to Grand Basileus Coulon's administration taking on this sensitive task. After Jesse Blayton's shameful acts, it is easy to understand why membership would be highly suspicion of all financial transactions. Members vehemently complained that they had sent in money and completed forms etc. as required and were not able to get credit for it in a reasonable time or in some instances, where money in the form of checks had been sent, simply never got credit for their payments at all.

Grand Basileus Coulon, after having this circumstance thoroughly analyzed and investigated found the genesis of the problem. He reported to the membership that, "these problems occurred not because money had been stolen, but primarily because it had been inefficiently and irresponsibly placed to the side, in drawers and as a result stacked up and was not kept up with by the office staff which caused lengthy and unreasonable time delays in processing." The antiquated hand driven manual labor process that was prevalent in headquarter was suspect. Grand Basileus Coulon decided it was time for Omega to correct this continuing disaster. His administration was successful in finding better ways to quickly process money and various other paperwork processing etc, and in turn was able to dramatically improve the organization's performance in these areas.

These items may seem small now in hind sight but then, the membership felt very, very strongly about them and was openly vocal in driving the point home that this situation had to change. And, when they were corrected by Grand Basileus Coulon and the headquarters' staff, it played a major role in improving morale and lifting the spirits of the membership throughout the organization. **Grand Basileus Coulon unselfishly credits PETE REEDER for the outstanding job he did as Executive Director during his tenure**. According to Grand Basileus Coulon, It was he who found and hired good dedicated staff such as Mrs. Dorothy Bynes and along with great Omega men like Daryl Stoutamier they rolled up their sleeves, burned the mid night oil on many occasions. And, they got the job done. These people (Dorothy Bynes, and the newly hired headquarter staff did a super job along with Pete Reeder and Grand Basileus Coulon, who routinely rolled up his sleeve and physically pitched in, in improving the over-all efficiency of the organization.

Brother Coulon in leaving out of the chief executive officer position gave a powerful message to young people interested in going up in the organization. Simply stated, he said "It is not easy!" However, this special service to Omega has it own gratifying rewards for a special kind of person. It is a constant developmental process with service to others as its center and prime directive. Grand Basileus Coulon also wanted young people to know that service to Omega Psi Phi Fraternity is all about sacrifice and hard work. He stated that many a night he would be on the lonely dangerous rode driving from one place to another in the dangerous dark of the night working for Omega up until the wee hours of the morning. The latter was most especially true in his former position as District Representative. He stated, he often worked late doing the business of Omega. Getting into his soft and warm bed long after one or two in the morning was his norm, only to have to get up a 6 A.M. to go to his regular job. Even still, he would recommend this torturous labor of love to all.

The Fraternity under grand Basileus Coulon's administration endowed its first Academic Chair in 1981 at Rust College, Holly Springs, and Mississippi. The Omega endowed Chair at Rust was headed by Brother **WILLIAM MCMILLAN**. This Omega chair was established to recognize scholarship and to support the establishment of professors who teach and inspire youth in the area of the Humanities. President W.A. McMillan stated that the Chair would be used to promote the humanities. The fraternity also completed its 250,000 dollars contribution to the United Negro College Fund, an organization under the direction of Christopher Edley, and approved a plan to continue the annual gift of 50,000 dollars to that organization in perpetuity. The latter contribution to the organization was derived from chapter assessments. The Fraternity also accelerated its support for other historical civil rights organizations like the NAACP and the National Urban League. Many chapters completed their life membership payments during this period.

Omega also continued to participate in Operation Big Vote. A national coalition of civic, fraternal and educational, political and civil rights organizations campaigned to increase Black voter turnout in 1980, an election year. The social action committee spearheaded the Fraternity's involvement. [55]

CHAPTER VI

(OMEGA FLEXES ITS POLITICAL MUSCLES, SOME PLEDGE PROGRAMS CALLED A DISGRACE TO OMEGA & THE Q-DOG IMAGE OUTLAWED)

The L. Benjamin Livingston, (the 32nd Grand Basileus of Omega Psi Phi Fraternity) era begins: (Term 1982-1984)

Grand Basileus Livingston was initiated into Omega Psi Phi Fraternity at Phi Psi Chapter at Langston University. He was affectionately known throughout the organization as "Ben the Big Q of the Desert." He was very well liked and as a result of his enormous popularity was able to lead and inspire Omega men to great heights. Grand Basileus Livingston served Omega Psi Phi Fraternity, Inc. in many capacities at the chapter, district and international level. It was said by those Omega men around him that knew him best, that he served Omega with all the energy, gusto and resources available to him. Grand Basileus Livingston, simply stated, was a gentle man of the people, "A brother's brother." Someone who young aspiring Omega men flocked to and wanted to model themselves after. In spite of his goodness

---

[55] Reginald E. Vance, Donald Ray Hornbuckle and Michael Lyles are contributing writers on this chapter.

and extreme popularity, Grand Basileus' Livingston's metal would be tested during his administration with the serious challenges that lie before it.

The 61ˢᵗ Grand Conclave was held in August 1982 in Miami Florida with the same officers from the 60ᵗʰ Grand Conclave presiding. The theme of the Conclave that year was **"Reconstruction Revisited: Black Survival in Spite of Reaganomics."** This Conclave resulted in further tightening and accountability procedures for funds collected during Conclaves and across the board in Omega Psi Phi Fraternity, Inc. in general. Omega was still reeling and extremely sensitive and suspicious in areas of finances, given the Jesse Blayton tragedy in the seventies.

The incoming Elected Grand officers were: Grand Basileus **L. BENJAMIN LIVINGSTON**, 1stVice Grand Basileus Moses C. Norman, Sr.; 2nd Vice Grand Basileus Lee Willis; Grand Keeper of Records and Seal, Walter G. Amprey; Grand Keeper of Finance Kenneth M. Taylor; Grand Counselor, Elbert A. Walton, Jr.

The theme of Grand Basileus Livingston's administration was, **"Unity, Brotherhood, and Fraternal Growth through commitment, accountability, responsibility and reaffirmation of our four cardinal principles."**[56] Brother Livingston shared his personal creed regarding life in Omega with the membership. He said: "I don't have many answers but I do have some sense of direction and this much I can say, I believe that Omega Psi Phi Fraternity is the greatest experience that has happened to any of us. I also believe that to live, one must care."

I believe that my behavior, my attitudes, my life are in themselves significant. I believe that other persons, especially the Brotherhood of Omega Psi Phi Fraternity, present the only concrete opportunity for love and service to mankind and that love and service of others is the most sincere form of worship I know. I believe that every person must make decisions and must live by their consequences. In these days of pressure and complexities, I need humility in the face of great ignorance, love for others in the face of great need, courage in the face of never fully knowing. These, my brothers comprise my dreams for me; I share them with

---

[56] L. Benjamin Livingston-State of The Fraternity Address Aug. 16, 1983, 62ⁿᵈ Grand Conclave

you.[57]"

The latter publicly released feelings by the new in coming Grand Basileus, after the very bad feeling still lingering in the air like a fowl smell regarding the Jesse Blayton incident, was like a soothing, pain relieving, healing balm on a hurting open sore. Grand Basileus Livingston seemed to be saying, "Evil had tested us. But had failed. It was now time for good and decent men to go on the offensive and show that they could make it right." His administration's openness and positive tone set the stage for the organization to move forward into the hope of a brighter, new dawning day.

After getting Omega Psi Phi Fraternity moving back in the right direction, it was thought that it was time for Omega to look outward and begin to flex it unified muscles/manpower and turn its attention to the political process. Grand Basileus Livingston also publicly expressed that it was time for Omega to make its presence known in the still smoldering civil rights battle in a big way. The black man was suffering many injustices. As a result, one of Omega's own, Jesse L. Jackson, hinted to the organization that he may enter the presidential arena in the immediate future. Omega encouraged this favorite son and the membership prepared itself and it neighbors for battle. **Voter registration efforts and voter rolls ALL ACROSS THE NATION** increased significantly as a direct result of Omega Psi Phi Fraternity's efforts. A major march of Washington D.C. by Black Americans was also planned to make its grievances known.

Out of the blue, just when Omega thought it was safe to go full blast externally, new serious internal problems surfaced and came to the fore regarding the pledging process. Omega could not ignore this threat to its very existence. It would have to handle this internal matter as well as find a way to honor its commitment and play a big role in the civil rights struggle. This is what great organizations do! The leadership and brain trust of Omega found a way to do both. Serious hazing allegations were beginning to surface that indicated serious flaws in the current pledging process. More direct training initiatives headed by the Second Vice Grand Basileus and District representatives proved to be a positive step in the efforts to curb pledging violations and to challenge undergraduates to high achievement. As if one internal problem was not enough, Omega was hit with another serious internal issue. The fiscal management of the organization came under more scrutiny in 1982 as the Fraternity was audited by the Internal Revenue Service. The Fraternity hired outside accountants to assist in handling the audit. Omega had implemented new financial accounting practices after the Jesse Blayton incident. Thank God! They stood up to intense scrutiny. Omega survived the Internal Revenue Service audit. A review of the accounting of the 61st Grand Conclave resulted in tightening accountability procedures for funds collected during conclaves.

The fraternity accelerated its financial support to the National Urban League. Mr. **JOHN JACOBS**, Executive Director of the Urban League, participated in Grand Conclaves on a regular basis. Additionally, **JESSE JACKSON**, former president of Operation PUSH and founder of the Rainbow Coalition, attended Grand Conclaves on a regular basis and received support from Omega Psi Phi Fraternity for these organizations.

From August 13 – 20, **1983, the Fraternity held its 62nd Grand Conclave in Kansas City Missouri**, in the Eighth District, under the leadership of 8th District Representative, **JESSE L. HIGH**. **1983 and 1984 were notable years for the Fraternity, mostly due to the U.S. presidential campaign of the first African American man to endeavor to do so, Omega Fraternity Brother JESSE L. JACKSON.**

Supreme Council officers elected at this Grand Conclave were:

L. Benjamin Livingston - Grand Basileus

Moses C. Norman – First Vice Grand Basileus; Mark A. Iles – Second Vice Grand Basileus; Walter G. Amprey – Grand Keeper of Records and Seal; Cameron Wade – Grand Keeper of Finance; Melvin C. Zeno - Grand Counselor; Harold Holliday, Sr.-Grand Marshal; Joe N. Cole, Sr. - Grand Chaplain; Thierry Fortune - Undergraduate Rep; David A. Brown-Undergraduate Rep; Darrel

G. Comer-Undergraduate Rep; Burnel L. Coulon immediate past Grand Basileus

DISTRICT REPRESENTATIVES

1ST District - Leroy C. Williams; 2nd District - Walter F. Wrenn, III; 3rd District-Vernon Johnson; 4th District - Frank Williams; 5th District - Willie A. Smith; 6th District - Joseph W. Harper; 7th District - Dorsey C. Miller; 8th Jesse L. High; 9th - Jethro L. Hills; 10th District - John S. Epps; 12th District - James A. Grady

Omega as a committed organization, strongly supported civil rights and participated heavily in the planning of the commemorative March on Washington in August 27, 1983. This March retraced the steps and memorialized for the nation the twentieth anniversary of the historic 1963 March on Washington lead by Dr. Martin Luther King and organized by Bro. **BAYNARD RUSTIN**, Asa Phillip Randolph, Dorothy Height and many others in the Civil Rights Movement. More than 217 delegates attended the Greek Leadership Conference on Civil Rights and Economic Issues." Officially representing Omega Psi Phi Fraternity were **L. BENJAMIN LIVINGSTON**, Judge **H. CARL MOULTRIE, MOSES C. NORMAN, WALTER AMPREY, ELBERT A. WALTON, KENNETH TAYLOR AND MARK A. ILES.**[58]

During the Conclave year, the Fraternity was able to acquire the home of **COL. CHARLES YOUNG**. The purchase of the fifty-eight acre parcel along with the house, which was a station on the famous Underground Railroad, was a major moment in Omega history and one for which much credit was given to Bro. **FRANK C. WILLIAMS**, Fourth District Representative for bringing to the attention of the Fraternity the availability of the property. The eighteen room home was declared a historic landmark in the State of Ohio and was immediately put under the management of the Omega Psi Phi Housing Authority. On March 30, 1974, the Colonel Charles Young House, located on Columbus Pike between Clifton and Stevenson Roads, was listed with the National Register of Historic Places.

---

[58] The Oracle-Fall 1983 Ed. p. 4-5

The 1983 Conclave was also notable in that it was the kick off of the 100th Anniversary of the birth of Omega's late Founder Dr. Ernest Everett Just. Mr. Kenneth Manning, a biographer of Just's life was on hand at the Conclave to discuss his research and his book on Brother Just- "Ernest Everett Just: The Black Apollo of Science." Other noted programs advocated by the Livingston council were support for the NAACP and the creation of a joint program of support between Omega and the Boys Club of America, lead by Brother **PELTON STEWART** and **Brother FILMORE GRAHAM**. Grand Basileus Livingston also recommended to the Conclave that a 60 year recognition ceremony and ring acknowledging continued service to Omega be approved.

Brother **H. CARL MOULTRIE** accepted appointment to chair a committee responsible for revising and updating the constitution and by-laws of the Fraternity as well as reviewing general policies and procedures and to establish policy that will guide the Grand Basileus and other's behavior in carrying out the work of the Organization. Brother **WILL SUTTON, JR.** was appointed to update the History of the Omega Psi Phi Fraternity beginning at the point where Brother Gill left off.

<<>>

The International Omega Man of the YEAR for 1983 was Brother **ROBERT S. SHOFFNER. He w**as recommended by the 12th District after being chosen for the same honor by his chapter, Sigma Iota of Oakland, Ca. He was initiated into Omega Psi Phi Fraternity, Inc. on March 26, 1971.

<<>>

On June 28, 1983, **FRED B. PAYTON**, Omega's 1st Traveling Representative enters Omega chapter. He was initiated into Omega Psi Phi Fraternity, Inc, in 1926 in Birmingham, Alabama via Alpha Phi Chapter.

<<>>

Many good things happened to the Fraternity in 1983. One example is Mrs. Mabel Coleman, the wife of Founder **FRANK**

COLEMAN, leaving $5,000 in her will to the Fraternity that was earmarked for the Omega Psi Phi Scholarship Fund.

<><>

THE OMEGA LIFE MEMBERSHIP FOUNDATION, INC.

The Omega Life Membership Foundation, Inc. was established in 1984. It was chartered to aid organizations involved in charitable, educational, scholastic and scientific pursuits. In its twenty year plus history, it has had tremendous growth and success and has been of significant benefit to those groups whose work it has been privileged to support. There have been numerous young people, gifted in the performing arts, and in scholastic pursuits who were able to continue their progress, as a result of the generous, philanthropic work of the Foundation. It has supported a number of Uplift and Scholastic projects and initiatives started and endorsed by the Omega Psi Phi Fraternity, Inc.

The Articles of Incorporation were filed in the District of Columbia on September 8, 1984 and Amended Articles of Incorporation filed on Marc 14, 1985. The purposes for which the corporation is organized are to take, receive, acquire, own, have, and hold the life membership estate, assets, funds, principal, income monies, accounts, grants, donations, gifts and properties both real and personal, tangible and intangible, for such uses and purposes and with such powers, duties, and obligations as are set forth in the Charter and corporate bylaws. [59]

<><>

The 63rd Grand Conclave was **held December 1984** in Louisville, Kentucky. This was the last winter Conclave. The bi-annual summer meetings were voted into effect in August 1983 beginning with the summer of 1986, the 75th anniversary. This was the last conclave with Benjamin Livingston as Grand Basileus.
In his final state of the Fraternity Address,

---

[59] Omega Life Membership Foundation website http://www.olmf.org/index.html

Grand Basileus Livingston stressed ridding the Fraternity of the NASTY-Q-DOG IMAGE.

In the 1980s and again in the 1990s, **the Fraternity reaffirmed its policy against the use of a canine (dog) reference in association with the organization.** The Fraternity looked with disfavor upon members who violated this policy by wearing paraphernalia with a canine image. Further, it forbided the wearing of any such paraphernalia at its meetings and advised the general public that persons so attired or who make such references did not represent the Omega Psi Phi Fraternity, Inc. in their actions.

<<>>

A Statement of Position against the Canine Reference was established and publicized by Omega Psi Phi Fraternity Inc.,
It is as follows:

WHEREAS, the Omega Psi Phi Fraternity is an organization of college-trained men: and,

WHEREAS, the Omega Psi Phi Fraternity has always sought, and continue to seek, men of similar high ideals of manhood, scholarship, perseverance and uplift to be members of the organization, and

WHEREAS, the Cardinal principles of Manhood, Scholarship, Perseverance and Uplift are deemed, in and of themselves, to be adequate symbolisms and representations for the organization and its members, now, therefore,

BE IT RESOLVED, that the Omega Psi Phi Fraternity, Inc. does not have, nor has it ever endorsed, a mascot of any type to be representative of the organization, and

BE IT FURTHER RESOLVED, that the Omega Psi Phi Fraternity, Inc. expressly denounces and vehemently opposes the

use of any canine (dog) representation associated with the organization's name, symbols, or crest (escutcheon), and
BE IT FURTHER RESOLVED, that the Omega Psi Phi Fraternity, Inc. forbids admission to any of its programs or events, or to the program or events of its chapter, to any person who wears paraphernalia which might depict association of a canine reference with the organization, and,

BE IT FURTHER RESOLVED that the Omega Psi Phi Fraternity, Inc. considers any person who wears Omega Paraphernalia with a canine reference to be in violation of Fraternity policy.[60]

Acting consistent with the organization's constitution and by-laws, operating procedures and ritual, Grand Basileus Livingston in his final address to the membership as Grand Basileus, insisted that the greatest problem Omega faced was what to do about our pledging program. He noted, quoting Former Grand Basileus Ed Braynon..."**Omega's pledge program is more destructive than productive."**

Grand Basileus Livingston further stated that during the previous two and one half years, many chapters and brothers were suspended or placed on probation for violations of the fraternity rules. Many more escaped detection each hereby convincing members and non-members of the Omega Psi Phi, neither has the desire or ability to enforce her rules and regulations.

Grand Basileus Livingston in his last official Conclave address stated that the pledge programs of some chapters are a disgrace to Omega Psi Phi. They completely repudiate our constitution, the cardinal principles, the motto and they defy the laws of common sense and decency. We must bring an end to all of the undesirable and irresponsible practices of chapters and brothers. As your Grand Basileus I have used my ability to raise the consciousness of many brothers and attempted to effectively deal with the problem in the Fraternity.

Omega Psi Phi Fraternity, Inc. Statement of Position on Hazing was officially established and published. It is as follows:

---

[60] Winter/Spring 1992 Oracle

The Omega Psi Phi Fraternity, Inc. embraces the principles contained in the Statement of Position on Hazing as promulgated by the Fraternity Executives Association.

However, for its own Position own intent and purposes, the Omega Psi Phi Fraternity, Inc. espouses the following as its official Statement of Position on Hazing; to wit:

Omega Psi Phi Fraternity, Inc. strictly prohibits and expressly denounces the practice of members against any person seeking admission to the organization. "Hazing" is defined as any reckless or intentional action taken or any situation created which produces mental or include, but are not limited to, paddling in any form; creation of excessive fatigue; creating or inflicting physical and/or psychological shocks; conducting quests, treasure hunts, scavenger hunts, road trips or any other such activities carried on outside the confines of a house/domicile; public wearing of any apparel or paraphernalia which is conspicuous, not normally in good taste or otherwise banned; engaging in public stunts and buffoonery; morally degrading or humiliating an individual(s) through words or deeds; conducting late (after establishing hours) sessions which interfere with or prohibit the pursuit of scholastic attainment or productive work; and the conduct of any activities, expressed or implied, which are not consistent with the Cardinal Principles espoused by the fraternity or the academic missions of colleges or universities where chapters of the Fraternity may exist.

The expressed or implied consent of a person to any such actions shall not be considered as an exception to this policy and is not defensible as a violation thereof.

<<>>

Brother **DORSEY MILLER JR.**, Seventh District D.R. at that time, was appointed to head up a special committee to bring recommendations as to how to leverage the fraternal strength to solve the pledge program problem. Our pledging activity needs to provide meaningful opportunity to participate in programs of uplift. There is much to be uplifted in our community and in our world. Most of all, our pledging activity must provide a chance to experience firsthand brotherly love.

Brother Miller asked the membership to remember the feeling and the fellowship we shared in moments of our fraternal life where we truly understood brotherly love. He also asked members to be reminded that the District Representatives are constitutionally mandated to see that no corporal punishment is inflicted on potential members at any time. He went on to say that it would better if each of us at this moment takes a pledge to personally see to it that our chapter and we sponsor productive pledging activities of a positive nature, designed to uphold our cardinal principles. Out of this stirring and passionate dialogue, a revised pledge program was offered for consideration by the Conclave.

Brother **VERNON JOHNSON** was appointed to assist with the updating of the Fraternity History. Other projects which were urged to continue and expand upon were the Assault on Illiteracy Project and an increased commitment to problems facing the continent of Africa. Grand Basileus Livingston brought forth several recommendations for consideration at the Conclave: Creation of at-large membership; 2, Honorary membership; 3. Supreme Council no-voting membership for Past Active Grand Basilei; 4. Omega Foundation established as a non-profit;[61]

<<>>

Other additional accomplishments of Omega men during this period:

November 1982 THOMAS MANN, JR. of Mu Omicron Chapter in Des Moine, Iowa became the first Black person elected to the Iowa State Senate.

<<>>

Brother **FRED RICE, JR.** of Sigma Omega Chapter appointed Chicago's fist Black Superintendent of Police in 1983.

<<>>

Voter registration and working with candidate **JESSE L.**

---

[61] L. Benjamin Livingston-State of the Fraternity Address- 63rd Grand Conclave, Louisville, Ky.

JACKSON was a major theme of the 1983-84 year. Omega was flexing it political muscles via its support of favorite son and Omega brother, Jesse L. Jackson.

Financial assistance was also initiated to Operation PUSH (People United to Save Humanity, under the leadership of Brother **JESSE L. JACKSON,**

Jesse Jackson a Member of Omega Psi Phi Fraternity, Inc., in July 1983 received public support from the Fraternity in his campaign for the presidency of the United States in 1984.

National Social Action Theme: "Omega striving for excellence in Every Endeavor."

<<>>

February 1, 1984 United States Postal Service Issues first **CARTER G. WOODSON** Stamp.

<<>>

The Seventy-fifth Anniversary Grand Conclave celebration was deemed the single most significant event on Omega's horizon. The dates selected were July 25-August 1, 1986 in Washington, D.C., the city of Omega's birth. It was the largest Conclave ever. Being planned as the largest conclave ever.

CHAPTER VII

(FRATERNAL EVANGELISM INTRODUCED & PLEDGING IS ABOLISHED)

The Moses C. Norman Sr. (the 33rd Grand Basileus of Omega Psi Phi Fraternity) era begins: (Term 1984-1990)

Grand Basileus **MOSES C. NORMAN, SR., PH.D. AND AREA SUPERINTENDENT OF THE ATLANTA PUBLIC SCHOOLS,** was elected at the 1984 Louisville Kentucky, 63rd Grand Conclave. He was initiated into Omega Psi Phi Fraternity, Inc on December 13th, 1954 in Beta Psi Chapter at Clark College, Atlanta Georgia. He is the father of three sons who, like him, are all Omega men. Grand Basileus Norman has the unique distinction to have served three consecutive terms as Grand Basileus of Omega Psi Phi Fraternity, Inc. At one point in Omega Conclave history, elections occurred every year; then it went to eighteen months and from there two years. This voted on change occurred during this administration. In the transition, Omega men felt so approving and comfortable with Grand Basileus Norman that he was elected to a third term at the Dallas, Texas, Grand

---

[62] *Contributing writers for this chapter are Omega men Dr. Reginald E. Vance, Donald Ray Hornbuckle and Michael Lyles

Conclave in 1988 One of Grand Basileus Norman's favorite sayings was **"The Lamp is aflame, the candles are lit, the pearls are aglow, and our hearts are warm and filled with love of brotherhood. Let us capture the moment for Omega."** And capture it he did! A [63] great deal of Omega's highly significant and lasting history was made during Grand Basileus Norman's extraordinary leadership.

Grand Basileus Norman initiated and was a strong and vocal advocate for what he called **Fraternal Evangelism** in Omega. This powerful positive concept centered around his publicly expressed desire and demonstrated public actions to heal the rifts that had formed between the men of Omega across America. Some of the problems sprung from the divisions and district related pride that manifested itself from political campaigns and the many subsequent appointments that often occurred as men moved into office and selected people they knew best. Additionally, many selections also followed voting patterns that often resulted in the selection of brothers from the bigger districts. The latter factor also inflamed the rift between the men of Omega.

It was Moses C. Norman who fought the good fight and healed this widening destructive rift during his tenure as Grand Basileus. He is credited with ushering in a more harmonious climate and productive period in Omega. Further, the accomplishments of Grand Basileus Norman's Supreme Councils in many other critically important areas during his three terms with Omega, are indeed numerous and worthy of historical note.

For example, two revised methods of bringing members into the fraternity were approved by the organization.[64] **Pledging was abolished and the new Membership Selection and Education Program came into being on August 1, 1985. The Membership Intake policy was adopted by the Grand Conclave in Detroit in 1990 and was implemented beginning in April, 1991.** A brief moratorium on initiations was instituted during this period.

Under Grand Basileus Norman, initial plans were begun for the writing of an updated history of the Omega Psi Phi Fraternity, Inc.

H. CARL MOULTRIE, I, Executive Secretary Emeritus, **RONALD E. MCNAIR**, noted Astronaut; **DON Q. PULLEN, W. MERCER COOK, ROY WILKINS and many other great Omega men** entered Omega Chapter during this period. Ah, what a great gathering this had to have been at the doors of the beautiful pearly gates of heaven. I can just see the Supreme Basileus and the Founders now, smiling broadly and singing along, as Don Q. Pullen led these good brothers through the gates of heaven singing the Omega hymn. What a welcome home party these great Omega men had. My, my my!

Newly Elected Supreme Council officers at the 63rd Grand Conclave in Louisville, Kentucky were:

MOSES C. NORMAN – Grand Basileus
C. Tyrone Gilmore – First Vice Grand Basileus
Anthony Brazile - Second Vice Grand Basileus
Willie A. Smith, Grand Keeper of Records and Seal
J. Cameron Wade – Grand Keeper of Finance
Melvin C. Zeno – Grand Counselor; Thomas Sears – Grand Chaplain; Grand Marshal – Edward Clements.

Among the noted speakers for the 63rd Grand Conclave were Rev. **JESSE LOUIS JACKSON**, Democratic Candidate for President of the United States,; Attorney **BENJAMIN L. HOOKS, Executive Director of the NAACP**,[65]

and John Jacobs, President of National Urban League. Each speaker in his own way shared an outstanding message for all of those in attendance. In a closed session with Jesse Jackson and Greek Letter Representatives, Grand Basileus Dr. L. Benjamin Livingston informed them that Omega Psi Phi Fraternity is leading the way and serving thousands of youths and organizations across the land (PUSH, Urban League and NAACP by coincidence at this point in time all are headed by Omega men). The theme for the Founders' Banquet was "The Importance of Black Political Action Now."[66]

Grand Basileus Norman, immediately after his election, appointed a committee to review the structure and operations of the Fraternity as a means of future focus. That Comprehensive

---

[65] Benjamin L. Hooks Institute for Social Change/http://benhooks.memphis.edu/biography.html
[66] The 1985 Summer/Fall Oracle
*

Review Committee included such brothers as H. Carl Moultrie, Father H. Albion Ferrell, Wiley Branton, Edward J. Braynon, Lloyd J. Jordan among others. As previously mentioned, in 1985 the Membership Selection and Education Program **replaced the pledge method of initiating new members into the fraternity.** Its process was conceived from the idea that Omega men are sought carefully from among the rank and file of otherwise worthy men on the college campus as well as from the post-baccalaureate community, and that those men who join the organization should already possess the qualities of an Omega man.

The program was replaced in the 1990s as part of an agreement reached by the eight Black Greek Letter fraternities and sororities upon the recommendation of the Council of Presidents which was chaired by Grand Basileus Norman. One pivotal impetus behind this overarching change was the position taken by the American Council of Education that fraternities and sororities were becoming liabilities to colleges and universities, especially through actions taken during the pledging process. The mere existence on their campuses was conditioned upon the change in the process of bringing members into those organizations. Thus, Omega's future was dependent upon this change; however, that change did not come without considerable debate and opposition from within the brotherhood.

In the summer 1985 Oracle, Brother Norman discussed the focus of his administration. He outlined several thrusts that are shown below:

-Raising and enhancing the image and esteem of Omega.
-Improving the operation of the international Headquarters
-Improving the spirit of brotherhood
-Including brothers from all age groups and Districts in the leadership of Omega
-Improving communications within Omega
-Upgrading programs at all levels
-Reclaiming at least 6,000 brothers by August 1986.
-Initiating only men who possess the qualities desired in Omega men.
-Operating the brotherhood in a more business-like manner.
-Impacting the social, political, academic, economic, morale and cultural order everywhere through aggressive and responsible programs.

Also, as a result of the internal activism of Moses C. Norman and his desire to restructure the operations of the Fraternity administration, the Fraternity accomplished an extensive program during this period including the following:

- Recommended employment of John S. Epps as National Executive Secretary to replace Brother "Pete" Reeder.
- Undergraduate brothers were appointed to serve as vice-chairmen of most Fraternity Committees at the National and District levels.
- The Fraternity resolved to provide significant support for UNCF, Afri-Care Program, Anti-Apartheid Movement in South Africa, Assault on Illiteracy, National Coalition of Black Voter Participation, and programs aimed at stemming the growing problem of teenage pregnancy
- Four Endowed Omega Chairs named in honor of the founders of Omega Psi Phi Fraternity, approved under the leadership of Grand Basileus Edward J. Braynon and initiated under the leadership of Grand Basileus Burnel Coulon, were recommended to be funded at the annual rate of not less than $5,000 each, effective the 1988 fiscal year
- The Omega Psi Phi Federal Credit Union was established.
- The Carter G. Woodson Memorial was established.
- An Economic Development Committee was established.
- The Fraternity sought to reclaim at least 6,000 brothers.
- The Colonel Young Home in Zenia, Ohio, was renovated and added to the National Historic Registry
- A new membership intake program, "Selection and Education", was created to replace the eight week pledge program and the Lampados Club tradition.

This Conclave was also responsible for dealing with the widely-discussed *plight of the undergraduate members* by refocusing Fraternity resources to their benefit in the areas of academics and leadership. **The Fraternity established the Ronald E. McNair Scholarship and the Herman S. Dreer Scholarship within the Charles R. Drew Memorial Scholarship Awards Program.** Grand Basileus Norman recommended and the 75th Anniversary Grand Conclave approved the Leadership Training Institute to be conducted during non-conclave years. National, district, and chapter officers, particularly Basilei, Keepers of Records and Seal, Keepers of Finance, and chapter reporters, along with national committee chairs, would be required to attend and participate.

Dr. JOHN S. EPPS was selected as the fifth Executive Director of Omega Psi Phi Fraternity, Inc. in 1984. In this capacity, he would follow in the great foot steps of such previous men in that office, including H, Carl Moultrie, the first and long-term holder of that office. Brother Epps was tasked to manage the daily activities of the fraternity, the World Center staff, and be responsible for planning the organization's annual meetings etc... Prior to being named Executive Director, Dr. Epps was an administrator and professor of medicine at Southern Illinois University School of Medicine. He had successfully held many other high level administrative jobs outside of Omega, such as being a consultant to the U.S. Department of Health, Education and Welfare. Dr. Epps had a sterling record of thirty years of consecutive service to Omega Psi Phi Fraternity. He was Tenth District Representative from 1982-1984, was the district's Omega Man of the Year, and was the International Omega Man of the Year for 1982 -1983.

John Epps had also been the Basileus of three different chapters and was an extremely active participant and highly effective in the leadership of the Tenth District for fifteen years. He chaired the tenth District's scholarship committee and by-laws committee and was also the director of public relations. It is very clear, that once again, Omega's leadership chose very well and had found a rare and precious gem in the dedicated and hard working Dr. Epps. Executive Director Epps was initiated into Omega Psi Phi fraternity in Nu Chi chapter in 1965.

<<>>

Major cultural events during this period contributed to Omega's continued growth and development: In 1984 the Vietnam War Memorial opened in Washington, D.C. "The Cosby Show" which featured Omega man Bill Cosby, debuts and becomes the longest running most successful sitcom about Black family life in history -- starting a trend of more realistic portrayals of African Americans in Television and Cinema. Vanessa Williams becomes the first Black Miss America, but resigns her crown after nude photos of her are made public. Her career survives and she thrives as a renowned and popular actress and R&B singer despite the negative publicity.

<<>>

Brother RAY ARMSTEAD represented the United States in the XXIII Olympiad in Los Angeles California in 1984. He was a graduate of Northeast Missouri State. Brother Armstead was a member of the U.S. 4x400 Meter Relay Team which won gold medals with a 2:57.91 time.

<<>>

Two revised methods of bringing members into the fraternity were approved by the organization. **PLEDGING WAS ABOLISHED, and the new Membership Selection and Education Program came into being on August 1, 1985.**

<<>>

The Seventy-fifth Anniversary Grand Conclave celebration was deemed the single most significant event on Omega's horizon. The dates selected were July 25-August 1, 1986 in Washington, D.C., the City's birth.

<<>>

In 1985 Crack Cocaine emerges as the second scourge of the eighties to wreak havoc in black communities. It is not until the late 1990's that the cheap homemade illegal drug and its attendant drug wars begins to subside.

<<>>

On February 8, 1986 the Fraternity was presented **a Charter** for the first national Fraternity Federal Credit Union established as the Omega Psi Phi Fraternity Federal Credit Union. Brother **KENNETH M. TAYLOR** of Alpha Omega Chapter was elected as the first President and Chairman of the Credit Union's Board of Directors. By 1988 the Credit Union had over 800 members and had awarded 50 loans, with a majority being for life membership. By 1989 the credit union had provided nearly a quarter of one million dollars in loans.

<<>>

The 64th Grand Conclave – July 25 – August 1, 1986, the 75th Anniversary or Diamond Anniversary Celebration, which marked the Fraternity's 75th year of existence, was in Washington, DC. The city of the Fraternity's birth. Up until this point in time in Omega history, it was the largest Conclave ever.

The grand officers elected in Louisville, Kentucky, (the 63rd Grand Conclave in 1984 and who presided at this 64th Grand Conclave) were:

33rd GRAND BASILEUS - **MOSES C. NORMAN, SR**.
1st VICE GRAND BASILEUS - C. Tyrone Gilmore
2nd VICE GRAND BASILEUS – Anthony Brazeale.
GRAND KEEPER OF RECORDS AND SEAL - Willie A. Smith
GRAND KEEPER OF FINANCE - J. Cameron Wade
GRAND COUNSELOR - Melvin C. Zeno; GRAND CHAPLAIN – Thomas Sears ; GRAND MARSHAL-Edward Clements; IMMEDIATE PAST GRAND BASILEUS-L. Benjamin Livingston; Undergraduate Representative-Carl Wright Undergraduate Representative-Kevin Cherry

<<>>

DISTRICT REPRESENTATIVES

1ST District – Donald F. Harris; 2nd District – Andrew Ray: 3rd District – Robert W. Fairchild; 4th District – Jarrett A. Thomas; 5th District – Clearthur Morris; 6th District – William H. Hoffler, DDS; 7th District – Astrid K. Mack; 8th District – Lloyd Jordan, Esq; 9th District – Marshal Grady; 10th District – Johnnie D. Washington; 12th District – Lewis J. Sears, PH.D

INITIATIVES/EVENTS

The theme of the Conclave was **"A Heritage Celebrated and a Legacy Enhanced."**

At that 75th Anniversary Grand Conclave, history was made when Moses C. Norman, Jr., popularly known as "Conrad," was elected to the office of Undergraduate/Intermediate Representative to the Supreme Council, joining his father as the first father-son duo on the Supreme Council in the storied history of Omega Psi Phi Fraternity, Inc. He served four years in that capacity through the 66th Grand Conclave in Detroit in 1990.

One highlight of that Conclave was the March on the South African Embassy in protest of the racist policies of that country.

<<>>

April 9th. 1986, Executive Secretary Emeritus H. Carl Moultrie enters Omega Chapter.

<<>>

In 1986 the National Aeronautics and Space Administration (NASA) Shuttle Program built around reusable payload space vehicles was well underway. The Shuttle named Challenger had a unique crew comprised of women, African Americans and Asians for the first time. Brother Ronald E. McNair was among the crew. The disastrous explosion of the space craft on January 28, 1986, while the world watched, killed all aboard, including, Omega man, and beloved brother. The Challenger disaster, as it came to be called, consumed the attention of the American public and the U.S. Space Program. The tragedy was a low point in Omega, in the Black Community, as well as for the NASA Space Program, which remained stalled for several years following. In his honor a scholarship was created by the Fraternity for undergraduate brothers who excelled in academics. His name and life will always have a special place of honor in the hearts of all Omega men.

Brother Ronald E. McNair, a distinguished astronaut and scientist, was born in Lake City, South Carolina where he graduated from Carver High School. He did his undergraduate work at North Carolina Agricultural and Technical State University in Greensboro, North Carolina graduating Magna Cum Laude. He pursued further studies at E'cole D'ete Theorique de {Physique, Les Houshes France; and earned a Ph.D. in Physics from Massachusetts Institute of Technology.

Before his selection as one of the first Black Astronauts by NASA, he was a physicist at the Hughes Research Laboratories where he developed lasers for isotope separation and photochemistry utilizing non-linear interactions in low-temperature liquids and optical pumping techniques. Brother McNair published several papers and gave numerous lectures in the United States and Europe on lasers and molecular spectroscopy.

A few of his honors include: presidential Scholar; Ford Foundation Fellow; National Fellowship Fund; Omega Psi Phi Scholar; and honorary doctorate degrees from North Carolina A&T University, Morris College and the University of South Carolina. Ronald E. McNair epitomized the kind of academic excellence and courage envisioned by the founding fathers of Omega, and was an exemplary model for undergraduate brothers to emulate. **Brother McNair was initiated into the Fraternity through Mu Psi Chapter at North Carolina A&T on December 4, 1969.** Ronald E. McNair was an active member of

Rho Beta Beta Chapter in Houston, Texas when he entered Omega Chapter.

In Ronald E. McNair's honor, there have been many schools, federal facilities, parks, libraries, etc. that now wear his name across America. Dr. Ronald E. McNair is buried in his beloved home town of Lake City South Carolina at the Ronald E. McNair Memorial on E. Main street. Ronald E. McNair's burial site also includes an extraordinary technological water display. Ronald E. McNair is a nationally mourned hero. Omega men in that area or visiting the city should visit his grave site and insure its stateliness for all time.

<<>>

The **first Leadership Training Institute, later the Leadership Conference,** was convened by Grand Basileus Norman in New Orleans in 1987.

<<>>

On October 19, 1987, the Stock Market Crash signals the largest economic downturn of the Twentieth Century since the great depression. The stock market plunged 22%. This day would be forever etched into the socio-economic conscience of America and become know as Black Monday.

<<>>

The **65th Grand Conclave was held July 23-29, 1988** in Dallas, TX. The Grand Officers presiding were:

GRAND BASILEUS: MOSES C. NORMAN, SR.
1st VICE GRAND BASILEUS: C. Tyrone Gilmore, Sr.
2nd VICE GRAND BASILEUS: Alonzo Carter, Jr.
GRAND KEEPER OF RECORDS AND SEAL: Willie A. Smith
GRAND KEEPER OF FINANCE: J. Cameron Wade
GRAND COUNSELOR: Melvin C. Zeno, GRAND MARSHAL: Billy J. Ratcliff, GRAND CHAPLAIN: Thomas Sears, Undergraduate Intermediate Rep: M. Conrad Norman, Jr. Undergraduate Immediate Rep; Kevin Cherry; Michael Carrauthers; and 32nd Grand Basileus L. Benjamin Livingston

INITIATIVES/EVENTS

One feature by Grand Basileus Norman during of the Grand Conclave in Dallas was the Tribute to Black Colleges Presidents sponsored jointly by the Anheuser Bush corporation and the Southern Education Foundation of which Brother Dr. Elridge McMillan was president/CEO.

- The history of the fraternity was under revision and updated by brother Vernon Johnson and was directed to be completed by the 1990 Grand Conclave in Detroit.
- The second Endowed Founders Academic Chair was funded to become operational in the fall of 1988 at a Black college/university
- The Fraternity directed that each chapter initiate a "Project Manhood" for the mentoring of African American young men and boys in their communities.
- Through the Recommendation Committee, the Brotherhood recommended the establishment of an Omega Resources and Education Foundation with 501(C) 3 tax status. The non-profit received $10,000 from Anheuser-Busch through the Southern Education Fund
- The Brotherhood recommended the Africare Project annual contribution of $50,000 solicited from chapters
- The Fraternity directed that an official partnership program between undergraduate and nearby graduate chapters be commenced
- Life membership dues were increased from $750 to $1,000
- It was resolved and passed that the constitution be amended to limit the term of grand officers to no more than two successive terms effective at the Grand Conclave, 1990 in Detroit, Michigan.

Following the 1988 Grand Conclave in Dallas, Texas, Grand Basileus Norman expanded the international scope of the Fraternity by convening a December 1988 meeting of the Supreme Council in Heidelberg, West Germany, during which a chapter was chartered in Wurzburg, and visits were made to Nuremberg and Frankfurt.

In the area of membership development, a recommendation at the Conclave sought to re-establish the membership category of honorary membership as it was prior to the Constitutional revision in 1969. **It should be noted that Colonel Charles Young, Carter G. Woodson and Count Basie all became members through the Honorary Membership Initiation Process.** Grand Basileus Norman proposed that the concept of general membership first proposed by former Grand Basilei **BURNEL E. COULON** and **L. BENJAMIN LIVINGSTON** be given serious review and approved at the 65th Grand Conclave in Dallas, in 1988. The Conclave also proposed and it was accepted that the Fraternity dues be raised from $15 to $30 for undergrads, and $40 to $60 for Graduate brothers.

Of special note, the Fraternity under **MOSES C. NORMAN'S** direction completed the renovation of the Colonel Charles Young Home in Xenia, Ohio, that was purchased under the term of Grand Basileus L. Benjamin Livingston for $90,000. The home was added to the national Historic Registry and was set aside to be utilized by the Fraternity and to have a significant presence in the community. as a museum, satellite fraternity office, retreat site and adult community complex.[67]

CONCLAVE REPORT presented to the **66th Grand Conclave in 1990** contained a membership summary which detailed the efforts of the Norman administrations to make good on its membership growth initiatives.

Membership Summary

October 31, 1985
    Graduates   8,989
    Undergraduates 2,522

---

[67] Oracle-Summer/Fall 1985 edition p. 74

Life Members   2,000
Total   13,508

October 31, 1986
Graduates   8,080
Undergraduates   2,487
Life Members   2,113
Total   12,570

October 31, 1987
Graduates   7,090
Undergraduates   2,199
Life Members   1,381
Total   10,670

October 31, 1988
Graduates   7,758
Undergraduates   2,789
Life Members   2,383
Total   12,930

October 31, 1989[68]

---

[68] Conclave Report to the 66th Grand Conclave p. 15

Graduates   7,944
Undergraduates   2,617
Life Members   1,868
Total   12,429

Membership as of the 1988-89 fiscal year comprised 671 chapters, which represented an increase of 8 chapters from the previous period. Undergraduate and intermediate chapters made up 318 of the total number of chapters.

. Brother **MELVIN ZENO** requested changes to the Ritual to comport with the Fraternity's new rules stance against hazing. A policy on brands was adopted by the Supreme

Council, essentially outlawing the practice and applying it to Lampados club members as well as to members of the Fraternity. The policy considered all branding as hazing violations.

<<>>

The first Youth Leadership Conference (YLC) was held in Dallas, Texas in 1988 under the leadership of Brother **ARNOLD BUTLER** who was appointed by Grand Basileus Norman as Chairman of the International Social Action Committee.

Omega continued to lend its financial support to the National Urban League. Mr. **JOHN JACOBS**, Executive Director of the Urban League, participated in Grand Conclaves on a regular basis. Brother JESSE L. JACKSON SR., former Second Vice Grand Basileus and president of Operation PUSH and founder of the Rainbow Coalition, attended Grand Conclaves on a regular basis and received support for these organizations as well as for his 1984 and 1988 campaigns for the presidency of the United States.

<<>>

FAMOUS OMEGA MEN WITH ACCOMPLISHMENTS OF SPECIAL NOTE DURING THIS PERIOD ARE AS FOLLOWS:

Rev. Jesse L. Jackson
Born 1941
Initiated in Pi Psi Chapter-1960

Clergyman, Civil Rights Leader, Politician and the Black presidential candidate was Born in Greenville, SC. He received his BA from North Carolina A&T, and Honorary D.D. Degree from the Chicago Theological Seminary. Jesse Jackson was ordained to the ministry of the Baptist Church in 1960. He also was the

Southeastern Field Representative for the Congress of Racial Equality (CORE). Two years later, he was appointed by his mentor, Martin Luther King Jr., to be the National Director of Operation Breadbasket, the economic branch of the Southern Christian Leadership Conference. **Brother Jackson led an unsuccessful bid for President in 1984. He blazed a trail for modern day presidential candidate, Barack Obama.**

Michael Jordan
Born in 1963.
Was initiated in Omega Psi Phi Fraternity Inc. via Omicron Alpha Chapter-1987. He is an extraordinary
Athlete, internationally known NBA super star and Corporate Executive.

Michael Jordan was born in Brooklyn, NY, but grew up in Wilmington, NC. He was cut from his Laney high school varsity team as a sophomore. His junior year he grew 5 inches and set a new school scoring record, and was named as a high school all-American. Jordan attended the University of North Carolina at Chapel Hill, and his last second winning jump shot in 1982 gave the Tarheels the National Championship. Michael Jordan was **named the College Player of the Year in 1983 - 1984. He also won an Olympic gold medal in 1984.** Michael Jordan won six NBA Championships as a professional with the Chicago Bulls, and has been awarded virtually every individual honor the league has. He is the best recognized personality in the world.

Ronald E. McNair
Born 1950 - 1986
Initiated into Omega via Mu Psi Chapter-1969
Famous Physicist, Astronaut

THE OMEGA PSI PHI FRATERNITY INC. 145

Omega man Ronald McNair was born in Lake City, SC. He received his BA in physics from North Carolina A&T in 1971, where he graduated Magna Cum Laude. He went on to earn a doctorate in physics from MIT in 1976. Dr. McNair was named a: Presidential Scholar, a Ford Foundation Fellow, a National Fellowship Fund Fellow, a NATO Fellow and a winner of the Omega Psi Phi Scholar of the Year Award. Dr. McNair was an expert in laser physics. He studied in France and worked as a staff physicist with Hughes Research Laboratories in Malibu, CA, before being selected for the Astronaut Corp. in 1978. He was a fourth degree Black Belt in Karate and taught the sport. He also played saxophone in a swing band.

Vernon Jordan
Born 1935
Initiated into Omega via Zeta Phi Chapter-1956
Attorney, Corporate Executive, Civil Rights Leader

Vernon Jordan was born in Atlanta, GA. He led a boycott of Augusta stores that refused to hire blacks. He headed the Voter Educational Project of the Southern Region. **Chaired the United Negro College Fund in 1970** and also was President and Executive Director of the National Urban League. During his leadership, the National Urban League expanded its focus to include such topics as energy and the environment, while retaining its impetus on social services. He was shot and wounded by a sniper in 1980. He was an advisor to President Bill Clinton and was in charge of his transition team.

L. Douglas Wilder
Born 1931
Initiated in Omega in Zeta Chapter-1950
Politician, Governor of Virginia

Omega man Wilder was born in Richmond, Virginia, was Educated at Virginia Union and Howard Law School. He saw action during the Korean War where he participated in the famous battle of "Pork Chop" Hill. A decorated war hero, Wilder received a Bronze Star for his bravery. He was the first African-American elected to the Virginia State Senate since reconstruction. **In 1985 L Douglas Wilder became the State's first African-American Governor.** In 1991 he became a candidate for President of the United States.

<<>>

Additional pertinent events and/or Omega accomplishments during this period:

Omega man, Rev. **HERMAN S. DREER**, Omega Historian, enters Omega Chapter on **AUGUST 7, 1981**.

<<>>

Omega man, **ROY WILKINS**, civil rights leader, enters Omega Chapter on **August 08, 1981**.

<<>>

9th Grand Basileus **JASPER ALSTON ATKINS** enters Omega Chapter on **June 28, 1982**.

Omega man, Hon. **OSCAR E. ADAMS, JR**. becomes the 1st African American Supreme Court Judge in the state of Alabama on **October 10, 1980**.

<<>>

Jesse Hill Jr.

President and Chairman of the Board of Atlanta Life Insurance Company; first African American to serve as Chairman of the president of the Atlanta Chamber of Commerce

<<>>

Omega man, **THOMAS MANN, JR.** wins primary election and becomes, the 1st African American elected to Iowa State Senate on **November 08, 1982.**

<<>>

Omega man, Capt. **JOE D. HOWZE** of Tau Phi University of Arkansas, Pine Bluff, Arkansas was cited as Outstanding Young man of America **for 1983.** He received this prestigious honor from the organization of Outstanding Young men of America (OYMA). Howze was also selected as the Omega Man of the Year in 1975 by the Omicron Pi chapter. He is also a recipient of the Army Commendation Medal (second bronze oak leaf cluster). Howze was the Commander of HHS, 20th Engr Bde, Ft. Bragg, N.C. from 1979 to 1980.

<<>>

Omega man, **JOSEPH R. DOUGLASS**, named 1st African-AMERICAN Postmaster in Orangeburg. SC, October 22, 1983.

<<>>

Omega man **Dr. RONALD E. MCNAIR** served as "mission specialist" on his 1st Mission in space on **January 03, 1984**.

<<>>

Omega man**, JAMES L. USRY, becomes** 1st African-American mayor of Atlantic City, NJ on **March 13, 1984**.

<<>>

Omega man, **WILLIAM "COUNT" BASIE,** famous bandleader and Composer, enters Omega chapter on **April 26, 1984**.

<<>>

Omega man, **Col. FREDRICK D. GREGORY,** (USAF) serves as "pilot" on his 1st mission in space **April 29, 1985**.

<<>>

Omega man, **HERBERT B. DIXON, JR**. SWORN IN AS AN Associate Judge of the Superior Court of the District of Columbia on **June 07, 1985.**

<<>>

Dedication of the **NU OMICRON**, Omega Psi Phi Fraternity Day Care Center, November 18, 1985.

<<>>

Omega man and U.S. Hall of Fame Astronaut, **Commander CHARLES F. BOLDEN, JR.**

1st mission in space occurred January 12, 1986. Brother Bolden went on to have several other very successful space flights. He has the distinction of being **the first African American to command a U.S. Space Shuttle.** For his extraordinary efforts as one of the pioneers in the space program, **he was inducted into the United States astronaut's hall of fame on May 06, 2006.**

<<>>

And thus ends the chapter about the Grand Basileus with the GOLDEN VOICE.
The great **MOSES C. NORMAN Sr., the 33rd Grand Basileus of Omega Psi Phi Fraternity, Inc.**

<<>>

CHAPTER VIII

THE ROARING NINETIES
1990-1999

OMEGA, LED BY A MAN OF VISION, TAKES A DARING LEAP OF FAITH INTO THE UNKNOWN

The C. TYRONE GILMORE, SR. (the 34TH Grand Basileus of Omega Psi Phi Fraternity Inc.) era begins: (Term 1990-1994)

In Detroit, Michigan at the 66th Grand Conclave, **C. TYRONE GILMORE, SR.** was elected the 34th Grand Basileus of Omega Psi Phi Fraternity Inc.. Upon assuming office, he and his Supreme Council embarked upon a program to enhance the image and productivity of the organization. Grand Basileus Gilmore was initiated in Omega Psi Phi Fraternity via Lambda Psi chapter, at Living Stone College in 1962. Although he would say he was some what small of stature at the time, Grand Basileus Gilmore had an outstanding career in college football at the tailback and quarterback position. The latter is a testament to the strong and extraordinary will and intestinal fortitude of this great Omega man. These attributes would serve him well in his leadership of Omega Psi Phi Fraternity.

Elected officers at the 66th Grand Conclave in Detroit Michigan were:

C. TYRONE GILMORE, Sr. – 34th Grand Basileus

Dorsey C. Miller – First Vice Grand Basileus; Clement M. Osimetha – Second Vice Grand Basileus; Adam E. McKee – Grand Keeper of Records and Seal; Kenneth A. Brown – Grand Keeper of Finance; Lloyd J. Jordan - Grand Counselor; Darryl L. Bell – Undergraduate/Intermediate Rep; Kurmmel W. Knox – Undergraduate/Intermediate Rep; Willie Rockward – Undergraduate. Intermediate Rep; Moses C. Norman - Immediate Past Grand Basileus; James C. Lane – Grand Chaplain; Joseph Strawbridge - Grand Marshal; John S. Epps – Executive Director

DISTRICT REPRESENTATIVES

Sylvester Wilkins - 1st District; George K. McKinney -2nd District; Marion Barnwell-3rd District; Raymond Tillery- 4th District; Mark A. Bishop-5th District; Robert C. Williams-6th District; Henry A. Spears, Sr. 7th District; Douglas D. Williams-8th District; Charles Christopher-9th District; Vernon G. Smith-10th District; Raymond Gibson-12th District; Richard Smith – International Chapters Rep

Under the strong leadership of C. Tyrone Gilmore, Sr., a site for the new Omega World Center and International Headquarters in Decatur, Georgia was identified. Also, the fraternity structure was revamped and the International Chapters were transformed into the 13th District. During his tenure as Grand Basileus, brother Gilmore also initiated the "Omega 2000" project, a program designed to lead the fraternity well into the 21st Century.

An accomplishment that will forever venerate Grand Basileus Gilmore with Omega members is that his administration identified the location of and from there aggressively led the effort for the acquisition of the Omega World Center headquarters in Decatur, Ga. THIS DARING INITIATIVE AND THE BEAUTIFUL site for the current international office (HQ) in Decatur Georgia was identified and courageously set in motion under his leadership.

Grand Basileus Gilmore also credits **MILT JOHNSON, JOE STRAWBRIDEG, JOHN S. EPPS, DORSEY C. MILLER** and

LEON BABRIDGE as instrumental in this re-location project. Several areas such as Memphis, Indianapolis and Charlotte were closely scrutinized before Omega man **HENRY BROWN** invited Grand Basileus Gilmore to visit the Georgia Educational Building in Decatur Georgia that was up for sale at the time. The first trip out to the site by these two Omega men, they will laughingly tell you, was in the AM, oddly enough.

Grand Basileus Gilmore stated it was a massive and extremely beautiful building when he first saw it. It appeared to be drawn directly; it seemed, from his dreams. He said to himself, "this is it!!!" Ah, like an incredibly beautiful woman, calling to you in the sexiest way imaginable; There it was, standing right there in front of his eyes. His wildest dreams for Omega Psi Phi Fraternity as its leader had just presented itself. As he sat with folded arms as if forever just staring at the building, he dared to day dream even further.

The building seemed to tease him. It began to effortlessly float in front of him, just a few inches from his grasp. "Man oh Man" he said. Omega had to have it!!! "That was the way it happened," he said, sitting in the building's parking lot in the wee early morning hours, eyes a glaze with a full moon glistening and hanging just over the building in the background. Ump, Ump, Ump what a rush! This incredible building would be perfect for the organization and it would also establish an extremely positive corporate image for Omega Psi Phi Fraternity that would prove to be head and shoulders above all other fraternities and sororities in America (black or white) even to the writing of this update.

The vision/dream had now been seen. The building had been located. The price and circumstance was right. Almighty God had put everything in place. Now would come the hard part of selling this mammoth vision to the Omega membership. Grand Basileus Gilmore asked that this issue be put on the agenda at the Cleveland 1994 Grand Conclave. He said, "We must do what is right and good for Omega." One positive point that Grand Basileus Gilmore frequently makes and lives by is that to be an effective leader one must be born with the God given gift to lead and convince others. He summoned all he had to ready himself for the battle that would certainly come. He didn't know if the brothers would be ready for such a giant leap of faith into the unknown.

The idea of a move to Georgia from the strategic and popular Washington D.C. location was, as he thought it would be, initially not well received by the Omega membership. Former Grand Basileus, Burnel E. Coulon initially opposed the move but ultimately gave in to this out of the box thinking but potentially risked filled wild idea. The up front money it would take alone, to buy the building, regardless of a great deal or not, could be a definite deal breaker. We were talking millions of dollars. Omega had never put out this type of money before and gone so far out on a financial limb in a venture. I can just see my good friend and mentor former Grand Basileus Coulon now, saying, "Somebody bring me the Pepto Bismol." Grand Basileus Gilmore took a brace and from there drew on his considerable communication skills, innovative financial advise from those in his corner and consensus building skills to achieve success for this forward thinking giant step. It was not an easy battle but the move was approved at the Cleveland Conclave.

Grand Basileus Gilmore asserted that several key safe guarding features would be included to insure the long term success of this venture. He proposed that no future Grand Basileus acting unilaterally could sell the location without the approval of the Conclave in session. He also included several income generating features into this venture so that it could financially sustain itself.

This idea, (the move to Georgia by Grand Basileus Gilmore) has proven itself in hindsight to be a stroke of sheer genius and an enormous success for Omega Psi Phi Fraternity. This move has also been an enormous economic boom for the city of Decatur Georgia and many other surrounding areas.

Grand Basileus Gilmore also became president of The Council of Presidents for the national Pan-Hellenic Council during his tenure. One major accomplishment he initiated while there was that cities that entertained/hosted their conventions would pay for organizations to come to their city. This was an enormous financial success that uplifted many Greek Letter organizations and ultimately helped Omega Psi Phi Fraternity as well. **Once again Omega was found leading the way.**

In 1991, Grand Basileus Gilmore also initiated the approved idea of Grand Basileus rings and lapel pins. A broach was also included at the 1992 Conclave for wives in a ceremony for the ring and broach for the wives. Grand Basileus Gilmore felt the latter innovative initiative went a long way to honor wives for their often unsung support and commitment that they give in supporting their Omega men.

Another powerful concept that is attributed to Grand Basileus Gilmore's administration was asking brothers/membership to adopt a more positive attitude and behavior that would lend itself to having the utmost mutual respect for their leadership as well as all other members so that in turn all membership top to bottom would benefit and receive the utmost respect. He felt that this concept also enabled America during his administration to gain even greater respect for Omega and its membership as a result of this infectious feeling throughout the organization.

Another initiative attributed to Grand Basileus Gilmore was to bring back all former Grand Basilei so that their wealth of experience, knowledge, talents and skills could be more effectively utilized by current and future Omega leadership. This was the first time this had been done. The first assignment given to the former Grand Basilei was to re-do the rituals. The charge for the Grand Basilei was to determine what to leave in, add or take out of the long standing and sacred Omega rituals. Sounds innocent and simple, but believe me it was not. This task could have been very explosive where the membership was concerned due to their loyalty and desire to hold on to the past. Grand Basileus Gilmore knew what he was doing when he picked these greatly admired men for this in the line of fire duty.

As a result of the tremendous goodwill, high regard, love the membership had for these men and their outstanding knowledge, wisdom and in sight, significant positive changes occurred in the ritual that were generally well received. The changes, oddly enough, lifted the spirits of the membership at the Conclave and set a great tone that lead to a productive meeting. One of Grand Basileus Gilmore's platform issues was having a strong 3R's program; meaning Reclamation, Retention and Recruitment. There was no question in his mind that the Omega membership needed to increase. He asked his members to join him in taking this issue seriously and adopting the posture that each active member will reclaim or recruit one member. This effort he firmly communicated to the members, would add to the strength and longevity of our beloved fraternity.

As previously mentioned, Grand Basileus Gilmore was also the initiator of Omega 2000. It was his blueprint for success in the 21st century for Omega Psi Phi Fraternity Inc. It was a bold plan that involved three goal areas. 1. A Face Lift for the International Headquarter. 2. Restructuring of the Fraternity's International Committees. 3. A broader base of membership involvement.

<<>>

SIGNIFICANT EVENTS DURING THIS PERIOD:

Omega man, **L. DOUGLAS WILDER** becomes the first African American to be elected Governor of a major U.S. City on January 13, 1990. He became the sixty six governor of Virginia. Additionally, in 1969 he was elected as the first African American state senator in Virginia since Reconstruction.

<<>>

Omega man, **THURBERT E. BAKER**, was appointed First Black Attorney General for the State of Georgia. He was sworn in on June 01, 1997. He is an active member of Kappa Alpha Alpha chapter.

<<>>

Omega Announce Expulsions, Suspensions: Respond to alleged hazing Incidents in its Summer/Fall 1997 Oracle. Grand Basileus Miller re-affirms the fact that Omega Psi Phi fraternity, Inc. is serious about stopping hazing.

<<>>

In June 1990 the **COLONEL CHARLES YOUNG** Home Restoration Project in Xenia, Ohio was completed. It was dedicated as a National Historic Landmark.

<<>>

In 1990, **the title Executive Secretary** of Omega Psi Phi fraternity was changed to Executive Director.

<<>>

In April 1991, **the new Membership Intake Program** was implemented.

<<>>

The 1992 Grand Conclave in Atlanta Georgia-Elected Supreme Council Officers:

C. TYRONE GILMORE – Grand Basileus;
Dorsey C. Miller-First Vice Grand Basileus; James Edmonds, III: Adam E. McKee Grand Keeper of Records and Seal; Warren G. Lee –Grand Keeper of Finance; Lloyd J. Jordan – Grand Counselor; Clement M. Osimetha – Undergraduate/Intermediate Rep; Cedric A. Portis – Undergraduate/Intermediate Rep; Willie Rockward – Undergraduate/Intermediate Rep; James C. Lane – Grand Chaplain; Frank C. Williams – Grand Marshal

The 67th Grand Conclave in Atlanta Ga. held from July 31st thru August 6th 1992, was described by men and women within and outside the Fraternity at the time as the "greatest" convention the organization had ever held. The "Fun City" lived up to its advance billing as also a friendly city. Brother **ANDREW RAY** was brought in by Grand Basileus Gilmore to lift the spirits of the membership. He knew the rituals of Omega by heart, which is truly a feat in itself. He opened the meeting and from there went on to astound the brothers with his great performance and with his incredible knowledge of the voluminous rituals **by reciting everything purely by heart.** This lifted the brothers' spirit tremendously. While a great time was had by all, a lot of work got accomplished as well. Below are just a few of the financial changes from this meeting.

1. Dues were raised for graduates and undergraduates, effective November 1, 1992.
2. The cost to become a life member was raised, effective November 1, 1992.
3. The annual cost to be an International member (Member at large) was set at $200.00
4. Dues for any fiscal year must be received at the International Headquarters by December 31, or they must be accompanied by a late fee of $5.oo per man.

Initiatives that sprung from the Atlanta Conclave were developed by the Comprehensive Review Committee composed of former Grand Basilei. This Committee was chaired by Moses Norman for the revision of the Ritual. Brother Norman then relinquished the chair to Herbert Tucker, the senior Grand Basileus for the self discovery meeting. He encouraged each past Grand Basileus to share their views for improving the state of Omega. They completed their task of revising the fraternity's Rituals. Upon completion of the latter task, the committee explored problems facing the fraternity in the area of growth and development with possible solutions from an apolitical viewpoint. A running agenda was structured including the following items for solutions.[69] The ideas that came out of these sessions were far reaching. They were submitted to Grand Basileus Gilmore and to the Supreme Council for review and implementation consideration. Below are the improvement ideas for the everyday operations for Omega Psi Phi Fraternity, Inc.

A. Developing new paradigms for Omega's future.

B. Revising the Constitution in keeping with Conclave changes.

C. Securing full insurance for all officers of the Fraternity.

---

[69] Winter/Spring Oracle 1994 Article by Grand Basileus Burnel E. Coulon

D. Redistricting of districts with parity to determine if such a move would aid in stability.

E. Reclamation under the direction of the National Office with local follow-up and a national goal for growth and financial incentives.

F. To explore new ways of doing what we do and devising a plan to increase efficiency and effectiveness for the operation.

This committee also reviewed in broad terms the future of Omega. It explored much of the reality of the fraternity's everyday operation, both administratively and financially as shown below.

1. A mandatory audit with constitution intervention by Supreme Council if an administration fails to have an audit;
2. Immediate development to aggressively pursue the International Membership;
3. Conclave revitalization with emphasis on development and enhancement for Brothers and families;
4. Increasing Oracles feature articles on life skills;
5. Program promotion in the Bulletin as a major communication tool to each Brother on a monthly or quarterly basis with a "How To" format;
6. A Director of Undergraduate Activities to spearhead their leadership.
7. A program of character values and ethics as part of the Undergraduate development
8. Funding for a Director of Development to expand Omega's scope and influence through fundraising, internally and externally, and the rethinking of the role of the Executive Director.

<<>>

RICHARD "Dick" SMITH named National Assistant
Executive Director at the 67th Grand Conclaves in Atlanta Ga. 1992.

<><>

July 1993, Founding Father ERNEST E. JUST was inducted into the Black South Carolina Hall of Fame.

Omega Man, Freeman, Bosley Jr. becomes the First Black Mayor of St. Louis, July 1993

<<>>

A quote from the Executive Director of Omega Psi Phi Fraternity, Inc. **JOHN S. EPPS**.

"The shining light of Omega serves as a beacon of hope and direction at the crossroads of determination. This is the gift of our Founders and the legacy of those elders upon whose shoulders Omega men now stand."

<<>>

CHAPTER IX

1990-1999 CONTINUATION
Omega Psi Phi Fraternity's Move From Washington D.C. to Georgia & The Growing Divide Between Grad & Under Grad Men

The DORSEY C. MILLER Jr. (the 35TH Grand Basileus of Omega Psi Phi Fraternity) era begins: (TERM 1994-1998)

Dorsey C. Miller, Jr. was elected the 35th Grand Basileus at the Cleveland Grand Conclave in 1994. He was initiated into Omega Psi Phi Fraternity at Psi Chapter at Morehouse College in 1962. Grand Basileus Miller's administration was responsible for **closing the sale in regard to the acquisition of the Omega World Center** and International Headquarters at 3951 Snapfinger Parkway, Decatur, Georgia 30035, **and the disposition of the property located at 2714 Georgia Avenue, N. W., Washington, D.C.** The Georgia Avenue location in Washington had served as the headquarters of the fraternity for thirty-one years.

Among Grand Basileus Miller's many accomplishments was the fact that his administration fought an up hill battle to lobby for and ultimately achieved approval to move the Omega headquarters from Washington DC to where it currently resides. As previously stated, this idea to move from Washington D.C. to Georgia and its approval and ultimate implementation by Grand Basileus Miller was not a popular decision among the Omega Psi Phi membership initially. However, Grand Basileus Miller through his wisdom, extraordinary communications skills, tenacity and the outstanding support, trust and faith he enjoyed and skillfully garnered from the organization's membership, was able to accomplish this move and ultimately prove the lingering nay Sayers wrong. While the latter accomplishment is now well celebrated, popular and has been proven a blessing for Omega, Grand Basileus Miller's unbelievable efforts behind the scenes to achieve it are little known. He personally had to travel to many chapters across the nation and engage in head to head battles with members to get them to see the wisdom in approving not only the move to Georgia from Washington DC, but also the $200.00 assessment fee that had brothers enraged, up in arms and loaded for bear.

Brother Miller shared with me in his interview that there were some very scary moments in his visits to the local chapters, most especially where convincing the brothers to approve the $200.00 assessment was concerned. Brothers were angry, openly opposed to the assessment and were eager to let him know it at every stop. Man, oh man oh man what a dilemma!!! Many members were hard core and just simply were refusing to pay it. In some cases/local chapters, Brother Grand (who is some what slight in stature) was facing what amounted to angry mobs all by his self, in some cases. God was with him though! He did not blink or stutter when making his case. He stood his ground! In the end, the Almighty once again calmed the angry waters and yes even parted the mighty red sea as he had for his faithful servant Moses to achieve this much needed decision for the organization. Probably took some years off his life, but Brother Miller faced the angry brothers and explained the issue from A to Z, eye ball to eyeball in a cool, calm and intelligent manner. He got it done.

The new Omega headquarters was purchased for $2.5 million dollars. The 1994 Grand Conclave approved a mandatory special assessment for all members, payable within two fiscal years.

The Supreme Council Members elected at the Cleveland Grand Conclave were:

DORSEY C. MILLER JR. – Grand Basileus
Adam Mckee, Jr. D.V.M – First Vice-Grand Basileus Mark E. Jackson – Second Vice-Grand Basileus; Robert W. Fairchild – Grand Keeper of Records and Seal; Warren G. Lee – Grand Keeper Finance; Calvin L. Brown – Grand Counselor; Terrance L. Hamilton – Undergraduate/Intermediate Rep; Darryl G. Moore –Undergraduate/Intermediate Rep; Mark E. Stevens – Undergraduate/Intermediate Rep; C. Tyrone Gilmore. Sr. – Immediate past Grand Basileus; Ferrel J. Duncombe – Grand Chaplain; Tony Collins – Grand Marshal

DISTRICT REPRESENTATIVES

Rodney J. Russel – First District Representative;
Calvin C. Zellars – Second District Representative
Gary Clark – Third District Representative
Henry W. Glaspie Jr. – Fourth District Representative
Ralph E. Johnson – Fifth District Representative
John H. Scott – Sixth District Representative
George Grace – Seventh District Representative
Delvert T. Neal – Eighth District Representative
Virgil Robinson - Ninth District Representative
Ronald J. Hughes – Tenth District Representative
Ricky L. Lewis – Twelfth District Representative
Peter L. Mitchell – International Chapter Representative

Grand Basileus Miller convened a special Strategic Planning Meeting, September 8-10, 1994 in Fort Lauderdale Florida, to develop an action plan to be a road map to ensure that "Omega 2000" would be a success. The primary focus of the meeting was undergraduate leadership, public relations, membership benefits, corporate involvement, economic development, leadership training and last but certainly not least, the acquisition of the new World Headquarters. A very ambitious agenda was planned for the meeting.

Another very serious area of concern for Grand Basileus Miller was the relationship between undergrads and graduate brothers. Many undergrads were not trusting or respectful of graduate brothers because they felt graduate brothers did not look upon them as equal brothers in Omega due to their youth. Graduate brothers felt that many undergrads were not responsible and serious minded when it came to living up to the high standards established by the Founders.

For years, rumors had surfaced regarding a growing rift between graduate brothers and undergrads that had somehow turned to an inappropriate and illegal practice called WRECKING. This was where undergraduate brothers, feeling that some grad brothers were not up to true Omega standard because they had been initiated in graduate chapters, would challenge these Omega men. This practice began in the northeast and slowly drifted across America. Younger brothers would challenge graduate brothers with off the cuff charges (questions about Omega's history and/or its escutcheon; some made up and some legitimate) and if the brother didn't answer to their liking, he could be beaten or threatened out of his frat shirt etc. or threatened with any number of other physical and or verbal intimidations for not knowing Omega material.

This cancer grew into other practices where brothers (Grad or under grad) often verbally and/or physically challenged newer brothers and even each others 'manhood by violently wrestling with each other to prove who was the strongest. This inappropriate behavior was not brotherly and was a direct contradiction to our beloved Founders intentions.

In the 1997 Summer/Fall Oracle issue Grand Basileus Miller stated to the Omega membership that, "You are aware, no doubt, of the existence of a group of members of Omega Psi Phi who seek to undermine the Four Cardinal Principles upon which we were founded. This group comprised mostly, but not entirely, of undergraduates, are in the process of destroying Omega Psi Phi as we know it. We have worked too hard, fought too long and struggled too much to allow those who do not truly love Omega to destroy our beloved Fraternity. I solicit your support and your prayers in helping to wipe out this cancer." An all out official effort was initiated to stop this illegal and officially publicly denounced practice dead in its tracks. The practice and all similar practices and/or manifestations were officially deemed in clear violation of the organization's Code of Conduct.

In commenting to the membership in the Oracle, Grand Basileus Miller said, "Let us never forget that ours is an organization of **men** from every walk of life – **men** who have accomplished and **men** who are in the process of accomplishing. So let us come together and resolve our differences. **We must always remember that Omega is much bigger than any brother, chapter or district and we have an obligation to remain true to our oath."**

Grand Basileus Miller went on to say, "President Lincoln was right, a house divided against itself cannot stand. If Omega is to survive the decade of the nineties and beyond we must put aside our petty differences. Omega is a union of men, not a federation of men. We are all Omega Men, Graduate brothers, Undergraduate brothers, and life members-WE ARE ONE!!! NORTH, SOUTH, EAST AND WEST, WE ARE ONE!!!"

These profound words were echoed throughout Omega Psi Phi Fraternity. They helped to bring the Omega family closer together. To further emphasize his concern over the rapid divide that was forming between grads and under grads, Grand Basileus Miller also spoke an ancient Chinese phrase to his membership and followed it with a rousing message that rang true and thundered like Abraham Lincoln's famous Gettysburg Address to America. **Four score and seven years ago our fathers brought forth on this continent, a new nation, conceived in Liberty, and dedicated to the proposition that all men are created equal. Now we are engaged in a great civil war, testing whether that nation or any nation so conceived and so dedicated, can long endure......** [70]

Abraham Lincoln, of course, was DESPERATELY trying to save and heal a nation ravaged by civil war. Grand Basileus Miller, as far back as his office as Vice Grand Basileus was fighting with all he had to keep Omega from an ever widening divide between young and old. His speech was sobering and served as a solid point of argument to unite and energize the organization for not only the many great challenges that lie before it but for the sanctity of brotherhood. Brother against brother would not rule the day in his administration as it did in America's civil war. Grand Basileus" Miller's ringing, inspiring additional words are as follows:[71]

"A journey of a thousand miles must begin with one step." It is my hope, indeed, it is my fervent prayer, that when

---

[70] Abraham Lincoln online
[71] The Summer/Fall ORACLE/The Grand Basilues Speak/Dorsey C. Miller

Mother History dips her pen in the river of time, she will be able to write that during the 1994-1996 Conclave year, the men of Omega Psi Phi Fraternity Inc. became concerned about the state of their fraternity, America, and the world and decided that they would take the first step. Men may one day write that during this period in Omega's history we tried and failed – but we must ensure that they will never be able to write that we failed to try. With God's help and yours we will be a viable force in the 21st Century and beyond."

Grand Basileus Miller's effort, as time would tell, would prove successful in that this circumstance's growth was slowed significantly. His diligent efforts in confronting this gigantic problem was sobering for Omega's membership and helped the organization to unify and move rapidly forward. Grand Basileus Miller also expressed concern over the vast number of un-financial members in the organization. He vowed that Reclamation, Retention as well as Recruitment would be major priorities of his administration. H directed several initiatives to relieve this internal concern.

The main accomplishments of Grand Basileus Miller's first term were the dedication of the new Omega World Center. Other pertinent projects/accomplishments were 1. Project for the Perpetuation of the Black Male, which would provide crucial educational, cultural and life skills experiences for 500 young black males. 2. The Senior Citizen Project which is a program for Omega chapters to adopt a senior citizen nursing home in the community and develop nurturing programs and activities for home residents. 3. The Habitat for Humanity Project which is a long standing national effort to build and renovate affordable housing for the poor. 4. The South Africa Project which was Omega's effort to provide educational, medical and health-related assistance to South Africa.

The Theme for the 1996 Conclave in Los Angeles was "On to California-Battlefield for Affirmative Action." The publicly expressed intent by Grand Basileus Miller and his administration was that this Conclave would be a forum for discussion, debate and exchange of ideas on the most important public policy issues of the day. [72] [73]

---

[72] Oracle Spring 1996/The Grand Basileus Speaks/Dorsey C. Miller
[73] From the mighty 9th .org website/Patrick B. Smith

A special dedication ceremony was planned to herald the official grand opening of the Omega Psi Phi Fraternity Inc. World Center. The new Headquarters is located at 3951 Snapfinger Parkway in Decatur, Georgia. It sits on six acres. It is located in suburban Dekalb Count, approximately 10 miles east of Downtown Atlanta. It has 415 parking spaces, compared to the 7 designated spaces at the old Washington Location.

In addition to the dedication of the New World Center, other activities were planned such as the unveiling of the Ernest E. Just Stamp, the Special Intake Program, the Prayer Breakfast, the Quettes Luncheon and the Omega Gala. Oh what a great day for Omega Psi Phi fraternity Inc. Brother Miller's administration did a fantastic job in this effort. On December 30, 1995 Omega Psi Phi fraternity stood head and shoulders above all other fraternities and sororities (black or white) with its grand opening of the new World Headquarters Building. Omega men from all across America came in for this event. Brothers wishing to have their names inscribed on the Founders' Wall paid $1000.00 for this lasting honor. The latter effort in itself was a significant financial boom for Omega.

One major income producing feature that was initiated by Grand Basileus Miller was from the lease of remote property on the acreage for a cell phone tower. Cell phones had just come on the scene and had become very popular. Grand Basileus Miller and Gilmore came up with an ingenious idea to charge for a cell phone tower to be placed on the property. A Lease agreement was arranged between Omega Psi Phi fraternity and Bell South. Grand Basileus Miller and Executive Director John Epps successfully negotiated the contract with them. This out of the box thinking idea brought in a fair amount of income for the organization. It was managed through the Friendship Foundation (another extraordinarily innovative idea by Brother Miller's administration) that was formed in 1997.

Grand Basileus Miller gave a special public recognition to the men who, along with his own hard work, were the driving force in making this dream come true. He cited **JIM ELAM, MILTON JOHNSON, JOHN EPPS, C. TYRONE GILMORE, ROBERT FAIRCHILD, WARREN LEE, CALVIN BROWN, TONY GRANT, KERMIT WARDELL, LEON BABRIDGE, GEORGE GRACE, JOE STRAWBRIDGE, CLARENCE**

LAWRENCE, AL ROSIER, ADAM MCKEE, WALTER WRENN, THOMAS MONTGOMERY and **ANDREW GRIFFINS**. Hat's off to these Omega men. We should forever give them our gratitude for their outstanding work on this monumental project.

Thanks to the vision and foresight of former Grand Basilei C. Tyrone Gilmore, Moses C. Norman, Grand Basileus Dorsey Miller, past and present Supreme Councils, the men shown above and the approving Conclave membership, Omega, with the opening of its New World Center, is ready to move into the 21St century. [74]

The new Omega headquarters dwarfed the old Washington D. C. Location. Although the Washington location served Omega well and was a credit to Omega in its day and time, it simply was no comparison to the new Decatur, Ga. building. It (the old Washington D.C. location) had 6907 square feet and the new World center had a mammoth 73,340 sq. ft.

The plan was for Omega to occupy the first two floors of approximately 36,000 feet. This would leave three complete floors to bring in revenue from rental to other businesses. There is an attached 7,536 sq. ft auditorium that will also be used to generate income from banquets, receptions and meetings by the community.

The building was free and clear of liens as verified by a due diligence study conducted by the fraternity. The property, at the time of purchase, was appraised at $2.9 million dollars for tax purposes. The market value at the time of purchase was approximately 3.5 million dollars, giving Omega substantial equity in the property when the deal was consummated.

Another accomplishment of the Miller administration was the development of **a strategic plan** to pay off the loan for the Omega World Center by November 30, 1995, while at the same time saving the fraternity over three million dollars in interest etc.

Grand Basileus Miller is also credited with implementing the first phase of Omega's African Project. A team headed by then 1st Vice Grand Basileus, **ADAM E. MCKEE**.

---

[74] The new World Center management team from the Spring 1995 Oracle

First Vice Grand Basileus, Adam E. McKee

This dream team also consisted of Brothers **WALTER JOHNSON, CHARLES CHRISTOPHER** and **WALTER J. WRENN**. This was a mission of hope. Omega Psi Phi Fraternity knew that it had to reach out to the world and be about a mission far greater than just it itself. **Brother McKee was indeed the right man for this job**. He was known for his extraordinary compassion for others, hard work and his strong desire to set the world ablaze with the brilliantly burning light of Omega. He and his team were sent to South Africa in March 1995 to make arrangements for a visit by a group of Omega physicians and other health providers in March 1996.

The group would also meet with internationally known Bishop Tutu and other top African officials to discuss the construction of an Omega Village and a health clinic. Their efforts were revolutionary and fruitful. Omega Psi Phi fraternity's name was now on the lips of many kids and adults in Africa. It would come to be a beacon and symbol of hope for a desperately struggling people far from the founding location of Omega. There is no doubt that the Founders of Omega Psi Phi Fraternity would be greatly pleased by the work of its sons, led by an Omega hero, Adam McKee.

<<>>

The 1996 Grand Conclave was at Los Angeles California;
The elected Supreme Council members were:

DORSEY C. MILLER JR. – Grand Basileus

Adam McKee-First Vice Grand Basileus; Lewis Anderson-Second Vice Grand Basileus; Robert W. Fairchild –Grand Keeper of Records and Seal; Warren Lee-Grand Keeper of Finance;
Calvin L. Brown-Grand Counselor; Tamer Ahmed Mokhtar-Undergraduate/Intermediate Rep; Zeldrix Jason Palmer-Undergraduate/Intermediate Rep; C. Tyrone Gilmore, Sr.-Immediate past Grand Basileus; Ferrell J. Duncombe-Grand Chaplain; Ronald J. Butler-Grand Marshal

DISTRICT REPRESENTATIVE

1st District – Rodney J. Russel; 2nd District – Michael Freeman; 3rd District – James A. Peterson; 4th District – Christopher M. Cooper; 5th – District – Ronald Griffin; 6th District – Charles Holmes; 7th District – William C. Brassfield; 8th District – Robert L. Robinson; 9th District – Virgil Robinson; 10th District – Larry B. Boyd; 12th District – Ricky L. Lewis; International Chapter Rep – Peter L. Mitchell;

Grand Basileus Miller sought to awaken the unified consciousness of Omega and make it a great political uplifting force in America.

Grand Basileus Miller stated that Omega was on the move!

THE MIGHTY PI CHAPTER ON THE MOVE FOR OMEGA DEAR!

So let us move forward with great enthusiasm he said, for "enthusiasm is more important than any other commodity. It will find solutions when none are apparent, and it will achieve success when none is thought possible." These words were truly a rallying cry for the men of Omega, given their extraordinary accomplishment during this period.

To perpetuate this premise further Grand Basileus Miller initiated Economic Summits be held in Washington D.C. for Omega Psi Phi Fraternity. These meetings were held during the same time that The Congressional Caucus held their meetings. The combination of this powerful Caucus where the movers and shakers in America were brought into play with Omega Psi Phi Fraternity proved to be highly successful in enabling Omega to accomplish its strategic objective in raising the economic consciousness and actual involvement of its membership. Grand Basileus Miller's words did not fall on deaf ears. Omega Psi Phi Fraternity members increased their political involvement and as a result set the stage for Omega becoming a strong force to be reckoned with by all national and local political parties.

To clearly demonstrate his intentions for Omega, Grand Basileus Miller in the 1997 Summer/Fall Oracle urged all Chapters to participate in Omega's Strategic Plan by doing the following:

- Adopt a senior citizen home
- Establish and implement programs for the perpetuation of the black male.
- Participate in the Habitat for Humanity project.
- Initiate a strong reclamation, retention and recruitment program
- Develop and implement other programs that will help uplift our people.

These efforts would help the Omega membership to focus itself for the long hard journey before it.

Accomplishments by Grand Basileus Miller during his tenure as Omega's leader were truly incredible. His hard work, dedication and extraordinary out of the box thinking and love for Omega led to many first for the organization. Just to name a few:

The first Economic Summit was held in 1997 in Miami Florida under Grand Basileus Miller's leadership.

The first Undergraduate Summit was held in January 1998 in Atlanta Georgia.

During Grand Basileus Miller's administration, a **one year moratorium on pledging was imposed in 1997** to allow Omega to better assess allegations, train and correct problems that surfaced in the pledging program. After the moratorium period expired, a requirement for undergraduate chapters to participate in future pledging programs stipulated that they attend and participate in training etc. at the newly established Undergraduate Summit

Two Foundations were created under Grand Basileus Miller's strong, cerebral leadership,

- The Omega Development Corporation was formed in 1996. It dealt with social issues and charities to get funding scholarships, and various other social action out reach projects. The perpetuation of the Black Male and African Project were products from this great idea.

The Omega Friendship Foundation was also formed **in 1997** under Grand Basileus Miller's administration. **It is** an independent corporation charged with the

Responsibility of managing The Omega World Center, (the tenant leased spaces, the building and property day to day operations, the physical plant and equipment and the staff. The Omega World Center is located at 3951 Snapfinger Parkway, in Decatur Georgia. It is the home of the Omega Psi Phi Fraternity International Headquarters. The Supreme Council of the fraternity appoints the Board of Directors. The board of Directors serves an overlapping term of 3 or 4 years. The seven member board elects its own officers. [75]

The Omega Friendship Foundation also manages other properties such as the Colonel Young estate and the Bell South cell tower lease properties. This organization is a brain child of Grand Basileus Miller and his fine administration.

<<>>

The beautiful James A. Elam Auditorium is contained within the Omega World Center: Omega man **JAMES A. ELAM,** successful business man and CEO and Founder of Elam Testing Company, was a generous contributor that was key in enabling Omega Psi Phi Fraternity to purchase the building. He has also used his keen business skills and helped Omega conduct several other highly successful financial ventures. He is a graduate of Central State University and a proud member of the fourth District.

The James A. Elam Auditorium in the Omega World Center

ADDITIONAL SIGNIFICANT EVENTS DURING THIS PERIOD:

GRAND BASILEUS MILLER & JOHN EPPS, Executive Director of Omega Psi Phi Fraternity at the time successfully negotiate contract for the sale of cell phones for Omega. This innovative deal reaped significant income for Omega and was an enormous success.

---

[75] Omega Friendship Foundation reference-The Oracle, Winter 2002

Omega man, **WILLIAM "BILL" CAMPBELL** becomes Mayor of Atlanta Georgia a major American City. He successfully served as Atlanta Mayor from 1994 to 2002.

<<>>

Omega man, **WILLIAM E. "KIP" WARD**, named the 82ND Airborne Division assistant Commander for Support in **1997**.

<<>>

Omega man, Brigadier General **CHARLES F. BOLDEN Jr.**, Assistant Wing Commander, 3rd Marine Aircraft Wing was honored and awarded the prestigious Yuri A. Gregarin Medal from the National Aeronautic Association on **April 28, 1997.**

<<>>

Omega man, astronaut **RONALD E. MCNAIR**, who was tragically killed in the NASA Challenger disaster, was inducted into South Carolina Hall of Fame on **February 03, 1997**.

<<>>

Omega man, MARCUS W. SHUTE receives the 1999 National Society of Black Engineers' Golden Touch Award for Engineering Excellence on **March 26, 1999**. He was initiated into the fraternity through Iota Chi, in 1986. He became a life member in 1988.

<<>>

Omega men, DORSEY C. MILLER III and ERIN TUCKER were inducted into the University of Florida Hall Of Fame on **December 03, 1998**. Both men were also selected for Who's Who among Students in American College and Universities

<<>>

Omega man, **JAMES W. NAPPER, JR.** was inducted into Johnson C. Smith University Sports Hall of Fame in 1998.

CHAPTER X
(OMEGA FACES DESTRUCTION FROM LEGAL BATTLES)

The 36TH Grand Basileus of Omega Psi Phi Fraternity, Inc. (LLOYD J. JORDAN, ESQ) era begins: (TERM 1998-2002)

Lloyd J. Jordan, Esq. became the 36th Grand Basileus of Omega Psi Phi Fraternity in 1998 at the 70th Grand Conclave in New Orleans, Louisiana. He was the youngest Omega to be elected to the head of the Fraternity in modern times. He was initiated at Omicron Sigma Chapter in 1975 in St. Louis Missouri. His administration had an enormous impact on the Fraternity. During his tenure, Grand Basileus Jordan reformed the way the Fraternity conducted its operations leading to unprecedented efficiencies and service to the brotherhood.

Equally as important, Grand Basileus Jordan and his administration skillfully guided Omega Psi Phi Fraternity with a study and courageous hand through some very difficult legal battles as a result of some unfortunate hazing allegations his administration inherited. With the financial saving generated from the operational changes He was able to successfully combated litigation resulting from illegal hazing activities, thus keeping the fraternity's infrastructure intact. Grand Basileus Jordan stated, "there were many, many sleepless nights and extremely agonizing and nauseating moments he and his administration went through to save Omega and protect it from the very serious law suits and judgments that threatened it." **The wolf was definitely at the door, huffing and puffing like crazy and at the point of almost kicking it in when he took over.** Grand Basileus Jordan vowed to his membership that there was **no way, (NO WAY!!) that he would let Omega die or down while he was its leader.** Grand Basileus Jordan, although extremely battered and bruised in the fight, kept his promise to Omega and his brothers.

Supreme Council Officers elected in the 70th Grand Conclave:

LLOYD J. JORDAN, ESQ. – Grand Basileus, John H. Scott – 1st Vice Grand Basileus Aaron E. Price - 2nd Vice Grand Basileus George H. Grace – Grand Keeper of Records and Seal Alcindeor R. Rosier – Grand Keeper of Finance; Melvin C. Zeno – Grand Chaplain; R. Steve Bowden Esq. – Grand Counselor Dorsey C. Miller, Ed.D – Immediate Past Grand Basileus Burnel E. Coulon – Grand Marshal; Christopher E. Benjamin - Undergraduate/Immediate Rep; Benjamin G. Dirden - Undergraduate/Immediate Rep Lenord A. Robinson – Undergraduate/Immediate Rep

DISTRICT REPRESENTATIVES

Rodney J. Russell – 1st District; Terrel D. Parris – 2nd District; Rayfield L. Harris – 3rd District; Albert L. Jordan – 4th District; Henry F. Jackson, Jr. – 5th District; Melvin Pinn – 6th District; S.M. "Chucky" Wilson – 7th District; Melvin L. Jenkins – 8th District; Wendel, V. Smith – 9th District; Charles Bruce – 10th District; Keith W. Neal – 12th District; Edouard T. Delagarde – 13th District

Grand Basileus Jordan in an interview that this author held with him stated that his election as Grand Basileus of Omega was primarily on the strength of objective, independent thinking Omega men who supported him. He also prides himself on the fact that to get elected he made no deals or built no secret coalitions. Prior to his election, he felt that the latter methods were overtly used and was a common political practice in Omega.

He is grateful that he was seen as a brothers' brother during his election campaign, and as a result was rewarded by the vast membership by putting him into office. In hindsight Grand Basileus Jordan also stated, **"I am now aware of God's hand working behind the scene to put me in office."** "God knew exactly what he was doing by making certain that Lloyd Jordan, an experienced, battle hardened lawyer and a person who could intimately understand the potentially lethal legal issues of the day, was elected Omega's leader during the coming legal storms that threatened its very existence during his tenure."

Lloyd Jordan's administration was successful in creating a financial and operational plan that reduced the cost of operating the Fraternity by 43%. At the same time, Brothers received unprecedented improve service from the International Headquarters. For example brothers received their financial cards within seven days and returned inquiries within 24-hours. Under Brother Jordan, the Fraternity began the use of telephone and internet conferencing. Once a month Grand Basileus Jordan held "Talk to the Grand Basileus" telephone conferences where the entire Fraternity had the opportunity to dial in and ask the Grand Basileus questions or they could simply just talk to the Grand Basileus. His administration created a $900,000 cash surplus in the Fraternity Treasurer.

This cash surplus helped Grand Basileus Jordan to combat litigation from illegal hazing activities. **Omega as a direct result of the potential devastating affects, if successful from the weighty legal judgments, was clearly facing its end**. If not for the dynamic thinking and legal mind of the then Grand Basileus, along with his legal counsel and administration, Omega could have been put in receivership or be forced into bankruptcy. This was not a generally known fact by the membership. The over whelming majority of Omega's membership slept easy in their beds at night not knowing just how close the organization had come to its utter destruction. Grand Basileus Jordan and his administration are unsung heroes/saviors of Omega for their successes during this period.

In the name of prudence, the names and specifics associated with the law suits will not be named in this book. The statues of limitations, as of the writing of this book, have not quite run out on several of the cases and we would not want their case issue examples etc. to be used in future suits. Suffice it to say, the financial stakes were high enough that any one of several successful suits would have been enough to destroy Omega Psi Phi Fraternity financially. With God's grace and mercy, the organization dodged these big litigation bullets via some outright knock down, drag them out victories and settlements that were very favorable for the organization.

Grand Basileus Jordan's administration was also very instrumental in getting the Omega membership more involved in local and national politics. He often stated to the membership that, "Omega Psi Phi Fraternity is the perfect organization to lead Black People because of its proven strong history in leading Black men. Lloyd Jordan challenged Omega and said that, "The year 2000 will test our leadership and our ability to serve as leaders of our community." He further stated, "Now is the time to accept that we must step into the void of Black leadership, **NOT JUST FOR OMEGA's sake, BUT ALSO, FOR ALL African-Americans."** This phrase resonated strongly with the Omega membership.

During this administration Omega Psi Phi Fraternity joined with the NAACP in a nationally stated goal to register ONE MILLION VOTERS. Kweisi Mfume, the NAACP president and CEO at the time publicly commended Omega Psi Phi Fraternity and Grand Basileus Jordan in particular for this noble under taking. He stated, " I truly admire your efforts to encourage Omega Men to play dynamic roles in the activities of the NAACP. Your organization has definitely exemplified a solid plan of action to obtain minority participation in addressing NAACP issues."

On December 5th, 1999, the Grand Basileus formalized the appointment of Brother **HENRY A. SPEARS**, along with Brothers **MARION BARNWELL, JAMES GALLMAN, JOHN HATCHER AND WILLIAM VICK** to serve on this crucially important committee. Brother **Henry A. Spears, the chairman of the Omega International NAACP committee aggressively took on the million voter goal.** He stated to the members of Omega Psi Phi Fraternity, "This should be an all-out, full-court press by our organization. It is our hope to execute a plan of action in partnership with the NAACP at the local, state, district and national levels." **Brother Spears performed nobly in galvanizing the intelligence and chapter level abilities of Omega to bring this organization closer with the NAACP.**

The Omega International NAACP committee in its mission statement had a high priority on improving social action collaboration with the NAACP with special emphasis on the survival of Black males and political empowerment, a charge publicly set forth by Grand Basileus Lloyd J. Jordan.

Grand Basileus Jordan cautioned in one of his many public addresses to the membership that "Too many times, no matter how much a candidate might have done in the past that was right, we (meaning Black people) turn our backs on them over one thing that they might have done that we disagree with. In doing this, many times we find ourselves in a worse position than what we were before. He often cited a recollection he had experienced in an election in Missouri where Black people decided to turn their backs on a candidate for senate because he took one position out of a dozen contrary to the wants of some Black people. The NAACP, church groups and other Blacks in the community decided to support the other senatorial candidate who had never done anything positive for the Black community in Missouri. This bad candidate nevertheless won the election with the Black community's support. He proved to be one of the most detrimental senators for Blacks in the U.S. Senate, although Blacks were the ones that helped put him in office. They allowed that one issue to steer them from the candidate who best represented their interests. Grand Basileus Jordan used this circumstance to employ the Omega membership to think carefully in electing our officials.

The 36TH Grand Basileus of Omega Psi Phi Fraternity, Inc. - LLOYD J. JORDAN, ESQ era continues: (TERM 1998-2002)
The 71st ^{Grand} Conclave was held in INDIANAPOLIS, 2000,
The elected Supreme Council members were;

LLOYD J. JORDAN Esq. – Grand Basileus
John H. Scott – First Vice Grand Basileus; Aaron Price – Second Vice Grand Basileus – George Grace – Grand Keeper of Records and Seal; Alcindor Rosier – Grand Keeper of Finance; R Steve Bowden – Grand Counselor; Christopher E. Benjamin – Undergraduate/Intermediate Rep; Benjamin G. Dirden – Undergraduate/Intermediate; Leonard A. Robinson – Undergraduate/Intermediate; Dorsey C. Miller – Immediate past Grand Basileus; Melvin Zeno – Grand Chaplain; Burnel E.

Coulon- Grand Marshal; S. Earl Wilson – Executive Director; Richard "Dick" Smith – Assistant Executive Director;

DISTRICT REPRESENTATIVES

James Owens – 1st District; Lee A. Bernard Jr. – 2nd District; Rayford L. Harris, Jr. – 3rd District; Albert L. Jordan – 4th District; Henry F. Jackson, Jr. – 5th District; Melvin Pinn – 6th District; S.M. "Chucky" Wilson – 7th District; Melvin L. Jenkins - 8th District; Jerry W. Rutherford – 9th District; Charles Bruce – 10th District; Keith W. Neal – 12th District; Edouard T. Delagarde – 13th District

In year 2000, Omega Psi Phi Fraternity, Inc. in a giant step towards communicating anti-hazing policies aired its anti hazing position with television, radio PSA announcements. The Supreme Council led by forward thinking Grand Basileus Lloyd Jordan wanted to be very clear to everyone in America that hazing is not tolerated in any form in Omega Psi Phi Fraternity, Inc.. Grand Basileus Jordan publicly announced to his membership and to the world, "Omega Psi Phi Fraternity recently produced television and radio public service announcements (PSA's) encouraging prospective members to know their rights and report any questionable intake practices. The PSA's were distributed to the top 25 television and top 100 radio markets in the country."

Omega Airs Anti-Hazing Position With Television, Radio PSA Announcements

We want to be very clear to everyone in America, hazing is not tolerated in any form and any questions concerning our practices should be directed to our international headquarters.
Grand Basileus Lloyd Jordan

Grand Basileus Jordan, Lincoln University President Dr. Ivory V. Nelson, the 2nd District DR, Terrel Parris and hosting 2nd D brothers.

Taped at Lincoln University in Philadelphia, the public service announcements featured Grand Basileus Lloyd Jordan. He firmly stated in the PSA's that, "African-American Greek-letter organizations for the last 20 years have wrestled with the issue of hazing, and despite clear anti-hazing messages, extensive education programs concerning membership and intake and enforcement measures, we are still trying to get the upper hand." He further stated that, "Any hazing activity is illegal. Most of it comes from renegades who actually are not members of Omega Psi Phi." **The Omega Psi Phi Fraternity public service announcements initiative was the first such anti-hazing national mass communication action by a Black Greek-letter organization."**

Grand Basileus Jordan defined hazing as any activity that humiliates, degrades abuses or endangers an individual regardless of their willingness to participate. He further stated that, "Omega Psi Phi Fraternity has worked diligently to address hazing by holding biennial leadership and education conferences on this subject. We've even had internationally famous, Omega man, **STEVE HARVEY** address Omega brothers on this critically important matter. Omega Psi Phi's anti-hazing disciplinary policy includes expulsion and prosecution to the full extent of the law. Grand Basileus Jordan told the world that, Omega Psi Phi Fraternity, Inc. is a proud organization. **Make no mistake about it; we are the premiere organization addressing issues relating to the Black male in America**. Collectively, our 700 plus chapters provide over a million dollars each year in scholarship money and we also contribute substantially to the NAACP and the United Negro College Fund."[76]

Grand Basileus Jordan's Supreme Council during this term voted to approve relaxed restrictions on the previous Omega canine ban. Omega men could now wear paraphernalia that referenced the previously banned canine and/or its image. This reversal was primarily based on the fact that enforcing the previous restriction had been found to be almost impossible given the extreme popularity of the image and the lack of and the unique logistics associated with enforcement throughout the organization. The only remaining restriction was that this image not be worn or used at formal gatherings. The Dog image was, for all practical purposes, millions of dollars in advertising for Omega that had been restricted and outlawed by previous administrations. The pros and cons of the previous ban were many. Omega, would now seek to find away to clean up the image and from there

---

[76] The Oracle Summer 2000 article by Brother larry Smallwood.

benefit from the world wide popularity of its canine image and reference.

Grand Basileus Jordan was also a tireless champion of improved brotherhood in the membership. He made a point of raising this issue at many of his opportunities at the podium. He emphasized that as true brothers living and dying with a creed of brotherhood, the men of Omega Psi Phi Fraternity must continue to strive to do better in this area. He stated in the 2000 issue Spring/Summer Oracle that; "A true Omega reaches down and lifts his fellow brother up so that he can stand." He went on to speak on brothers who had some public troubles and the negative reaction of some brothers to distance themselves from them. He also spoke on brothers who are unemployed and brothers not trying to help them or even inquire about their families and ask how they are making it in the tough times. He also specifically spoke on the subject of a brother who may have fallen ill and no one showing concern for him or his family. Or, how brothers talk about a brother with an addiction without offering him help. He felt that although gossip, rumors, jokes about a brother's misfortune is commonplace, **this is not an Omega envisioned by our Founders.** He publicly fought to bring his membership out of this terrible darkness and bad way of thinking. Grand Basileus Jordan often raised brotherhood improvement issues at the podium when he addressed the omega membership.

Grand Basileus Jordan frequently stated, "**A true Omega man sees his brother in need, has pity on him and seeks to help him, and not further destroy him. A true Omega man does not condemn another Omega man because he has a different idea, seeks to run for office or speaks in opposition to proposals etc.. A true Omega man recognizes that our brotherhood is to strive to remove burners of self conceit, wealth, station and class. A true Omega man likens his love for his brothers to that which existed between David and Jonathan. A true Omega man knows that Friendship is indeed Essential to the Soul.**" He employed all Omega men to seek to achieve, maintain and hold this level up in their fraternal lives, personal lives to all around them and as a beacon to the world.

Another noteworthy initiative of Grand Basileus Jordan under his leadership was demonstrated at the seventh annual biennial Leadership Conference in Memphis. **Omega Psi Phi Fraternity**

entered into a historic national partnership with the U.S. Census Bureau to engage in complete count awareness campaigns across the country to help ensure that every individual is counted. Grand Basileus Jordan went on to express to the membership this partnership is historic because it engages Omega with a political process that will impact the distribution of federal funds to communities where our chapters are active in the civil infrastructure.

As the premiere African American organization concerned with the proper development of the Black males, Omega's partnership with the Census Bureau is one step in our plan to help strengthen our community. Grand Basileus Jordan further stated that, "We (Black America) should not under estimate the power of an accurate census. [77] Every individual with a heart beat must be counted. We are all dependent upon each other to ensure that Black America does not lose out on federal programs and dollars. Omega's involvement is not race based. Our motives center around the known fact that minorities are most likely to be under-counted. Federal and state governments use the Census count to determine where funds are spent and how much money is given to programs that are desperately needed in the Black community and/or crucial organizations such as Community Development Block Grants to build our neighborhoods."

Grand Basileus Jordan's administration and his Supreme Council also continued the highly successful Business & Economic Summits and moved it to Washington DC. These summits were highly successful in accomplishing the goal of enlightening and providing sound financial methods and practices for the Omega membership. They allowed the Omega membership additional opportunities to interface with highly successful people who had obtained various degrees of success in the business community.

The September 2000 Business & Economic Summit is notable. It was held in Washington D.C. at the same time that the Congressional Black Caucus was held. This enabled Omega men to interact with the movers and shakers in America. Grand Basileus Jordan's accomplishments were indeed many and far reaching.

---

[77] The Winter 2000 Oracle, Grand Basileus Corner

Significant Events and/or Omega Accomplishments During This Period.

"Upon the resignation of Dr. John Epps, on October 5, 1998 Brother **ALONZA BENNETT** was appointed as the 6th International Executive Director, a position he held on an interim basis until May 30, 2000. Bro. Bennett was very instrumental in assuring that the policies and programs of Grand Basileus Jordan were executed."

On June 1, 2000, **SYLVESTER EARL WILSON** began his tenure as the Executive Director of Omega Psi Phi Fraternity.

On September 13, 2000 a Joint Position Statement against Hazing was signed by all members of the Council of Presidents National Pan-Hellenic Council, Inc. of which Omega Psi Phi Fraternity, Inc is an active member.

September 10, 1999, Omega Psi Phi fraternity Inc. **launches the Hall Of Fame for African American Business champions** with five Omega Men inductees. They are **EARL GRAVES,** Publisher of Black Enterprise Magazine, **BYRON LEWIS**, CEO of Uniworld Group, Inc., **JAMES ELAM**, CEO Elam testing Company, **TONY GRANT**, President African-American banking Group-Bank Of America, and **EDWARD LEWIS,** Chairman & CEO Essence Communications.

THE OMEGA PSI PHI FRATERNITY INC.

<<>>

Omega man, **L. DOUGLAS WILDER,** inaugurated, 1st African-American Governor in the U.S. (VA) **January 13, 1990.**

<<>>

Omega man, **Dr. WILLIAM MONTAGUE COBB,** renowned medical scholar, enters Omega Chapter on **November 20th 1990.**

<<>>

Omega man, **Hon. TOMMY JEWEL,** becomes the 1st African-American District Court Judge in the state of New Mexico on **September 05, 1991.**

<<>>

Omega man, **KEVIN M. CHERRY**, former Undergraduate/Intermediate Representative enters Omega Chapter on **November 01, 1991.**

<<>>

OMEGA PSI PHI FRATERNITY, Inc. presents **$100,000.00** check to the United Negro College Fund **on December 28, 1991.**

<<>>

Establishment of the **CHARLES R. DREW**, Chair in Surgery at Howard University, College of Medicine on **March 08, 1992.**

<<>>

Omega man, **RICHARD "DICK" SMITH** appointed National Assistant Executive Director of Omega Psi Phi Fraternity on **August 03, 1992.**

<<>>

Omega man, **WILLIAM "PARLEZ-VOUS" JONES**, renowned educator, enters Omega Chapter on **February 03, 1994.**

35th **Grand Basileus, DR. DORSEY C. MILLER JR.**, elected: the 1st former, Vice & 2nd Vice Grand Basileus elected Grand Basileus on **July 27, 1994.**

<<>>

Omega man, **NATHANIEL GLOVER, JR.** 1st African-American elected Sheriff in the State of Florida on **April 11, 1995. Initiated into Omega at Edward Waters College**

<<>>

29th **Grand Basileus, Hon. MARION WINSTON GARNETT**, enters Omega Chapter on November **09, 1995.**

<<>>

DEDICATION OF THE NEW OMEGA PSI PHI FRATERNITY, INC. WORLD CENTER at 3951 Snapfinger Pkwy, Decatur, Ga. occurred on **December 09, 1995.**

<<>>

Founder, DR. ERNEST E. JUST, becomes the 19th African-American, Honored with a U.S. Postal Black Heritage Stamp on **February 1, 1996**.

<<>>

Omega Man **LEROY T. WALKER** named President of the 1996 Centennial Olympic Games in Atlanta Ga. To the roar of the crowd at the 1996 Olympics, Brother Walker, A Black man, a proud Omega man, led the American Olympic team into the stadium for the opening ceremony.

<<>>

Fifth District Omega man, **L.A. WESLEY**, principal broker of Westley & Associates, Inc. Realtors became the first African American president of the organization's 2500-member Memphis

Area Association of Realtors in 1996. At the Sixty-six Grand Conclave he received his forty year plaque.

<<>>

Omega man, **RICHARD "DICK" SMITH Day** designated in Vicksburg, Mississippi on **May 11, 1996**.

<<>>

Omega man, Hon. **THURBERT E. BAKER**, 1st African-American appointed Attorney General for the State of Georgia on **June 01, 1997**.

<<>>

1st. National Undergraduate Summit held at the Omega Psi Phi Fraternity, Inc. World Center on **January 20, 1998**.

<<>>

Omega man, **DR. JOSEPH C. SANDERS** Day dedicated in Moncks Corner, S.C. (1 of only 3 days ever dedicated in honor of a person) on **March 23, 1998**.

<<>>

Omega man, **MICHAEL JORDAN**, the greatest professional basketball player of all times, wins his 6th NBA Championship Final with the Chicago Bulls on **June 14, 1998**.

<<>>

Omega man, **CHARLES F. BOLDEN JR**. in July 1998, is promoted to the rank of MAJOR **GENERAL** in the United States Marine Corps.

Brother Bolden's rank of Major General was the highest ever obtained of any African American in the U.S. military up until this time. He assumed his duties as the Deputy Commander, U.S. Forces in Japan. Prior to obtaining the rank of Major General, he was a Brigadier General in the USMC. Brother Bolden also has the distinction of being the first African American Commander of a U.S. Space Shuttle. Major General Bolden's then served as the Commanding General, <u>3rd Marine Aircraft Wing</u>, He retired from the military in August 2004.

<<>>

Omega man, Judge **ALOYISUS LEON HIGGINBOTHAM, Jr.** enter Omega Chapter **<u>December 14, 1998</u>**. Also known as A. Leon Higginbotham, Jr. of Pennsylvania. Born in Trenton, <u>Mercer County</u>, N.J., <u>February 25, 1928</u>. He received the <u>Presidential Medal of Freedom</u> in 1995; received the Spingarn Medal in 1996.

<<>>

Omega man, **EARL G. GRAVES,** (Publisher of Black Enterprise magazine) is selected as 84th recipient of the NAACP Spingarn Medal **on July 15, 1999.**

<<>>

CHAPTER XI

2002 TO 2008
THE DAWN OF A NEW MILLENNUIM: AN ERA OF STRONG ECONOMIC RESURGENCE FOR OMEGA

The George H. Grace, (the 37th Grand Basileus of Omega Psi Phi Fraternity, Inc.) era begins:
(Term 2002-2006)

Grand Basileus **GEORGE H. GRACE**, the 37th Grand Basileus of Omega Psi Phi Fraternity Inc., will be forever remembered in the annals of Omega history for the extraordinary economic success of his administration. In his own words, he stated, "My administration was able to do some extraordinary things with some very ordinary talents and less than ordinary means. Their accomplishments indicate that God has his protective arms around Omega and its leadership. Omega Psi Phi fraternity's finances was dramatically improved and achieved great budgetary surplus as a result of Grand Basileus Grace's financial brilliance and leadership during this period. Without a doubt he delivered on his campaign promise to bring economic prosperity to Omega. Grand Basileus Grace was initiated into

Omega Psi Phi Fraternity in 1973 at Pi Nu Chapter, in Miami Florida.

Brother Grace also gives credit for his administration's great success to the outstanding members of his administration, undergrads and District Representatives included. He stated that he and his administration worked very well cooperatively and from there went about the business of getting the job done in excellent fashion for Omega. Grace believed his ability to surround himself with accomplished supporters was central to his success. "They wanted the same things that I wanted and the record showed that." He also credits his fine relationship with the former Grand Basilei who mentored him closely during his tenure for his administration's success. He cites that their relationship was almost like a very tight knit family. Each former Grand Basileus made time for him and shared their pearls of wisdom with him.

Having learned hard work and teamwork as a young man, George H. Grace, the 37th Grand Basileus of the Omega Psi Phi Fraternity, understood well what a strong united brotherhood of African Americans could accomplish. "To succeed you need a good team," "with everyone committed to the same objectives." Grand Basileus Grace believed that the men of Omega Psi Phi fraternity, living and dying by four shared principles: manhood, scholarship, perseverance, and uplift, with an organization of over 200,000 initiates, would succeed and lift the black race, where many other organizations etc. have failed. This was the aim of Omega's Founders as they so intricately designed the purpose of Omega Psi Phi Fraternity so many years ago. George Grace became Grand Keeper of Records and Seal in 1998 and was then elected Grand Basileus of Omega Psi Phi Fraternity in 2002. "I never sought to be an officer," he said. "It was a course of events and I was in the right place at the right time." But he added: "I was asked because of my track record."

In his rise to become the Grand Basileus of Omega Psi Phi Fraternity, Inc., George H. Grace guided the organization through its purchase of the first black fraternity house at the University of South Carolina and also led discussions with Hilton Hotel for the construction of the first black conference center and resort in the United States. Located in Zenia, Ohio, near Wilberforce and Central States colleges, two of the oldest historically black colleges in the country, this 59-acre parcel of landmark property is the former homestead of Colonel Charles Young, one of the nation's first black military officers.

Of significant historical note, during Grand Basileus Grace's first term, his administration brought forth **a ground breaking initiative that increased the District Scholar awards from $1000.00 to $10,000.00 each and a program to award Undergrads on the Supreme Council scholarships of $10,000.00 each. Brother Grace was a very out spoken champion of these two land mark successes.** He felt that there was a need to better support our cardinal principle of Scholarship and better support our undergrads on the supreme council. These actions and similar actions during his administration soundly demonstrated Grand Basileus Grace's commitment to Omega's future via it young people.

Elected officers at the 72nd Grand Conclave in Charlotte N.C. were:

GEORGE H. GRACE – Grand Basileus

Warren G. Lee – First Vice Grand Basileus; Ademuyiwa Bamiduro – Second Vice Grand Basileus; Terrel D. Parris – Grand Keeper of Records & Seal; Carl A. Blunt – Grand Keeper of Finance; Aubrey Nick Pittman – Grand Counselor; Lloyd J. Jordan Esq. – Immediate Past Grand Basileus; Farrell Duncombe – Grand Chaplain; Dylan Bess – Undergraduate/Intermediate Rep; Anthony Washington- Undergraduate/Intermediate Rep; Wilson White – Undergraduate/Intermediate Rep; Charles B. B. Shelton – Grand Marshal; S. Earl Wilson – Executive Director; Richard "Dick" Smith – Assistant Executive Director; Isaiah Robinson – Editor to the Oracle

District Representatives

Stafford Thompson, Jr. – 1st District; Benjamin Jeffers – 2nd District Representatives; Curtis A. Baylor – 3rd District Representative; Gregory D. Epps – 4th District; Richard Jones – 5th District; Antonio Knox – 6th District; Edgar L. Mathis Sr. – 7th District; Kenneth Patterson – 8th District; Donald Davis - 9th

District; Dwight E. Pointer – 10th District; Lymus D. Capehart, Jr. – 12th District; Cipriani A. Phillip, Jr. – 13th District

Grand Basileus Grace's administration, shortly after assuming leadership, mapped out a strategy to partner with other groups and powerful organizations that had similar interest across America .
This administration was determined for Omega to be a political force in America. Omega, under his leadership, would work to identify and actively support candidates to insure our desired outcome for the 2004 elections. The administration saw the need to develop a structured political action program for our Fraternity. The Grace administration held its first Omega Political Summit with four Omega men in the Florida Senate and House (Brother Hill and Siplin in the Senate and Brother Holloway and Peterman in the House) He also determined that Omega Psi Phi Fraternity needed to improve its financial position so that it could be strong enough to accomplish its stated theme.

Grand Basileus Grace's theme for his administration was, "Economic Empowerment bringing about Political and Social Change." This powerful concept was soundly demonstrated in reality during Grand Basileus Grace's administration. George Grace believed the way to economic empowerment is to look at how you spend your dollar, where you spend it, and what you are spending it for; Omega Psi Phi Fraternity Inc. can make a difference if we use our buying power in a different way." Grand Basileus, Grace has focused on changing the economic plight of minorities in America through better education, greater involvement in the political process, and early training in economics and money management. "We should not blame others for our own short comings," he often proclaimed. Grand Basileus Grace has often said to the members of Omega Psi Phi Fraterntiy, "We can change a lot of things ourselves; no one is going to do it for us."

Grand Basileus Grace's administration was able to pay off over one million dollars in debt, while acquiring a beautiful corporate facility in the Atlanta area which is, as of this writing, debt free. The acquisition of a corporate residence has been a heaven sent, financial bonanza for Omega Psi Phi Fraternity in saving temporary hotel expenses for member training and lodging in the Atlanta area.

This administration also eliminated the debt on the Colonel Young property. Grand Basileus Grace stated, given the latter accomplishments, "We were in God's hand in a mighty way. In addition he further stated, "God has allowed Omega Psi Phi Fraternity, Inc. to improve and hire additional staff, while improving Omega's financial position". Grand Basileus Grace also credited the fraternity's fine relationship with Omega man Banking genius, Tony Grant, as well in taking Omega to over a twelve million dollar net worth in just four years.

Grand Basileus Grace in answering why he brought Omega man Tony Grant in to assist Omega, stated, "Omega Psi Phi Fraternity had tried for eight months to no avail to refinance the property in Decatur, Georgia. The decision was made to hire Grant Business Strategies. Within two weeks after retaining Tony Grant's firm, we had over three to five firms commit letters from financial institutions agreeing to provide financing to Omega Psi Phi Fraternity, Inc. Now, that's results! He further went on to say that Brother Grant's firm was responsive to our needs, result oriented and as a result of their good work saved Omega Psi Phi Fraternity, Inc. a lot of money.

Omega Psi Phi Fraternity, under Grand Basileus Grace's hands on style of leadership was also able to automate our major training areas and allow its membership to take advantage of some much-needed training without leaving the comfort of their homes. The accomplishments of this administration were indeed many and earth shattering. At his side and playing a key role in his administration's success was First Vice Grand Basileus, Warren G. Lee. They complimented each other well and along with a super Supreme Council, as a result of their fantastic team work, the organization prospered.

Grand Basileus Grace also analyzed our congressional districts to learn where we were strong and weak so that Omega could organize and target those areas to reach its goals. He and his administration realized and clearly understood the need for Omega's membership to be involved in the political process of America.

In this effort to empower minorities, which included a big push by black fraternities and sororities to register 1.5 million unregistered and uncommitted voters for the 2004 U.S. presidential election, Grand Basileus Grace firmly said to the members of Omega Psi Phi Fraternity at each opportunity: **"Brothers! Omega Men! We've got to get out and vote**." To the victor goes the spoils; that's how this country works." Omega Psi Phi members as a result of this battle cry, reached out in a unified way to urge citizens in their communities to vote. They also went many steps further and advised citizens in black communites all across America on their rights as voters. Omega men also offered transportation to ensure that anyone who wanted to get to the polls could. All they had to do was step forward and ask an Omega man. And, it was done![78]

The 73rd Grand Conclave in St. Louis, Missouri:

Elected and/or re-electedSupreme Council officers were:

GEORGE H. GRACE – Grand Basileus

Warren G. Lee – First Vice Grand Basileus; Ademuyiwa Bamiduro – Second Vice Grand Basileus; Terrel D. Parris – Grand Keeper of Records & Seal; Carl A. Blunt – Grand Keeper of Finance; Aubrey Nick Pittman – Grand Counselor; Lloyd J. Jordan Esq. – Immediate Past Grand Basileus; Farrell Duncombe – Grand Chaplain; Dylan Bess – Undergraduate/Intermediate Rep; Anthony Washington- Undergraduate/Intermediate Rep; Wilson White – Undergraduate/Intermediate Rep; Charles B. B. Shelton – Grand Marshal; S. Earl Wilson – Executive Director; Richard "Dick" Smith – Assistant Executive Director; Isaiah Robinson – Editor to the Oracle

District Representatives

1st District – Stafford Thompson, Jr.; 2nd District – Benjamin Jeffers; 3rd District - Curtis A Baylor; 4th District – William Comeaux; 5th District – Richard Jones; 6th District Antonio Knox; 7th District – Edgar L. Mathis Sr.; 8th District – Larry Burks ; 9th District – Donald Davis; 10th District – Dwight E. Pointer; 12th District – Lymus D. Capehart, Jr.; 13th District Cipriani A. Phillip, Jr.

---

[78] http://biography.jrank.org/pages/2411/Grace-George-H.html// Brief Biographies :: African American Biographies Vol 2

This conclave was dedicated to political candidate forums Initiatives of the 2004 St. Louis Grand Conclave were;

- **State of the Nation & Omega's Impact on it**
- **Economic Empowerment Continued**
- **Leadership,**
- **Voter Registration**
- **Public Policy and the Economy**
- **Credit Training**

In 2004, George Grace was re-elected to his position as Grand Basileus and began the Undergraduate Economic Summit initiative with the Minority Business Office of the Department of Commerce, whose director is a fraternity member. The plan was to spread Omega's lessons in money management into historically black college campuses. This positive germ hopefully would spread across America.

Teaching underprivileged kids about home ownership and credit was a key component of Grand Basileus Grace's initiative. Each year the fraternity also held a Youth Economic Summit in Washington, D.C., offering seminars on topics like first-time home purchasing and managing credit. "We need to talk about these things before it's too late, to make sure African-American youth never get credit problems," Grace says. "Home ownership is a key to success. Our members absolutely must take this message back to the community.

Omega Psi Phi Fraternity, under Grand Basileu's Grace's leadership has gone into high schools with this message, and it has paid off. The kids learn about buying habits and investing; then they take it home to the parents. **Not everything is found in a book.** It's about being exposed to people like our fraternity members." Through these seminars young African Americans are able to hear brothers like Earl Graves, Sr., president and CEO of Black Enterprise, and many many other successful Omega men share their expertise in creating wealth and controlling one's own destiny. This valuable experience would be a comodity more valuable than gold to them when they needed.

<<>>

Another significant historical achievement of Grand Basileus Grace was the grand opening of the John H. Williams museum at the 2005 Leadership Conference in Atalnta Georgia. The museum honors distinguished Omega man **JOHN H. WILLIAMS AND HIS EXTRAORDINARY WORK AS WELL AS many other HISTORICALLY SIGNIFICANT ACCOMPLISHMENTS OF THE MEN OF OMEGA PSI PHI FRATERNITY.** John Williams was appointed by the 29th Grand Basileus, **MARION W. GARNETT,** as Omega Psi Phi Fraternity's International Photographer. He has retained that illustrious title since 1973.

Brother Williams has captured the soul of Omega Psi Phi fraternity in the good times as well as in bad times. In faithfully doing his work, he was so close to the action that he tasted the tears of many of our brothers and leaders as they wept at the passing and burials of our beloved Founders. He has walked with giants (the Founders and various other movers and shakers) in our organization as well as with Kings and presidents out in the world.

Not only did Brother Williams not lose his common touch and composure. in being the ultimate professional that he is, he managed to anchor and enhance those around him and in the process also give us a rare glimpse of history in the making along the way. **God has touched/blessed Brother Williams and in doing so gave him a UNQUE talent for photography that has no equal in his field.** Omega has been a beneficiary of this blessing. Omega men across the world are grateful to Brother Williams for being their eyes and are indeed proud to number this extraordinary man, as one of their own.

John H. Williams has served nobly as the Omega Psi Phi International Photographer and his experiences, travels, historic occasions and achievements have been captured and chronicled in the much celebrated pictorial, The Omega Psi Phi Fraternity, Inc. 1950-1994. His work has also appeared in the Fraternity's video, "A Summary of the History and programs of the Omega Psi Phi Fraternity, Inc. His extraordinary work has also appeared extensively for the last several decades in both the Omega Psi Phi Oracle and the NAACP Crisis magazines.

Brother Williams was born October 26, 1918 in Monroe, North Carolina. He was intimately acquainted with the struggles of African-Americans for equality. Being a Black man in his field in the early 1900 was not easy. John H. Williams in spite of the

THE OMEGA PSI PHI FRATERNITY INC.

blatant and mean spirited racism that he often experienced while honing his skills, was able to fight his way to the top of his profession.

The John H. Williams museum is a fitting testament to the greatness of this Omega man. The opening was made available to the general public as well as to all our Omega brothers. A grand ribbon-cutting ceremony was conducted to herald this historical achievement.

<<>>

The 2006, 74th Grand Conclave in Little Rock Arkansas was presided over by Grand Basileus Grace and his administration. Below is his state of the Fraternity Financial report; and the Conclave's report.

Grand Basileus Grace's extraordinary financial accomplishments are shown by the following:

Grand Basileus State of the Fraternity Address

The Grand Basileus, Bro. George H. Grace, presented his State of the Fraternity address to the Grand Conclave indicating:

Membership & Finances
- As of June 30, 2006 the Fraternity has 17,000 financial members.
- The Fraternity's financial situation has made a dramatic turnaround during the period 2002 – 2006. In August 2002, the debt position reported by the Grand Basileus was:

Expense Item Description	Amount
Amount owed in 2002 Conclave Expenses	$X00,000
Amount owed to OLMF	$X00,000
Amount owed to Districts	$X25,000
Amount owed to Friendship Foundation	$X0,000
Amount owed in Back Legal Expenses	$X25,000
Amount owed to Bro. Jim Elam	$X75,000
TOTAL	**$X,315,000**

The Grand Basileus went on to say,
- As of May 31, 2006 the fraternity had over $X,047,000 in its operating account with no outstanding long term debt. **The Grand Basileus attributed this remarkable improvement** to several things such as:
    1. Administrative operating cost improvements
    2. Refinancing the debt on the IHQ building in Decatur, Georgia resulting in lowering the monthly payment from $25,000/mo to $19,000/mo.

3. Real estate investments at the University of South Carolina, the Col. Charles Young property in Ohio and a future looking housing development project in Ensley, Alabama.
4. The Rewards Program providing a revenue stream for the Fraternity and savings on services to the Brothers who participate. These opportunities resulting from collaborations and partnerships with corporate entities.
5. Direct contributions and sponsoring assistance from public and private sources

The benefits derived have been retained, maximized and shared with the Membership with savings through:
1. Purchase of a corporate residential property in Atlanta, GA. The property will be principally used by members of the Supreme Council when they travel to Atlanta, GA for Fraternity business. The corporate residential property is debt free with no mortgage obligation.
2. The Fraternity will donate 15 laptop computers to Arkansas Baptist College at the conclusion of the 74th Grand Conclave
3. The IHQ building and property in Decatur, Georgia has increased in value from $2.2 million dollars (circa 2002) to $6.5 million dollars per a 2006 appraisal.
4. The registration fee for the Undergraduate Summit has been eliminated as a classic demonstration of how the Fraternity's success is shared with the Membership.

- The Fraternity held "Omega Days" at the US Capital in Washington, DC September 26 – 27, 2006. It was noted the presence of the Fraternity and its Leadership was essential in the renewal of the 1965 Voting Rights Act.

Brother Grace's theme was Economic Empowerment

An excerpt from the 37th Grand Basileus Speaks..... (The Oracle/Fall 2003) Message from Brother George H. Grace " Can't See The Forest for the Trees: In passionately speaking on the subject of how the public see Omega and how we as members should behave, Grand Basileus Grace quoted the old saying. "Can't see the forest for the Trees" The hazing incidents and poor behavior is often the only thing highlighted or given attention by the media. Often the poor behavior is the thing reinforced and seen by the public and copied by some of our brothers.

Grand Basileus Grace further stated, "We should make it our mission to cut a path through the trees and let this beautiful Omega forest show through. We can do this if we are vigilant and committed to the task of keeping the positives about Omega at the forefront. These positives tremendously out weigh the negative behavior of a few, but we must remain committed and dedicated to the ideals of our Founders." He went on to say in this article that we must also make certain that all the positive programs that Omega Psi Phi Fraternity routinely perform should be made available to the public. Finally, Brother Grace proclaimed in this article that we must tell everyone that Omega men are leaders in all walks of life and we must also remember we reproduce what we reinforce and Omega Psi Phi Fraternity has a beautiful forest when one really gets to see it.

<<>>

Omega held it 4th annual Celebrity Golf Tournament at Mill Cove Golf Course in Jacksonville, Florida on June 10-11, 2005. A special tribute to Golf legend Calvin Peete was held. Several other initiatives such as Sickle Cell, HIV/Aids and Erectile Dysfunction were also highlighted at this event. **Brother T.C. Newman** at the time of this writing was the proprietor of this beautiful golf course.

<<>>

AND JUST WHEN WE THOUGHT EVERYTHING IN OMEGA LAND AND THE WORLD WAS ALL ROSY AND GOING OH SO GREAT, THEN KABOOM!!!! LIKE A SONIC BOOM EXPLOSION. HURRICANE KATRINA UNMERCIFULLY STRUCK, KNOCKED US ALL OFF OUR FEET AND RAVAGED THE GULF COAST LIKE NEVER BEFORE.

ALMOST AS DEVASTATING AS TERRORISTS DROPPING A NUCLEAR BOMB IN THE HEART OF AMERICA, HURRICANE KATRINA ON AUGUST 29TH 2005 showed the world the sheer terror, ferocity and unmatched strength of Mother Nature. My God, My God, My God, what a horrific sight to behold! The unbelievable pain and suffering this event caused was gut wrenching for the entire nation as it played itself out on national television. All of America was riveting to their television sets witnessing the unthinkable. Eighty percent of this famous and beloved city was flooded. Thousands were left homeless and wondering aimlessly in the flooded streets of New Orleans as in a daze, slashing through up to five feet of nasty, disease filled water in its aftermath as a result of levies in New Orleans breaking and causing much of New Orleans to be flooded. The Mississippi Gulf Coast as well as Alabama were knocked to their knees and rendered helpless as well. Thousands in the three state affected areas were killed and many even till this day are missing.

The news media and the world could not get enough of this incredible story. Black Americans were sickened to the core at the sight of their fellow neighbors going through such a horrendous ordeal. People caught in the middle of this life or death circumstance were desperately begging for help and assistance on national television. Many homes were completely under water and roof tops all across the city of New Orleans in particular, showed people who had, out of desperation, cut holes out the top of their roofs, standing on them and clinging to anything they could get their hands on to save their lives. Dead bodies were floating in the water and many were left lying out on the streets in full view, abandoned by their own family members who simply could now, just do all they could to save themselves and the living.

Many sought refuge in the almighty Super Dome at the beginning of the hurricane's onslaught. But to no avail. **Hurricane Katrina was just too much for this man made, seemingly God defying object.** Its roof gave way and yes many many people suffered and were forced to under go pure hell to fight to survive. These were our brothers and sisters and we, who were forced to watch helplessly at home, could do nothing at that moment. What a horrendous sight this national tragedy was. And in the mist of this terrible human tragedy, people, yes despicable people, were seen looting in the streets. Sure, justification was found. But almighty God will certainly be the judge of the guilty. And people, yes, our people, African Americans of which many were our dear Omega brothers suffered oh so dearly.

Hundreds of thousands of people were hastily dispersed on buses all across America to try to get them immediate help. Babies were ripped from the arms of their mothers and old and sick people in the panic were forced on to buses that they had no idea of their destination. Many people who were hastily relocated did not know where their family members were for months after the move.

Hurricane Katrina without a doubt, would become one of the greatest natural disasters the United States had ever experienced. This was the first time in American history that an entire city was mobilized and impacted in such a manner. Thousands were left scarred for life as a result of this national tragedy. Many faulted the government and president George W. Bush in particular, for not acting quickly enough. History would show that there was plenty of blame to place. The Director of FEMA's head rolled. Yes he was fired for incompetence in not being able to provide adequate and timely relief to the victims of Katrina. President Bush's already low popularity, plummeted like a rock. The female Governor of Louisiana so racked with guilt and shame, could not bring herself to run for another term. Ray Nagin, an African American mayor, of this city that the world loved so dearly, was not sparred. At public hearings across the city, he was lambasted for his lacking performance in this disaster. He along with the U.S. CORP. of Engineers shouldered their share of the blame as well.

As soon as humanly possible Omega Psi Phi Fraternity rushed itself to the scene to help not only its members, but all needing assistance as well. Food, money, clothes, physical assistance, homes were made available and in many instances, almost burst at the seams with over flowing crowds. Omega Psi Phi Fraternity did its part magnificently, as many other Americans and various other organizations did. Local chapters of Omega, particularly those neighboring the disaster areas leapt fearlessly head on into this spiraling nightmare.

Grand Basileus George Grace at the international level and his extraordinary administration went all out to insure that Omega was at the fore front in uplifting its brothers and fellow Americans. Omega Psi Phi Fraternity provided over $100,000.00 to begin with to the Katrina relief Fund along with tons of food and clothes. Each chapter would also contribute in addition to the enormous generosity they had independently given $1000.00 outright or pledged $200.00 installments for up to a five year period. Brothers who were directly affected filled out relief assistance forms and as a result got financial assistance. Omega's International Headquarters was utilized as a collection and distribution point for providing additional non-monetary items such as clothes, food etc. Brothers in need of insurance counseling as a result of Katrina were given much needed assistance given the utter devastation. Creation of email addresses that brothers could use to direct inquiries regarding any need or construction issues during the rebuilding process were made freely available for all who needed it. **Yes, Omega Psi Phi Fraternity did its part and much much more in excellent fashion.**

And, as if Hurricane Katrina wasn't enough, Hurricane Rita decided it would wade ashore just west of New Orleans and kick the crap out of America once again, just a month later. Just prior to coming ashore, because of the uncertainty of where it would actually hit, hundreds of thousands of people fled Houston, Texas creating another human disaster as a result of the chaos of so many fleeing at one time. Over a million people flooded the highways at one time in an effort not to be in a Katrina type situation. Cars were jammed together in no certain order, all over the highway. It took hours at less than a snail's pace to get just a few hundred yards.

It took this author thirty eight hours to drive what would normally take seven and half hours to Jackson Mississippi from Houston Texas. It was pure hell. People reduced themselves to barbarian, kill or be killed behavior to get food, water, right of way, bath room rights and gas for themselves and their families. Fists fights broke out every mile of the way and guns were drawn and some instances fired. Several elderly people died on the highways as a result of heat exhaustion, stress and sheer fatigue. Their bodies could be seen in their cars with their love ones begging for help and crying frantically over them. I had never seen anything like it. And I hope to God that I never ever do so again!

It was like the end of the world had come. Highways were packed with cars trying to flee the city. People were panicking and driving wildly all over the place. Many cars ran out of gas or broke down completely from the heat and strain. What were meant to be four line highways became ten lane highways with people driving off the side of the road, in fields and not necessarily going in the same direction. Cars and trucks run out of gas and were abandoned where they stopped, people whose cars had given out of gas, were walking all over the place, with no idea of where they were going or where they were. Fist fights broke out and utter chaos was seen as people (black, white, yellow, brown) reached their boiling point. Lawlessness reigned; people were screaming and crying. **Again, as in the case of Katrina, Omega Psi Phi Fraternity, when the smoke cleared and order was restored, once again stepped up and played a role in assisting its own as well as all who needed it**. God bless Omega Psi Phi Fraternity, Inc, its Founders who created such a helping, uplifting vehicle and the extraordinary generous members that call Omega their own. Omega served its God given purpose on these two occasions. These were shining moments that Omega men all across America can point to with pride regarding the relevance and worthiness of their organization.

<><>

The 74th Grand Conclave:

The second plenary session was called to order at 2:30 PM on Monday, 7/24/2006. The second plenary session focus was a presentation on health initiatives, moderated by Bro Charles Christopher (MD). The guest speaker was Dr. Gerald DeVaughn, President of the American Association of Black Cardiologists; a medical association with a mission to decrease the rate of incidence of cardiovascular disease, a leading cause of death among Black Americans.

Also of significance during the Second Plenary Session was the nomination process for the Grand Officer positions. The nomination process was Chaired by Past Grand Basileus, Bro. Moses C. Norman, Sr. (33rd Grand Basileus). Note: District Caucus sessions were held on Tuesday July 25, 2006 at various locations in the Convention Center. The actual elections were held on Wednesday July 26, 2006 (starting at 7:30 AM) with a run-off for the Offices of 1st Vice Grand Basileus and Grand Keeper of Records and Seal held in the early evening of that same day.

The Undergraduate Caucus determined the identification and election of the 2nd Vice Grand Basileus and Undergraduate Representatives to the Supreme Council. Nominations for the Office of Grand Keeper of Finance was closed on one nominee, however, the name of that nominee, Bro. Antonio F. Knox, did still appear on the ballot and received votes. The formal announcement of the election results was read to the Grand

Conclave on the morning of Thursday, July 27, 2006. For brevity and clarity, the results of the nomination process, election and election run-off are indicated together below. (Winners are indicated by all capital letters in bold print.)

Nominees

GRAND BASILEUS Votes
Bro. WARREN G. LEE, JR. 641
Bro. Kenneth A. Brown 498
1ST VICE GRAND BASILEUS
RUNOFF
Bro. Carl A. Blunt 454 **Bro. CARL A. BLUNT 571**
Bro. Terrell D. Parris 401 Bro. Terrell D. Parris 310
Bro. Aubrey Nick Pittman 150
Bro. Alcindor R. Rosier 115
Bro. Inaki Bent (on ballot as Inaki Vent) 20
2ND VICE GRAND BASILEUS
Bro. BRIAN GUNDY (Elected by Undergraduate Caucus)
GRAND KEEPER OF RECORDS AND SEAL
RUNOFF
Bro. Mandrid N. Williams, Jr. 79
Bro. Edgar L. Mathias, Sr. 335 Bro. Edgar L. Mathias, Sr. 328
Bro. Charles A. Bruce 398 **Bro. CHARLES A. BRUCE 554**
Bro. Marcus W. Shute 326
GRAND KEEPER OF FINANCE
Bro. ANTONIO F. KNOX (Unopposed) 979
GRAND COUNSELOR
Bro. Christopher M. Cooper 560
Bro. MICHAEL R. D. ADAMS 578 KRS
The Undergraduate Caucus also elected the Undergraduate
Representatives to the Supreme Council. Those new Supreme Council Members are:
        Bro. BENJAMIN L. HART (7th District)
        Bro. JOSEPH F. BOWERS, Jr. (10th District)
        Bro. JAMES McKOY (6th District)
The Grand Conclave activities of Monday, July 24, 2006 ended with the presentation of the International Talent Hunt Program and the wonderful performances by the District Winners.

<u>**GRAND MARSHAL REPORT**</u>
Brother Derek Lewis, the Grand Marshall of the 74th Grand Conclave, presented his report. The pre-audit registration figures for the 74th Grand Conclave were:

Total Number of Pre-Registered Brothers	1288
Total Number of On-Site Registrations	168
Total Number of Registered Brothers	**1456**

SIGNIFICANT EVENTS AND OMEGA ACCOMPLISHMENTS DURING THIS PERIOD:

Omega Psi Phi Fraternity Inc holds its first Annual Omega Celebrity Weekend June 1-2, 2001, in Atlanta Ga.

<<>>

Omega man, **KENDRICK B. MEEKS** elected to U.S. Congressman, House of Representatives – 17th District of Florida in 2002.

<<>>

Omega man, **JOSEPH "JAKE" SUGGS** was voted to the CIAA Hall of fame during the annual meeting of CIAA Football Officials held **July 24-26, 2003**. He was a 25 year member of the Omega Psi Phi Fraternity, Pi Phi chapter, sixth District at the time of this honor.

<<>>

IN 2005, SYLVESTER EARL WILSON'S tenure as the Executive Director Omega Psi Phi Fraternity Inc. ends. The order for Executive Directors for Omega Psi Phi fraternity was 1. H. Carl Moultrie, I, He was the first Executive Secretary. His tenure lasted from 1949-1972. Brother Moultrie did such an excellent job in this position that he was granted emeritus status. Then came Harold Cook, Willie Wright, Pete Reeder, John S. Epps and finally, Earl Wilson. As of this writing the permanent position is vacant and a candidate is actively being sought,

<<>>

Omega man **GEORGE A. SMITH** initiated into Omega Psi Phi Fraternity in 1972 on the Auburn University charter line was brought in October 2005 as Acting Executive Director under George H Grace. He, as of the writing of this book, is acting in this capacity running the day to day operation of the International Office and managing the staff. George Smith was selected due to his outstanding track record of performance and dedication in Omega. During the 73rd St Louis Conclave brother Smith worked diligently and successfully to pass resolutions to revise the mandated programs to insure Omega focused on a specific slate of approved programs from year to year, rather than adopt new ones as new administrations come in. This innovative effort will insure significant and continuous long term successes and strides by Omega Psi Phi Fraternity in making a difference in the lives of black people. Under the Warren Lee Administration, Brother Smith's duties and title at the International Headquarters changed to Liaison to the Grand Basileus.

<<>>

32nd Grand Basileus **L. BENJAMIN LIVINGSTON** enter Omega Chapter on December 04, 2005

<<>>

Omega man, General **WILLIAM E. "KIP" WARD** takes over as Deputy Commander, of the U.S. European Command on 05/03/06.

<<>>

Omega Man, **CHARLES F. BOLDEN JR.**, Astronaut and retired Major General, United States Marine Corps. **was inducted into the U.S. Astronauts Hall of Fame for his heroic space exploits and outstanding career on May, 06, 2006.** He was initiated into Omega Psi Phi fraternity in Gamma Nu chapter in 1983. ***UPDATE-On May 28th 2009, newly elected president Barack Obama nominated Omega man Charlie F. Bolden to head NASA.** This is an extraordinary honor and accomplishment. Brother Bolden is the first African American to be considered for this government agency.

<<>>

Omega man, Colonel **WILLIAM E. MOSLEY** made Commander, 607th Air Support Group; Director of Logistics, Seventh Air Force and Assistant Chief of Staff, Logistics, Air Component Command, of an Air Base, Republic of Korea. He was initiated in Omega Psi Phi Fraternity, fall 1968 at Lambda Gamma Chapter, Elizabeth City State University, North Carolina.

Brother Dr. CHARLES A. CHRISTOPHER

Omega's First Surgeon General

In 2006, Grand Basileus George H. Grace appointed Brother **Dr. CHARLES A. CHRISTOPHER** as Omega's first Surgeon General. A pressing need was identified for a medical leader of Omega Psi Phi Fraternity. In this position as well as, as chairman of the Health Initiative committee, Brother Christopher has done an extraordinary job of looking out for the health of our members and their families. Since that time, Brother Christopher and his outstanding committee have organized and put on extremely valuable health fairs/workshops and published numerous health enhancing articles that have been highly effective in improving the health of members of Omega Psi Phi Fraternity. We must assume that, as a result of the fine work of Brother Christopher, many Omega lives and their family members with them have been saved and/or prolonged. Praise be to God for guiding the hands and mind of this outstanding, dedicated, hard working and skilled medical man. Brother Christopher was initiated into Omega Psi

Phi Fraternity by way of Huston-Tillotson College in Austin, Texas, December 07, 1962.

The 74th Grand Conclave was officially approved and scheduled for Little Rock Arkansas. Former United States President Bill Clinton (The affectionately named first Black president because of his high popularity by African Americans) helped the city in welcoming Omega Psi Phi Fraternity to their city with great fanfare. **One incident that occurred prior to the arrival of thousands of Omega men to the city was a nasty email that was circulated by a white female** that claimed that the crime rate in Little Rock, Arkansas would more than triple during the convention and that white residents should be on the alert during this period. This unfounded email circled the nation and made for some bad feelings from all sides. Only time would prove this email to be utter nonsense. Omega men proved themselves to be extraordinary guests.

<<>>

Grand Basileus Grace's parting words in 2006 as Grand Basileus to his membership were very prophetic. He warned Omega that the future would bring with it some important challenges for African-Americans in the economic, political and social arenas. Omega Psi Phi Fraternity, Inc must be ready and be at the forefront to ensure that it and America remains great by demonstrating to everyone that this land of equal opportunity is for everyone. Omega Psi Phi Fraternity, Inc. can help to insure this by supporting those corporations that support African Americans and exposing and dealing accordingly with those who don't. We must make certain that the political process works for African-Americans. To this end, Grand Basileus Grace's administration left the scene and turned over the reins to his good friend and the in coming Grand Basileus, Warren G. Lee, by saying that, "Omega Psi Phi Fraternity's continued progress in the critically important area of Economic Empowerment will indeed lead to Political and Social Change."

CHAPTER XII

(OMEGA: TODAY, TOMORROW & FOREVER)

GRAND BASILEUS WARREN G. LEE
(TERM 2006 to 2010)

The Warren G. Lee, (the 38th Grand Basileus of Omega Psi Phi Fraternity Inc.) era begins:

Grand Basileus **WARREN G. LEE** was elected at the 74th Grand Conclave in Little Rock Arkansas in July 2006. He has been an incredible performer in several Grand level administrations for over three decades in Omega Psi Phi Fraternity. He served as First Vice Grand Basileus just prior to being elevated to the chief executive officer position. He served flawlessly as the Second Vice Grand Basileus as well as in various other positions at the local, district and national level. The 38th Grand Basileus of Omega Psi Phi Fraternity hails from the ninth District and was initiated into Omega in Eta Theta chapter at the University of Texas on December 18th, 1971.

Omega men are known for their unique levels of diverseness, character, humbleness, honesty, leadership and extraordinary integrity. These are just a few of the outstanding qualities that describe Brother Warren G. Lee. One of his most passionate focus is "Making a difference in the lives of Black Americans" As the leaders of one of the most powerful African American organizations in the world, he has done and vows to continue to do great things for Omega and the Black race before his tenure is over. He has publicly stated that he looks forward to continuing Omega's great legacy of serving the global community. Grand Basileus Lee's theme for leading this Omega Psi Phi Fraternity is: "Three Looks, One Focus: Family/Fraternity/Friends. He is confident that if Omega keeps these three critical elements as its core values its future will be limitless.

Grand Basileus Lee has also publicly stated that, "if Omega Psi Phi Fraternity, Inc. is to become the most recognizable voice of our people, we must reinforce our organizational "top-down" leadership style. In order to lead our people effectively, we must constantly strive to improve our communications methodologies that support and enhance this style. Working together, there is no doubt, that our great organization will continue, "Making a Difference in the Lives of Black People."

Grand Basileus Lee has continued to build on the great foundation laid by his very successful predecessor and good friend George H. Grace, (the 37th Grand Basileus) which is Economic Empowerment Leading to Social and Political Change. Grand Basileus Lee has soundly demonstrated this commitment by developing a highly innovative platform that encompasses an internal focus as well as external focus. Internally he has implemented programs/initiatives to strengthen our communities, infrastructure, accountability and efficiency. Externally he has embarked on a course to display Omega's strengths as a powerful uplifting positive force out in the Black community.

The Lampados Club Initiative & Pilot, Coaches for Cancer, the Clarion Call, The Prostate Cancer Initiative, The Book Reading Initiative, The Grand Basilei Interviews, the Grand Basileus News letter the Sword and Shield, The Grand Opening of the John H. Williams Museum, the highly successful 2007 Philadelphia Leadership Conference, which was the largest Conference to date with over 760 registered brothers, as well as numerous other innovations and initiatives are very positive products of his administration that have helped to galvanize, mobilize and energize Omega Psi Phi Fraternity's membership in this his first term. We will explore the aforementioned initiatives in more detail as the chapter progress.

Grand Basileus Lee is big on Leadership. His continuing mantra to the Omega membership is, "Everything Rises and Falls on Leadership. He has strongly emphasized this and insist that it be demonstrated daily from not just his position but from top to bottom in the organization. He is an avid reader and as a result, he has constantly recommended excellent developmental and inspirational books to read and has espoused their intelligence enhancing content to his membership from the podium. This extremely innovative practice has been valuable for the men of Omega.

Grand Basileus Lee is also known and respected for the fact that he is constantly urging his members to read more. It is clear he feels that the more knowledge Omega men obtain, the better the organization will be and the better Omega men can go back to their families and communities and uplift them with their new found intellectual growth. Omega Psi Phi Fraternity's past performance in helping the Black race without a doubt, is well documented. This performance will be improved. Grand Basileus Lee and his administration have planned a strategic road map that will insure Omega's greatness not only for today but long into the future.

Supreme Council members elected at the 74th Grand Conclave in Little Rock Arkansas:

[79]

WARREN G. LEE – Grand Basileus

Carl A. Blunt - 1st Vice GRAND BASILEUS; Brian S. Gundy – 2nd Vice Grand Basileus; George H. Grace - Immediate Past Grand Basileus; Charles Bruce – Grand Keeper of Records and Seal Antonio F. Knox – Grand Keeper of Finance; Michael R. Adams - Grand Counselor; Ferrel Duncombe – Grand Chaplain; Joseph F. Bowers – Under Graduate Immediate Rep; Benjamin L. Hart – Under Graduate Immediate Rep; James McKoy – Under Graduate Immediate Rep; *Walter Body – Grand Marshal ,75th Conclave;

DISTRICT REPRESENTATIVES

Vaughn M. Willis -1st District; Marvin Dillard – 2nd District; Mark E. Jackson – 3rd District; Jesse Junius – 4th District; Horace W. Chase 5th District: Charles Worth - 6th District; Joseph T. Williams – 7th District; Jeffrey T. Smith – Todd S. Clemons – 9th District; Glenn A. Matthews – 10th District; Charles Peevy – 12th District; Jonathan N. Griffin Sr. – 13th District

    The 74th Grand Conclave in Little Rock Arkansas proved to be a smashing success for all involved. Omega leadership had once again proved and soundly demonstrated its outstanding metal. Even the naysayers (racist whites who did not want Omega in their fair city and even some Omega brothers, who felt that they would not be able to enjoy themselves in a city with such a notoriously bad past racial history) had to smile and admit they were wrong about Little Rock. The mayor and the good people of Little Rock welcomed Omega with open arms, the brothers had a great time, no incidents occurred, the little Rock Nine salute and program was nothing short of sensational and a great time was indeed had by all. Millions of Omega dollars were happily spent and left in Little Rock.

    A city that could definitely use the money was improved greatly, a great organization had a very productive meeting while having a little fun in the process and more importantly, human nature once again demonstrated that people (black and white, regardless of past history) can, with a little faith and prayer, indeed get along. **What the Devil meant for bad, God turned**

---

[79] Spring 2008 Oracle/ The Omega Grand Officers

it into good. God is good my brothers! And, it's obvious that he, the Holy Spirit and Jesus, loves Omega Psi Phi fraternity very, very much. For the stiff neck doubter, you only have to be truthful and/or objective, and from there open your eyes, brain and heart to see the holy Trinity's guiding and protective hand in our beloved organization. What God has put together, let no man put asunder!

Immediately after being elected Grand Basileus, **Warren Lee commissioned the update of the Omega History book project for the period 1960 to 2008.** Vernon Steve Weakley, noted nationally known author and Omega man, was appointed History Book chairman and assigned this task. The last time the History of Omega Psi Phi Fraternity was done was 1963 by Dr. Robert Gill. Prior to that time, it was done by Herman Dreer in 1940. Forty eight years have passed since Omega's illustrious history has been officially published. Since that time no less than six other official chairmen and committees have attempted this task and failed. It, as can see, has been accomplished. Credit goes to Grand Basileus Lee and his administration for commissioning this difficult, Herculean task.

Additionally, Grand Basileus Lee committed to accomplishing the following in the first one hundred days of his administration.

1. Send a letter to all financial members outlining our short-term goals and strategies
2. Establish and use Phone Tree R to deliver broadcast messages directly to members
3. Establish web casting as a communication vehicle
4. Introduce a new publication and identify new staff
5. Refresh the editorial emphasis of the Oracles (aristocracy of the intellect)
6. Maintain the Bulletin (members only)
7. Institutionalize the Newsletter as a vehicle for new member activity.

BROTHER CHARLES JOHNSON

In 2007, Omega Psi Phi fraternity takes a giant step to shape and better perfect its internal and external COMMUNICATIONS and image by selecting the golden voice and extraordinary and innovative creative communication skills and God given talents of Brother **CHARLES JOHNSON** of Theta Alpha chapter of Dallas Texas. Brother Johnson's outstanding work in producing videos and highly professional promotional productions have raised Omega's external image significantly in a positive way to corporate America and city, federal, and state governmental agencies. This action has and will pay enormous financial dividends to Omega Psi Phi Fraternity for many years to come. Brother Johnson has had many successful years in communications in corporate America.

<<>>

Omega Psi Phi Fraternity, Inc.'s Coaches vs. Cancer Initiative:

In March 2007, during the height of March Madness, the Supreme Council of Omega Psi Phi Fraternity, Inc. was in attendance at the MEAC Tournament in Raleigh, North Carolina. During the reception and the Friday evening portion of the MEAC Tournament, there was a presentation of a $20,000 check by the Grand Basileus to the MEAC Scholarship Foundation.

When Grand Basileus Warren G. Lee, Jr. noticed that the coaches were wearing business suits and sneakers, he asked why? The answer led to a conversation that culminated in a partnership between the American Cancer Society, the National Association of Basketball Coaches and Omega Psi Phi Fraternity, Inc.

Coaches vs. Cancer is a nationwide collaboration between the American Cancer Society and the National Association of Basketball Coaches (NABC) that empowers basketball coaches, their teams, and local communities to make a difference in the fight against cancer. The program leverages the personal experiences, community leadership, and professional excellence of basketball coaches nationwide to increase cancer awareness and promote healthy living through year-round awareness efforts, fundraising activities, and advocacy programs.

Grand Basileus Lee was quick to see an opportunity to raise awareness about a health issue affecting Black males and to advance the cause of medical research focused on the black community. A partnership was born when Omega Psi Phi Fraternity, Inc. agreed to support the Coaches vs. Cancer project. This year, in recognition of our efforts, the ACS will donate a significant portion of the funds raised to support research on colon and prostate cancer as it affects black males. "We will use our vast network of brothers to sell 100,000 t-shirts at $20 each in support of this venture," Grand Basileus Lee proclaimed. In true Omega style, we have created some incentives to encourage Districts, Chapters, and Individuals to get moving. [80]

Omega Psi Phi Fraternity has also placed great emphasis on the improvement of prostate health for its members as well as all African Americans. The Fraternity leadership asked all chapters within the organization to promote awareness of prostate cancer and raise money for cancer research. Omega man, Charles A. Christopher, MD is a staff physician at Texas State University, Student Health Center. He also serves as Omega Psi Phi's Surgeon General. Researchers have determined that black males have the highest rate of prostate cancer in the world and the lowest rate of survival. In America black men are 1.5 times more likely to develop this terrible disease and are three times more likely to die of it. This is totally unacceptable!

"Everyone else is living longer" proclaims Grand Basileus Warren G. Lee, "But black men are dying sooner." Omega Psi Phi Fraternity must make a difference in the lives of black people

---

[80] Omega Psi Phi Fraternity, Inc, Internation Web site

and make a stand in correcting this problem. To this end, numerous workshops have been held to improve over-all nation wide performance with this particularly devastating cancer. Additionally, major news/press releases were initiated by Grand Basileus Lee and his Supreme Council via its Communication's Director Ben Holbert. We think the statistics pertaining to prostate cancer are alarming and we want to alert men that it is important that they get checked," said Grand Basileus Lee. Omega Psi Phi Fraternity is indeed working hard to make a difference in its community.

<<>>

In June 2007, Omega Psi Phi fraternity led by Grand Basileus Warren G. Lee demonstrates extraordinary courage and compassion by adopting the "**Stop The Violence Initiative.**" This ground breaking project will go along way in stopping domestic violence across America.

<<>>

As previously stated, **the 2007 Leadership Conference** was the most well attended of any previous Omega Leadership Conference. The 2007 conference was held in Philadelphia, PA. It was extremely informative for the Omega leadership. Guest speakers included, Coast Guard, Rear Admiral Manson K. Brown, Florida State Senator Anthony C. Hill, Former New Jersey State Attorney General, Peter C. Harvey, Esq, and Dr. Joseph E. Marshal. Workshops for the conference were Preparing for Leadership (Presenters Terrel D. Parris, Eric Lewis and Alfonso Cornish; Critical Issues Impacting African American Men (Presenters Farrel Duncombe, Rueben C. Warren and Bleu Colquitt), Medical Panel, (Presenters Dr. Charles A. Christopher and Dr. Alfred D. Dennis; Leadership In Business, (Presenters Dave Duerson, Eddie Bickham and Robb Harvey) and MSP Seminar and Lampados Club Pilot, (Presenters Keith W. Neal, Raymond Bourgeois, Dorsey Miller Jr. and Joseph T. Williams.

The men of Omega were enhanced immensely by the outstanding wealth of valuable information provided at this conference. **The ninth District, led by District Representative Willie F. Hinchen, received several top awards for its**

outstanding performance in having the highest attendance etc. at this conference.

Leadership Conferences/Workshops that were not a part of Grand Conclaves began in 1987 in New Orleans Louisiana. They have proven to be a highly effective tool in significantly improving Omega Leadership at the local and district levels. Grand Basileus Lee shared with his membership and the world his feelings regarding Omega Psi Phi Fraternities outstanding work in our community, specifically work that has sprung from our successful leadership conferences. He states, "the extraordinary success of Omega's leadership conferences have been a hallmark of Omega's commitment to the communities we serve, which is evidenced by the recent projects conducted by the organization such as:

- Partnering with the University of South Carolina to construct a two-million dollar dormitory on campus.

- Building up to 75 affordable homes in Ensley Alabama.

- Sponsoring a Celebrity Golf Tournament and Health Symposium/Fair in Jacksonville Florida.

- Funding a research project at the International Theological Center in Atlanta Ga. The theme, "Crisis Facing the Black Male."

- Sponsoring a Leadership Summit for male undergraduates in Atlanta Ga.

- Co-Sponsoring the Mid-Eastern Athletic Conference Basketball Tournament in Raleigh, N.C.

Omega Psi Phi Fraternity's outreach efforts have had significant positive impact in uplifting the Black community. One significant initiative that is currently being reviewed and piloted is the change in the Membership Intake Program to the Lampados Club. This initiative if approved and successful, will be a major change in how new members are selected and processed into Omega Psi Phi Fraternity, Inc. This initiative represents the bold new thinking of this Supreme Council. It will be up for approval consideration at the 75th Grand Conclave.

Brother John H. Williams: A Giant Among Men [81]

The second opening of the JOHN H. WILLIAMS Museum- January 26, 2007, was held at the beautiful Omega World Center (International Headquarters) at Snapfinger Drive in Decatur Georgia. This new re-opening initiative by Grand Basileus Lee and his administration prompted by the collection of newly received and found rare artifacts will be one that earns Omega praise and renown for many, many years to come. John Williams was appointed by the 29th Grand Basileus, **MARION W. GARNETT,** as Omega Psi Phi Fraternity's International Photographer, and he has retained that illustrious title since 1973.

The John Williams Museum second opening occurred during the Undergraduate Summit in Atlanta Georgia. It was a smashing success. The enormous crowd that witnessed the museum's opening was unbelievable! Cameras were flashing and all were totally enthralled at this awesome historical display of Omega Psi Phi Fraternity's golden history. Omega's former Grand Basilei and current Grand Basileus, Warren Lee signed autographs and graciously shared their pearls of wisdom with the sea of undergrads that attended the opening and adoringly

---
[81] The Oracle Summer 2000/John H. Williams

gathered around them. It was truly a thing of beauty and a shinning moment in Omega history.

Once again, Omega Psi Phi Fraternity was found leading the way for all the other Greek organizations. There is nothing out there in Greekdom that can compare to the beautiful Omega Headquarters **and now, to the new John Williams Museum.** Omega man, **JARVIS R. GREEN, at the time of this writing,** is the Chairman of the John H. Williams Museum at the international headquarters in Decatur Ga. I think the Omega brotherhood needs to know that Omega Psi Phi Fraternity has an EXTRAORDINARY "official" Omega Museum that honors famous and lesser known brothers for their achievements. For every **PERCY JULIAN** and **ERNEST E. JUST**, we have a **HILDRUS POINDEXTER**, for every "SHAQ" and **MICHAEL JORDAN**, we have a **CLARENCE 'BIG HOUSE" GAINES** and a **NEVIL SHEDD**, for every **STEVE MCNAIR** and **ED "TO TALL" JONES**, we have a **BOB FERGUSON** and **BRICE TAYLOR** and for every **COL. YOUNG, CHARLIE F. BOLDEN** and "KIP" WARD, we have a **THOMAS DENT** and a **MANSON BROWN**. Our museum covers the full spectrum of our Omega membership (undergraduate and graduate) from the very beginning to the present day. No one or segment is left out. In this, Omega men the world over, should all be proud!

All Omega men should beam with pride when they see the incredible historical display of memorabilia in the new John Williams international museum and the inspiring history that we Omega men can proudly call our own. The Colonel Young exhibit and the many other historical items displayed, are nothing short of breath taking. All Omega men should make a pilgrimage to the Omega International Headquarters and see this amazing mind blowing display of Omega history. Mere words cannot do it justice. You have got to see it for yourself. I believe the beloved Founders of Omega Psi Phi Fraternity and the world would be extremely pleased with the John Williams Museum, the extraordinary work of **JOHN H. WILLIAMS** and our leaders. This new Museum and the incredible efforts that produced it is an outstanding testament to Omega's greatness that should and will last for all time.

<<>>

Another very important initiative of the Warren G. Lee administration was the historic VIDEO INTERVIEWS AND TAPING OF ALL LIVING GRAND BASILEI in both individual and joint roundtable settings.

This historic event was accomplished on January 26, 2006 in Atlanta Georgia by the International History committee, chaired by Vernon Steve Weakley. Grand Basilei, Warren G. Lee, George H. Grace, Lloyd Jordan, Dorsey Miller Jr., C. Tyrone Gilmore, Burnel E. Coulon, Moses C. Norman, Edward Braynon and James S. Avery, participated. Pictures of this event are shown below.

These video recorded interviews (joint and individual) were extremely enlightening, inspiring, thought provoking, enthralling and nothing short of sensational. This forward thinking, Bridge Builder project is the brain child of and was initiated by Grand Basileus, Warren G. Lee. The actual interview phase of this never done before project was completed January 27th, 2007, in Atlanta Georgia during the Undergraduate Summit. **This project will enable Omega Psi Phi Fraternity Inc. to have the extraordinary combined wisdom of our legendary former Grand Basilei** to guide, inspire, instruct, enlighten and warn if necessary, our future leadership and our Omega membership for many, many years to come.

Behind the scene key International History committee members, organizers and participants in this project were, Carl A. Blunt, Curtis Lawrence (photographer and Video production manager), Reginald E. Vance, Lee Bernard Jr. Curt Childers, Michael Lyles, Kevin Rolle and Vernon (Bop Swalos) Weakley, project chairman. Charles Johnson of Theta Alpha chapter and Dylan Bess were the interviewers for this historic undertaking.

<<>>

March 2007, Omega Charities honors active Omega Men in the field of Sports and Entertainment As Lifetime Achievers at the 2007 NBA All-star Game

Honorees are as follows:

Vince Carter
Michael Jordan
Alonzo Mourning
John Salley

Bill Cosby
Steve Harvey
Shaquille O'Neal
Ricky Smiley
Maurice "Mo" Vaugh

Joe Torre
Steve McNair
Ahmad Rashad
Terrence Trammel

<<>>

FIRST VICE GRAND BASILEUS
Brother Carl A. Blunt

Brother Blunt was initiated into Omega Psi Phi Fraternity through Sigma Iota chapter in Oakland, California on April 7th, 1978. He "came up" through the ranks of Omega by serving in extraordinary fashion in many positions in Omega at the local, district and national level. He was elected and served as the 12th District Representative an unprecedented two non-consecutive terms. He was the 12th District DR at the Cleveland, New Orleans and Indianapolis Conclaves and is on the cornerstone of the IHQ building. These are extraordinary accomplishments. First Vice Grand Basileus Blunt has served on the Supreme Council under five different Grand Basilei and as the International Social Action Chairman. Prior to his selection as First Vice Grand Basileus, he served as Grand Keeper of Finance. His financial genius and years of mortgage financing experience played a role in the great financial success of the Grace administration.

First Vice Grand Basileus Blunt has been a tremendous partner, help mate and asset for Grand Basileus Lee in this administration. Understanding that he is only a heart beat away from the chief executive officer position in Omega, all of Omega breathes easy knowing that the organization would not skip a beat with Carl Blunt at the helm. He is extremely knowledgeable, fiercely dedicated to Omega, popular with the membership, known for his hard work and creativity, has very high standards of excellence, is self motivated, and is a born leader who is highly regarded throughout the organization as a brother's brother. He is, as Grand Basileus Lee was under former Grand Basileus George Grace, an intricate part of the amazing success of this administration.

A copy of Vice Grand Basileus Blunt's Summary Report for the 2008 District Meetings is as follows:

LEADERSHIP

Performed all First Vice Grand Basileus duties as required by the Constitution and as directed by the Grand Basileus which included:

1. Managed & Chaired the Philadelphia Leadership Conference Committee, which delivered the largest Conference to date, with over 760 registered brothers.

2. Chaired International. Committee meeting during the Leadership Conference, with 100% of Chairmen reporting.

3. Chaired Reception Committee that successfully hosted over 150 SG Rho's @ IHQ during their 85thCelebration.

4. Coordinated w/ Centennial Committee to develop fundraising proposals for 2011.

5. Coordinated w/ Omega Museum committee to create an "Omega's In Civil Rights" exhibit for 2008 Conclave.

6. Organized the successful delivery of "Custom "Converse shoes to the brotherhood & coordinated w/ UG Council to successfully submit names for the Converse Summer Intern Program.

7. Conducted FVDR Officer Training & Conference calls. Organization & Coordination

FIRST VICE GRAND BASILEUS SUMMARY

•Cooperation and honest communication was the major reason for successful projects.
•Everyone I called on delivered and proved that "Brothers in true Brotherhood is still the Fraternity's # 1 Asset". Thanks for your continued support, and I again ask for your vote to re-elect me in Birmingham as your First Vice Grand Basileus. I remain yours in Friendship & Fraternity.

             Carl A. Blunt

<<>>

2nd Vice Grand Basileus
Brian S. Gundy

Additionally, of particular encouraging and historical note during this administration was the outstanding performance of Brother Brian S. Gundy who was elected 2nd Vice Grand Basileus of Omega Psi Phi Fraternity, Inc, at the 74th Grand Conclave in Little Rock Arkansas in July 2006. During his tenure in this position, he helped to galvanize the undergraduate brothers and be an effective voice for them bridging the gap between new school and old school with his frankness and extraordinary leadership.

Brian Gundy was initiated into Omega Psi Phi fraternity at Gamma Gamma chapter at Grambling University IN SPRING 2003. His election was an extraordinary uplift to undergraduate brothers internationally given his strong leadership, dedication to excellence, hard work, openness, outstanding intelligence, team building skills, vision and analytical insight. This brilliant, up and coming young Omega super star epitomizes the germ of greatness as well as the realized and future dreams of Omega Psi Phi Fraternity's that our beloved Founders Ernest E. Just, Oscar J. Cooper, Edgar A. Love and Frank Coleman envisioned. We expect even greater things from Brian S. Gundy where Omega is concerned long into the future.

Another two outstanding and impressive successes of the Warren Lee administration involved the highly successful and well organized 2006 and 2007 Undergraduate Summits that were held in Atlanta Georgia in January of the respective years. Both summits were very well attended. Theses meeting were presided over by Second Vice Grand Basileus Brian S. Gundy, **Bro. BENJAMIN L. HART** (7th District) **Bro. JOSEPH F. BOWERS, Jr.** (10th District) **Bro. JAMES McKOY** (6th District). Undergraduate members left energized and renewed with the Omega spirit and the enormous information they received at these productive meetings.

OMEGA'S FUTURE IS LOOKING VERY BRIGHT!

The Warren G. Lee administration has, to the date of this writing, done great things for Omega Psi Phi Fraternity Inc.

Its success is due to the hard work of Grand Basileus Lee and his superb grand officers and Supreme Council members.

<<>>

38TH Grand Basileus, Warren G. Lee was re-elected for a second term at the 75th Grand Conclave in Birmingham Alabama.

Grand Officers re-elected or elected with him were:

Carl A. Blunt - 1st Vice GRAND BASILEUS; Jamin Powell - 2nd Vice Grand Basileus; Lewis Anderson – Grand Keeper of Records and Seal; Antonio F. Knox – Grand Keeper of Finance; Michael R. Adams - Grand Counselor; Ferrel Duncombe – Grand Chaplain; Under Graduate Immediate Rep; Philip Merchant – Under Graduate Immediate Rep; James Swinson – Under Graduate Immediate Rep – Alexander Gibson; George H. Grace - Immediate Past Grand Basileus;

DISTRICT REPRESENTATIVES

1st District - Carlton Pickeron; 2nd District - James W. (Scappy) Jordan; 3rd District - Mark E. Jackson; 4th District - Dewey Ortiz; 5th District - Edward C. Morant; 6th District - Octavio Miro; 7th District - Keith R. Jackson; 8th District – Glenn E. Rice; 9th District – Willie F. Hinchen; 10th District – Climent J. Edmond, Jr.; 12th District – Charles C. Peevy; 13th District - Jonathan N. Griffin, Sr.

<<>>

On January 14th, 1963, Alabama Governor, George C. Wallace (a well known segregationist at the time) gave a speech that contained the racist statement, "Segregation Now, Segregation Tomorrow, and Segregation Forever." The 2007 Leadership Conference Theme; Leadership, Today Tomorrow and Forever" was a play on that statement and a reminder that only 45 years since that speech, members and families of Omega Psi Phi Fraternity, Inc. converged on Birmingham Alabama for the 75th Grand Conclave in July 2008, having long since defeated legal segregation. This and many similar actions like this are a testament to the relevance of Omega Psi Phi Fraternity in our modern day society.

The 75th Grand Conclave was held in Birmingham Alabama in July 2008. More than 10,000 members of Omega Psi Phi fraternity Inc. came to Birmingham for this conclave. It was held from July 10-17. The host chapter was Alpha Phi of Birmingham. The Grand Marshal for this conclave was brother **WALTER BODY**.

The city opened its heart to Omega and with that was showered in a beautiful sea of purple and gold. The 75th Conclave began on July 11th, with a Career and Health Fair and was followed by a concert by the nationally known artists Joe and Zap.

One of several highlights of this conclave was the "Omega Men in the Civil Rights Struggle" exhibit that was displayed at the Birmingham Civil Rights Institute. It was an awesome display of civil rights accomplishments and contributions. Omega men who have played significant roles were dignified and saluted in an elaborate grand visual wall display in the museum. This highly successful effort was led by First Vice Grand Basileus Carl A. Blunt along with a special committee composed of Keath Neal, Jarvis Green, and others. Brother Vice Grand stated, " According to Dreer, the first historic step the Founders took in establishing this great fraternity was to select men that after graduation were going back into their communities to take up positions of leadership to combat the injustices and discrimination that were barriers to human progress. What better place than Birmingham, which is highly regarded as a starting spark for the civil rights movement, to honor and remember those that went before us." The extraordinary bravery and efforts of the great Omega Men displayed will ring for all time in the annals of American history. Let there be no doubt that Omega Psi Phi Fraternity Inc. has done its part in making a difference in the lives of Black people.

On July 12th, a Comedy Show and Step Competition was hosted by internationally known comedian and Omega man, **RICKY SMILEY.**

SMILEY TORE DOWN THE HOUSE WITH HIS FUNNY ANTICS! The competing brothers from all across the nation, of course, were true to long standing Omega stepping excellence by putting on shows that kept the enormous crowd electrified.

During this conclave, Omega Psi Phi Fraternity, in its long standing tradition, also held a Youth Leadership Conference at Miles College. It was well attended by over 150 eager and bright eyed high school age young men from all over the country. Additionally, Omega Psi Phi Fraternity held several community service projects throughout Birmingham during the conclave that included blood drives, the rehabilitation of three houses and a very well received project that involved Omega Psi Phi Fraternity Inc. generously opening up its heart, yet again, and providing a week's worth of groceries to over 400 needy families in the Birmingham area.

This Conclave also included an off sight bus trip to Selma Alabama by hundreds of Omega men and their families to re-trace the steps of those who endured the "Bloody Sunday March" on March 7, 1965, by making a symbolic walk across the Edmund Pettus Bridge and also attending the Brown Chapel A.M.E. Church which was a staging point for this famous march. Both events were powerful reminders of the struggle and the courage and efforts of those who actually participated in the march. In Addition, bus loads of Conclave participants and their families took an enthralling journey back in time to the Slavery and Civil War Museum in Selma. This tour was nothing short of incredible.

Historians view the 1965 Selma to Montgomery Voting Rights March as one of the last great grassroots campaigns for human rights and as the summit of the modern civil rights movement that originated in the 1950s. This off site tour ended with Omega men and their families visiting the Montgomery State capitol area and while there hearing rousing speeches from Omega men Tony Hill of the Florida State Senate, and Alabama's own Fred Gray, a legendary civil rights icon and Omega man, just to name a few.

Special thanks was given from Omega Psi Phi leadership to Brother **LARRY DANCY**, Chairman Historic Site Tour Committee, Brother **RAYFORD MACK**, Alabama State

Representative, **COLLIN PETTAWAY**-Basileus of Omega Chi Chapter, Robert Smiley-Basileus of Omega Iota, Iota Chapter, Rev. **FERREL DUNCOMBE**–Grand Chaplin and Basileus Sigma Phi Chapter, and **HOWARD ROBINSON**, History and Archives Chairman, State of Alabama for making the Selma to Montgomery Historic tour a memorable experience for Omega Psi Phi Fraternity during the 75th Conclave.

<<>>

The speaker at the 75th Grand Conclave Undergraduate Luncheon was Brother **ROBERT HOLMES**, Senior Vice President for Ethics and Cooperate Concerns Alabama Power and Light. His speech was uplifting and enlightening. Brother Holmes challenged our undergrads to strive to achieve higher heights.

<<>>

Special thanks was given from Omega Psi Phi leadership to brother **LARRY DANCY**, Chairman Historic Site Tour Committee, brother **RAYFORD MACK**, Alabama State Representative, **COLLIN PETTAWAY**-Basileus of Omega Chi chapter, Robert Smiley-Basileus of Omega Iota, Iota chapter, Rev. **FERREL DUNCOMBE**–Grand Chaplin and Basileus Sigma Phi chapter, and **HOWARD ROBINSON**, History and Archives Chairman, State of Alabama for making the Selma to Montgomery Historic tour a memorable experience for Omega Psi Phi Fraternity during the 75th Conclave.

<<>>

The speaker at the 75th Grand Conclave Undergraduate Luncheon was brother **ROBERT HOLMES**, Senior Vice President for Ethics and Cooperate Concerns, Alabama Power and Light. His speech was uplifting and enlightening. Brother Holmes challenged our undergrads to strive to achieve higher heights.

<<>>

PERTINENT RECOMMENDATIONS APPROVED AND/OR NOT APPROVED AT THE 75TH GRAND CONCLAVE :[82]

-. Lampados Program (not Club) was passed with the current MSP eligible (2.5, 36 credits)

- Mobility of National Undergraduate Summit - want to rotate it throughout the country. FAILED (Result - will continue to be held in Decatur/Atlanta)

- Grandfather Housing Assessment - FAILED (Result -All brothers still responsible for paying or providing proof of payment)

- Undergraduate Advisor of the Year Award - PASSED (Result - create new award recognizing the Advisor of the Year).

- 60 Year Registration Waiver - PASSED (Result- brothers that have been active for 60 years will not have to pay to register for District and National Meetings).

- Proposed Budget to be provided 30 days before Conclave - PASSED (Result - report to be provided to chapters 30 days before Conclave so it can be properly reviewed PRIOR to the Conclave)

- Due Process Expulsion - PASSED. - Brother shall not be limited in his membership rights and privileges without being afforded due process with respect to allegations made against him. Prior to any expulsion or suspension, a Brother shall be afforded written notice of the allegations against him sent to his last known address by certified mail, return receipt and a hearing pursuant to the Fraternity's Member Code of Conduct and Disciplinary Policy. The Supreme Council shall have exclusive authority to expel any Brother from the Fraternity. If any member of the Supreme Council has initiated or approved the charges against the Brother, that member(s) shall be precluded from voting for any reason in regards to the Supreme Council's decision as to

---

[82] Goldboot Digest #2421/GoldbootQue@aol.com <GoldbootQue@aol.com/Bro. John Berkley, Basileus Pi Omega Chapter, Baltimore

expulsion.) Submitted by 12th District Counselor Lawton Connelly.

- One Man One Vote - Committee ruled this one was not presented by the deadline (120 days before Conclave). Will be considered at next Conclave.

OTHER ISSUES PRESENTED:

Lampado's Club - PASSED (Result - New Lampados Club will be implemented starting September 2009. Until then, ALL Chapters must perform MSP for initiation, including former Lampado's Club Pilot program chapters.)

- Fraternity Assessment - PASSED. (Result - There will be an assessment/review of the Fraternity's way we conduct business, IHQ operations, Executive Director duties required, etc., to determine the changes needed.)

<<>>

SIGNIFICANT OMEGA EVENTS AND/OR ACCOMPLISHMENTS DURING THIS PERIOD:

RICHARD "DICK" SMITH, Assistant Executive Director of Omega Psi Phi Fraternity enters into Omega Chapter on November 5, 2006. He was a tireless and dedicated worker for

Omega Psi Phi Fraternity at the international office up until his retirement and even up until his untimely death. Dick Smith was also very instrumental in establishing Omega chapters in Europe.
Brother Smith, among many of the honors he held, was also the Theta Rho International Chapter's "Omega Man of the Year in 1988." He also received the Department of the prestigious Army's Commander's Award for Public Service in 1991. Brother Smith served as president of the NAACP in Frankfort Germany from 1981 to 1987. This was the oldest and largest NAACP chapter outside of the U.S. He was initiated into Omega Psi Phi fraternity in 1954, via Eta chapter at Alcorn State University.

COLONE PEARSON, Nu Omega Chapter member, former Chairman of the Detroit Omega Foundation, Inc. (DOFI), and Executive Director of DOFI, transitioned to Omega Chapter. He entered Omega Chapter at 12 Noon on 12-14-2006 in Detroit. He was made (initiated into Omega Psi Phi Fraternity) in 1968 at Delaware State and was active in grad chapters in Connecticut, Psi Nu in Alexandria, VA. He was active in Nu Omega for 12 years up until his death.

The highly successful movie "Stomp The Yard" breaks onto the movie screen and creates an enormous interest in the public and movie going scene where stepping is concerned. **Brother GREGORY ANDERSON was initiated at Upsilon Psi Chapter of Omega Psi Phi Fraternity, Inc. on the campus of Florida A&M University, summer, 1994.** His screenplay writer project "Stomp the Yard" acts as the spark to bring this heretofore African American fraternity art form to the public eye. Writer, producer and distributor, Omega man Gregory Anderson, was the driving creative force behind the number one movie for two weeks at the box office in 2006. Anderson's Stomp the Yard documented him as the first African-American writer to have a film based on a screenplay that placed number one at the box office.

<<>>

***HERBERT E. TUCKER JR.,** the 23rd Grand Basileus of Omega Psi Phi Fraternity Inc. entered Omega chapter March 1st, 2007. Grand Basileus Tucker was an electrifying force while in Omega Psi Phi Fraternity, especially where leading its members to stand up and take action against resource. A mass of people without training, without polish, without direction, without leadership is no more useful than un-mined ore he explained! "

Although this incredibly powerful and courageous force has gone from us to Omega Chapter, his words and teaching will never be forgotten by the men of Omega Psi Phi Fraternity.

Gaining a reputation as an extraordinary judge in the judicial system for many many years, Judge Herbert E. Tucker, Jr., was born in Boston on August 30, 1915. After graduating from the Boston Latin School, Tucker attended Northeastern School of Law, earning his J.D.

In 1960, Brother Tucker was appointed by Senator John F. Kennedy to the civil rights section of his 1960 presidential campaign. In 1969, Tucker became commissioner of the Massachusetts Department of Public Utilities and was named chairman in 1972. The following year, Brother was named special justice to the Municipal Court of Dorchester, and in 1974 he became the presiding justice of the district. Leaving Dorchester, Tucker became the presiding judge of the Edjartown District Court in 1979, where he remained until his retirement in 1985. Tucker served with distinction as the Grand Basileus of Omega Psi Phi Fraternity from 1955 to 1958.

<<>>

March 2007, Omega Man **SAMUEL C. HUNTER Jr.** received **the Congressional Gold Medal** at Tuskegee Airmen Ceremony. He at the time of this writing is one of only a few living original members of the heroic and legendary Tuskegee Airmen. Brother Hunter was initiated into Omega **On the 9th day of December, 1937, at West Virginia State College, through Theta Psi Chapter.** He is, as of this writing, a founder and an active member of the Xi Pi chapter.

<<>>

The movie, **"The Great Debaters"** held the number #1 movie rating for several weeks in 2007. Its primary focus, A highly controversial figure, challenging the social issues of the time, **Professor MELVIN TOLSON an Omega man initiated** at Beta chapter. (played by popular actor Denzel Washington) He used unconventional and ferocious teaching methods to shape a highly decorated debate team at Wiley College, a small African American university in Texas during the 1930s. Fighting against all odds and paving their way to success, the team reaches a pivotal moment when they are faced with one of their greatest challenges yet: going up against Harvard University's critically acclaimed national championship debate team.

<<>>

Omega man, **KENNETH L. HALE** receives the NAACP Military Award, Xi Alpha Chapter in Charleston, WV. Brother

Major Kenneth L. Hale, was presented the Roy L. Wilkins Renown Service Award by the NAACP on July 18, 2006 during the groups' 31st Annual Armed Services and Veterans Affairs Awards Dinner in Washington, D.C.

Brother Hale's father was a member of the Tuskegee Airmen, a group of dedicated young black men who enlisted at a time when many thought black men lacked the skill and intelligence to be military aviators. History debunked this myth, and men like Hale's father became known as pioneers in the fight for freedom – against the Axis powers overseas and against racism and prejudice at home. According to Brother Hale, the Buffalo Soldiers and Tuskegee Airmen were trail blazers in the fight for equal rights in the military and true African-American patriots. "It makes me very proud to know that I stand on the shoulders of those who've gone before me," he said. Brother Hale is among a distinguished group of military members to receive the Wilkins award.

<<>>

LEGENDARY JAZZ DRUMMER, MAX ROACH, an Omega man, enters Omega chapter August 16th, 2007 in New York at the age of 83.

<<>>

Brother Edward Hanas Taylor

EDDIE H. TAYLOR enters Omega chapter September 07th, 2007. Born Tuesday January 12, 1909 in Brooklyn, New York, Brother Edward H. Taylor was duly initiated on Saturday November 17, 1928 into the Omega Psi Phi Fraternity, Incorporated through Alpha Chapter, at Howard University in

Washington, D.C. At the time of his unfortunate death due to illness, he was the oldest living member of Omega Psi Phi Fraternity Inc for many years. This was a distinction that Eddie Taylor said he really enjoyed.

In November 1949, Brother Taylor, along with other distinguished Omega Men, helped to charter Alpha Upsilon Chapter to serve as the graduate chapter in Brooklyn, New York, where he served as the Basileus for two years, and the Keeper of Records and Seal for thirty years. Brother Taylor served as the Chaplain and Keeper of Records and Seal Emeritus for Alpha Upsilon Chapter and as a Special Advisor to the Second District Representative. Outside of Omega, Brother Taylor faithfully served as a teacher and guidance counselor for the New York City Board of Education for thirty-four years.

Up until May 2006, Brother Taylor had not missed a Chapter meeting with Alpha Upsilon Chapter since 1950. He always sat in the front row to keep the Basileus in line. In 1959, Brother Taylor served as the New York City Grand Conclave Grand Marshal.

Brother Taylor has been honored or received the following awards and distinctions: Omega Man of the Year, Zeta Psi Chapter 1967; Forty Year Award, Conclave Charlotte, NC 1968; Omega Man of the Year, Alpha Upsilon Chapter, 1970 and 1984; Fifty Year Award, Conclave New Orleans, LA 1978; Sixty Year Award, Conclave Dallas, TX 1988; Founders Award – Stand in for Brother Love at the Second District conference 1989; Seventy Year Award, Conclave New Orleans, LA 1998; Brother Grant Reynolds Lifetime of Courage Award 1999; Special Honoree, Alpha Upsilon Chapter 50th Anniversary 1999; Iota Xi Chapter Award 2000; Outstanding Participation Award, Zeta Theta Chapter 2001; Outstanding Service to Omega Award, Theta Omicron Chapter 2001; Undergraduate Summit – Keynote Speaker 2003; Supreme Council – Keynote Speaker 2003; Special Honoree, Alpha Upsilon Chapter 55th Anniversary 2004.

*In 2004, Alpha Upsilon Chapter established the Brother Edward H. Taylor Lifetime Achievement Award to serve as Brother Taylor's Legacy in the Chapter and the Fraternity in recognition of his many years of service and deeds to Omega. This recognition is to be awarded to Men affiliated with Alpha Upsilon Chapter who have served Omega faithfully and tirelessly for at least twenty-five years, and embody the Cardinal Principals of Manhood, Scholarship, Perseverance and Uplift.

No biography could ever adequately capture the true essence of what Brother Taylor has done for Omega throughout his seventy-eight years of loyal service to her. Brother Taylor held the distinction of being the oldest living active and financial member of our Omega Dear at the time of his death, and we hope and pray to the Supreme Basileus of the Universe that this is a distinction that he holds for many years to come.

<<>>

On October 1st, 2007, Omega man, **Brother GENERAL KIP WARD** became the first Commanding General for the United States Army African Command. (AFRICOM)

<<>>

35th Grand Basileus, **DORSEY C. MILLER**, JR. received U.S. Census Bureau Appointment, in 2007 for the 2010 Census.

<<>>

Omega man, **SEAN P. HOGGS** named one of the top ten 2007 Outstanding Young Man of the Year by the United States Junior Chamber (Jaycees), September 22, 2007.

<<>>

* It is with deep regret that we inform the WORLD AND MOST ESPECIALLY the loyal membership of Omega Psi Phi Fraternity of the passing of **Mrs. Willa Mae Cooper-Hampton, the widow of our Founder Oscar J. Cooper on January 24, 2008.** She was 89 years old. Funeral Services was held on Monday, January 28, 2008, 10:30AM At the African Episcopal Church of Saint Thomas, 6361 Lancaster Ave Philadelphia, PA 19151.

<<>>

JEREMIAH A. WRIGHT, JR. (born September 22, 1941) an Omega man, (1960, Zeta Chapter, Virginia Union University, and current Life Member). is a former pastor of the Trinity United Church of Christ (TUCC), a megachurch in Chicago with around 10,000 members. In early 2008, Wright retired after 36 years as the pastor of his congregation.[1][2] Following retirement, Wright's beliefs and manner of preaching were scrutinized when segments from his sermons were publicized in connection with presidential candidate Barrack Obama. Obama addressed the matter in his "A More Perfect Union" speech. To lay his actual positions on various social issues before the nation, Rev.Wright gave a speech before the NAACP on April 27th, 2008.

April 28th, 2008 Reverend Dr. **JEREMIAH A. WRIGHT JR.,** an Omega man, and former pastor of democratic presidential candidate Barrack Obama, in a nationally publicized Washington D.C. Meet the Press interview makes comments that cause Barrack Obama to publicly distance and completely separate himself from him. During the press conference Jeremiah Wright flashed an Omega sign that makes the cover of front pages of many major newspapers and television programs all across America. In previous frequently nationally publicized sound bites that had been viewed, Jeremiah Wright comes to national prominence as it relates to his relationship with presidential candidate Barrack Obama. He completely dominates talk radio and all U.S television airways for a significant period with his revelations about many serious issues such as the role of the Black church, the difference between the races, etc.

<<>>

Rep. **JAMES E. CLYBURN** of South Carolina (a member of Omega Psi Phi), the highest-ranking black member of Congress, publicly announces his support for presidential candidate Barack Obama in May 2008.

<<>>

On June 03, 2008 Barack Obama in a very hard fought battle with Senator Hillary Clinton, the last candidate standing and many other previous candidates for the presidency of the United States, reaches the required number of primary delegates to become the presumptive Democratic nominee for President of the Unites States of America. He is the first man of African American descent to achieve this honor. Many (both black and white and other wise) in America and across the world, celebrated this extraordinary first.

On September 2nd, 2008, Barack Obama officially received the presidential nomination from the Democratic National Convention. It is the first time in American history that an African American was nominated FOR PRESIDENT by a major political party in the United States.

*****Omega Psi Phi Fraternity, Inc. via its leadership led by Grand Basileus Warren G. Lee, publicly and officially endorses Barack Obama on**

September 2008 for President of the United States of America.

Barack Obama's candidacy was aggressively supported by the men of Omega Psi Phi Fraternity. In this, we believe, the beloved Founders of Omega Psi Phi Fraternity, in us, would be well pleased. Grand Basileus Warren G. Lee proudly and courageously led thousands of Omega men in stellar fashion in this glorious historic cause.

Below is a letter from the Grand Basileus to the Omega membership encouraging all Omega men to step to the fore and do their duty to vote in this historic election.

Brothers:

On Thursday, October 16, 2008, we held our first National Chapter Basileus conference call. The call was a joint effort between Omega Psi Phi Fraternity and the Barack Obama Campaign. **Now, it is time for action!**

As I said on the call, I am also encouraging you to work within your sphere of influence to get out the vote. Make sure your eligible family members, church members, neighbors, and friends are committed to voting in this election. We can impact the outcome of this election by continuing our voter education efforts, and by going to the polls in record numbers.

When the votes are tallied, I want to report, with confidence,

100% of our active Omega men voted in this election!
If you are already volunteering with a campaign, please send an email to communications@oppf.org and include your Name and control number, Chapter, Name of the campaign you are working with, Location (City, ST, Zip)
Alternatively, go to http://www.surveymonkey.com/s.aspx?sm=2FyDTRhRe4Sx8x79sKWXGQ_3d_3d and complete the survey there.

If you are not working with a campaign and you are interested in doing so, please go to www.voteforchange.com and sign up. When you have signed up, then go to http://www.surveymonkey.com/s.aspx?sm=2FyDTRhRe4Sx8x79sKWXGQ_3d_3d and complete the survey there.

Brothers who are Attorneys could assist with Voter Protection Program. Lawyers will be deployed across the country to monitor all voter activities and address matters such as
voter disenfranchisement, fraud, intimidation, etc. Voters can report irregularities via hotline or website. Training will be provided for lawyers interested in participating. Please contact former Grand Basileus, Lloyd Jordan at loyd.jordan@hklaw.com or our Grand Counselor, Michael Adams at michael@decuirlaw.com .

Fraternally,
Warren G. Lee, Jr.
38th Grand Basileus
Omega Psi Phi Fraternity, Inc.

On November 04th, 2008, Barack Obama was elected President of the United States of America.

This was indeed a historic day for all Americans, but most especially it was a very special day for all African Americans. The world also openly celebrated this event. Our beloved Founders, Ernest E. Just, Edgar A Love, Frank Coleman and Oscar Cooper, would most certainly be pleased with this extraordinary accomplishment.

Omega Psi Phi Fraternity's position from 38th Grand Basileus Warren G. Lee:

November 4, 2008

Brothers:

It's Official!

We have a new President. History will record that the men of Omega Psi Phi Fraternity, Inc. played a pivotal role in the Presidential Election of 2008.

I am very pleased that we have actively participated in the election process in our communities. Across the country, we have helped to register voters, conducted voter education seminars and given of our time and resources to get citizens to the polls.

I applaud you and thank you for coming together to galvanize our efforts on a very significant project. Now I encourage you to let your voices be heard as we move steadily toward another historic milestone – Our Centennial Celebration. Just as we needed every Omega Man to make this Presidential election a memorable one, we also need every Omega Man to make our Centennial a memorable one.

Now it is time for a reconciliation strategy for our country. I expect that we will be an integral part of that conversation as well. The only question is – "How much of a difference do you want to make in the lives of our people and all of humanity?" The only answer is – "Yes, we can!"

Yours in Friendship and Fraternity,

Warren G. Lee, Jr.

Warren G. Lee, Jr.

38th Grand Basileus

Omega Psi Phi Fraternity, Inc.[83]

This Omega Psi Phi History Book Update revision will end here on November 04th, 2008 on the election date of the first African American President, Barack Obama. Omega Psi Phi Fraternity and its members proudly and publicly endorsed his historic selection as President of the United States of America. **Omega Psi Phi Fraternity's** glorious history from this point forward is yet to be written. It will unfold however, right before our eyes. We all will be intricate parts of it and bare witness to it as it reveals itself.

<<>>

---

[83] Official Omega Psi Phi Fraternity Inc. International Website

OMEGA PSI PHI FRATERNITY INC.
PROUDLY MAKING A DIFFERENCE IN THE LIVES OF BLACK PEOPLE!

Long Live Omega Psi Phi Fraternity Inc.

AND WITH IT THE DREAM OF ITS GREAT FOUNDERS

Ernest E. Just
    Edgar A. Love
        Frank Coleman
           Oscar J. Cooper

<<>>

ALL PRAISE BE TO THE SUPREME BASILEUS OF THE UNIVERSE FOR BLESSING AND PRESERVING OUR BELOVED FRATERNITY.

<<>>

APPENDIX SECTION

APPENDIX A

THE SUPREME COUNCIL OF THE OMEGA PSI PHI FRATERNITY(*ELECTED AT THE 2008, 75TH GRAND CONCLAVE IN BIRMINGHAM, ALABAMA

GRAND OFFICERS

Warren G. Lee Jr.
Grand Basileus

Carl A. Blunt
First Vice Grand Basileus

Jamin Powell
Second Vice Grand Basileus

Lewis Anderson
Grand Keeper of Records and Seal

Antonio F. Knox
Grand Keeper of Finance

Rev. Farrell Duncombe
Grand Chaplain

Michael R. Adams
Grand Counselor

Walter Body
Grand Marshal

George H. Grace
Immediate Past (37th)Grand Basileus

Lloyd Jordan ESQ.
36th Grand Basileus

Dr. Dorsey Miller
35th Grand Basileus

C. Tyrone Gilmore, SR
34th Grand Basileus

Dr. Moses C. Norman
33rd Grand Basileus

Burnel E. Coulon
31st Grand Basileus

Dr. Edward Braynon, Jr.
30th Grand Basileus

James Avery
28th Grand Basileus

UNDERGRADUATE REPRESENTATIVES

Alexander Gibson
Undergrad/Intermediate Rep.

Phillip Merchant
Undergrad/Intermediate Rep.

James Swinson
Undergrad/Intermediate Rep.

DISTRICT REPRESENTATIVES

Carlton Pickron
1st District Representative

James W. Jordan
2nd District Representative

Mark E. Jackson
3rd District Representative

Dewey Ortiz
4th District Representative

Edward C. Morant
5th District Representative

Octavio Miro
6th District Representative

Keith R. Jackson
7th District Representative

Glenn E. Rice
8th District Representative

Willie F. Hinchen
9th District Representative

Climent J. Edmond, Jr.
10th District Representative

Charles C. Peevy
12th District Representative

Johnathan N. Griffin, Sr.
13th District Representative

THE SUPREME COUNCIL OF THE OMEGA PSI PHI FRATERNITY (*ELECTED SHOWN) (2006, 74TH GRAND CONCLAVE)

WARREN G. LEE JR. - GRAND BASILEUS
4708 FOREST BEND ROAD
DALLAS, TX 75244
OMEGAWARRENLEE@OPPF.COM
QUETTE – LORAINE

CARL A. BLUNT - 1ST VICE GRAND BASILEUS
8912 E. PINNACLE PEAK ROAD
SUITE 413
SCOTTSDALE, AZ 85255-3649
QSIGHCAB@AOL.COM
QUETTE- JACQUELINE

BRIAN S. GUNDY - 2ND VICE GRAND BASILEUS
P O. BOX 1070
GRAMBLING, LA 71245
BGUNDY71245@YAHOO.COM

CHARLES A. BRUCE – GRAND KEEPER OF RECORDS AND SEAL
421 FORSHEER DRIVE
CHESTERFIELD, MO 63017
CHARLES.BRUCE@EMOTORS.COM
QUETTE - SANDRA

ANTONIO F. KNOX – GRAND KEEPER OF FINANCE
2304 HOOT OWL COURT
RALEIGH, NC 27603
TONYKNOXSR@YAHOO.COM
QUETTE-ANGELA

MICHAEL R. ADAMS.- GRAND COUNSELOR
5536 VALLEY FORGE AVENUE
BATON ROUGE, LA 70808
MICHAEL@DECUIRLAW.COM
QUETTE-BRUNETTA

JOSEPH F. BOWERS JR. - UNDERGRADUATE REPRESENTATIVE
22412 RAY
DETROIT, MI 48223
DOCTOR_JOSEPH_BOWERS@MAIL.COM
JOSEPH-BOWERSJR@HOTMAIL.COM

BENJAMIN L. HART - UNDERGRADUATE REPRESENTATIVE
411 CHANDLER ST
INVERNESS, MS 38753
MAILING ADDRESS:
1914 SHADY LANE
JACKSON, MS 39204
OMEGALOVE_3@YAHOO.COM

JAMES MCKOY - UNDERGRADUATE REPRESENTATVE
5114 COPPER RIDGE DRIVE
APT. 302
DURHAM, NC 27707
MCKOY6TP04@YAHOO.COM

GEORGE H. GRACE - IMMEDIATE PAST GRAND BASILEUS
P. O. BOX 970187
MIAMI, FL 33157
QUEGRACE@BELLSOUTH.NET

OMEGAGRACE@AOL.COM
QUETTE – BARBARA

REV. FARRELL DUNCOMBE- GRAND CHAPLAIN
4271 LAWNWOOD DRIVE
MONTGOMERY, AL 36108
DUNCOMBE1@AOL.COM
QUETTE – JUANITA

GRAND MARSHAL-74TH GRAND CONCLAVE
Brother Derek Lewis - Little Rock, Arkansas

<<>>

74TH GRAND CONCLAVE DISTRICT REPRESENTATIVES

VAUGHN M. WILLIS - 1ST DISTRICT REPRESENTATIVE
53 ROBIN HILL LANE
HAMDEN, CT 06518
(VEELOVE88@AOL.COM

MARVIN C. DILLARD- 2ND DISTRICT REPRESENTATIVE
284 KATHERINE STREET
ENGLEWOOD, NJ 07631
MARVINDILLARD@YAHOO.COM
QUETTE – ROBIN

MARK E. JACKSON - 3RD DISTRICT REPRESENTATIVE
4314 4TH STREET, NW
WASHINGTON, DC 20011-7302
MARK.JACKSON@BTA.MIL
OMEGA2000@AOL.COM
QUETTE – LASONYA

JESSE JUNIUS - 4TH DISTRICT REPRESENTATIVE
1470 CORNELL DRIVE
DAYTON, OH 45406
JUNIUS.JESSE@MBCO.COM
JJJJUNO@AOL.COM
QUETTE – CAROLYN

HORACE W. CHASE-5TH DISTRICT REPRESENTATIVE
49 BRIDLEWOOD COVE
JACKSON, TN 38305

HCHASE@JSCC.EDU
QUETTE – BARBARA

CHARLES J. WORTH. - 6TH DISTRICT REPRESENTATIVE
P.O. BOX 411
MANSON, NC 27553
AGGIEWORTHQUE@AOL.COM

JOSEPH T. WILLIAMS - 7TH DISTRICT REPRESENTATIVE
103 PINE STREET
TUSKEGEE, AL 36083
JTWILLQ@BELLSOUTH.NET

JEFFREY T. SMITH - 8TH DISTRICT REPRESENTATIVE
4935 URSULA WAY
DENVER, CO 80239
(303) 513-4437 - CELL
JSMITTYQUE@YAHOO.COM
QUETTE - SHELIA

TODD S. CLEMONS - 9TH DISTRICT REPRESENTATIVE
4208 BEAU CHENE DRIVE
LAKE CHARLES, LA 70605
(TODD.CLEMONS@USDOJ.GOV
QUETTE – STEFANIE O.

GLENN A. MATTHEWS-10TH DISTRICT REPRESENTATIVE
2601 N 9TH ST
MILWAUKEE, WI 53206
GMQUE1@AOL.COM
GLENN.MATHEWS@PHOENIX.EDU

CHARLES C. PEEVY -12TH DISTRICT REPRESENTATIVE
1344 E SAN REMO AVE
GILBERT, AZ 85234-8715
CCPEEVY1@MINDSPRING.COM

JONATHAN N. GRIFFIN SR. - 13TH DISTRICT REPRESENTATIVE
CMR 480 BOX 7
APO, AE 09128
JONATHANGRIFFIN0@MSN.COM
J-SGRIFFIN1@T-ONLINE.DE
QUETTE - SHARRON

<<>>

DISTRICT REPRESENTATIVES ON 06/03/08

Carlton Pickeron
1st District Representative

James W. (Scrappy) Jordan
2nd District Representative

Mark E. Jackson
3rd District Representative

Dewey Ortiz
4th District Representative

Edward C. Morant
5th District Representative

Octavio Miro
6th District Representative

Keith R. Jackson
7th District Representative

Glenn E. Rice
8th District Representative

Willie F. Hinchen
9th District Representative

Climent J. Edmond, Jr.
10th District Representative

Charles C. Peevy
12th District Representative

Jonathan N. Griffin, Sr.
13th District Representative

<<>>

APPENDIX B

DISTRICTS OF OMEGA, THEIR 2008 DRs, STATES & Histories when submitted.

1st District: Connecticut, Maine, Massachusetts, New Hampshire, Rhode Island and Vermont

DISTRICT REPRESENTATIVE-Carlton Pickron

<<>>

2nd District - Delaware, Maryland, New Jersey, New York and Pennsylvania
Bro. James W. (Scrappy) Jordan

Second District
Historical Sketches 1947-1973

The Second District Conference, was founded in Brooklyn, N.Y. in 1947 shortly after being transferred from the First District which included Massachusetts, Rhode Island and Connecticut.

When formed the District was composed of five states: New York, New Jersey, Pennsylvania, Delaware and the Eastern Shore of Maryland. When the newly formed District was transferred there were eleven chapters and in 1973 there were forty-four chapters (twelve undergraduate, three Intermediate, and twenty-nine Graduate Chapters).

During the period of 25 years since its transfer changing times and with the growth of Chapters, our distinguished Omega Men in the District assumed competence and proper in all the basic fields of endeavor. Many of the brothers grew in strength and wisdom and it produced growth in the various communities and the Second District became a stronger organization.

THE FIRST OFFICERS OF THE DISTRICT WERE: Brother Nathaniel Burrell, a Forty year Honoree was elected the first President of the District Conference. However, at the next District meeting in Syracuse, N.Y., this office was abolished because the District Parliamentarian ruled that this office did not exist constitutionally.

The late Brother Mifflin T. Gibbs of Mu Omega Chapter in Philadelphia, PA was elected the first District Representative. His duties and responsibilities were clearly defined in Omega's Constitution. The duties of the other District Officers were defined in the Second District By-Laws.

Brother Marion English, of Brooklyn, N.Y. a YMCA Secretary was the first elected DKR & S and he was succeeded by Brother National Burrell and he held this office for ten years. Brother Burrell was succeeded by James L. Murray and both were cited for their meritorious service to the District.

Brother Richard E. Carey, Esq., of Xi Phi Chapter and the former Grand Counselor was the first District Counselor. Brother Carey also wrote with the assistance of other brothers the first District By-Laws and Constitution.

Brother H. Albion Ferrell (Grand Chaplain) was elected as the first District Chaplain. His successor was William C. Jason, Jr. (deceased) of Mu Omega Chapter of Philadelphia, PA. Brother Jason later became Chairman of the Recommendations Committee and he served with distinction.

<<>>

3rd District: Virginia and Washington, DC

3rd District Representative – Mark E. Jackson Sr.

<<>>

4th District: Ohio and West Virginia

Brother Dewey Ortiz 4th District Representative

4th District
Ohio and West Virginia

4th District History

In late 1919 to early 1920, Kappa Chapter was founded at West Virginia State Teachers College in Institute, West Virginia. In 1923 Kappa Chapter was moved to Syracuse, New York. West Virginia State Teachers College was given the name of Theta Psi Chapter. Xi Alpha Graduate Chapter was founded by several aspiring Omega men, many of them from Cleveland, Ohio, in the 1930s.

On March 6, 1923, Bro. Nathaniel Bowen and other young Omega Brothers came together and established Zeta Omega Chapter as the first graduate chapter in Ohio. On April 1st, 1923 these young men established the first undergraduate chapter in Ohio as Upsilon Chapter at Wilberforce University. In the 1920s and 30s, Ohio and West Virginia were part of the 10th District which also consisted of Indiana and Illinois. In the 1940s Ohio, West Virginia and Western Pennsylvania were part of the 11th District. The state of Virginia comprised the 4th District during this period. In 1945 the 4th District became Ohio and West Virginia. Some of the early District Representatives were called traveling DRs.

Bro. E.S. Donaldson (1928 –)
Bro. Ellis A. Weatherless (1933 -) 9th District
Bro. Baskerville (1935 -)   9th District
Bro. A.P. Hamblin (1937-39) # 1   10th District
Bro. Henry Rowland (1939-40) # 2   10th District
Bro. Bro. Chester Gray (1940 -1943) 11th District
Bro. Boling (1943-1944)   11th District
Bro. J. Douglas Anderson (1944-1948)
In 1945 Ohio and West Virginia becomes the 4th District
Gap in Years
Bro. Leonard Holland (1948-60) # 3 Columbus, Ohio

Bro. William Moore (1961-65) # 4   Cincinnati, Ohio

Bro. Clark Beck (1965-68) # 5   Dayton, Ohio
Bro. Robert Thomas (1968-1969) Dayton, Ohio (**Served only part of his term**)
Bro. John Fuller (1969) # 6   Charleston, West Virginia (**Finished out the term**)
Bro. Dr. Floyedlh Anderson (1970-72) # 7   Charleston, West Virginia
Bro. William Hunter (1972-75) # 8   Canton, Ohio
Bro. Dr. R. Charles Byers (1975-78) # 9   Charleston, West Virginia
Bro. Richard Jenkins (1978-80) # 10   Cleveland, Ohio
Bro. Dr. Frank Williams (1980-84) # 11 Cleveland, Ohio
Bro. Kenneth Wilson (1985-87) # 12   Akron, Ohio
Bro. Jarrett Thomas (1987-90) # 13   Dayton, Ohio
Bro. Raymond Tillery, Sr. (1990-92) # 14 Columbus, Ohio
Bro. Malvin Jones (1992-94) # 15   Dayton, Ohio
Bro. Henry "Hank" Gillespie Jr. (1995-96) # 16 Cincinnati, Ohio
Bro. Mel Kendall McCray (1996-97) # 17   Cleveland, Ohio
Bro. Christopher Cooper Esq. (1997-99) # 18   Columbus, Ohio
Bro. Albert Jordan (1999-01) # 19   Dayton, Ohio
Bro. Dr. Gregory Epps (2001-03) # 20 Charleston, West Virginia
Bro. William Comeaux (2003-05) # 21 Cleveland, Ohio
Bro. Jesse Junius (2005-07) # 22   Dayton, Ohio
Bro. Dewey Ortiz (2007-09) #23   Columbus, Ohio
Bro. Rufus Heard (2009-   #24   Cleveland, Ohio

The only 4th District Grand officers known are:

Bro. George V. Johnson 1937 Grand Marshall - Cleveland, Ohio

Bro. Leonard V. Holland 1948 Grand Marshall - Columbus, Ohio

Bro. Paul A. Jones 1953 Grand Marshall – Cincinnati, Ohio

Bro. Charles P. Lucas 1958 Grand Marshall – Cleveland, Ohio

Bro. C. Franklin Spurill – Attorney (Grand Counselor)   He was initially appointed to the position and **wasn't re-elected** at the next conclave. He probably served in the 1960s.
He was probably a member of Xi Chi Chapter, Akron, Ohio.

Bro. Dr. Frank C. Williams served as Grand Marshall for the 68th Grand Conclave
held in Cleveland, Ohio in 1994.

Bro. Darryl Moore – 1996-98 Undergraduate/Intermediate Representative
Supreme Council Member

Today the 4th District continues to thrive in various outreach and communities activities. This includes focusing our attention on accomplishing the fraternity's mandated programs, Achievement Week, and Talent Hunt Programs.

4th District Officers:

Bro. Rufus Heard – District Representative (Cleveland, OH)
Bro. Stanford Williams – First Vice District Representative (Cincinnati, OH)
Bro. Sean Strong – 2nd Vice District Representative (Kent, OH)
Bro. Darryl Cameron - District Keeper of Finance (Youngstown, OH)
Bro. Christopher Welch - District Keeper of Records and Seal (Dayton, OH)
Bro. Christopher Cooper – District Counselor (Columbus, OH)
Bro. Jerry Kennebrew – District Editor to the Oracle (Cleveland, OH)
Bro. Mikle Brown – District Keeper of Peace (Cincinnati, OH)
Bro. David Reliford - District Chaplain (Canton, OH)
Bro. Dewey Ortiz - Immediate Past District Representative (Columbus, OH)
2009 – Delta Alpha (Dayton,OH)
2008 – Psi Omicron (Youngstown,OH)
2007 – Xi Tau (Toledo,OH)
2006 – Zeta Kappa Kappa (Beachwood/Cleveland, OH)
2005 – Xi Chi (Akron,OH)

2004 – Mu Iota (Columbus,OH)
2003 – Beta Iota (Cincinnati,OH)
2002 – Zeta Omega (Cleveland,OH)
2001 – Xi Iota Iota (Troy/Piqua/Sidney)
2000 – Xi Alpha (Charleston,WV)
1999 – Delta Alpha (Dayton,OH)
1998 – Mu Chi (Springfield/Xenia)
1997 – Kappa Tau (Canton,OH)
1996 – Mu Iota (Columbus,OH)
1995 – Xi Tau (Toledo,OH)
1994 – Beta Iota (Cincinnati,OH)
1993 – Xi Alpha (Charleston,WV)
1992 – Zeta Omega (Cleveland,OH)
1991 – Mu Iota (Columbus,OH)
1990 – Xi Chi (Akron,OH)
1989 – Psi Omicron (Youngstown,OH)
1988 – Delta Alpha (Dayton,OH)
1987 – Xi Tau (Toledo,OH)
1986 – Unknown
1985 – Beta Iota (Cincinnati,OH)
1984 – Mu Chi (Springfield/Xenia, OH)
1983 – Unknown
1982 – Mu Iota (Columbus,OH)
1981 – (Beckley/Bluefield, WV)
1980 – Xi Chi (Akron,OH)
1979– Delta Alpha (Dayton,OH)

<<>>

5th District - Kentucky and Tennessee

District Representative - Edward C. Morant

A Brief High Level History of the Fifth District
Bro. Edward C. Morant

this is a brief outline history of the Fifth District of the Omega Psi Phi Fraternity, Inc. It is not intended to be a complete istory. The available documents are sketchy at best and in some cases nonexistent. However, I've done some research, using the GILL book and the Omega Men of Distinction book that I received from Brother Carl Blunt, 1st Vice Grand Basileus. This document should provide a starting point from which to develop a complete history of the district going forward.

In 1919 Delta Chapter in Nashville, Tennessee, was the first chapter to be established in what is now the 5th District, under the 7th Grand Basileus Brother Raymond G. Robinson. Delta was organized with twenty chartered members. Nashville can also be considered the birth place of what is now known as "Black History Month". It was in Nashville at the 1920 Conclave that Carter G. Woodson delivered an inspiring address entitled, "Democracy and the Man Far Down". The address was so eloquent and moving, that the Fraternity decided to devote a week each year to focus on disseminating accurate information on the life and history of the Negro.

Authority was given the Grand Basileus in 1922 to appoint representatives of the Grand Chapter, called District Representatives, to assist in the supervision of the chapters. Five such representatives were appointed at the time. The representatives were Charles W. White, (New England States), Carter L. Marshall (Mid Atlantic States), L.R. Hill (Central States), William J. Faulkner (Southern States) and George L. Vaughn (Western States). It is unclear which Representative supervised the states of Tennessee and Kentucky at that time. The year 1922 also saw the establishment of Theta Omega Chapter in Louisville, Kentucky during the administration of the 9th Grand Basileus, J. Alston Atkins. Brother Atkins was also a charter member of Delta Chapter. No other chapters that are currently in the 5th District were established until 1925, when Epsilon Phi in Memphis and Gamma Phi in Nashville were formed under the 11th Grand Basileus Brother George E. Vaughn.

The most significant movement toward forming the 5th District as we know it today came during Grand Basileus Z. Alexander Lobby's administration (1940 – 1945). Brother Looby served during the challenging years of World War II. Despite the dwindling number of active Brothers and potential members because of the war, Brother Looby was successful in establishing 14 new chapters. Among the chapters that were formed are Theta Iota (Jackson, TN) in 1944 and Kappa Iota (Chattanooga, TN) in 1945. The first attempt to structure the Fraternity into Districts occurred in 1937.

Brother Looby served as the first 5th District Representative from 1938 to 1941. In 1937 the Fraternity was organized with 11 Districts. At this point the state of Tennessee was in the Fifth District along with Mississippi and Arkansas. The state of Kentucky was placed in the 8th District along with Kansas, Minnesota, Colorado and Missouri.

In 1945 the Fraternity made the decision to re-organize into 12 Districts. It was at this point that the 5th District in its present form, with the states of Tennessee and Kentucky was created. The first 5th District Representative after the re-organization was Brother L. W. Beasley, who served from 1945 to 1960, which remains the longest term served by any 5th District Representative. In 1984 Brother Willie A. Smith, who served as the 11th 5th District Representative was elected Grand Keeper of Records and Seal at the 74th Grand Conclave in Louisville, KY, thus making him the second 5th District Brother to become a Grand Officer.

The following is the list of District Meetings, Grand Conclave cities and 5th District Brothers who served as Grand Officers.

5th District Grand Officers

Office	Name	Year Elected
Grand Basileus	Z. Alexander Looby	1940
Grand KRS	Willie A. Smith	1984

<<>>

6th District: North Carolina and South Carolina

District Representative - Octavio Miro

<<>>

7th District - Alabama, Florida, Georgia and Mississippi

DISTRICT REPRESENTATIVE – KEITH R. JACKSON

Seventh District History

In 1922, Grand Basileus J. Alston Atkins divided our fraternity into five districts. At that time they were The New England States, The Middle Atlantic States, The Central States, The Southern States, and The Western States. In 1935, a redistricting occurred and the seventh district was created. M.R. Austell was appointed the first seventh district representative in 1935. On April 24, 1936 the first seventh district meeting occurred on the campus of Fort Valley State University in Fort Valley, GA. There were twelve delegates present at that first meeting; ten were from the state of Georgia and two from the state of Alabama. The seventh district at that time was composed of three states: Alabama, Florida, and Georgia. The state of Mississippi was added to the seventh district in 1941.

The longest serving district representative in the seventh district and even in the fraternity is J.T. Brooks who served approximately twenty-seven years. Bro. Brooks appointed W.A. McMillan to the position of state supervisor of chapters in 1958 in the state of Florida. However, it appears that Bro. McMillan served as the supervisor of chapters throughout the district. In 1963, Bro. Brooks renamed this position to state representative and appointed the first state representatives. He continued using W.A. McMillan for the state of Florida and appointed Samuel Sheffey for the state of Alabama, Robert Church for the state of Georgia, and Charles Jones for the state of Mississippi.

The first chapters in the seventh district were: Phi Chapter at Talladega College in 1921 in the state of Alabama, Chi Omega Chapter at Tallahassee in 1924 in the state of Florida, Eta Chapter composed of students at Atlanta University, Morehouse College, and Clarke University in 1919 in the state of Georgia, and Beta Alpha in 1933 at Alcorn in the state of Mississippi. The state of Florida was the first state to create a state organization of Omega Psi Phi in 1974. Alabama did the same in 1977, Georgia in 1980 and Mississippi was the last to do so in 1992.

Although the seventh district has been the largest district in our fraternity, it took forty years before a brother from the seventh district was elected Grand Basileus. In 1976, Bro. Edward Braynon was elected Grand Basileus. Since that time three other brothers from the seventh district have served our fraternity as Grand Basileus and they are: Bro. Moses C. Norman, Bro. Dorsey C. Miller, and Bro. George Grace.

The seventh district through the years has been one of the great standard bearers in the fraternity. We do it so well that our international headquarters will often implement changes in how they do things after witnessing our example here in the seventh district. The ideas of the Lampados Club, the Leadership Conference, an inspector general, data based mechanization for membership, a modernized registration process with photos on identification badges, state organizations, and utilization of CD in lieu of paper reports originated in the seventh district.

<<>>

8th District - Colorado, Iowa, Kansas, Missouri, Nebraska, New Mexico, North Dakota and South Dakota

GLEN E. RICE-30TH EIGHT DISTRICT REPRESENTATIVE
<<>>

9th District: Arkansas, Louisiana, Oklahoma and Texas

THE MIGHTY NINTH DISTRICT WAS ESTABLISHED MAY 5 AND 6, 1937 at the Moorland Branch YMCA in Dallas, Texas. The mighty 9th District, as of the writing of this book, is led in exceptional fashion by its 21st District Representative,

Willie F. (Mercenary) Hinchen
District Representative

The 9th District was established under the direction of Brother J. D. Bowles of Nu Phi Chapter of Houston, Texas. Brother Bowles was appointed Ninth District Representative by the 16th Grand Basileus, the late Brother Albert W. Dent. What a glorious day that was for all of us here in the 9th District.

We are extremely proud of Grand Basileus Warren Lee and many other exceptional modern day 9th District brothers such as Brian Van Gundy, Michael Adams, Aubrey "Nick" Pittman Esq., Melvin Zeno, Clement Osmethia and Lee G. Willis who have held international office in Omega Psi Phi Fraternity Inc. Brothers, it is very unique and is a distinct honor to have major international Grand Officers from the same district in office at the same time no less which was the case for several of them. **The mighty, mighty 9th District is proud of the fact that it has played and is playing a major role in leading Omega Psi Phi Fraternity Inc. to greatness.**

The mighty 9th District is filled with interesting stories, legends, extraordinary Chapters and exceptional Omega Men who have accomplished great things in their Chapters, the District as well as in their personal lives and gallant exploits across the nation. For example, we have had two Grand Basileus come from our ranks. **The late Brother Albert W. Dent of Rho Phi Chapter, New Orleans, Louisiana, was elected the 16th Grand Basileus in 1937. Warren G. Lee was elected Grand Basileus in the 2006, 74th Grand Conclave in Little Rock Arkansas.**

OMEGA PSI PHI FRATERNITY Inc. was re-districted to provide for 12 districts during World War II and post World War years 1941-1951. The Ninth District consisted of the states of Texas, Louisiana, Oklahoma and California at that point in time in its history.

OMEGA PSI PHI FRATERNITY Inc. was re-districted again for 11 districts during the post war years. The Ninth District became the states of Texas, Louisiana, Oklahoma, and Arkansas. It remains that way up until the date of this writing.

<<>>

10th District - Illinois, Indiana, Michigan, Minnesota and Wisconsin

DISTRICT REPRESENTATIVE-CLIMENT J. EDMOND JR.

<<>>

12th District - Alaska, Arizona, California, Idaho, Montana, Nevada, Oregon, Utah, Washington and Wyoming

DISTRICT REPRESENTATIVE-CHARLES C. PEEVY

<<>>

13th District: Hawaii; Monrovia, Liberia; Nassau, Bahamas; Okinawa, Japan; Panama Canal Zone; South Korea; The Virgin Islands; and Germany

DISTRICT REPRESENTATIVE- JONATHAN N. GRIFFIN SR.

<<>>

CHAPTERS OF OMEGA PSI PHI FRATERNITY INC.

DIS_ID	CHP_ID CHARTER #	CHAPTER NAME	LOCATION	ADDRESS	CITY	STATE	CHARTER DATE
03	000001	Alpha	Howard University	2400 Sixth St. NW	Washington	DC	15THDec1911
02	000002	Beta	1570 Old Baltimore Pike	OXFORD PENN	Lincoln University	PA	06-Feb19
01	000003	Gamma	BOSTON MASS				13-Dec-16
05	000004	Delta	Meharry Medical College	P.O. Box 1911	Nashville	TN	15-May-18
02	000005	Epsilon	P.O. Box 22867		Brooklyn	NY	18-Apr-19
03	000006	Zeta	VA Union University	1500 North Lombardy Street	Richmond	VA	19-Oct-19
07	000007	Eta	Alcorn A & M College	P.O. Box 255	Alcorn State	MS	27-Dec-19
09	000008	Theta	Wiley College	P.O. Box 1941	Marshall	TX	17-Dec-22
10	000009	Iota	Iota Chapter	P.O. Box 201266	Chicago	IL	01-Nov-23
02	000010	Kappa	Syracuse University	P.O. Box 37031	Syracuse	NY	01-Oct-22
12	000011	Lambda		P.O. Box 43418	Los Angeles	CA	03-May-23
02	000012	Mu	3939 Baltimore Avenue		Philadelphia	PA	01-Oct-20
02	000013	Nu	State College of Pennsylvania	122 Grange Building	University Park	PA	15-Mar-21
10	000014	Xi	University of Minnesota	300 Washington Ave. S.	Minneapolis	MN	01-Oct-21
02	000015	Omicron	Columbia University	140 Claremont Avenue	New York	NY	01-Oct-21
02	000016	Pi	Morgan State University	P.O. Box 66337	Baltimore	MD	24-Oct-23

THE OMEGA PSI PHI FRATERNITY INC. 263

06	000017	Rho	Johnson C. Smith University	P.O. Box 1034	Charlotte	NC	01-Oct-21
10	000018	Sigma	Michigan State University	P. O. Box 6493	East Lansing	MI	01-Oct-25
07	000019	Tau	P.O. Box 7369		Atlanta	GA	01-May-22
04	000020	Upsilon	Wilberforce University	P.O. Box 750	Wilberforce	OH	01-Apr-23
10	000021	Phi	University of Michigan	539 S. State	Ann Arbor	MI	01-Jan-22
07	000022	Chi	Edward Waters College	P O Box 694	Jacksonville	FL	01-Oct-21
07	000023	Psi	Morehouse College	830 Westview Drive Box 140076	Atlanta	GA	07-Apr-22
09	000024	Alpha Psi	Huston-Tillotson College	P.O. Box C161	Austin	TX	01-Oct-22
07	000025	Beta Psi	Clark Atlanta University	223 James P. Brawley Dr. Box 1520	Atlanta	GA	20-Dec-23
07	000026	Gamma Psi	P.O. Box 90207		Talladega	AL	01-Oct-21
06	000027	Delta Psi	Shaw University	P.O. Box 28792	Raleigh	NC	09-Jan-24
08	000028	Epsilon Psi	Wichita State University	P.O. Box 8	Wichita	KS	01-Feb-68
02	000029	Zeta Psi		P.O. Box 380922	Brooklyn	NY	24-Dec-24
05	000030	Eta Psi	Fisk University	P.O. Box 331503	Nashville	TN	01-Oct-26
04	000031	Theta Psi	West Virginia State College	Gore Hall Room 222	Institute	WV	22-May-26
04	000032	Iota Psi	Ohio State Universtiy	314 Ohio Union 1739 N. High St.	Columbus	OH	17-Mar-26
03	000033	Kappa Psi	P.O. Box 73364		Washington	DC	19-Nov-26
06	000034	Lambda Psi	Livingstone College	701 West Monroe Street	Salisbury	NC	01-Oct-27
06	000035	Mu Psi	North Carolina A&T State	P.O. Box 5110	Greensboro	NC	01-Oct-27

			University				
03	000036	Nu Psi	P.O. Box 768		Petersburg	VA	12-Dec-27
06	000037	Xi Psi	South Carolina State University	P.O. Box 7431	Orangeburg	SC	10-Mar-28
02	000038	Omicron Psi	University of Pittsburgh	P.O. Box 7234	Pittsburgh	PA	01-Mar-28
05	000039	Rho Psi	Tennessee State University	P.O. Box 117	Nashville	TN	01-Oct-30
10	000040	Pi Psi	Univ of Illinois at Urbana	P.O. Box 2636	Champaign	IL	01-Oct-28
04	000041	Sigma Psi	University Athens Ohio	204 Baker Center	Athens	OH	15-May-68
06	000042	Tau Psi	North Carolina Central University	P.O. Box 602	Durham	NC	01-Oct-32
07	000043	Upsilon Psi	Florida A&M Universirty	833 Liberty Street	Tallahassee	FL	01-Oct-32
09	000044	Phi Psi		P O Box 837	Langston	OK	21-Jul-33
05	000045	Chi Psi	P.O. Box 80	807 Walker-Lemoyne-Owen College	Memphis	TN	01-Oct-34
05	000046	Psi Psi	Kentucky State University	400 East Main Street	Frankfort	KY	01-Oct-36
07	000047	Alpha Sigma	Morris Brown College	643 Martin Luther King Jr. Dr	Atlanta	GA	25-May-35
09	000048	Beta Sigma	Southern University and A&M College	P O Box 10999	Baton Rouge	LA	28-Feb-36
07	000049	Gamma Sigma	Alabama State University	P O Box 23	Montgomery	AL	01-Apr-36
05	000050	Delta Sigma	Eastern Kentucky University	Powell Bldg. Stud. Act. Office	Richmond	KY	02-May-36
02	000051	Epsilon Sigma	14000 Jericho Park Rd.		Bowie	MD	02-May-36

THE OMEGA PSI PHI FRATERNITY INC. 265

04	000052	Zeta Sigma	Bluefield State College		Bluefield	WV	16-May-39
08	000053	Eta Sigma	Lincoln University	P.O. Box 29	Jefferson City	MO	06-May-36
09	000054	Theta Sigma	Dillard University	P.O. Box 45	New Orleans	LA	01-Oct-36
08	000055	Iota Sigma	Central Missouri State University	P.O. Box 18 Student Union	Warrensburg	MO	01-Oct-37
05	000056	Kappa Sigma	Lane College	P.O. Box 914	Jackson	TN	03-Dec-37
06	000057	Lambda Sigma	Claflin College	P.O. Box 4112	Orangeburg	SC	21-May-38
06	000058	Mu Sigma	Allen University	1530 Harden Street	Columbia	SC	01-Oct-36
10	000059	Nu Sigma	Wayne State University	5221 Gullen Mall SCB	Detroit	MI	01-Oct-38
09	000060	Xi Sigma	1 Drexel Drive	P.O. Box 117	New Orleans	LA	01-Oct-38
08	000061	Omicron Sigma	P.O. Box 150346		St. Louis	MO	01-Oct-42
09	000062	Pi Sigma	Philander Smith College	1 Trudie Kibbe Reed Drive	Little Rock	AR	01-Oct-42
10	000063	Rho Sigma	Purdue University Stewart Center	P.O. Box 657	West Lafayette	IN	19-Apr-42
09	000064	Sigma Sigma	Texas College	P O Box 4500	Tyler	TX	01-Oct-42
09	000065	Tau Sigma	University of Arkansas @ Pine Bluff	1200 N. University Dr P.O Box 4952	Pine Bluff	AR	01-Oct-43
07	000066	Upsilon Sigma	Fort Valley State University	P.O. Box 4700	Fort Valley	GA	01-May-46
04	000067	Phi Sigma	Western Reserve University	P.O. Box 06244	Cleveland	OH	01-May-46
10	000068	Chi Sigma	Indiana State University	Jones Hall - Box 6236	Terre Haute	IN	01-May-46
10	000069	Psi Sigma	Northwestern University	1914 Sheridan Rd	Evanston	IL	03-Jan-47
12	000070	Alpha Epsilon	University of Arizona	P. O. Box 26209	Tucson	AZ	01-Oct-46
05	000071	Beta Epsilon	Knoxville	901	Knoxville	TN	01-Oct-46

				College	College Street Box 322			
03	000072	Gamma Epsilon	Hampton University	P. O. Box 88	Hampton	VA	12-Feb-47
04	000073	Delta Epsilon	Bowling Green University	440 Saddlemire Student Svc Bld.	Bowling Green	OH	01-Oct-47
06	000074	Epsilon Epsilon	Benedict College	1600 Harden Street- Box 120	Columbia	SC	01-Oct-47
10	000075	Zeta Epsilon	Indiana University	P.O. Box 5192	Bloomington	IN	20-Oct-47
07	000076	Eta Epsilon	Miles College 5500 Myron Blvd	P.O. Box 47	Birmingham	AL	01-Oct-47
01	000077	Theta Epsilon	Brown University	P.O. Box 1147	Providence	RI	27-Jun-47
02	000078	Iota Epsilon	Towson State Univ.	P.O. Box 1972	Towson	MD	01-Oct-47
06	000079	Kappa Epsilon	St. Augustine College	P.O. Box 25126	Raleigh	NC	17-Apr-48
07	000080	Lambda Epsilon	Tuskegee University	P.O. Box 1056	Tuskegee	AL	22-Dec-47
06	000081	Mu Epsilon	Winston-Salem State University	P.O. Box 19328	Winston Salem	NC	01-Oct-48
07	000082	Nu Epsilon	Alabama A&M University	P. O. Box 674	Normal	AL	01-Oct-48
10	000083	Xi Epsilon	Bradley University	P O Box 5162	Peoria	IL	03-May-57
07	000084	Omicron Epsilon	640 Mary McLeod Bethune Blvd		Daytona Beach	FL	01-Apr-48
02	000085	Pi Epsilon	Univ. of Maryland Eastern Shore	Student Activities	Princess Anne	MD	03-May-47
07	000086	Rho Epsilon	Tougaloo College	500 West County Line Road	Tougaloo	MS	01-Oct-48
06	000087	Sigma Epsilon	Barbar Scotia College	145 Carrus Ave West	Concord	NC	01-Oct-48
09	000088	Tau Epsilon	Texas Southern Univ., 3100	P.O. Box 1112	Houston	TX	01-May-48

THE OMEGA PSI PHI FRATERNITY INC. 267

			Cleburne				
07	000089	Upsilon Epsilon	Jackson State University	P. O. Box 17127	Jackson	MS	10-Oct-49
02	000090	Phi Epsilon	Buffalo State University	P.O. Box 1257	Buffalo	NY	01-Oct-49
07	000091	Chi Epsilon	Albany State University	504 College Drive	Albany	GA	01-Oct-49
02	000092	Psi Epsilon	1200 North Dupoint Highway	P.O. Box 86	Dover	DE	17-Dec-46
04	000093	Omega Epsilon	University of Toledo	1110 Coventry Ave.	Toledo	OH	01-Nov-49
07	000094	Alpha Gamma	Savannah State University	P.O. Box 20675	Savannah	GA	28-Apr-49
02	000095	Beta Gamma	Cheyney State College	P O Box 436	Cheyney	PA	12-Feb-50
09	000096	Gamma Gamma	Grambling State University	P.O. Box 84	Grambling	LA	01-Oct-51
06	000097	Delta Gamma	Fayetteville State University	P.O. Box 15468	Fayetteville	NC	18-May-51
03	000098	Epsilon Gamma	St Paul's College	115 College Drive	Lawrenceville	VA	18-Mar-51
04	000099	Zeta Gamma			Youngstown	OH	11-Mar-51
04	000100	Eta Gamma	Central State College	P.O. Box 157	Wilberforce	OH	01-Oct-51
10	000101	Theta Gamma	Eastern Michigan University	P O Box 140	Ypsilanti	MI	15-May-52
02	000102	Iota Gamma	Trenton St College- Student Ctr.	c/o P O Box 2335	Trenton	NJ	01-Oct-52
07	000103	Kappa Gamma	Florida Memorial College	15800 NW 42nd Ave, Box 707	Miami	FL	08-May-54
06	000104	Lambda Gamma	Elizabeth City State University	P.O. Box 135	Elizabeth City	NC	15-May-54
09	000105	Mu Gamma	Bishop College	SCHOOL CLOSED	Dallas	TX	12-Dec-57
10	000106	Nu Gamma	Oakland University	P.O. Box 63202	Rochester	MI	01-Apr-59
12	000107	Xi Gamma	San Jose	1840	Oakland	CA	03-Feb-63

			State College	Scott Blvd Apt #1			
03	000108	Omicron Gamma	University of DC	1231 Harvard Street NW	Washington	DC	10-Sep-62
03	000109	Pi Gamma	Norfolk State University	P.O. Box 2873	Norfolk	VA	30-Sep-62
07	000110	Rho Gamma	Stillman College	P.O. Box 1430	Tuscaloosa	AL	11-Jan-63
08	000111	Sigma Gamma	University of New Mexico	P.O. Box 4	Albuquerque	NM	26-Apr-65
10	000112	Tau Gamma	Southern Illinois University	P.O. 1553	Edwardsville	IL	01-Apr-65
10	000113	Upsilon Gamma	Western Michigan University	Box 200 ,Student Serv. Bldg.	Kalamazoo	MI	29-Feb-68
09	000114	Phi Gamma	University of North Texas	UNT Station 310371	Denton	TX	16-Dec-68
10	000115	Chi Gamma	University of Detroit	8200 West Outer Dr.	Detroit	MI	26-Mar-69
04	000116	Psi Gamma	1865 Algonguin Place		Kent	OH	01-Apr-69
09	000117	Omega Gamma	West Texas State University	P.O. Box 515	Canyon	TX	29-Mar-69
12	000118	Alpha Theta	Arizona State University	PO. BOX 1144	Tempe	AZ	29-Mar-69
07	000119	Beta Theta	14000 Highway 82 West	P.O. Box 5007	Itta Bena	MS	01-Dec-69
05	000120	Gamma Theta	Western Kentucky University	P.O. Box 8166	Bowling Green	KY	03-Jul-69
03	000121	Delta Theta	Southeastern University MUSU	1231 Harvard Street N.W.	Washington	DC	03-Sep-69
10	000122	Epsilon Theta	University of Wisconsin	716 Langdon Street	Madison	WI	15-Sep-69
07	000123	Zeta Theta	Georgia State University	P.O. Box 1911 Univ. Plaza	Atlanta	GA	16-Sep-69
09	000124	Eta Theta	University of Texas	P O Box 288	Austin	TX	02-Dec-69

THE OMEGA PSI PHI FRATERNITY INC.

09	000125	Theta Theta	East Texas State University	Box I - E. T Station	Commerce	TX	01-Feb-70
08	000126	Iota Theta	Northeast Missouri State College	P.O. Box 221	Tarkio	MO	15-Jan-70
10	000127	Kappa Theta	Buter University (Indiana)	INACTIVE	Indianapolis	IN	15-Jan-70
04	000128	Lambda Theta	Shepard College		Shepardstown	WV	17-Jan-70
08	000129	Mu Theta	Iowa State University	P.O. Box 1323	Ames	IA	01-Feb-70
10	000130	Nu Theta	Lawrence Institute of Technology	INACTIVE	Detroit	MI	11-Feb-70
04	000131	Xi Theta	Ashland College		Ashland	OH	11-Mar-70
10	000132	Omicron Theta	Southern Illinois University	P.O. Box 636	Carbondale	IL	10-Apr-70
10	000133	Pi Theta	Northern Michigan University	INACTIVE -SEE CHAPTER FILE	Marquette	MI	10-Apr-70
09	000134	Rho Theta	Prairie View A&M University	P. O. Box 2811	Prairie View	TX	25-Apr-70
06	000135	Sigma Theta	Voorhees College	P O Box 678 - Box 83	Denmark	SC	14-May-70
10	000136	Tau Theta	Eastern Illinois University	1262 1/2 Jackson Avenue	Charleston	IL	12-Apr-70
09	000137	Upsilon Theta	Lamar University	P. O. Box 10714	Beaumont	TX	22-May-70
04	000138	Phi Theta	Cleveland State University	2121 Euclid Avenue	Cleveland	OH	01-Aug-70
07	000139	Chi Theta	Florida State University	P.O. Box 67013	Tallahassee	FL	19-Aug-70
04	000140	Psi Theta	University of Cincinnati	CHARTER REVOKED	Cincinnati	OH	01-Aug-70
09	000141	Omega Theta	4800 Calhoun	P.O. Box 106	Houston	TX	11-Nov-70
05	000142	Alpha Beta	Murray State University	P. O. Box 2431	Murray	KY	06-Jan-71
04	000143	Beta Beta	University of Akron	P.O. Box 13797	Akron	OH	08-Jan-71

07	000144	Gamma Beta	Paine College	P.O. Box 2507	Augusta	GA	08-Jan-71
02	000145	Delta Beta	Coppin State College	2500 West North Avenue	Baltimore	MD	15-Jan-71
10	000146	Epsilon Beta	Western Illinois University	Student Union	Macomb	IL	04-Feb-71
04	000147	Zeta Beta			Dayton	OH	19-Feb-71
05	000148	Eta Beta	University Tennessee Chattanooga	P. O. Box 150	Chattanooga	TN	22-Feb-71
05	000149	Theta Beta	Vanderbilt University	P.O. Box 351522 Station B	Nashville	TN	01-Mar-71
05	000150	Iota Beta	University of Tennessee Knoxville	P.O. Box 16450	Knoxville	TN	01-Apr-71
07	000151	Kappa Beta	Rust College	150 Rust Ave	Holly Springs	MS	01-Apr-71
08	000152	Lambda Beta	Colorado State University	P.O. Box 8448	Denver	CO	20-Apr-71
09	000153	Mu Beta	Univ. of Texas at Arlington	Box 19348	Arlington	TX	04-May-71
04	000154	Nu Beta	Marshall University		Huntington	WV	14-May-71
09	000155	Xi Beta	Henderson State University	P.O. Box 6547	Arkadelphia	AR	12-May-71
10	000156	Omicron Beta	Central Michigan University	P.O. Box 65	Mt Pleasant	MI	26-May-71
10	000157	Pi Beta	Illinois State University		Normal	IL	01-Jun-71
09	000158	Rho Beta	McNeese State University	P.O.Box. 90549	Lake Charles	LA	15-Sep-71
10	000159	Sigma Beta	Indiana Purdue University		Indianapolis	IN	07-Oct-71
02	000160	Tau Beta	Ramapo College of NJ		Camden	NJ	20-Oct-71
10	000161	Upsilon Beta	Ball State University	Box 158, Student Center	Muncie	IN	11-Nov-71
09	000162	Phi Beta	Jarvis Christian	P.O. Box 154	Hawkins	TX	18-Nov-71

THE OMEGA PSI PHI FRATERNITY INC. 271

			College				
12	000163	Chi Beta	California State College	1250 Bellflower Blvd	Long Beach	CA	14-Jan-72
05	000164	Psi Beta	Morehead State University	P.O. Box 2419	Morehead	KY	12-Jan-72
09	000165	Omega Beta	Stephen F. Austin University	P.O. Box 1470	Lufkin	TX	09-Mar-72
09	000166	Alpha Delta	Dallas Baptist College	1820 East 8th Street	Austin	TX	09-Mar-72
09	000167	Beta Delta	University of Central Arkansas	P.O. Box 2034	Conway	AR	18-Mar-72
09	000168	Gamma Delta	University of Southwestern Louisiana	P. O. Box 41643	Lafayette	LA	07-Apr-72
08	000169	Delta Delta	Kansas State University	204 Holt Hall	Manhattan	KS	19-Apr-72
08	000170	Epsilon Delta	University of Missouri	V. Tatum - A022 Brady Commons	Columbia	MO	19-Apr-72
08	000171	Zeta Delta	Kansas State Teachers College	1200 Commercial-Emporia State	Emporia	KS	20-Apr-72
10	000172	Eta Delta	Indiana University Northwest		Gary	IN	01-May-72
09	000173	Theta Delta	Northwestern Louisiana State Univ	P.O. Box 4119	Natchitoches	LA	15-May-72
10	000174	Iota Delta	Southern Illinois University		Dekalb	IL	16-May-72
07	000175	Kappa Delta	HUC 440 1530 3rd Avenue South		Birmingham	AL	07-Oct-97
10	000176	Lambda Delta	Eureka College		Eureka	IL	25-May-72
08	000177	Mu Delta	University of Iowa		Iowa City	IA	30-May-72
07	000178	Nu Delta	Columbus College	P.O. Box 6644	Columbus	GA	12-Jun-72

09	000179	Xi Delta	P.O. Box 1323	601 University Drive	San Marcus	TX	18-Sep-72
07	000180	Omicron Delta	University of Miami	P. O. Box 2487106 Bldg. 21E	Coral Gables	FL	19-Sep-72
09	000181	Pi Delta	University of Oklahoma	900 Asp Ave Box 2747	Norman	OK	22-Sep-72
09	000182	Rho Delta	Texas A&M University	P O Box 2384	Kingsville	TX	15-Feb-73
07	000183	Sigma Delta	Auburn University	P.O. Box 1372	Auburn	AL	02-Mar-73
06	000184	Tau Delta	Wofford College	429 N. Church Street	Spartanburg	SC	02-Mar-73
07	000185	Upsilon Delta	University of South Florida	Office of Greek Life CTR256	Tampa	FL	19-Mar-73
03	000186	Phi Delta	Virginia Commonwealth University	P.O. Box 27331	Richmond	VA	20-Mar-73
02	000187	Chi Delta	University of Maryland	PO Box 135	College Park	MD	22-Mar-73
06	000188	Psi Delta	450 Ridge Road Suite 1125	CB#5100	Chapel Hill	NC	22-Mar-73
02	000189	Omega Delta	West Chester State College	Box 3095	West Chester	PA	29-Mar-73
09	000190	Alpha Zeta	Arkansas State University	P. O. Box 4827	Jonesboro	AR	11-Apr-73
07	000191	Beta Zeta	216 Memorial Hall		Athens	GA	11-Apr-73
07	000192	Gamma Zeta	Mercer University		Macon	GA	02-May-73
02	000193	Delta Zeta	Villanova University	INACTIVE	Philadelphia	PA	21-May-73
06	000194	Epsilon Zeta	Univ. of No. Carolina Charl.	Caucus Room	Charlotte	NC	31-Jul-73
06	000195	Zeta Zeta	P.O. BOX 85128	Campus Activities Center	Columbia	SC	31-Jul-73
07	000196	Eta Zeta	University of Mississippi	P.O. Box 6111	University	MS	31-Jul-73
05	000197	Theta Zeta	East Tennessee State	P.O. Box 23514	Johnson City	TN	07-Sep-73

			University				
05	000198	Iota Zeta	University of Tennessee	P.O. Box 98	Martin	TN	07-Sep-73
09	000199	Kappa Zeta	Southeastern OK State Univ.		Durant	OK	10-Sep-73
03	000200	Lambda Zeta	University of Virginia	P.O. Box 400416	Charlottesville	VA	10-Sep-73
05	000201	Mu Zeta	Middle Tennessee State University	E089	Murfreesboro	TN	21-Sep-73
04	000202	Nu Zeta	West Virginia University	P.O. Box 389	Morgantown	WV	28-Sep-73
05	000203	Xi Zeta	University of Memphis	Campus Postal Station Box 1046	Memphis	TN	28-Sep-73
07	000204	Omicron Zeta	University of Florida	P.O. Box 13073	Gainsville	FL	05-Nov-73
04	000205	Pi Zeta	Baldwin Wallace College		Berea	OH	06-Nov-73
02	000206	Rho Zeta	Keene College	INACTIVE	Union	NJ	06-Nov-73
10	000207	Sigma Zeta	University of Wisconsin	264 University Center	Whitewater	WI	03-Nov-73
02	000208	Tau Zeta	Rutgers University	418 Ervin-Turner Blvd	Newark	NJ	06-Nov-73
06	000209	Upsilon Zeta	East Carolina University	P.O. Box 1309	Greenville	NC	11-Dec-73
10	000210	Phi Zeta	Ferris State College	P.O. Box 12	Big Rapids	MI	11-Feb-74
06	000211	Chi Zeta	Clemson University	P.O. Box 2306	Clemson	SC	06-Apr-74
02	000212	Psi Zeta	Delaware University		Newark	DE	18-Apr-74
06	000213	Omega Zeta	Duke University	P.O.Box 2452	Durham	NC	12-Apr-74
02	000214	Alpha Eta	East Stroudsburg State College	Box 866	E Stroudsburg	PA	07-Sep-74
07	000215	Beta Eta	University of Alabama	P.O. Box 866122	Tuscaloosa	AL	
09	000216	Gamma Eta				AR	18-Feb-75
09	000217	Delta Eta	Southern Arkansas	P.O. Box 8599	Magnolia	AR	18-Feb-75

10	000218	Epsilon Eta	Chicago State University	3304 West Beach	Chicago	IL	18-Feb-75
09	000219	Zeta Eta	Paul Quinn College	P O Box 1346	Waco	TX	05-Apr-75
08	000220	Eta Eta	N. Mexico State University	P.O. Box 15067	Las Cruces	NM	19-Apr-75
07	000221	Theta Eta	Jacksonville State University	P.O. Box 3031	Jacksonville	AL	19-Apr-75
02	000222	Iota Eta		17 Mission St	Montclair	NJ	20-Jul-75
02	000223	Kappa Eta	Seton Hall University	324 Valley Street	S. Orange	NJ	20-Jul-75
06	000224	Lambda Eta	Wake Forest College	P.O. Box 8832	Winston Salem	NC	10-Sep-75
07	000225	Mu Eta	Daniel Payne College	SCHOOL CLOSED	Birmingham	AL	12-Nov-75
07	000226	Nu Eta	University of Southern Mississippi	P.O. Box 8387	Hattiesburg	MS	12-Nov-75
09	000227	Xi Eta	Texas State University	4111 17th St. #110	Lubbock	TX	15-Nov-75
01	000228	Omicron Eta	University of Connecticut	West Campus - Box 8	Storrs	CT	15-Nov-75
10	000229	Pi Eta	Lewis University	Rt. 53 Box 39	Romeoville	IL	22-Mar-76
08	000230	Rho Eta	University of Kansas	P.O. Box 2395	Lawrence	KS	10-Apr-76
12	000231	Sigma Eta	University of California	1132 W. Blaine St., Apt. 101 #9	Riverside	CA	10-Apr-76
08	000232	Tau Eta	Drake University	1319 30th Street	Des Moines	IA	01-Oct-97
06	000233	Upsilon Eta	Lander College	P.O. Box 6189	Greenwood	SC	11-May-76
05	000234	Phi Eta	University of Louisville	SAC 301W	Louisville	KY	10-Apr-76
08	000235	Chi Eta	University of Northern Iowa	P.O. Box 452	Cedar Falls	IA	01-Jul-76
06	000236	Psi Eta	A&T State University		Greensboro	NC	01-Jul-76
07	000237	Omega Eta	Augusta College	P O Box 3105	Augusta	GA	15-Aug-76
10	000238	Alpha Kappa	Marquette		Milwaukee	WI	15-Aug-76

THE OMEGA PSI PHI FRATERNITY INC.

02	000239	Beta Kappa	Frostburg State University	C/O 122 Hitchins Admin Bld FSU	Frostburg	MD		13-Oct-76
02	000240	Gamma Kappa	Salisbury State College	Box 50 College Center	Salisbury	MD		13-Oct-76
07	000241	Delta Kappa	Georgia Inst of Technology	221 Student Svcs. Bldg.	Atlanta	GA		13-Oct-76
02	000242	Epsilon Kappa	Clarion State College	2006 Shaal Avenue	Erie	PA		20-Nov-76
07	000243	Zeta Kappa	University os S. Alabama	P.O. Box 82094	Mobile	AL		20-Nov-76
02	000244	Eta Kappa	Millersville State College	8E Brookwood Ct. Aptmts.	Millersville	PA		12-Mar-77
09	000245	Theta Kappa	Louisiana State University	P O Box 20672	Baton Rouge	LA		12-Mar-77
09	000246	Iota Kappa	Southern University	P O Box 10807	Baton Rouge	LA		12-Mar-77
07	000247	Kappa Kappa	West Georgia	P.O. Box 10028	Carrollton	GA		12-Mar-77
06	000248	Lambda Kappa		219 W. Weaver Street	Durham	NC		28-Apr-77
12	000249	Mu Kappa	Cal. Poly State College	P.O. Box 12226	San Luis Obispo	CA		01-May-77
09	000250	Nu Kappa	P.O. Box 750355		Dallas	TX		31-Aug-77
02	000251	Xi Kappa	Pennsylvania State College	P.O. Box 282	California	PA		31-Aug-77
08	000252	Omicron Kappa	P.O. Box 787		Springfield	MO		01-Sep-77
09	000253	Pi Kappa	University of Little Rock	2801 South University	Little Rock	AR		01-Mar-78
05	000254	Rho Kappa	Austin Peay State University	P.O. Box 4746	Clarksville	TN		10-Mar-78
09	000255	Sigma Kappa	P O Box 1614		Edmond	OK		10-Mar-78
08	000256	Tau Kappa	University of Nebraska at Omaha	P.O. Box 11566	Omaha	NE		01-Mar-78

10	000257	Upsilon Kappa	University of Wisc-Oshkosh		Oshkosh	WI	01-Oct-78
02	000258	Phi Kappa		P O Box 667	Glassboro	NJ	15-Sep-78
02	000259	Chi Kappa	P.O. Box 1443		Baltimore	MD	15-Sep-78
06	000260	Psi Kappa	Winthrop College	P.O. Box 5092	Rock Hill	SC	09-Mar-79
09	000261	Omega Kappa	Nicholls St University	P O Box 2582	Thibodoux	LA	09-Mar-79
09	000262	Alpha Lambda	Southern University	P.O. Box 1453	Marrero	LA	06-Aug-79
06	000263	Beta Lambda	University of South Carolina		Aiken	SC	06-Aug-79
04	000264	Gamma Lambda	West Virginia Inst. Technical	P.O. Box 281	Montgomery	WV	06-Aug-79
01	000265	Delta Lambda			New Britain	CT	06-Aug-79
06	000266	Epsilon Lambda	CPO Box 1061	100 West College Street	Sumter	SC	06-Aug-79
12	000267	Zeta Lambda	University of Washington	P.O Box 22249	Seattle	WA	06-Aug-79
03	000268	Eta Lambda	Virginia Polytech Univ	P.O. Box 11182	Blacksburg	VA	06-Aug-79
06	000269	Theta Lambda	Western Carolina University	P O Box 777	Cullowhee	NC	22-Sep-79
06	000270	Iota Lambda	Univ of N.C. at Wilmington	P O Box 7111	Wilmington	NC	17-Dec-79
06	000271	Kappa Lambda	N.C. State @ Raliegh	P.O. Box 50265	Raleigh	NC	15-Mar-80
06	000272	Lambda Lambda		P.O. Box 100547	Florence	SC	15-Mar-80
09	000273	Mu Lambda	Northeast Louisiana Univ.	P.O. Box 5418	Monroe	LA	17-Dec-79
10	000274	Nu Lambda	Univ of Wisconsin	WM Union, BX 293-P.O. Box 413	Milwaukee	WI	15-Mar-80
02	000275	Xi Lambda	Shippensburg State College	Cumberland Union Bldg.	Shippensburg	PA	15-Mar-80
09	000276	Omicron Lambda	179 Student Union	P.O. Box 1025	Stillwater	OK	28-Feb-80

THE OMEGA PSI PHI FRATERNITY INC.

09	000277	Pi Lambda	University of Texas @ El Paso	P O Box 57	El Paso	TX	28-Feb-80
05	000278	Rho Lambda	University of Kentucky	P.O. Box 418	Lexington	KY	15-Mar-80
09	000279	Sigma Lambda	Texas Christian College	P O Box 32337	Fort Worth	TX	13-Sep-80
03	000280	Tau Lambda	Old Dominion College	P.O. Box 6181	Norfolk	VA	13-Sep-80
02	000281	Upsilon Lambda	Univ of Maryland Baltimore County	PO Box 24091	Baltimore	MD	15-Oct-80
12	000282	Phi Lambda	PO BOX 6830	Mailbox 237	Fullerton	CA	03-Nov-80
05	000283	Chi Lambda	Tennessee Tech University	P.O. Box 5253	Cookeville	TN	01-Mar-79
02	000284	Psi Lambda	P.O.Box 553	Robert Bolden, Advisor	Pomona	NJ	26-Dec-80
02	000285	Omega Lambda				PA	30-Dec-80
12	000286	Alpha Mu	Stanford University	P.O. Box 7528	Stanford	CA	11-Aug-81
06	000287	Beta Mu	College of Charleston	P.O. Box 1271	Charleston	SC	11-Aug-81
02	000288	Gamma Mu	Indiana Univ. of Pennsylvania	Folger Hall Box 1649	Indiana	PA	25-Jun-82
02	000289	Delta Mu	Cornell University		Ithaca	NY	25-Jun-82
12	000290	Epsilon Mu	University of Berkeley	102 Sproul Hall	Berkeley	CA	13-Feb-82
12	000291	Zeta Mu	California State University	P.O. BOX 191922	Los Angeles	CA	23-Oct-82
09	000292	Eta Mu	Sam Houston State University	P. O. Box 2730 SHSU #50	Huntsville	TX	15-Feb-83
09	000293	Theta Mu	University of New Orleans	P.O. Box 276	New Orleans	LA	15-Feb-83
12	000294	Iota Mu		4408 Truxel Rd. #42	Sacramento	CA	27-Mar-83
10	000295	Kappa Mu	University of Illinois	P O Box 6330	Chicago	IL	27-Mar-83
05	000296	Lambda Mu	American	1908	Hermitage	TN	27-Mar-83

08	000297	Mu Mu	Baptist College	Hermitage Park Drive			
12	000298	Nu Mu	University of Pacific	P.O. Box 580822	Modesto	CA	27-Mar-83
12	000299	Xi Mu	Univ of Cal. Santa Barbara	7288 Tulumne Street	Goleta	CA	01-Jun-83
12	000300	Omicron Mu	Weber State University	1984 East 5875 South	Ogden	UT	15-Aug-83
12	000301	Pi Mu	San Diego State University	4299 Spring, St #59	La Mesa	CA	15-Aug-83
09	000302	Rho Mu	University of Arkansas	P.O. Box 3458	Monticello	AR	24-Oct-83
06	000303	Sigma Mu	Elon College	P.O. Box 1039	Elon	NC	18-May-84
02	000304	Tau Mu	Fairleigh Dickinson University	S.U.D 733	Teaneck	NJ	15-Jun-84
02	000305	Upsilon Mu	S.U.N.Y. Old Westbury College	P.O. Box 210	Old Westbury	NY	27-Jun-84
08	000306	Phi Mu	Washburn University	P.O. Box 1696	Topeka	KS	29-Sep-84
06	000307	Chi Mu	Pembroke State	P O Box 5107	Pembroke	NC	29-Dec-84
06	000308	Psi Mu	Appalachian State University	ASU Box 8988	Boone	NC	29-Dec-84
07	000309	Omega Mu	Georgia College		Milledgeville	GA	01-Jul-85
09	000310	Alpha Delta Delta	Louisiana Tech. University	P. O. Box 3118	Ruston	LA	07-Dec-85
03	000311	Beta Delta Delta	James Madison University	P.O. Box 8171	Harrisonburg	VA	07-Dec-85
01	000312	Gamma Delta Delta	University of Massachusetts	P.O. Box 1053	Amherst	MA	28-Feb-87
07	000313	Delta Delta Delta		P.O. Box 623/800 Wheatley St.	Americus	GA	28-Feb-87
10	000314	Epsilon Delta Delta	c/o Omicron Rho Chapter	P. O. Box 3205	Flint	MI	06-Dec-87
07	000315	Zeta Delta Delta	P O Box 8097	Georgia Southern	Statesboro	GA	05-Dec-87

THE OMEGA PSI PHI FRATERNITY INC. 279

				University			
03	000316	Eta Delta Delta	George Mason University	P. O. Box 796	Fairfax	VA	29-Jul-88
07	000317	Theta Delta Delta	Mississippi State University	P O Box 1469	Starkville	MS	29-Jul-88
08	000318	Iota Delta Delta	Southeast Missouri State University	1127 Indian Tmils Dr.	Olivett	MO	09-Dec-88
08	000319	Kappa Delta Delta	University of South Colorado	P.O. Box 232	Pueblo	CO	17-Feb-90
08	000320	Lambda Delta Delta		P.O. Box 8448	Denver	CO	15-Oct-91
10	000321	Mu Delta Delta	Campus Life Building, Suite 180		DeKalb	IL	07-Dec-91
09	000322	Nu Delta Delta	P.O. Box 5688	Aggieland Station	College Station	TX	29-May-92
10	000323	Xi Delta Delta		P.O. Box 83	Houghton	MI	28-Oct-92
02	000324	Omicron Delta Delta	William Patterson University	300 Pompton Road	Wayne	NJ	05-Dec-92
07	000325	Pi Delta Delta	Drawer B	Emory University	Atlanta	GA	23-Jul-94
07	000326	Rho Delta Delta	Troy State University	P.O. Box 820333	Troy	AL	12-Jul-95
07	000327	Sigma Delta Delta		2801 NW 24TH AVE	OAKLAND PARK	FL	06-Dec-95
07	000328	Tau Delta Delta	Valdosta State University	P.O. Box 1712	Valdosta	GA	08-Jun-96
07	000329	Upsilon Delta Delta	P.O. BOX 1241		Cleveland	MS	12-Jul-97
05	000330	Phi Delta Delta	Cumberland University	P.O. Box 2464	Lebanon	TN	11-Jul-98
09	000331	Chi Delta Delta		P.O. Box 1346	Waco	TX	05-Dec-98
06	000332	Psi Delta Delta	Charleston Southern University	P.O. Box 60756	North Charleston	SC	21-Dec-01
02	000333	Omega Delta Delta	Temple University	P.O. Box 56334	Philadelphia	PA	06-Jun-03
09	000334	Alpha Delta Epsilon	SLU 11436		Hammond	LA	22-Jan-04
06	000335	Alpha Delta Zeta	Univ. of N. Carolina @ Greensboro	P.O. Box 26170	Greensboro	NC	22-Jul-04
07	000336	Alpha Delta	Florida	P O Box	Miami	FL	01-Nov-04

		Eta	International University	652726			
09	000337	Alpha Delta Theta	Arkansas Technical University	P.O. Box 6253	Russellville	AR	02-May-05
07	000338	Chi Tau Tau	P.O. Box 160157		Orlando	FL	
07	000339	Alpha Delta Iota	Univ. of West Alabama	P.O. Box 4849	Livinston	AL	04-Dec-05
06	000340	Alpha Delta Kappa	Coastal Carolina University	P.O. Box 51053	Myrtle Beach	SC	21-Jul-06
09	000341	Alpha Delta Lambda	P.O. Box 100837		San Antonio	TX	
14	000499	3951 Snapfinger Parkway			Decatur GA		30035
03	000501	Alpha Omega	Benjamin Franklin Station	P.O. Box 90158	Washington	DC	01-Oct-22
08	000502	Beta Omega	P.O. Box 46129		Kansas City	MO	01-Oct-22
03	000503	Gamma Omega	P. O. Box 2392		Lynchburg	VA	01-Oct-23
03	000504	Delta Omega	P.O. Box 2163		Petersburg	VA	14-Dec-23
06	000505	Epsilon Omega	P.O. Box 1182		Orangeburg	SC	01-Oct-23
04	000506	Zeta Omega	P.O. Box 91271		Cleveland	OH	01-Oct-23
07	000507	Eta Omega	P. O. Box 50521		Atlanta	GA	27-Dec-19
05	000508	Theta Omega	P.O. Box 307		Louisville	KY	12-Dec-22
07	000509	Iota Omega	P.O. Box 831155		Tuskegee	AL	03-Dec-23
02	000510	Kappa Omega	P.O. Box 60333		Harrisburg	PA	25-Jan-23
03	000511	Lambda Omega	937 Norfolk Square		Norfolk	VA	20-Jun-20
02	000512	Mu Omega	P.O. Box 42615		Philadelphia	PA	01-Oct-20
10	000513	Nu Omega	P.O. Box 2484		Detroit	MI	01-Oct-23
09	000514	Xi Omega	P.O. Box 6087		Tulsa	OK	01-Oct-23
03	000515	Omicron Omega	P.O. Box 155		Lawrenceville	VA	01-Oct-23
02	000516	Pi Omega	P.O. Box 23952		Baltimore	MD	01-Oct-21
09	000517	Rho Omega	P. O. Box 958		Shreveport	LA	02-Sep-23
10	000518	Sigma Omega	P. O. Box 497068		Chicago	IL	01-Oct-21
06	000519	Tau Omega	P. O. Box		Greensboro	NC	01-Oct-23

THE OMEGA PSI PHI FRATERNITY INC.

			20381		o		
08	000520	Upsilon Omega	P.O. Box 150346		St. Louis	MO	01-Oct-21
02	000521	Phi Omega	Central Park Station	P O Box 1193	Buffalo	NY	01-Oct-23
07	000522	Chi Omega	P.O. Box 6252		Tallahassee	FL	15-Dec-24
07	000523	Psi Omega	P.O. Box 2507		Augusta	GA	09-Aug-25
07	000524	Alpha Phi	P.O. Box 1741		Birmingham	AL	01-Oct-24
06	000525	Beta Phi	P.O. Box 2091		Durham	NC	15-Dec-24
05	000526	Gamma Phi	P.O. Box 22674		Nashville	TN	01-Oct-25
08	000527	Delta Phi	2501 SW WESTPORT DRIVE		Topeka	KS	01-Oct-25
05	000528	Epsilon Phi	152 East McKellar	P.O. Box 17123	Memphis	TN	01-Oct-25
10	000529	Zeta Phi	P. O. Box 691		Indianapolis	IN	25-Apr-25
01	000530	Eta Phi	P.O. Box 255819	Uphams Corner	Dorchester	MA	01-Jul-25
07	000531	Theta Phi	P.O. Box 41151		Jacksonville	FL	01-Oct-25
02	000532	Iota Phi	P.O. Box 1054		Moon Township	PA	01-Oct-25
10	000533	Kappa Phi	2661 North 2nd Street	P.O. Box 12455	Milwaukee	WI	15-Apr-53
07	000534	Lambda Phi		P O Box 5141	Macon	GA	01-Oct-26
07	000535	Mu Phi	P.O. Box 1363		Savannah	GA	01-Oct-26
09	000536	Nu Phi	P.O. Box 1468		Houston	TX	01-Oct-26
02	000537	Xi Phi	P. O. Box 616	Hamilton Grange Station	New York	NY	11-Nov-26
06	000538	Omicron Phi	P.O Box 4686		Columbia	SC	01-Oct-26
06	000539	Pi Phi	P O Box 16308		Charlotte	NC	27-Jan-27
09	000540	Rho Phi	1616 1/2 Treasure St.		New Orleans	LA	01-Oct-27
07	000541	Sigma Phi	P O Box 4613		Montgomery	AL	16-Apr-27
09	000542	Tau Phi	P.O BOX 7853		Pine Bluff	AR	15-Mar-27
02	000543	Upsilon Phi	P.O. Box 716		Newark	NJ	27-Oct-27

03	000544	Phi Phi	P.O. Box 25685		Richmond	VA	01-Oct-27
08	000545	Chi Phi	P.O. Box 8448		Denver	CO	26-Dec-27
06	000546	Psi Phi	PO Box 21271		Winston-Salem	NC	23-Jan-32
03	000547	Alpha Alpha	P.O. Box 9351		Hampton	VA	01-Oct-32
07	000548	Beta Alpha	P.O. Box 146		Jackson	MS	01-Oct-33
03	000549	Gamma Alpha	P.O. Box 12501		Roanoke	VA	04-Apr-33
04	000550	Delta Alpha	P.O. Box 2817		Dayton	OH	01-Oct-24
09	000551	Epsilon Alpha	P. O. Box 15927		Fort Worth	TX	01-Oct-32
06	000552	Zeta Alpha	P.O. Box 791		Oxford	NC	01-Oct-34
08	000553	Eta Alpha	PO Box 105865		Jefferson City	MO	01-Oct-34
09	000554	Theta Alpha	P.O. Box 227083		Dallas	TX	01-Oct-35
05	000555	Iota Alpha	P.O. Box 6824		Knoxville	TN	01-Oct-35
06	000556	Kappa Alpha	P.O. Box 11165		Rock Hill	SC	09-May-53
09	000557	Lambda Alpha	725 North Foster Drive		Baton Rouge	LA	01-Sep-36
06	000558	Mu Alpha	P.O. Box 22523		Charleston	SC	01-Oct-36
06	000559	Nu Alpha	P.O. Box 551		Plymouth	NC	01-Oct-36
04	000560	Xi Alpha	P.O. Box 178		Institute	WV	01-Oct-36
06	000561	Omicron Alpha	P. O. Box 10373		Wilmington	NC	01-Dec-36
02	000562	Pi Alpha	29669 Scotts Blvd	P O Box 353	Princess Anne	MD	01-Oct-38
07	000563	Rho Alpha	P.O. Box 787		Mobile	AL	01-Oct-38
07	000564	Sigma Alpha	P O Box 680577	Gratigny Station	Miami	FL	01-Oct-39
06	000565	Tau Alpha	P.O. Box 5141		Salisbury	NC	01-Oct-39
02	000566	Upsilon Alpha	P.O. Box 1424		Atlantic City	NJ	01-Oct-39
06	000567	Phi Alpha	P O Box 8424		Greenville	SC	01-Oct-40
04	000568	Chi Alpha	P.O. Box 1752		Bluefield	WV	01-Oct-39
09	000569	Psi Alpha	P.O. Box 200337		San Antonio	TX	01-Nov-40
03	000570	Alpha Iota	P.O. Box 1453		Suffolk	VA	01-Oct-40
04	000571	Beta Iota	P.O. Box 32139	University of Cincinnati	Cincinnati	OH	01-Oct-40
06	000572	Gamma Iota	PO Box 2152		Sumter	SC	01-Oct-40

THE OMEGA PSI PHI FRATERNITY INC.

06	000573	Delta Iota	P.O. Box 2426		Elizabeth City	NC	01-Oct-41
09	000574	Epsilon Iota	P O Box 140044		Austin	TX	15-Nov-41
03	000575	Zeta Iota	P.O. Box 1313		Portsmouth	VA	01-Oct-41
09	000576	Eta Iota	P.O. Box 54636	Sharrel Station	Oklahoma City	OK	10-Apr-42
05	000577	Theta Iota	P.O. Box 7123		Jackson	TN	01-Oct-44
06	000578	Iota Iota	P.O. Box 27353		Raleigh	NC	01-Oct-44
05	000579	Kappa Iota	P.O. Box 822		Chattanooga	TN	01-Oct-45
07	000580	Lambda Iota	P.O. Box 6644		Columbus	GA	01-Oct-45
04	000581	Mu Iota	P.O. Box 16203		Columbus	OH	01-Oct-45
09	000582	Nu Iota	P.O. Box 1941		Marshall	TX	01-Oct-45
03	000583	Xi Iota	P O Box 6291		Charlottesville	VA	12-Apr-46
02	000584	Omicron Iota	P.O. Box 241-H	Heathcote Station	Scarsdale	NY	01-Oct-46
07	000585	Pi Iota	P.O. Box 1093		Tampa	FL	15-Jun-46
03	000586	Rho Iota	P. O. Box 205l		Danville	VA	01-Oct-46
12	000587	Sigma Iota	P.O. Box 3	484 Lake Park Ave.	Oakland	CA	14-May-46
01	000588	Tau Iota	P.O. Box 1715		Hartford	CT	29-Jun-46
09	000589	Upsilon Iota	P.O. Box 837		Langston	OK	21-Oct-46
12	000590	Phi Iota	P.O. Box 3441		Phoenix	AZ	01-Oct-46
06	000591	Chi Iota	P.O. Box 3930		Florence	SC	16-Nov-46
02	000592	Psi Iota	P O Box 1049		Dover	DE	16-Nov-46
06	000593	Alpha Omicron	P.O. Box 2036		Rocky Mount	NC	11-Dec-46
07	000594	Beta Omicron	P.O. Box 9433		Pensacola	FL	01-Dec-46
09	000595	Gamma Omicron	P. O. Box 118		Minden	LA	01-Dec-46
09	000596	Delta Omicron	P O Box 3322		Beaumont	TX	01-Oct-48
09	000597	Epsilon Omicron	P.O. Box 1681		Wichita Falls	TX	16-Feb-47
03	000598	Zeta Omicron	P.O. Box 99		Hampton	VA	01-Oct-47
07	000599	Eta Omicron	P.O. Box 4606		Albany	GA	01-Oct-47
02	000600	Theta Omicron	P.O. Box 24888		Rochester	NY	27-Jul-55
07	000601	Iota Omicron	P.O.BOX 426		Lyon	MS	01-Oct-48

02	000602	Kappa Omicron		P.O. BOX 4153	Waterbury	CT	25-Sep-48
12	000603	Lambda Omicron	P.O. Box 43418		Los Angeles	CA	16-Dec-46
08	000604	Mu Omicron	P.O. Box 1842		Des Moines	IA	03-Aug-47
02	000605	Nu Omicron	P.O Box 230145		Hollis	NY	01-Oct-47
07	000606	Xi Omicron	P.O. Box 5193		Huntsville	AL	30-May-48
07	000607	Omicron Omicron	P.O Box 9571		Daytona Beach	FL	21-Mar-48
09	000608	Pi Omicron	P. O. Box 164238		Little Rock	AR	17-Dec-46
09	000609	Rho Omicron	P.O. Box 12751		New Iberia	LA	01-Oct-48
09	000610	Sigma Omicron	PO Box 5146		Tyler	TX	01-Oct-48
03	000611	Tau Omicron	P.O. Box 3249		Martinsville	VA	01-Oct-48
06	000612	Upsilon Omicron		185 Biltmore Ave.	Asheville	NC	10-Jul-54
12	000613	Phi Omicron	P.O. Box 741162		San Diego	CA	01-Nov-49
01	000614	Chi Omicron	P. O. Box 3263	Westville Station	New Haven,	CO	01-Oct-49
04	000615	Psi Omicron	P.O. Box 5932		Youngstown	OH	15-Jun-49
02	000616	Alpha Upsilon	P.O. Box 1700-63542	542 Atlantic Avenue Station	Brooklyn	NY	01-Oct-49
08	000617	Beta Upsilon	P.O. Box 11754	Downtown Station	Omaha	NE	28-Dec-49
08	000618	Gamma Upsilon	P.O. Box 8483		Wichita	KS	29-Dec-49
02	000619	Delta Upsilon	P. O. Box 2388		Trenton	NJ	30-Jan-50
06	000620	Epsilon Upsilon	P.O. Box 1304		Gastonia	NC	08-Mar-50
12	000621	Zeta Upsilon	P.O. Box 22249		Seattle	WA	19-Jul-50
08	000622	Eta Upsilon	P.O. Box 651		Ft. Leonard Wood	MO	19-Jul-50
09	000623	Theta Upsilon	P. O. Box 3432		Texarkana	TX	28-Nov-50
07	000624	Iota Upsilon	P. O. Box 3563		Gulfport	MS	17-Jul-52
07	000625	Kappa Upsilon	P O Box 2854		West Palm Beach	FL	28-Jan-50
02	000626	Lambda Upsilon	P.O. Box 90		Paterson	NJ	15-Feb-51

THE OMEGA PSI PHI FRATERNITY INC. 285

06	000627	Mu Upsilon	P O Box 82		Denmark	SC	21-Apr-51
02	000628	Nu Upsilon	P O Box 86		Wilmington	DE	18-Aug-51
09	000629	Xi Upsilon	P.O. Box 1311		Port Arthur	TX	07-Feb-52
09	000630	Omicron Upsilon	P O Box 1346		Waco	TX	17-Feb-52
09	000631	Pi Upsilon			Hawkins	TX	17-Feb-52
01	000632	Rho Upsilon	P.O. Box 3672	Beardsley Station	Bridgeport	CT	23-Mar-53
10	000633	Sigma Upsilon	P. O. Box 12277		Lansing	MI	17-May-52
10	000634	Tau Upsilon	P. O. Box 2001		Carbondale	IL	17-May-52
04	000635	Upsilon Upsilon	P.O. Box 823		Skelton	WV	01-May-52
02	000636	Phi Upsilon	P.O. Box 366		Neptune	NJ	15-Jun-52
02	000637	Chi Upsilon	P.O. Box 891		Camden	NJ	15-Jul-52
09	000638	Psi Upsilon	P. O. Box 1066		Lawton	OK	01-Oct-53
10	000639	Alpha Chi	P.O. Box 64440		Gary	IN	07-Jul-53
06	000640	Beta Chi	1100 Hillsborough Street	P.O. Box 1095	Fayetteville	NC	03-Oct-53
09	000641	Gamma Chi	P O Box 5191		Corpus Christi	TX	20-Nov-53
01	000642	Delta Chi	P.O. Box 1405		Springfield	MA	01-Apr-54
09	000643	Epsilon Chi	P. O. Box 5126		Alexandria	LA	01-Apr-54
07	000644	Zeta Chi	P.O. Box 100018		Ft. Lauderdale	FL	24-Apr-54
09	000645	Eta Chi	P. O. Box 8229		Longview	TX	01-Apr-55
09	000646	Theta Chi	P.O.Box 2147		Missouri City	TX	01-Feb-55
01	000647	Iota Chi	P.O. Box 380691		Cambridge	MA	01-Feb-55
09	000648	Kappa Chi	P.O. Box 572		Magnolia	AR	01-Mar-55
09	000649	Lambda Chi	P. O. Box 2884		Amarillo	TX	04-Feb-56
04	000650	Mu Chi	P. O. Box 3261		Fairborn	OH	05-Apr-55
10	000651	Nu Chi	P.O. Box 3302		East St. Louis	IL	10-Apr-55
04	000652	Xi Chi	P.O. Box 8259		Akron	OH	01-May-55
02	000653	Omicron Chi	P.O. Box 1434		Plainfield	NJ	01-Jan-55
12	000654	Pi Chi	2380 109th Ave		Oakland	CA	01-Jul-55
09	000655	Rho Chi	P.O. Box 1095		Lake Charles	LA	01-Jun-55
06	000656	Sigma Chi		P O	Reidsville	NC	24-Aug-55

13	000657	Tau Chi		Box 2666	Monrovia LIBERIA	LB	01-Dec-55
09	000658	Upsilon Chi	P.O. Box 177		Bentonville	AR	04-Feb-56
06	000659	Phi Chi	P.O. Box 1054		Concord	NC	06-Mar-56
06	000660	Chi Chi	PO Box 573		Camden	SC	26-Feb-58
07	000661	Psi Chi	P.O. Box 174		Ocala	FL	29-May-56
07	000662	Omega Chi	P.O. Box 2392		Selma	AL	01-Jan-57
07	000663	Alpha Tau	Post Office Box 1157		Tuscaloosa	AL	01-Apr-57
06	000664	Beta Tau	P.O. Box 1191		Mullins	SC	01-Apr-57
07	000665	Gamma Tau	P O Box 5626		Leesburg	FL	31-Dec-57
09	000666	Delta Tau	P.O. Box 387		Plaquemine	LA	05-May-58
09	000667	Epsilon Tau	P.O. Box 1632		Cedar Hill	TX	01-May-58
12	000668	Zeta Tau	P.O. Box 94712		Pasadena	CA	01-Sep-57
07	000669	Eta Tau	P.O. Box 522		Port Gibson	MS	01-Oct-57
07	000670	Theta Tau	P.O. Box 1561		Anniston	AL	10-Mar-59
06	000671	Iota Tau		P O Box 2604	Georgetown	SC	25-Apr-59
04	000672	Kappa Tau	P.O. Box 35051		Canton	OH	20-Jun-59
07	000673	Lambda Tau	P.O. Box 1642		Brunswick	GA	15-Oct-59
09	000674	Mu Tau	P.O. Box 3041		Monroe	LA	15-Nov-59
02	000675	Nu Tau	P.O.Box 341		Albany	NY	15-Nov-59
04	000676	Xi Tau	P.O. Box 864		Maumee	OH	06-Apr-60
07	000677	Omicron Tau	P.O. Box 775		Fort Pierce	FL	10-Oct-60
09	000678	Pi Tau	P O Box 202		Grambling	LA	01-Oct-60
10	000679	Rho Tau	P.O. Box 252		Gurnee	IL	03-Feb-61
09	000680	Sigma Tau	P.O. Box 6491		El Paso	TX	03-Feb-61
12	000681	Tau Tau	P.O. Box 59453		Los Angeles	CA	03-Feb-61
02	000682	Upsilon Tau	P.O. Box 2086		Poughkeepsie	NY	19-Mar-61
05	000683	Phi Tau	119 N.Lincoln Ave		Jonesboro	TN	01-Jun-61
07	000684	Chi Tau	P.O. Box 555949		Orlando	FL	08-Jan-62
05	000685	Psi Tau	P.O. Box 11981		Lexington	KY	01-Oct-62
12	000686	Alpha Rho	P.O. Box 56635		Haywood	CA	15-Mar-62

THE OMEGA PSI PHI FRATERNITY INC. 287

07	000687	Beta Rho	14000 HWY 82 W	P.O. BOX 5007	Itta Bena	MS	05-Apr-62
09	000688	Gamma Rho	P.O. Box 740426		New Orleans	LA	05-Apr-62
06	000689	Delta Rho	P.O Box 267		Kingstree	SC	29-Apr-62
10	000690	Epsilon Rho	P.O. Box 4548		St. Paul	MN	09-May-62
12	000691	Zeta Rho	P.O. Box 431358		Los Angeles	CA	11-Jun-62
07	000692	Eta Rho	P. O. Box 35184		St Petersburg	FL	11-Sep-62
13	000693	Theta Rho	c/oByron C. Mattews	HHC, 21ST TSC, UNIT 23203, BOX 294	APO	AE	15-Aug-62
09	000694	Iota Rho	P.O. Box 12181		Odessa	TX	01-Jun-63
06	000695	Kappa Rho	P.O. Box 877	500 Beaman Street	Clinton	NC	10-Oct-63
01	000696	Lambda Rho	Omega Housing Development	330 Bishop Street	Waterbury	CT	01-Mar-64
02	000697	Mu Rho	P.O. Box 4212		Annapolis	MD	01-Mar-64
08	000698	Nu Rho	P.O. Box 657		Albuquerque	NM	01-Apr-64
09	000699	Xi Rho	P. O. Box 5450		West Memphis	AR	01-Apr-64
10	000700	Omicron Rho	P.O. 13104		Flint	MI	01-May-64
12	000701	Pi Rho	P.O. Box 55093		Riverside	CA	07-Aug-64
06	000702	Rho Rho	P.O. Box 464		Ahoskie	NC	05-Sep-64
10	000703	Sigma Rho	P.O. Box 7421		Ann Arbor	MI	09-Nov-64
03	000704	Tau Rho	P.O. Box 1321	College Station	Fredericksburg	VA	07-Dec-64
09	000705	Upsilon Rho	P. O. Box 92595		Lafayette	LA	01-Oct-97
07	000706	Phi Rho	P.O. Box 17557		Hattiesburg	MS	26-Mar-65
02	000707	Chi Rho	C/O- KRS	P O Box 471	Wheatley Heights	NY	11-Aug-65
07	000708	Psi Rho	P.O Box 5001		Holly Springs	MS	03-Aug-65
01	000709	Alpha Nu	Box 445	304 Main Avenue	Norwalk	CT	11-Dec-65
06	000710	Beta Nu	P.O. Box 178		Proctorville	NC	01-Mar-66

07	000711	Gamma Nu	P.O. Box 771		Cocoa	FL	15-Mar-67
06	000712	Delta Nu	P. O. Box 1001		Morganton	NC	06-Apr-67
06	000713	Epsilon Nu	P O Box 1642		Spartanburg	SC	10-Jun-67
12	000714	Zeta Nu	P.O. Box 12440		Portland	OR	21-Jun-68
07	000715	Eta Nu	P.O. Box 547		Pompano Beach	FL	11-Jun-69
10	000716	Theta Nu	P.O. Box 4473		Muskegon Heights	MI	20-Dec-69
02	000717	Iota Nu	P.O. Box 373		Aberdeen	MD	
02	000718	Kappa Nu	Marcus Whitehurst	122 Grange Building	University Park	PA	01-Mar-70
03	000719	Lambda Nu	P. O. Box 351		Franklin	VA	01-Jun-70
02	000720	Mu Nu	P. O. Box 3330		Silver Spring	MD	23-May-70
02	000721	Nu Nu	P O Box 425		Willingboro	NJ	01-Aug-70
12	000722	Xi Nu	P.O. Box 6254		San Jose	CA	08-May-68
12	000723	Omicron Nu	P.O. Box 864		Seaside	CA	01-Jan-71
07	000724	Pi Nu	P.O. Box 570507		Miami	FL	17-Feb-71
09	000725	Rho Nu	P.O. Box 817		Galveston	TX	01-Apr-71
01	000726	Sigma Nu	Brown Universsity	P.O. Box 1147	Providence	RI	28-Jun-71
10	000727	Tau Nu	P.O. Box 12758		Fort Wayne	IN	16-Jul-71
03	000728	Upsilon Nu	P.O. Box 27955		Richmond	VA	12-Oct-71
02	000729	Phi Nu	Charles B. Bolden	P O Box 329	Mohegan Lake	NY	14-Jan-72
12	000730	Chi Nu	438 E. Shaw Avenue #323		Fresno	CA	19-Jan-72
03	000731	Psi Nu	P O Box 26162		Alexandria	VA	07-Apr-72
10	000732	Omega Nu	P O Box 1944		Springfield	IL	07-May-72
07	000733	Alpha Pi	P.O. Box 502		Florence	AL	12-Jan-73
07	000734	Beta Pi	P.O. Box 143143		Gainesville	FL	12-Jan-73
02	000735	Gamma Pi	P.O. Box 4072		Capitol Heights	MD	05-Mar-73
12	000736	Delta Pi	P O Box 44095		Tacoma	WA	15-Mar-73
02	000737	Epsilon Pi	P.O. BOX 1081		Chester	PA	23-Mar-73
02	000738	Zeta Pi	P.O. Box 877	Homer L Smith,	Erie	PA	27-Mar-73

THE OMEGA PSI PHI FRATERNITY INC.

				KRS			
02	000739	Eta Pi	PO Box 459		Montclair	NJ	02-May-73
12	000740	Theta Pi	P.O. Box 948		Vallejo	CA	31-Jul-73
10	000741	Iota Pi	PO Box 7789		Grand Rapids	MI	09-Mar-74
06	000742	Kappa Pi	P.O. Box 1212		Lancaster	SC	06-Nov-73
06	000743	Lambda Pi	P O Box 1583		Kinston	NC	21-Nov-73
06	000744	Mu Pi	P.O. Box 17582		Greenville	SC	09-Mar-74
10	000745	Nu Pi	P. O. Box 3934		Joliet	IL	09-Mar-74
08	000746	Xi Pi	P.O. Box 2288		Colorado Springs	CO	18-Jul-74
09	000747	Omicron Pi	P.O. Box 1105		Killeen	TX	18-Jul-74
10	000748	Pi Pi	P.O. Box 2243		Midland	MI	18-Feb-75
07	000749	Rho Pi		1044 Lobster Lane	Jacksonville	FL	17-Jan-75
06	000750	Sigma Pi	P.O. Box 491		Aiken	SC	17-Apr-75
02	000751	Tau Pi	P.O. Box 66		Columbia	MD	19-Apr-75
10	000752	Upsilon Pi	P.O. Box 51565		Kalamazoo	MI	20-Jul-75
09	000753	Phi Pi	P O Box 2038		Muskogee	OK	12-Nov-75
02	000754	Chi Pi	P.O. Box 6024	Teall Avenue Station	Syracuse	NY	12-Nov-75
05	000755	Psi Pi	P.O. Box 2903		Clarksville	TN	12-Nov-75
06	000756	Omega Pi	5300 McCormick Rd		Durham	NC	12-Nov-75
07	000757	Alpha Xi	P O Box 1633		LaGrange	GA	15-Nov-75
10	000758	Beta Xi	P.O. Box 5194		Evansville	IN	28-Jan-76
03	000759	Gamma Xi	P O Box 64535		Virginia Beach	VA	22-Mar-76
09	000760	Delta Xi	P.O.Box 8321		Greenville	TX	01-Apr-76
12	000761	Epsilon Xi	P.O Box 188765		Sacramento	CA	10-Apr-76
13	000762	Zeta Xi	P.O. Box 308775		St. Thomas	VI	15-Aug-76
07	000763	Eta Xi	P.O. Box 2241		Starkville	MS	13-Oct-76
10	000764	Theta Xi	P.O. Box 5162		Peoria	IL	13-Oct-76
02	000765	Iota Xi	P.O. Box 7905	FDR Station	New York	NY	20-Nov-76
12	000766	Kappa Xi	P.O. Box 270226		Las Vegas	NV	20-Nov-76
13	000767	Lambda Xi	PSC 450 Box 434	Korea	APO	AP	22-Feb-77

10	000768	Mu Xi	P.O. Box 2483		Glen Ellyn	IL	11-Mar-77
07	000769	Nu Xi	P O Box 1704		Natchez	MS	12-Mar-77
05	000770	Xi Xi	P.O. Box 511		Fort Knox	KY	25-Mar-77
08	000771	Omicron Xi	P.O. Box 11763		Kansas City	MO	03-Apr-77
13	000772	Pi Xi	c/o Eugene Horton, IBM Bahamas Ltd.	P. O. Box N 10369	Nassau	BA	17-Aug-77
09	000773	Rho Xi	P.O. Box 2043		Freeport	TX	31-Aug-77
10	000774	Sigma Xi	P.O. Box 2636		Champaign	IL	31-Aug-77
04	000775	Tau Xi	CHARTER REVOKED - DISBANDED		Cincinnati	OH	01-Jan-77
07	000776	Upsilon Xi	P.O. Box 91492		Lakeland	FL	01-Nov-77
08	000777	Phi Xi	P.O. Box 2006		Fort Riley	KS	10-Mar-78
10	000778	Chi Xi	P.O. Box 2011		Saginaw	MI	10-Mar-78
12	000779	Psi Xi	P.O. Box 5723		Oxnard	CA	10-Mar-78
02	000780	Omega Xi	P O Box 1464		Bethlehem	PA	10-Mar-78
14	000782	Life Members	Omega Psi Phi Fraternity Inc	3951 Snapfinger Parkway	Decatur	GA	01-Oct-97
03	000783	International Members	International Headquarters	3951 Snapfinger Parkway	Decatur	GA	02-Aug-90
04	000784	Alpha Alpha Alpha	P.O. Box 429		Shepherdstoen	WV	10-Mar-78
02	000785	Beta Alpha Alpha	P.O. Box 241		White Plains	NY	01-Oct-97
12	000786	Gamma Alpha Alpha	P.O. Box 201547		Anchorage	AK	15-Sep-78
12	000787	Delta Alpha Alpha	P.O. Box 22976		Tucson	AZ	16-Sep-78
09	000788	Epsilon Alpha Alpha	P.O. Box 452		Blytheville	AR	16-Sep-78
03	000789	Zeta Alpha Alpha	P.O. Box 866		Hampden-Sydney	VA	15-Aug-79
12	000790	Eta Alpha Alpha	P.O. Box 1863		Pomona	CA	30-Jul-79
05	000791	Theta Alpha Alpha	P.O. Box 50243		Bowling Green	KY	22-Sep-79
02	000792	Iota Alpha Alpha	4336 Russell Road		Hurlock	MD	22-Sep-79
07	000793	Kappa Alpha Alpha	P.O. Box 360260		Decatur	GA	22-Sep-79

THE OMEGA PSI PHI FRATERNITY INC. 291

07	000794	Lambda Alpha Alpha	P. O. Box 306		Boynton Beach	FL	15-Mar-80
12	000795	Mu Alpha Alpha	P. O. Box 2002		Artesia	CA	15-Mar-80
10	000796	Nu Alpha Alpha	P.O. Box 8542		Bloomington	IN	15-Mar-80
09	000797	Xi Alpha Alpha	P.O. Box 2682		Natchitoches	LA	15-Mar-80
10	000798	Omicron Alpha Alpha	P.O. Box 431189		Pontiac	MI	19-May-80
05	000799	Pi Alpha Alpha	601 Alfa Drive		Frankfort	KY	25-Apr-80
07	000800	Rho Alpha Alpha	P.O. Box 1978		Cleveland	MS	08-Aug-80
07	000801	Sigma Alpha Alpha	P.O. BOX 8330		Moss Point	MS	08-Aug-80
12	000802	Tau Alpha Alpha	PO Box 1521		Bakersfield	CA	08-Dec-80
07	000803	Upsilon Alpha Alpha	P. O. Box 1337		Panama City	FL	30-Dec-80
06	000804	Phi Alpha Alpha	P.O. Box 10245		Goldsboro	NC	30-Dec-80
12	000805	Chi Alpha Alpha	P.O. Box 142124		Spokane	WA	30-Dec-80
03	000806	Psi Alpha Alpha	P.O. Box 30876		Alexandria	VA	30-Dec-80
06	000807	Omega Alpha Alpha	P.O. Box 151		Beaufort	SC	30-Dec-80
06	000808	Alpha Beta Beta	P.O. Box 2284		Hartsville	SC	14-Mar-81
06	000809	Beta Beta Beta	P.O Box 1388		Wilson	NC	14-Mar-81
06	000810	Gamma Beta Beta	P.O. Box 882		Shelby	NC	14-Mar-81
10	000811	Delta Beta Beta	P.O. Box 321		Moline	IL	14-Mar-81
10	000812	Epsilon Beta Beta	P.O. Box 22		South Bend	IN	14-Feb-81
07	000813	Zeta Beta Beta	P.O. Box 5824		Athens	GA	15-Apr-81
06	000814	Eta Beta Beta	P.O. Box 165		Lexington	NC	15-Aug-81
01	000815	Theta Beta Beta	Dartmouth College-D. Thompson	Hinman Box 0663	Hanover	NH	25-Jun-82
06	000816	Iota Beta Beta	P.O. Box 1361		St. Stephens	SC	25-Jun-82
07	000817	Kappa Beta Beta	P.O. Box 38		Dothan	AL	25-Jun-82
13	000818	Lambda Beta Beta	P.O. Box 4694		Mililani	HI	25-Jun-82
07	000819	Mu Beta Beta	P.O. Box 2362		Thomasville	GA	08-Aug-82
02	000820	Nu Beta Beta	P.O. Box 1293		Teaneck	NJ	08-Aug-82

07	000821	Xi Beta Beta	P O Box 773		Dublin	GA	08-Aug-82
07	000822	Omicron Beta Beta	P.O.Box 2855		Ft Myers	FL	23-Oct-82
07	000823	Pi Beta Beta	P.O. Box 1902		Bradenton	FL	23-Oct-82
09	000824	Rho Beta Beta	P. O. Box 652		Houston	TX	23-Oct-82
02	000825	Sigma Beta Beta	P.O. Box 153		Westbury	NY	27-Mar-83
06	000826	Tau Beta Beta	P.O. Box 941		Weldon	NC	27-Mar-83
06	000827	Upsilon Beta Beta	PO Box 2481		Conway	SC	27-Mar-83
12	000828	Phi Beta Beta	P.O. Box 191922		Los Angeles	CA	27-Mar-83
10	000829	Chi Beta Beta	P.O. Box 226		Bloomington	IL	28-May-83
04	000830	Psi Beta Beta	P.O. Box 5525		Huntington	WV	25-Jul-83
07	000831	Omega Beta Beta	P O Box 550103		Orlando	FL	15-Aug-83
07	000832	Alpha Gamma Gamma	P.O. Box 67		Valdosta	GA	15-Aug-83
07	000833	Beta Gamma Gamma	P.O. Box 3281		Ft. Stewart	GA	06-Jan-84
10	000834	Gamma Gamma Gamma	P. O. Box 1494		Madison	WI	06-Jan-84
08	000835	Delta Gamma Gamma	P.O. Box 81661		Lincoln	NE	06-Jan-84
06	000836	Epsilon Gamma Gamma	812 Green St		Greenwich	SC	14-Jan-84
05	000837	Zeta Gamma Gamma	P.O. Box 4323		Oak Ridge	TN	01-Aug-84
08	000838	Eta Gamma Gamma	P.O. Box 834		Waterloo	IA	29-Sep-84
07	000839	Theta Gamma Gamma	P.O. Box 2353		Belle Glade	FL	29-Sep-84
09	000840	Iota Gamma Gamma	P.O. Box 3285		Fort Polk	LA	29-Dec-84
06	000841	Kappa Gamma Gamma	P.O. Box 1002		Anderson	SC	29-Dec-84
02	000842	Lambda Gamma Gamma	P.O. Box 1787		Clinton	MD	29-Dec-84
02	000843	Mu Gamma Gamma	P.O. Box 6322		Somerset	NJ	04-Oct-85
13	000844	Nu Gamma Gamma	P.O. Box 39118	Billings Bridge RPO	Ottawa	ON	05-Dec-85
12	000845	Xi Gamma Gamma	P. O. Box 2241		Oceanside	CA	13-Mar-85

09	000846	Omicron Gamma Gamma	P.O. Box 5792		Arlington	TX	21-Jan-86
05	000847	Pi Gamma Gamma	P.O. Box 386		Murfreesboro	TN	28-Feb-87
10	000848	Rho Gamma Gamma	P. O. Box 81265		Chicago	IL	01-Mar-87
13	000849	Sigma Gamma Gamma	PSC 482 Box 2554		FPO	AP	28-Feb-87
06	000850	Tau Gamma Gamma	P. O. Box 71930		Ft. Bragg	NC	06-Dec-87
07	000851	Upsilon Gamma Gamma	P.O. Box 7115		Fort Gordon	GA	06-Dec-87
13	000852	Phi Gamma Gamma	CFLCC C3 OPS	Camp Arifjan, Kuwait	APO	AE	29-Jul-88
07	000853	Chi Gamma Gamma	P O Box 71507		Marietta	GA	29-Jul-88
07	000854	Psi Gamma Gamma	841 Burgundy Drive		Columbus	MS	16-Dec-88
07	000855	Omega Gamma Gamma	P O Box 6728		Warner Robins	GA	09-Dec-88
09	000856	Alpha Iota Iota	P. O Box 795293		Dallas	TX	15-Sep-89
02	000857	Beta Iota Iota	P.O. Box 2091		Vineland	NJ	09-Dec-89
05	000858	Gamma Iota Iota	754 Hawks Road		Martin	TN	09-Dec-89
12	000859	Delta Iota Iota	P.O. Box 522		Tracey	CA	09-Dec-89
01	000860	Epsilon Iota Iota	P.O Box 6712		Hamden	CT	02-Aug-90
02	000861	Zeta Iota Iota		P.O. Box 4357	Cherry Hill	NJ	20-Jul-90
13	000862	Eta Iota Iota	P.O. Box 5511	Kingshill U.S.V.I.	St. Croix	VI	08-Dec-90
07	000863	Theta Iota Iota	P.O. Box 8163		Meridian	MS	08-Dec-90
12	000864	Iota Iota Iota	P.O. Box 581469		Salt Lake City	UT	08-Dec-90
03	000865	Kappa Iota Iota	P. O. Box 4682		Fort Eustis	VA	07-Dec-91
06	000866	Lambda Iota Iota	P.O. Box 1311		Bennettsville	SC	07-Dec-91
02	000867	Mu Iota Iota	P.O. Box 425		Fort Drum	NY	07-Dec-91
07	000868	Nu Iota Iota	P O Box 1795		Auburn	AL	07-Dec-91
04	000869	Xi Iota Iota	P.O. Box 36		Sidney	OH	07-Dec-91
08	000870	Omicron Iota Iota	P.O. Box 3222		Ft. Leavenwor	KS	29-May-92

07	000871	Pi Iota Iota	P. O. Box 51856	Fort Benning	GA	29-May-92
12	000872	Rho Iota Iota	P.O. Box 35542	Ft Wainwright	AK	07-Aug-92
12	000873	Sigma Iota Iota	P. O. Box 4775	Lancaster	CA	07-Aug-92
06	000874	Tau Iota Iota	P O Box 697	St George	SC	07-Aug-92
05	000875	Upsilon Iota Iota	P.O.Box 8141	Paducah	KY	28-Oct-92
09	000876	Phi Iota Iota	P.O. Box 405	LaPlace	LA	31-Dec-92
06	000877	Chi Iota Iota	P.O. Box 1943	Columbia	SC	18-Aug-93
07	000878	Psi Iota Iota	P.O. Box 615	Shalimar	FL	10-Apr-94
07	000879	Omega Iota Iota	P.O Box 201191	Montgomery	AL	23-Jul-94
10	000880	Alpha Kappa Kappa	P.O. Box 64572	Gary	IN	23-Jul-94
06	000881	Beta Kappa Kappa	P.O. Box 583	High Point	NC	23-Jul-94
06	000882	Gamma Kappa Kappa	P.O BOX 1873	Gaffney	SC	23-Jul-94
09	000883	Delta Kappa Kappa	P.O. Box 387	Hot Springs	AR	12-Jul-95
07	000884	Epsilon Kappa Kappa	P O Box 1391	Canton	MS	12-Jul-95
04	000885	Zeta Kappa Kappa	P.O. Box 22480	Beachwood	OH	12-Jul-95
09	000886	Eta Kappa Kappa	P.O. Box 3233	Lufkin	TX	03-Aug-95
10	000887	Theta Kappa Kappa	P.O. Box 5300	Evanston	IL	19-Aug-95
07	000888	Iota Kappa Kappa	P O Box 2841	Deland	FL	07-Dec-95
07	000889	Kappa Kappa Kappa	P. O. Box 1486	Swainsboro	GA	07-Dec-95
09	000890	Lambda Kappa Kappa	P.O. Box 53212	Baton Rouge	LA	07-Dec-95
12	000891	Mu Kappa Kappa	P.O. Box 487	Redwood City	CA	01-Oct-97
10	000892	Nu Kappa Kappa	P.O. Box 361	Butler	WI	02-Aug-96
07	000893	Xi Kappa Kappa	P.O. Box 1193	Yazoo City	MS	14-Dec-96
03	000894	Omicron Kappa Kappa	P. O. Box 3317	Reston	VA	14-Dec-96
02	000895	Pi Kappa Kappa	P.O. Box 204	Sicklerville	NJ	17-Apr-97
05	000896	Rho Kappa Kappa	P.O. Box 84	Spring Hill	TN	17-May-97
03	000897	Sigma Kappa Kappa	P.O. Box 15631	Chesapeake	VA	01-Oct-97

THE OMEGA PSI PHI FRATERNITY INC. 295

10	000898	Tau Kappa Kappa	P.O. Box 829		Southfield	MI	11-Jul-98
10	000899	Upsilon Kappa Kappa	P. O. Box 6463		Lafayette	IN	11-Jul-98
07	000900	Phi Kappa Kappa	P. O. BOX 90215		East Point	GA	05-Dec-98
09	000901	Chi Kappa Kappa	P.O.Box 2655		Slidell	LA	05-Dec-98
07	000902	Psi Kappa Kappa	P.O. Box 8150		Redstone Arsenal	AL	
00	000903	Omega Kappa Kappa				FS	
02	000904	Alpha Lambda Lambda	P.O. Box 1112		Frederick	MD	19-Oct-00
07	000905	Beta Lambda Lambda	P.O. Box 490488		Lawrenceville	GA	06-Dec-00
09	000906	Gamma Lambda Lambda	P O Box 963		Houma	LA	20-May-01
06	000907	Delta Lambda Lambda	P O Box 1437		Graham	NC	29-May-01
09	000908	Epsilon Lambda Lambda	P.O. Box 116		Opelousas	LA	01-Oct-01
13	000909	Zeta Lambda Lambda	P.O. Box 1982 HM HX		Hamilton, Bermuda		01-Oct-01
09	000910	Eta Lambda Lambda	P.O Box 2065		Red Oak	TX	12-Nov-01
07	000911	Theta Lambda Lambda	P O Box 2284		Peachtree City	GA	07-Jan-02
02	000912	Iota Lambda Lambda	Calder Square	P.O. Box 10295	State College	PA	27-Mar-02
13	000913	Kappa Lambda Lambda	P.O. Box N-255		Nassau	BA	09-Aug-02
07	000914	Lambda Lambda Lambda	P O Box 1574		Americus	GA	15-Oct-02
07	000915	Mu Lambda Lambda	P. O. Box 2452		Tunica	MS	06-Nov-02
02	000916	Nu Lambda Lambda	P O Box 15427		Jersey City	NJ	04-Jan-03
02	000917	Xi Lambda Lambda	P.O. Box 383		Pomona	NY	25-Sep-03
09	000918	Omicron Lambda Lambda	P.O. Box 55401		Little Rock	AR	22-Jan-04
03	000919	Pi Lambda Lambda	P O Box 663		Dumfries	VA	22-Jan-04
02	000920	Rho Lambda Lambda	P. O. Box 173		South Orange	NJ	22-Jan-04
05	000921	Sigma Lambda	2095 Exeter Road	Suite 80-208	Germantown	TN	28-May-04

		Lambda						
02	000922	Tau Lambda Lambda	P.O. Box 1624		Waldorf	MD	11-Jun-04
13	000923	Upsilon Lambda Lambda	GDS P. O. Box 92		APO	AP	22-Jul-04
06	000924	Phi Lambda Lambda	P.O. Box 369		Jacksonville	NC	10-Sep-04
10	000925	Chi Lambda Lambda	P.O. Box 336		Matteson	IL	07-Dec-04
02	000926	Psi Lambda Lambda	P.O. Box 595	College Station	New York	NY	20-Jan-05
05	000927	Omega Lambda Lambda	P O Box 1611		Madison	TN	20-Jan-05
09	000928	Alpha Mu Mu	P.O. Box 1731		Bryan	TX	21-Jul-06
12	000929	Beta Mu Mu			Las Vegas	NV	
09	000930	Gamma Mu Mu	P.O. 1025	179 Student Union	Stillwater	OK	
00	000999	Detached/Unknown	3951 Snapfinger Parkway		Decatur	GA	

<<>>

Founded 1986

"THE BEST FEDERAL CREDIT UNION FOR OMEGA MEN AND THEIR FAMILIES"

Omega World Center, 3951 Snapfinger Parkway, Decatur, GA 30035
(404) 289-1100 | Fax: (404) 289-3322

OPPFFCU President's Message
"Our Financial Security"

It is with great pleasure and pride to have the opportunity to serve as the President of the Omega Psi Phi Fraternity Federal Credit Union. With the potential of more than 100,000 members, it has opened up many financial avenues for the fraternity's members, families and employees. Working with an excellent team of dedicated members of the Board, and Committees, we now have a competitive, financially secure credit union. I encourage you to join, save, borrow and take advantage of all the services available to you.

In the future, we will continue to increase our services and welcome your ideas, input and suggestions to make this credit union the finest in the world at serving your needs.

Derrick Hostler, President
OPPFFCU

<<>>

APPENDIX C

Grand Basilei
Of
Omega Psi Phi Fraternity

	Name	Term of Office	
1st	Edgar A. Love	1911 - 1912	Deceased
2nd	Oscar J. Cooper	1912 - 1913	Deceased
3rd	Edgar A. Love	1913 - 1915	Deceased
4th	George E. Hall	1915 - 1916	Deceased
5th	James C. McMorries	1915 - 1916	Deceased
6th	Clarence F. Holmes	1917 - 1918	Deceased
7th	Raymond G. Robinson	1918 - 1920	Deceased
8th	Harold H. Thomas	1920 - 1921	Deceased
9th	J. Alston Atkins	1921 - 1924	Deceased
10th	John W. Love	1924 - 1924	Deceased
11th	George E. Vaughn	1924 - 1926	Deceased
12th	Julius S. McClain	1926 - 1929	Deceased
13th	Matthew W. Bullock	1929 - 1932	Deceased
14th	Lawrence A. Oxley	1932 - 1935	Deceased
15th	William E. Baugh	1935 - 1937	Deceased
16th	Albert W. Dent	1937 - 1940	Deceased
17th	Z. Alexander Looby	1940 - 1945	Deceased
18th	Campbell C. Johnson	1945 - 1947	Deceased
19th	Harry T. Penn	1947 - 1949	Deceased
20th	Milo C. Murray	1949 - 1951	Deceased
21st	Grant Reynolds	1951-1953	Deceased
22nd	John E. Potts	1953 - 1955	Deceased
23rd	Herbert E. Tucker. Jr.	1955 - 1958	Deceased
24th	I. Gregory Newton	1958 - 1961	Deceased
25th	Cary D. Jacobs	1961 - 1964	Deceased
26th	George E. Meares	1964 - 1967	Deceased
27th	Ellis F. Corbett	1967 - 1970	Deceased

28th	James S. Avery	1970 - 1973	
29th	Marion W. Garnett	1973 - 1976	Deceased
30th	Edward J. Braynon. Jr	1976 - 1979	
31st	Burnel E. Coulon	1979 - 1982	
32nd	L. Benjamin Livingston	1982 - 1984	Deceased
33rd	Moses C. Norman. Sr.	1984 - 1990	
34th	C. Tyrone Gilmore	1990 - 1994	
35th	Dorsey C. Miller	1994 - 1998	
36th	Lloyd J. Jordan	1998 - 2002	
37th	George H. Grace	2002 - 2006	
38th	**Warren G. Lee, Jr.**	2006 - 2010	

<<>>

APPENDIX D

FIRST VICE GRAND BASILEI
OF
OMEGA PSI PHI FRATERNITY INC.

#	NAME	YEAR
1	JOHN W. LOVE	1922
2	STERLING A. BROWN	1924
3	JULIUS S. MccLAIN	1925
4	J.D. STEWART	1927
5	MATHEW W. BULLOCK	1928
6	IRA DE A. REID	1930
7	WILLIAMS E. BAUGH	1932
8	JESSE O. THOMAS	1935
9	PARIS V. STERRETT	1937
10	MIFFLIN T. GIBBS	1939
11	JOHN H. CALHOUN, JR.	1944
12	MILO C. MURRAY	1948
13	GRANT REYNOLDS	1949
14	JOHN F. POTTS	1951
15	HERBERT E. TUCKER JR.	1953
16	JOSEPH T. BROOKS	1955
17	I. GREGORY NEWTON	1957
18	CARY D. JACOBS	1958
19	GEORGE E. MEARES	1961
20	ELLIS F. CORBETT	1964
21	JAMES S. AVERY	1967
22	MARION W. GARNETT	1970

23	EDWARD BRAYNON	1973
24	BURNEL E. COULON	1976
25	L. BENJAMIN LIVINGTON	1979
26	MOSES C. NORMAN	1982
27	C. TYRONE GILMORE	1984
28	MELVIN ZENO	1988
29	DORSEY C. MILLER	1990
30	ADAM McKEE	1994
31	JOHN H. SCOTT	1998
32	WARREN G. LEE	2002
33	CARL A. BLUNT	2006

<<>>

APPENDIX E

Second Vice Grand Basilei Of Omega Psi Phi Fraternity, Inc.

	Name	School	Chapter	Tenure
1st	Dexter D. Eure	West Virginia State	Theta Psi	1945 - 1946
2nd	Joseph T. Brooks, Jr.	Morehouse College	Psi	1946 - 1947
3rd	Thomas A. Lassiter	Johnson C. Smith Univ	Rho	1947 - 1948
4th	Malcolm L. Corrin	Morehouse College	Psi	1948 - 1950
5th	James N. Young	Morehouse College	Psi	1950 - 1952
6th	J. Heyward Harrison	Morgan State College	Pi	1952 - 1953
7th	Howard C. Davis	Howard University	Alpha	1953 - 1954
8th	Ralph Kelly	Central State College	Eta Gamma	1954 - 1955
9th	Ernest E. Reeves	West Virginia State	Theta Psi	1955 - 1956
10th	Fred Henderson Moore	Allen University	Mu Sigma'	1956 - 1957
11th	William T. Johnson	Virginia State College	Nu Psi	1957 - 1958
12th	Paul N. Johnson	New York University	Zeta Psi	1958 - 1959
13th	James L. Felder	Clark College	Beta Psi	1959 - 1961
14th	Robert H. Tucker	Clark College	Beta Psi	1961 - 1962
15th	Jesse L. Jackson	North Carolina A&T	Mu Psi[2]	1962 - 1964
16th	Dorsey C. Miller, Jr.	Morehouse College	Psi	1964 - 1965
17th	Harold D. Thompson	South Carolina State	Xi Psi	1965 -1967
18th	Lincoln C. Scott	Harris Teachers College	Omicron Sigma	1967 - 1968
19th	Daniel R. Thomas	Southern Illinois	Omicron Theta	1968 - 1970
20th	Richard L. Taylor	Boston University	Gamma	1970 - 1971
21st	Samuel W. Johnson	Univ of New Mexico	Sigma	1971- 1973

22nd	Christopher Dixon	Howard University	Gamma Alpha[3]	1973 - 1974
23rd	Warren G. Lee, Jr	Univ of Texas-Austin	Eta Theta	1974 - 1976
24th	K. Earl Ferguson	Howard University	Alpha	1976 - 1977
25th	Napoleon Darnell Smith	New Mexico State Univ	Eta Eta[4]	1977 - 1979
26th	Leon R. Frank	Johnson C. Smith Univ	Rho	1979 - 1980
27th	Lee G. Willis	Kansas State University	Delta Delta	1980 - 1983
28th	Mark A. Illes	Cal Poly San Luis Obispo	Mu Kappa	1983 - 1984
29th	Anthony W. Brazile	Oakland University	Nu Gamma	1984 - 1985
30th	Alonzo L. Carter, Jr.	Hampton University	Gamma Epsilon	1986 - 1990
31st	Clement M. Osimetha	Univ of Texas-Arlington	Mu Beta	1990 - 1992
32nd	James D. Edmonds III	Hunter College-CUNY	Epsilon	1992 - 1994
33rd	Mark E. Jackson	Southeastern Univ	Delta Theta	1994 - 1996
34th	Lewis Anderson	Pace University	Epsilon	1996 - 1998
35th	Aaron E. Price	Univ Dist. of Columbia	Omicron Gamma	1998 - 2000
36th	Michael Johnson	Bethune Cookman	Omicron Epsilon	2000 - 2002
37th	Ademuyiwa Bamiduro	Univ of Detroit	Chi Gamma	2002 - 2004
38th	Dylan Bess	Univ of South Carolina	Zeta Zeta	2004 - 2006
39th	Brian S. Gundy	Grambling University	Gamma Gamma	2006 - 2008
40TH	Jamin Powell	Va Union University	Zeta	2008 -

APPENDIX F

THE GRAND CONLAVES OF OMEGA PSI PHI FRATERNITY (1960 to 2008)

#	LOCATION	YEAR
47TH	SAN ANTONIO, TEX.	1960
48TH	WASHINGTON, D.C. (*50TH YEAR ANNIVERSARY)	1961
49TH	INDIANAPOLIS, IND.	1962
50TH	DETROIT, MICH.	1965
51st	BOSTON, MASS.	1967
52TH	CHARLOTTE, N.C.	1968
53RD	PITTSBURGH, PA	1970
54TH	HOUSTON, TX.	1971
55TH	ST. LOUIS, MO.	1973
56TH	PHOENIX, AZ.	1974
57TH	ATLANTA, GA .	1976
58TH	NEW ORLEANS, LA.	1977
59TH	DENVER, CO.	1979
60TH	SAN FRANCISCO, CALIF.	1980
61st	MIAMI, FLA	1982
62ND	KANSAS CITY, MO.	1983
63TH	LOUISVILLE, KY.	1984
64TH	WASHINTON D.C. (75 th Anniversar	1986
65TH	DALLAS, TX.	1988
66TH	DETROIT, MICH.	1990
67TH	ATLANTA, GA.	1992
68TH	CLEVELAND, OH.	1994
69TH	LOS ANGELES, CALIF.	1996
70TH	NEW ORLEANS, LA.	1998
71TH	INDIANAPOLIS, IND.	2000
72TH	CHARLOTTE, N.C.	2002
73RD	ST. LOUIS, MO.	2004
74TH	LITTLE ROCK, ARK.	2006
75TH	BIRMINGHAM, ALA.	2008

APPENDIX G

75TH GRAND CONCLAVE
OMEGA MEN WITH 75 YEARS OF SERVICE

FRANK T. COLEMAN- BETAC CHAPTER
H. ALFRED GLASCOR –IOTA PSI CHAPTER

<<>>

75TH GRAND CONCLAVE
OMEGA MEN WITH 70 YEARS OF SERVICE

AUBREY KEARNY
SAMUEL C. HUNTER

<<>>

75TH GRAND CONCLAVE
OMEGA MEN WITH 60 YEARS OF SERVICE

JAMES ATKINSON
CHARLES E. BRANFORD
ANTHONY CARY
FLETCHER COOMBS
JORDON CORBETT
WILLIAM DARITY
HUEY DREDD
EDWARD FULLER GIBBY, SR.
CLARENCE JARRELS
LESTER JOHNSON JR.
FLOYD LEWIS
ROBERT MEDLOCK
JOHN PEOPLES
ERNEST SIDNEY
GEORGE SMITH, JR.
ERNEST TOLDEN JR.
SAUL T. WILSON

CHARLES G. BRANTLEY, JR.
WILLIAM BROWN
ALEXANDER CLARKE
NOBLE COOPER SR.
SEYMOUR DANIEL, JR.
L. CLIFFORD DAVIS
CHARLES FALANA
CHARLES G. IRVINGS JR. JAMES WILLIAM GRAY, SR.
ALPHONSO JENKINS
MARSHAL LANIER
LOUIS MARION
JAMES MYERS
EDWARD I. SIMMONS
JOSEPH SMITH
WILLIAM R. SMITH
JAMES WADE
ALFRED WYATT, SR.

75TH GRAND CONCLAVE
OMEGA MEN WITH 50 YEARS OF SERVICE

WILLIAM T. ADAMS
JAMES AVERY
GERALD BRISCOE
KENNETH CARTER

RAMSEY ALEXANDER II
LYNN BECKWITH, JR.
J.B. CARTER, JR.
WALTER L. CARTER

THE OMEGA PSI PHI FRATERNITY INC.

HERBER CHENNAULT
HOSEA CRITTENDON
EARNEST DARBY, JR.
JOHN DAVIS
JAMES FELDER
SAMUEL GAINES
RAYMOND GIBSON
JAMES GILLIARDS
CLARENCE HANNA
SIDNEY HOLMES, JR.
LEONARD HOWIE
JOHN HUMES
EVANDER HUMPHREY
JIMMIE JAMES JR.
JAMES JOHNSON
MADISON LYLES, JR.
HENRY McKEE, JR.
LANES McLEAN
HARRY D. NELSON
DELANO O"BANNON
MORRIS O'KELLY
HAROLD PALMER
JOHN PHILLIPS
WILLIAM RICHARDSON
JOHN ROYAL
HAROLD SIMPSON
ELLIS SMITH
CHARLES SMALLS
HERBERT STOVER
JAMES SURRATT
WILLIE A. WALKER
GEORGE A. WATERS, JR.
DAVID WASHINGTON
JOHNNIE WASHINGTON
AMOS WESLEY III
LOUIS WRIGHT
DONALD McINTOSH
AMOS WESLEY III
JOHN MOORE

RICHARD CHUBB
JAMES CRUMP
GUION DAVIS, JR.
DEWEY DUCKETT, JR.
DANA FROE
JAMES GEORGE
WALTER GILL
ROBERT GRANT
LEON O. HARVEY
LEWIS HODGE
JERRY HUBBARD, SR.
BILLY LESTER
DONALD McINTOSH
JAMES JEFFERSON
EARL JONES, JR.
WILLIS McCOMBS
BOBBY McDOWELL
JOHN MOORE
VIRGIL NORRIS
ROOSEVELT D. ODOM
SYLVESTER PACE
LEWIS PERKINS
ELTON POINDEXTER
JAMES H. ROBINSON
WILLIAM C. SHORT
CHARLES SINGLETON
LONNIE SMITH
ROBERT H. SMITH ,JR.
JAMES SWIMPSON
WILLIAM VICK
WEBSTER WALLACE
JAMES WARD
RICHARD WATKINS
JOHN H. WATSON
MELVIN WHITE
HAROLD D. NELSON
LOUIS WRIGHT
KENNETH CARTER
WILLIAM C. SHORT

<<>>

75TH GRAND CONCLAVE
OMEGA MEN WITH 40 YEARS OF SERVICE

JACOB ALLEN
CLYDE A. BESS
HAYWOOD DUNLAP, JR.
JAMES GARNER
ELIJAH K. HILL
OLIVER JOHNSON
ROSCOE A. NANCE
DON C, OFFUTT
MERRITT ROBERTSON

JOHN BERRY, SR.
WALTER K. BROWN
HAYWOOD DUNLAP, JR.
CARL HAYWOOD
ROBERT HOLMES
DONALD A. JOLLY
JAMES M. NELLEMS
GERAUD PRINCE
HERBERT B. SHANNON

GEORGE B. WINSTON, III
DAN FAGAN, JR.
ROBERT HOLMES, JR.
KENNETH R. LEWIS
CHARLES RAINE
ERNEST JACKSON
HERBERT BESS
MARK BISHOP
WILLIAM LYONS
CHUCKY WILSON
LEWIS SEARS
ANDREW HOARD
HAROLD WHITE
JOB COLEMAN
DAVID CRAIG
GERALD MAYS
LARRY WALLS
GREGORY G. WEBB
MELVIN PINN, JR.
EDDIE MIMS
ROMMIE WHEELER
THOMAS GREEN, JR.
GERALD HILL
LAWRENCE JONES
ROGER HUDSON
JOHN BERRY, SR.
JOE ANDERSON
JEWELL CHAMBERS
CHARLES CURRY
CHARLES WORTH
ARTHUR RAY
RONALD ADRINE
RUFUS HEARD
FREDERIC WHITE, JR.
SAMUEL PAUL
RAYMOND M. BROWN
FREDERICK TODD
RONALD SARGENT
GODFREY L. EASON
KNOWLTON ATTERBEARY
TALMADGE R. STEWART
WILLIAM GREEN
FREDERICK TODD
LEONARD HUBBARD
RONALD SARGENT
HORACE HUNTLEY

WILLIAM L. GREEN
CLIFTON GRIFFIN
TOM LARKIN, ESQ.
AL MOORE
THOMAS BELL, JR.
EVESTER BAILEY
ANDREW HUGINE, JR.
CLEARTHER MORRIS SR.
ARCHIE COURSE
HAYWOOD DUNLAP, JR.
WILLIAM BARTLEY, III
DEE MADISON
DWIGHT FIELDS
HENRY FORTISON, JR.
HENRY JAMES, JR.
THEODORE GREER
REGINALD MORTON
WILLIAM DAVIS
OSCAR EPPS. JR.
JOE D. HOWZE
GALVIN CRISP
BALJEAN SMITH
MOSES PRIMUS
JOHN MITCHELL
MARK KIEL
BERNARD SNOWDEN
BELVIE BRICE
JAMES MOORE
MAURICE CRUMP SR.
WILLIE PLESE
DONALD GRAHAM
TERRY ARMSTEAD
JAMES NELLEMS
CLIFFORD JONES
FRED WILLIAMS
WILLIAM GREEN
LEONARD HUBBARD
HORACE HUNTLEY
SAMUEL PAUL
JAMES SPENCER
FRED WILLIAMS
DWIGHT LEWIS
BERNARD JUDGE
MICHAEL ROBINSON
LARRY HOLMAN
VERNON HUNT

75TH GRAND CONCLAVE
OMEGA MEN WITH 25 YEARS OF SERVICE

JOSHUA THOMAS

RALPH MAYES

THE OMEGA PSI PHI FRATERNITY INC.

- DAVID TONEY
- HERBERT TOWNES
- ANDRE L. DANIELS
- CHARLES MOSES
- ANDRE GAINES
- KENNETH DOLLAR
- KENZIE WALLACE
- MELVIN BRADLEY
- MICHAEL MAYS
- MICHAEL WRIGHT
- JEFFERY OWENS
- GERALD FOLSOM
- LARRY JEFFERSON
- KEITH CLARK
- RANDALL WILSON
- MICHAEL McCLINTON
- RONALD THOMPSON
- KENNY ROSE
- ALEXANDR EDMONDS III
- RONALD HAIRSTON
- LARRY PARKER, JR.
- MICHAEL ADAMS
- ALVIN REW
- JAMES MELVIN
- ULYSSES SWEENEY, IV
- DAVID FIELDS
- RAYMOND EDGERSON
- BRUCE SMITH
- REGINALD SULLIVAN
- MARVIN BROWN
- CARL PURCHELL
- CHESTER FAIR, JR.
- LYNDON LOVELACE
- NICHOLAS THOMPSON
- NORRIS MIDDLETON
- GREGORY BRADSHER
- J. AUGILLARD
- PHILLIP THOMAS
- ANDRE HOWARD
- CONRADO MORGAN
- JAMES DIXON, SR.
- RICKY ANDERSON
- ANTHONY DIXON, SR.
- KEVIN MATTHEWS
- JAMES BALL
- KENNETH PATTERSON
- JOSEPH WINSTON
- RAMADAN BAYYAN
- ANTHONY L. DIXON, SR.
- ALLEN LITTLE
- JONATHAN PHILLIPS
- MICHAEL F. WADE
- WILBERT McTIER
- MICHAEL ANDREWS
- RONALD BARTHOLOMEW
- HARRY JOHNSON
- EDDIE GRAY, III
- WESLEY SMITH
- ROBERT FITZPATRICK
- H. JOHN BALL
- MAURICE GIBSON
- TIMOTHY RUSH
- GRAYLAND FREDERICKS
- MICHAEL ARMSTEAD
- CLINTON VAUGHN JR.
- CLAUDE PAGE III
- KENNETH RODGERS
- CURTIS WHITTEN
- JOSEPH WILLIAMS
- LEONARD NELSON
- ANTHONY JORDAN
- LLOYD BOXLEY JR.
- WALT BUCKHANAN
- RAYNANDO BANKS
- ANTONIO WOMACK
- VICTOR GEE
- JOHN HUNTER
- WILLIE MITCHELL
- ARTHUR KENNERLY
- BENNIE SHOEMAKER
- LATHAN TURNER
- KENNETH TERRELL
- PAUL COAKLEY
- ARNOLD PLEASANT
- MICHAEL RANDALL
- AVON WHITE
- EDWARD ECHOLS
- KEVIN TOLBERT
- JAMES BLAIR
- ROBERT STEWARD
- CLINTON CRAWLEY
- J. GOINS SR.
- TERRENCE AUGILLARD
- GREGORY FRIZELL
- ANDRE HOWARD
- WILLIE MOORING, JR.
- KEITH JOHNSON
- MILES NICHOLSON
- KEITH BARNES
- JAMES GIBBS
- GILBERT DOUGLASS
- JAMES TURNAGE
- JOHNNY CARR
- ANTONIO DINKINS
- GERALD T. FOLSOM
- ALLEN J. MYLES
- CRAIG ROBERTS
- GERALD WILDER
- VICTOR BANKS
- JOSEPH BROWN
- CHARLES MIKELLL
- DARRYL ROBINSON

WALTER MILLER	JOHN JOHNSON
RANDALL LITTLE	JAMES BURCH
WILLIAM McMURRAY	INMAN OGLETREE
BRUCE GREY	ANTHONY SPRIGGINS

APPENDIX H

74TH GRAND CONCLAVE
MEN SERVING 70 YEARS OF SERVICE

EARL C. ANDERSON
WALTER L. JOHNSON

74TH GRAND CONCLAVE
MEN SERVING 60 YEARS OF SERVICE

JAMES W. ANDERS	WORSHAM N. CALDWELL, SR
CHARLES O. CHRISTIAN	SAMUEL COOK, Ph.D
LENORD M. DUNN	HENRY M. ELDRIDGE
HOWARD M. FITTS, JR.	HENRY W. GLASPIE II
WILLIAM J. GRIGGS	CHARLES W. HARGRAVE
JOHNNY B. JOHNSON	JAMES T. JONES
LUCIUS JONES	SEYMORE E. LOFTMAN
GEORGE H. LOVE	JOHN A. McCULLOUGH
ERNEST L. McKINNEY, SR.	BISHOP M. PATTERSON
GEORGE E. PUREFOY	THADDEUS L. THOMPSON
BORAH WALTON, JR.	WILLIAM WRIGHT

APPENDIX I

74TH GRAND CONCLAVE
MEN SERVING 50 YEARS OF SERVICE

LEVI ADAMS	WILLIAM L. ALLEN
ARTIS BASKIN	HENRY BELL, JR.-
JOHN BLACK, JR.	JAMES W. BURKS
DAVID D. COLE	WILLIAM L. COLMAN
FREDDIE C. COLEMAN	WILLIAM W. CROSBY
EDMOND C. DEAN	HERBERT E. DRUMMOND
JOHN W. FEAGIN'	PHILLIP FERGUSON
WALTER H. FULCHER, JR.	ROOSEVELT L. HOBBS

THE OMEGA PSI PHI FRATERNITY INC.

ROBERT W. HOWARD, SR	W. ROMANDO JAMES Ph.D
GEORGE P. KING	ROBERT H. KIRK
WILLIAM C. KEEN	LEONARD D. LAW, JR.
SAM L. LOVE	WILLIAM L. LYGHT
HERMAN McKINNEY	LAFAYETTE McKINNEY
ALEXANDER RAYE, JR.	JOHN W. REAVIS, JR.
HUBERT L. REYNOLDS	CHARLES H. SMITH
ALVIN STEVENSON	FRANK H. TAYLOR
FREDERICK W. THOMAS	JOHN G. TUCKER
HAROLD R. WATKINS	WILLIAM F. WILLIAMS
EARL J. WILLIS	SAMUEL M. WING
LUCIUS R. WINGATE	HAROLD B. WINSTON

<><>

APPENDIX J

74TH GRAND CONCLAVE
MEN SERVING 40 YEARS OF SERVICE

LARRY R. ABDULLAH	ALVIN R. ANDERSON
WILLIAM S. ARMSTEAD, III	JOHN ARRINGTON
GREGORY AUSTIN	THEODORE BACOTE
ROBERT A. BAILEY	WILSON BAKER
CARROLL BARTHOLMEW	CLARENCE BATES
CLEVELAND A. BLOUNT, JR.	DAVID BURCH
WAYNE P. BROOKINS	JOHN M. BRYANT
HARMAN N. CARROWAY	PHILLIP N. CHANCEY
PAUL K. COLE	HAROLD COOK
CHARLES A. COVERDALE	HERBERT B. DIXON, JR.
FRANKLIN DOUGLASS	ROBERT E. DOWNING
ARNOLD W. FAIRLY	CHARLES W. FINLEY
CHARLES D. FOWLER	JOSEPH FOWLER
JOHN FREDERICK	CLARK FROST
EDWARD E. GASKIN	LEE E. GIBSON
CHARLES C. HALL, JR.	DONALD F. HARRIS, JR.
JOHN T. HARPER	BADREA L. HANNAH
SAMUEL A. HAUGLER, JR.	JAMES L. JENNINGS
JOSEPH W. JOHNSON	RONALD E. JONES
ALFRED R. JUNIOR	MANLEY KHALEEL
ANDREW J. LEWIS	RICHARD H. LAYNE
BYRON T. LEGARDY	EUGENE W. LONG
IRVIN V. LONG	WILLIAMD J. MCHUGH, ESQ.
DAVID B. MAYES, SR.	LEON MILLS
DANNY MOSLEY, SR.	LEE E. MOSS
JOSEPH McCORD	CALVIN W. McLARIN
ALEXANDER NICHOLS, JR.	JAMES A. OWENS, JR.
LOUIS PARHAM	CHARLES C. PEEVY
OSCAR PENDLETON	KENNETH S. POWELL, DDS
LIONELL RANDOLPH	RALPH B. RANSOM
ANDREW A. RAY	RALPH T. REDRICK
LaCOLIS REED	ALSINDOR R. ROSIER, SR.
WILLIAM SCOTT	JAMES O. SHELLEY

JAMES H. SHELTON, JR. ---------- ALBEERT W. SMITH
EARL SMITH, JR. ---------- EDWARD U. SMITH
JIMMY L. SMITH, SR. ---------- RAYMOND SMITH III
KENNETH M. TAYLOR ---------- JARRET THOMAS
JOHN W. THOMAS ---------- OCIE ELLIS TOLSON
TALMADGE R. VARNADO ---------- CURTIS L. WALKER
EUGENE WASHINGTON ---------- WALTER C. WATKINS, JR.
CALVIN E. WEEMS, JR. ---------- PRICE W. WHITAKER, JR.
CLETUS W. WILKINS ---------- BILLY J. WILLIAMS
FRANK C. WILLIAMS, DDS ---------- ROBERT E. "BUTCH" WILLIAMS JR.
V.T. WILLIAMS ---------- EVERETT H. WILSON
JAMES C. WILSON ---------- ROBERT L. WOODS
MARCUS SHEPPARD, Sr ----------

<>

APPENDIX K

74TH GRAND CONCLAVE
MEN SERVING 25 YEARS OF SERVICE

LEROY J. ADKINS ---------- WILLIE A. BEST
LEE BROWN, JR. ---------- VICTOR BRUINTON
GREGORY D. BURNETT, SR. ---------- WALTER L. CARTER, JR.
HERBERT CHARITY ---------- ALBERT H. CICCEL, SR.
ELIAS W. COVINGTON ---------- CLIMENT J. EDMOND, JR.
PATRICK FRANKLIN ---------- ANTHONY FREEMAN
EMMANUEL G. GARRETT ---------- CALVIN GOLDEN
JONATHAN N. GRIFFIN, SR. ---------- RODERICK D. HENDERSON
CHARLES B. HOLLIS ---------- FRANK HOOKS, JR.
CURTIS M. INMAN ---------- HARRISON J. JONES
WILLIAM R. LESTER ---------- RICKY L. LEWIS
ROY C. LINDSEY ---------- DUANE H. LIVINGTON
DAVID MICHAELS LYLES, JR. ---------- ROOSEVELT Q. MEADS
LARRY L. MELTON, JR. ---------- KENNETH L. MINEFIELD
WILLIAM T. MITCHELL ---------- LONNIE JAMES MORRIS
DORS G. MUSGRAY ---------- OSCAR ODOM III
SYLVESTER L. PALMER ---------- EDIE PINCHBACK
CHARLES PRICE ---------- CLINTON RAINES
BRYAN O. RANDALL ---------- DAVID RICHARDS, JR.
STANLEY REED ---------- PERRY O. ROBINSON
BENJAMIN SILES ---------- MELVIN M. SLATER
JEFFREY T. SMITH ---------- TANTALOUS A. SMITH
HILLBURN SPARROW II ---------- FRANK H. STALEY
CURTIS JAMES STARKS, SR. ---------- FRED H. STROUD
WILLIAM A. TOLLIVER ---------- THOMAS TAYLOR
WILLIE A. TERREL, JR. ---------- WILLIAMS C. THOMAS
ROBERT L. WASHINGTON ---------- ROGER T. WATKINS
ZOLLIE WHITE, JR. ---------- THEODORE WILDER
MICHAEL A. WILLIAMS ---------- ANTHONY D. WILLIAMS
MILTON H. WILLIAMS III ---------- DeWAYNE K. WYNN
GARLAND E. YARBER ---------- WILLIAM C. YORK, JR.
CHARLES E. ZEIGLER ----------

APPENDIX L

BOOKS WRITTEN BY OMEGA MEN DURING THIS PERIOD
(Listed in Alpha order by Author)

"OTHERS THOUGHT I COULD LEAD" by
James S. Avery, Sr. – Published 2006 by Wheatmark Publishing
Initiated in Omicron Chi, summer 1957.

"THE BOOK OF AMERICAN CITY RANKINGS" by James S. Avery, John Marlin and Stephen T. Collins. Published by Facts on File 1983.

"MAKING CHURCH MATTER" By Reginald D. Bernard.
Pastor King Solomon Baptist Church, Vicksburg Ms. Published by IUniverse. . Upsilon Epsilon chapter 1991

"OMEGA MEN OF DISTINCTION" by
Carl A. Blunt, Keith W. Neal, Gerald G. Wood and Cleveland Palmer and many other Omega contributors. 1st printing 1998, 2nd printing 1999, 3rd printing 2002, 4th printing 2006
Carl Blunt, initiated 04/07/78, Sigma Iota Chapter

"RADICAL INTRODUCTIONS, BEGINNING BY GOING BACKWARDS" by Clarence T. Brown - Published by Clarence T. Brown/1st edition 2007
Initiated Lambda Sigma Chapter, Claflin College, Orangeburg, SC
March 1990

"RAISING A RADICAL CHILD" by
Clarence T. Brown - Published by Clarence T. Brown/1st edition 2007
Initiated Lambda Sigma Chapter, Claflin College, Orangeburg, SC
March 15, 1990

"BARBARA CHARLINE JORDAN": From the Ghetto to the Capitol by
Ira B. Bryant. Published by **D. Armstrong Co., Inc (1977)**

"ANDREW JACKSON YOUNG, MR. AMBASSADOR": United States Ambassador to the United Nations by Ira B Bryant. Published by Armstrong Co (1979)

TEXAS SOUTHERN UNIVERSITY: Its antecedents, political origin, and future by Ira B Bryan. Published by **Bryant (1975)**

"COME ON PEOPLE" On the path from victims to victors by Bill Cosby & Alvin F. Poussaint. Published by Thomas Nelson; 1 edition (October 9, 2007) Bill Cosby initiated Nu Zeta chapter

"THE MEANEST THING TO SAY": A Little Bill Book for Beginning Readers, Level 3 (Oprah's Book Club) by Bill Cosby and Varnette Hon Eywood

"GRANDDADDY'S DIRT" by
Brian Egeston - Published by Carter-Krall Publishing in 2000
Initiated Rho Psi chapter, Spring '92

"WHIPPINS SWITCHES & PEACH COBBLER" by
Brian Egeston – Published by Carter-Krall Publishing in 2001
Initiated Rho Psi chapter, Spring '92

"CATFISH QUESADDILLAS" by
Brian Egeston - Initiated Rho Psi chapter, Spring '92
Initiated Rho Psi chapter, Spring '92

"THE BIG MONEY MATCH" by
Brian Egeston - Published by Carter-Krall Publishing in 2003
Initiated Rho Psi chapter, Spring '92

"AN AUBURN AUTUMN" by
Brian Egeston – Published by Carter-Krall Publishing in August 2006, Initiated Rho Psi chapter, Spring '92

"I BURIED JOHN F. KENNEDY" by James L. Felder. Published by Lee Books Ltd (August 1994)

"They Call Me Big House" by
Clarence E. Gaines **and** Clint Johnson. Published by John F. Blair Publisher (September 2004)

"TIMELESS: a series of intimate love tales" by
Maurice S. Gibson Published by Maurice S. Gibson 2007

"JOGO THERAPY: Jogging as a Therapeutic Strategy," by
Frederick D. Harper. Published by Douglas Publishers 1980

"WHAT THE HELL IS HE THINKING?:
A view of the world through the eyes of a Black man." by
Rodney Garrett.
Published by CreateSpace, 2007

THE OMEGA PSI PHI FRATERNITY AND THE MEN WHO MADE IT'S HISTORY A CONCISE HISTORY
by Robert L. Gill.
Published by Omega Psi Phi Fraternity (1963)

"HOW TO SUCCEED IN BUSINESS WITHOUT BEING WHITE":
Straight Talk on Making It in America by Earl G. Graves.
Published by Collins (April 21, 1998).

"MY WIFE, MY PARTNER.(PUBLISHER'S PAGE)(VIEWPOINT ESSAY)": An article from: Black Enterprise
by Earl G., Sr. Graves.
Published and Distributed by Thomson Gale 2007.

"BUILDING OUR OWN SAFETY NETS.(PUBLISHER'S PAGE)": An article from: Black Enterprise by Earl G., Jr. Graves

"IN THE MATTER OF COLOR"
Race and the American Legal Process 1: The Colonial Period (Race and the American Legal Process) by
A. Leon Higginbotham, a study of the racial laws in six of the American Colonies before the Revolution. Published by Oxford University Press, USA; New Ed edition (May 29, 1980)

GROUNDWORK: Charles Hamilton Houston and the Struggle for Civil Rights by Genna Rae McNeil and A. Leon Higginbotham
Published by University of Pennsylvania Press (May 1, 1983)

SHADES OF FREEDOM: Racial Politics and Presumptions of the American Legal Process Race and the American Legal Process, Volume II (Oxford World's Classics, Vol 2) by A. Leon Higginbotham. Published by Oxford University Press, USA (June 11, 1998)

RACEING JUSTICE, EN-GENDERING POWER: Essays on Anita Hill, Clarence Thomas, and the Construction of Social Reality by Jr. A. Leon Higginbotham, Andrew Ross, Manning Marable, and Michael Thelwell

BLACK LAW JOURNAL **(Volume 7)** by
Jr. Judge A. Leon Higginbotham. Published by UCLA Center for Afro-American Studies; No. 1 edition (1980)

AN OPEN LETTER TO JUSTICE CLARENCE THOMAS FROM A FEDERAL JUDICIAL COLLEAGUE by A. Leon Higginbotham. Published by **s.n. (1992)**

AMERICAN EDUCATION AND AN OPEN SOCIETY: "So many deeds cry out to be done!" by A. Leon Higginbotham. Published by
ACT Publications (1973)

DE JURE HOUSING SEGREGATION IN THE UNITED STATES AND SOUTH AFRICA: The difficult pursuit for racial justice
by A. Leon Higginbotham.
Published by University of Illinois law review?] (1991)

FROM PRESIDENTIAL FACT-FINDING COMMISSIONS TO JUSTICE FOR BLACKS -: Can we bridge the gap? (J.A. Vickers, Sr., memorial lecture series) by A. Leon Higginbotham. **Published by University of Kansas (1971)**

HON. A. LEON HIGGINBOTHAM, JR: A ceremonial compendium : "the early years" and "the judicial years" (The oral history series) by A. Leon Higginbotham. **Published by WTL Productions (1995)**

RACIAL JUSTICE AND THE FOUNDING FATHERS: A moral duality? ([Herbert H. Lehman memorial lecture) by A. Leon Higginbotham. Published by Herbert H. Lehman College of the City University of New York (1981)

A TRIBUTE TO JUSTICE THURGOOD MARSHALL: (Harvard law review) by A. Leon Higginbotham. Published by The Harvard law review association (1991)

"**THE COLLECTED POEMS OF LANGSTON HUGHES,**" by Langston Hughes and Arnold Rampersad. Published by Vintage; 1st Vintage Classics Ed edition (October 31, 1995)

"SELECTED POEMS OF LANGSTON HUGHES," **by LANGSTON HUGHES. PUBLISHED BY** Vintage (September 12, 1990). Initiated in Xi Phi chapter.

"THE LANGSTON HUGHES READER," by LANGSTON HUGHES. PUBLISHED BY George Braziller (July 1981)
"**VINTAGE HUGHES,**" by LANGSTON HUGHES. Published by Vintage (January 6, 2004)

"FIVE PLAYS BY LANGSTON HUGHES," (Midland Books, No 121) by **LANGSTON HUGHES** and Webster Smalley. Published by Indiana University Press (June 1963)

"**ESSENTIAL LANGSTON HUGHES,**" CD (Caedmon Essentials) by LANGSTON HUGHES. Published by Caedmon (July 24, 2007)

"THE DREAM KEEPER AND OTHER POEMS," by LANGSTON HUGHES and Brian Pinkney. Published by Knopf Books for Young Readers (November 13, 2007)

THE BIG SEA: An Autobiography (American Century Series) by Langston Hughes and Arnold Rampersad. Published by Hill and Wang (August 1, 1993.

"LANGSTON HUGHES READS," by LANGSTON HUGHES (Audio Cassette - Mar 22, 2000) Published by **Caedmon; Abridged edition (March 22, 2000)**

"THE POEMS:" 1951-1967 (Collected Works of Langston Hughes, Vol 3) by **LANGSTON HUGHES and Arnold Rampersad.** Published by University of Missouri Press (June 2001)

"**THE WAYS OF WHITE FOLKS,": Stories** by LANGSTON HUGHES. Published by Vintage (September 12, 1990)

"I WONDER AS I WANDER:" An Autobiographical Journey (American Century Series) by LANGSTON HUGHES and Arnold Rampersad. Published by **Hill and Wang (August 1, 1993)**

"NOT SO SIMPLE: THE "SIMPLE" STORIES," by LANGSTON HUGHES and Donna Akiba Sullivan Harper. Published by University of Missouri Press; New Ed edition (August 1996)

"**PICTORIAL HISTORY OF AFRICAN AMERICANS," A: Newly Updated Edition** by LANGSTON HUGHES. Published by Crown; 6 Rev Sub edition (January 13, 1995)

"THE BOOK OF RHYTHMS" by LANGSTON HUGHES, Robert G. O'Meally, Matt Wawiorka, and Wynton Marsalis. Published by Oxford University Press, USA (December 21, 2000)

"NOT WITHOUT LAUGHTER,"by LANGSTON HUGHES. Published by Touchstone **(March 1, 1995)**

"HUGHES POEMS," (Everyman's Library Pocket Poets) by LANGSTON HUGHES. PUBLISHED by Everyman's Library (March 23, 1999)

"LANGSTON HUGHES AND THE *CHICAGO DEFENDER*:"Essays on Race, Politics, and Culture, 1942-62 by LANGSTON HUGHES and Christopher C Santis. Published by University of Illinois Press (July 1, 1995)

"IT'S ABOUT THE MONEY!: The Fourth Movement of the Freedom Symphony: How to Build Wealth, Get Access to Capital, and Achieve Your Financial Dreams by JESSE L. JACKSON. Published by Three Rivers Press (January 9, 2001). Initiated by Nu Pi chapter.

Virginia's Native Son: The Election of Governor L. Douglas Wilder of Virginia (West Lafayette, Indiana: Purdue University Press, 2000). by JUDSON L. JEFFRIES

Huey P. Newton, The Radical Theorist (Jackson, Miss: University Press of Mississippi, 2002) by

JUDSON L. JEFFRIES
Urban America and its Police (co-authored with Harlan Hahn (Bolder, Colorado: University Press of Colorado, 2003). by
JUDSON L. JEFFRIES

Black Power in the Belly of the Beast (Urbana, Illinios: University of Illinois Press, 2006) by
JUDSON L. JEFFRIES

Comrades, A Local History of the Black Panther Party (Bloomington, Indiana: Indiana University Press, 2007).
by
JUDSON L. JEFFRIES

" NEXT LEVEL PURSUIT" by
Kevin J. McKinnon – Published by LuLu Publishing, 2007
Initiated in Omega Tau Delta Delta chapter spring 85, (June 1,1985)- line name
Private Prez, Valdosta State University

"THE MISSISSIPPI BLACK BANKERS AND THEIR INSTITUTIONS" by
Jimmie James, Arther James and Robert James. Published by Arthur James, Arthur James and Jimmie James Jr. in 1996

"MEN WHO DARE TO MAKE A DIFFERENCE": Omega Psi Phi Fraternity, Inc. Membership Directory 2002 by Lloyd J Jordan. Published by Bernard C. Harris, 2002.

"QUOTABLE QUOTES OF BENJAMIN E. MAYS" by
Benjamin Mays. Published by
Vantage Press (June 1983)

" SECRETS MORTGAGE LENDERS DON'T WON'T YOU TO KNOW"
by
Derrick Miller – Published by Derrick Miller 2008
Initiated Iota Gamma chapter 04/18/1981

LEADERSHIP: WHY MANAGERS FAIL, 10 MISTAKESTO AVOID WHEN MANAGING PEOPLE
By
William L. Minix-Published by Starwise, Inc. 2008

"THE CRITICAL ZONE: *From High School to Career Success*" by
Alvin S. Perry published by Critical Zone Alvin Perry 2008
Initiated in Tau Delta Delta chapter, spring 1998, Valdosta State University

"MY WORLD OF REALITY": **An Autobiography** by Hildrus A. Poindexter. Published by
Publisher: BALAMP PUBLISHING (1973)

"WE HAVE TAKEN A CITY": The Wilmington Racial Massacre and Coup 1898, by

Sr. H. Leon Prather, Sr. and Kenneth Davis. Published by **Dram Tree Books** (February 15, 2006). H. Leon Prather, Sr., an Omega man, was initiated in Gamma Phi chapter.

"POLITICAL RELIGION" by
Charles R. Stith. Published by Abingdon Press in 1995. Initiated Omicron Sigma chapter in 1969,

"AFRICAN LEADERS STATE OF AFRICA REPORT 2002" by Jean Hennelly Keith and Charles R. Stith. Published by Boston University, 2002. Charles R. Stith Initiated Omicron Sigma chapter in 1969.

"THE HISTORY OF THE THETA EPSILON CHAPTER OF THE OMEGA PSI PHI FRATERNITY: AND ITS LEGACY IN THE STATE OF RHODE ISLAND, 1947-1989" : "A CRUST AND A CORNER" by Anthony Terrell Teat. Published by Theta Epsilon Chapter, Omega Psi Phi Fraternity] (1989)

"STANDING AT THE EDGE OF MADNESS" by
Vernon Steve Weakley – Published by ZWORLD-NET Publishing in 2001
Initiated 12/05/1969, Upsilon Epsilon chapter

"FEAR NO EVIL" by
Vernon Steve Weakley – Published by ZWORLD-NET Publishing 2004
Initiated 12/05/1969, Upsilon Epsilon chapter

"PAUL R. WILLIAMS": A Collection of House Plans (California Architecture & Architects) by Paul R. Williams. Published by Hennessey & Ingalls (October 15, 2006)

"THE NON-FICTION BOOK": How to Write & Sell it By Paul R. Reynolds by Paul R. Reynolds. Published by William Morrow (1970)

APPENDIX M

OMEGA MEN HONORED ON U.S. POSTAGE STAMPS

ERNEST E. JUST – Founder of Omega Psi Phi fraternity and internationally famous Biologist.

WILLIAM "COUNT" BASIE – Jazz Pianist, Bandleader, Composer –Xi Phi Chapter, (honorary)

LANGSTON HUGHES – Poet, Author – Xi Phi Chapter

CHARLES R. DREW – Pioneering surgeon, Medical Health Researcher – Alpha Psi Chapter

ROY WILKINS – Executive Secretary of the NAACP – Xi Chapter

CARTER G. WOODSON – Author, Educator, Historian – Alpha Chapter

PERCY LAVON JULIAN – Sciientist, Businessmen, Teacher – Sigma Omega Chapter

WILLIAM ALLISON DAVIS – Scientist, known for his work in IQ testing - Alpha Psi Chapter

APPENDIX N

OMEGA RECIPIENTS OF THE PRESTIGIOUS SPINGARN MEDAL

1915	ERNEST E. JUST	BIOLOGIST
1916	CHARLES YOUNG	ARMY MAJOR
1924	ROLAND HAYES	COMPOSER, PIANIST, SINGER
1926	CARTER G. WOODSON	HISTORIAN
1943	WILLIAM H. HASTIE	JURIST, EDUCATOR
1944	CHARLES DREW	SCIENTIST
1947	PERCY JULIAN	CHEMIST
1953	PAUL R. WILLIAMS	ARCHITECT
1958	DAISY BATES & THE LITTLE ROCK 9 (ERNEST GREEN)	STUDENT
1960	LANGSTON HUGHES	POET, AUTHOR, PLAYWRIGHT
1962	ROY WILKINS	CIVIC LEADER
1969	CLARENCE M. MITCHELL	CIVIC LEADER
1973	WILSON C. RILES	EDUCATOR
1982	BENJAMIN MAYS	EDUCATOR, THEOLOGIAN
1985	BILL COSBY	CIVIC LEADER
1986	BENJAMIN HOOKS	CIVIC LEADER
1989	JESSE L. JACKSON	CLERGYMAN, POLITICAN, ACTIVIST
1990	L. DOUGLAS WILDE	POLITICIAN
1996	A. LEON HIGGINBOTHAM JR.	JURIST, HISTORIAN

1999	EARL G. GRAVES SR.	PUBLISHER
2001	VERNON E. JORDAN	LAWYER, CIVIC LEADER
2005	OLIVER W. HILL	LAWYER, CIVIC LEADER

APPENDIX O

DISTRICT REPRESENTATIVES

12th DISTRICT

	NAME	CHAPTER	TERM
1st	Ralph A. Vaughan	Lambda	1942 -1943
2nd	Julian A. Bell	Detached	1942 - 1945
3rd	James P Perry	Lambda	1945 - 1948
4th	Thomas M. Dent	Sigma Iota	1948 - 1951
5th	W.I. Murray	Phi Iota	1951-1953
6th	Thomas G. Neusom	Lambda Omicron	1953 - 1956
7th	John C. Long	Iota Gamma	1956 - 1961
8th	J. Quentin Mason	Zeta Tau	1961 - 1973
9th	Percy H. Steele	Phi Omicron	1963 - 1965
10th	Limuary A. Jordon	Lambda Omicron	1965 - 1966
11th	Henry W. Sands	Zeta Rho	1966 - 1968
12th	Philmore Graham	Sigma Iota	1968 - 1970
13th	Thomas P. McPhatter	Phi Omicron	1970 - 1973
14th	Hayves Streeter	XiNu	1973 - 1974
15th	L. Benjamin Livingston	Pi Rho	1974 - 1977
16th	Godfrey B. James	Sigma Iota	1977 - 1978

17th	**Arnold Butler**	Zeta Rho	1978 - 1980
18th	**Edgar Bridges**	Zeta Upsilon	1980- 1983
19th	**James A. Grady**	Sigma Iota	1983 - 1985
20th	**Jewett Walker**	Lambda Omicron	1985 - 1987
21st	**Lewis J. Sears, Ph.D.**	Gamma Alpha Alpha	1987 -1990
22nd	**Raymond L. Gibson**	Phi Beta Beta	1990 - 1993
23rd	**Carl A. Blunt**	Sigma Iota	1993 - 1995
24th	**Ricky L. Lewis**	Tau Tau	1995 - 1998
25th	**Carl A. Blunt**	Phi Iota	1998 - 1999
26th	**Keith W. Neal**	Sigma Iota	1999 - 2001
27th	**Lymus Capehart**	Gamma Alpha Alpha	2001 - 2004
28th	**Grieg R. Boone**	Pi Rho	2004 - 2006
29th	**Charles C. Peevy**	Phi Iota	2006 - Present

DISTRICT REPRESENTATIVES
10th DISTRICT

10th District Representatives

	NAME	CHAPTER	TERM
1	Francis Dent *	Nu Omega/Detroit	1933-1934
2	George A. Isabell*	Nu Omega/Detroit	1934-1936
3	Charles E. Harry III	Zeta Phi/Indianapolis	1936-1939

4	**Corneff Taylor**	Sigma Omega/Chicago	1939-1942
5	**Cary D. Jacobs**	Zeta Phi/Indianapolis	1942-1945
6	**Chester Smith**	Nu Omega/Detroit	1945-1948
7	**G. Stevens Marchman**	Sigma Omega/Chicago	1948-1951
8	**A. M. Butler**	Epsilon Rho/St. Paul	1951-1954
9	**Thomas E. Watson**	Sigma Omega/Chicago	1954-1956
10	**Abraham Ulmer Jr.**	Nu Omega/Detroit	1956-1958
11	**Charles E. Johnson**	Nu Omega/Detroit	1958-1962
12	**Leo M. Zinn**	Sigma Omega/Chicago	1962-1965
13	**James S. Mullin**	Zeta Phi/Indianapolis	1965-1968
14	**Wilfred Anderson**	Sigma Upsilon/Lansing, MI	1968-1970
15	**Danny Thomas (undergraduate)**	Omicron Theta/Carbondale, IL	1970-1971
16	**Frederick Birth**	Nu Chi/E. St. Louis, IL	1971-1972
17	**Burnel E. Coulon**	Zeta Phi/Indianapolis	1972-1976
18	**Owsley G. Spiller**	Nu Omega/Detroit	1976-1979
19	**Abraham L. Reynolds**	Sigma Omega/Park Forest. IL	1979-1982
20	**John S. Epps**	Tau Upsilon/Carbondale, IL	1982-1985
21	**Leonard D. Law Jr.**	Zeta Phi/Indianapolis	1985-1987
22	**Johnnie D. Washington**	Omega Rho/Springfield, IL	1987-1989

23	Lawrence E. Moon	Omicron Rho/Flint, MI	1989-1990
24	Vernon G. Smith	Alpha Chi/Gary, IN	1990-1993
25	Ronald J. Hughes	Sigma Omega/Chicago	1993-1996
26	Larry B. Boyd	Nu Omega/Detroit, MI	1996-1999
27	Charles A. Bruce	Nu Chi/E. St. Louis, IL	1999-2001
28	Dwight Pointer	Alpha Kappa Kappa/Gary, IN	2001-2004
29	Kurmmell W. Knox	Tau Kappa Kappa/Southfield, MI	2004-2006
30	Glenn A Mathews	Kappa Phi/Milwaukee, WI	2006-2007
31	Climent J. Edmon Jr.	Mu Xi Glyn Ellen Illinois	2008-

*Appointed by Grand Basileus

9th District Representatives

Appointed 9th District Representatives

Name	Term
P.F. Midiane	1922 - 1926
Howard Payne Carter	1926 - 1937
J.D. Bowles	1937 - 1937

Elected 9th District Representatives

F. Ribers Barnwell	1937 - 1958
W.L.D. Johnson, Jr.	1958 - 1958

O. McCoy Gibb	1958 - 1962
U.S. Hammonds	1962 - 1966
Fletcher Morgan	1966 - 1969
C.D. Henry	1969 - 1972
Warren Berry	1972 - 1975
Samuel W. Prince	1975 - 1978
Walter L. Littlejohn	1978 - 1981
Clarence E. Wilson	1981 - 1983
Jethro Hills	1983 - 1986
Marshall Grady	1986 - 1989
Shelly Stewart	1989 - 1990
Charles Christopher	1990 - 1993
James L. Wise	1993 - 1995
Virgil Robinson	1995 - 1998
Wendell Van Smith	1998 - 2000
Jerry Rutherford	2000 - 2002
"Teflon" Don Davis	2002 - 2004
Todd S. Clemons	2004 - 2007
Willie F. Hinchen	2007 -

<<>>

8TH DISTRICT REPRESENTATIVES

George D. Brantley-St. Louis, MO	1928 - 1932 (3rd District)
J.A. Jones, Louisville, KY	1932 - 1933 (3rd District)
Herman Dreer-Upsilon Omega (MO, KS, CO, MN)	1933 - 1934 (8th District)

Ulysses S. Donaldson-Upsilon Omega	1934 - 1935
Alonzo V. Mercer-Chicago, IL (MO, KS, CO, IL, MN	1935 - 1936
Ulysses S. Donaldson-Upsilon Omega	1936 - 1941

Omega Goes to War - WWII

Elza H. Hunter - Pi Sigma (MO, AR, KS)	1947 - 1951
James A. Harris - Tau Sigma	1951 - 1953
H. Monroe Purnell - Eta Alpha	1953 - 1957
Curtis C. Crawford - Upsilon Omega (MO, KS, NE, IA)	1957 - 1959
H. Monroe Purnell - Eta Alpha	1959 - 1960
Harvey McDaniel - Chi Phi (MO, KS, CO, NE, IA, NM)	1960 - 1965
Alonzo Brown - Eta Alpha	1965 - 1967
Edgar A. Burnett - Upsilon Omega	1967 - 1974
William A. Bowers - Chi Phi	1974 - 1976
Lynn Beckwith, Jr. - Upsilon Omega	1976 - 1977
George I. Williams - Nu Rho	1977 - 1979
Charles I. Shelton, Jr. - Upsilon Omega	1979 - 1982
Jesse I. High - Omicron Xi	1982 - 1985
Lloyd J. Jordan - Upsilon Omega	1985 - 1988
Mandrid Williams - Beta Omega	1988 - 1991
Doug Williams - Upsilon Omega	1991 - 1992
Kenneth Carson - Nu Rho	1992 - 1994
Delvert T. Neal - Chi Phi	1994 - 1996

Robert Robinson - Eta Alpha	1996 - 1998
Melvin Jenkins - Beta Omega	1998 - 2001
Kenneth Patterson - Upsilon Omega	2001 - 2003
Larry Burks - Gamma UpsilonS	2003 - 2006
Jeffery T. Smith - Chi Phi	2006 - 2008
Glenn E. Rice	2008

7th District Representatives

M.R. Austil
John H. Calhoun
J.T. Brooks
William Gaines
J.T. Brooks
W. A. McMillan
Edward Braynon
Moses Norman
U.G. Horne
David Beckley
Dorsey Miller
Astrid Mack
J.B. Carter
George Grace
William Brassfield
S.M. "Chucky" Wilson
Edgar Mathis
Joseph T. Williams
Kenneth R. Jackson

<<>>

6th District Representatives

Name	Chapter	Term
S. Herbert Adams *	Pi Phi	1935 - 1943
E. Kermit Hightower *	Psi Phi	1943- 1944

A.I. Terrell *	Psi Phi	1944 - 1945
John Potts	Mu Alpha	1945 - 1947
H. Carl Moultrie *	Omicron Alpha	1947 - 1949
Dewey Duckkett *	Kappa Alpha	1949 - 1951
W.O. Yarborough *	Psi Phi	1951 - 1953
W.H. "Bubba" Young *	Pi Alpha	1953 - 1955
J. Alston "Jack" Atkins *	Psi Phi	1955 - 1957
J. Herbert Nelson *	Epsilon Omega	1957 - 1959
John H. Moore *	Pi Phi	1959 - 1961
Harold Boulware *	Omicron Phi	1961 - 1963
George W. Miller	Epsilon Upsilon	1963 - 1965
Lewie C. Roache	Epsilon Omega	1965 - 1967
John M. "Bing" Miller *	Beta Beta Beta	1967 - 1969
Thomas J. Crawford *	Epsilon Omega	1969 - 1971
Zoel S. Hargrave, Jr. *	Pi Phi	1971 - 1973
Charles T. Brooks	Omicron Phi	1973 - 1975
Mitchell E. Gadsden	Beta Chi	1975 - 1977
Holland W. Daniels *	Mu Alpha	1977 - 1979
S.P. Woodard *	Pi Phi	1979 - 1991
C. Tyrone Gilmore	Epsilon Nu	1981 - 1983
Joseph W. Harper III	Pi Phi	1983 - 1985
Leon B. Babridge	Omicron Phi	1985 - 1987
William H. Hoffler, Jr. *	Psi Phi	1987 - 1989
Ulysses S.G. Sweeney III	Beta Tau	1989 - 1991
Robert C. Williams	Beta Chi	1991 - 1993

Lonnie C. Holman	Epsilon Nu	1993 - 1995
John H. Scott	Beta Phi	1995 - 1997
Charles S. Holmes	Mu Alpha	1997 - 1999
Dr. Melvin T. Pinn Jr.	Pi Phi	1999 - 2001
Walter L. Funderburk, Sr.*	Epsilon Omega	2001 - 2002
Antonio F. "Tony" Knox	Iota Iota	2002-2004
John H. Williams, Jr.	Mu Pi	2004-2006
Charles J. Worth	Zeta Alpha	2006-2008
Octavio Miro		2008 -

* = Omega Chapter

<<>>

5th DISTRICT REPRESENTATIVES

Z. Alexander Looby	1938 - 1941
A. A. Branch	1941 - 1945
L. W. Beasely	1945 - 1960
Fred Pickett	1960 - 1964
L.A. Westly	1964 - 1968
Frank Royal	1968 - 1969
Albert Berry	1969 - 1971
Robert Jefferson	1971 - 1973
Frank Bowden	1973 - 1976
Roscoe Crump	1976 - 1978
Willie A. Smith	1978 - 1983
William R. Asbury	1983 - 1986

CleArthur Morris, Sr.	1986 - 1991
Mark A. Bishop	1991 - 1995
Ralph E. Johnson	1995 - 1997
Ronald Griffin	1997 - 1999
Henry F. Jackson Jr.	1999 - 2002
Richard Jones	2002 - 2005
Horace Chase	2005-2008
Edward C. Morant	2008-PRESENT

<<>>

4TH DISTRICT REPRESENTATIVES

Brother A.P. Hamblin (W.VA & OH-11th District)	1937 - 1939
Brother James Henry Rowland (11th Dis. W. VA & Ohio)	1939 - 1940
Brother Leonard L. Holland	1957 - 1960
Brother William J. Moore	1961 - 1965
Brother Clark E. Beck	1965 - 1969
Brother John L. Fuller	1969
Brother Dr. Floydelh Anderson	1970 - 1972
Brother William L. Hunter	1972 - 1975
Brother Dr. R. Charles Byers	1975 - 1978
Brother Richard Jenkins	1978 - 1980

THE OMEGA PSI PHI FRATERNITY INC. 327

Brother Dr. Frank C. Williams	1980 - 1984
Brother Kenneth Wilson	1985 - 1987
Brother Jarrett A. Thomas	1987 - 1990
Brother Raymond Tillery, Sr.	1990 - 1992
Brother Malvin Jones	1992 - 1994
Brother Henry W. Glaspie, Jr.	1994 - 1996
Brother Mel K. McCray	1996 - 1997
Brother Christopher M. Cooper	1997 - 1999
Brother Al Jordan	1999 - 2001
Brother Gregory Epps	2001 - 2003
Brother William Comeaux	2003 - 2005
Brother Jesse J. Junius	2005 - 2007
Brother Dewey Ortiz	2007 - Present

<<>>

3rd District Representatives
Listed alphabetically, Term provided where available

Marion L. Barnwell (1990 - 1993)
Curtis A. Baylor (2002 - 2004)
Sylvester W. Blue
George D. Brantley
Kenneth A. Brown (1978 - 1981)
Melvin Brown
Charles D. Chambliss Jr. (1976 - 1978)
Gary C. Clark (1995 - 1997)
James R. Clark, Sr. (1981 - 1983)

Ellis F. Corbett, (VA. 4th Dist.)
Robert W. Fairchild (1987 - 1990)
B. Thomas Garnette
Rayford Harris, Jr. (1999 - 2002)
Robert L. Howard, Sr. (1986 - 1987)
Mark Jackson
Vernon E. Johnson (1983 - 1986)
J.A. Jones
Robert H. Lewis (2004 - 2006)
Joseph C. McKinney (1993 - 1995)
Frederick Nance
Harry T. Penn
James A. "Pete" Peterson (1997 - 1999)
C.W. Seay, (VA. 4th Dist.)
Thomas Shields
Charles A. Shorter
Stanley S. Shorter
Melvin Washington
J.B. Williams
Mark E. Jackson

<<>>

2nd District Representatives

Name	Chapter	Term
C.R. Alexander		1937 - 1938
Roger M. Yancy	Upsilon Phi (NY/*NJ*/*CT*)	1938
Wendell P. Grisby	Iota Phi	1939

	(PA/MD/DE/DC)	
Mifflin T. Gibbs	Mu Omega	1946 - 1947
Nathaniel Burrell	Xi Phi	1947 - 1948
Mifflin T. Gibbs	Mu Omega	1948 - 1949
Herschel Day	Kappa Omicron	1949 - 1951
George Meares	Kappa Omicron	1953 - 1955
Ermon K. Jones	Phi Upsilon	1957 - 1960
Melvin Coleman	Alpha Upsilon	1960- 1962
Edward Waters	Pi Alpha	1962 - 1964
James S. Avery	Omicron Chi	1964 - 1967
Robert L. Johnson	Pi Omega	1967 - 1969
Norman Johnson	Iota Phi	1969 - 1971
Milton D. Johnson, II	Nu Omicron	1971 - 1973
James E. Grant	Pi Omega	1973 - 1975
Theodore N. Greer	Nu Upsilon	1975 - 1977
Frederick Scott	NuNu	1977 - 1978
Adam E. McKee, Jr.	MuNu	1978 - 1980
Walter G. Amprey	Pi Omega	1980 - 1982
Walter F. Wrenn, III	Mu Omega	1982 - 1984
John W. Maloney, III	Kappa Omega	1984 - 1986
Andrew A. Ray	Theta Omicron	1986 - 1988
Richard H. Johnson, Jr.	MuNu	1988 - 1990
George K. McKinney	Pi Omega	1990 - 1992
David B. Wharton, Sr.	Chi Upsilon	1992 - 1994

Calvin C. Zellars	Tau Pi	1994 - 1996
Michael A. Freeman	Pi Omega	1996 - 1998
Terrel D. Parris	Mu Omega	1998 - 2000
Lee A. Bernard, Jr.	Upsilon Phi	2000 - 2002
Benjamin Jeffers	Chi Pi	2002 - 2004
Gregory E. Ackles	Nu Nu	2004 - 2006
Marvin C. Dillard	Nu Beta Beta	2006 - 2008
James Jordan	Chi Pi	2008 -

1st District Representatives

Listed alphabetically, Term provided where available

Bernard Gilliam	1980 -1983
Donald F. Harris	1986 -1989
Raymond Hilton	1994 -1994
Ted Hogan	1976 -1980
Al Maule	
Claude McAdams	1941
Clifton Moore	1970 -1973
Jim Myers	
James Owens	2000 – 2002

Carlton Pickeron	2008 -
Rodney Russell	1994 - 2000
Stafford Thompson, Jr.	2002 - 2004
Herbert Tucker	1955 -1960
Sylvester Wilkins	1989 - 1994
L. C. Williams	1983 -1986
Vaughn M. Willis	2004 – 2008
*C. Everett Yates	1937

13th District/International Chapter Reps

Richard Smith
Peter L. Mitchell
Edouard T. Delagarde
Cipriani A. Phillips, Jr.
Jonathan N. Griffin, Sr.

<<>>

APPENDIX P

Early Highlights of Omega Psi Phi Fraternity

1911	Omega Psi Fraternity founded Friday, November 17th 1911. 1st African American Greek letter organization at a predominately African American campus.
1913	First fraternity house located at 322 T Street NW in Washington D.C. *
1914	First "official" Conclave held with delegates, December 28th.
1917	First "War" chapter established at Ft. Des Moines Iowa.
1919	First issue of Oracle published in the spring.
1920	First Graduate chapter established in November. Lambda Omega, Norfolk, VA
1921	Undergraduate chapters distinguished from Graduate chapters by Greek Letter placement.
1921	Omega Chapter reserved for deceased brothers.
1921	Omega Psi Phi becomes the Ist African American Greek Letter organization to span the American continent. Atlantic to Pacific Oceans.
1922	First revision of ritual by Bro. G.L. Lythcott at the Philadelphia Conclave.
1922	First District Representatives appointed by the Grand Basileus. (5)
1922	Office of the Vice Grand Basileus & Grand KRS established.
1923	Lambda Chapter established in Los Angeles.
1924	First International chapter established, Sigma, for undergraduates in Canada.
1925	Annual Achievement Week program established. Renamed from Negro History and Literature Week initiated in 1920.
1926	Bro. Colonel Young Memorial Dedicated at Arlington National Cemetery.
1926	Fraternity moves to restrict expansion.

1926	Memorial Service established to memorialize Bro. Col. Young's birthday
1929	Bro. Matthew W. Bullock elected as chairman of 1st permanent Panhellic Council. Temporary officers were elected in 1921.
1931	"Omega Dear" adopted as official Hymn.
1931	Escutcheon designed by Bro. Frederick Alston.
1933	Fraternity moves to reactivate inactive chapters.
1935	Ritual corrected to include Bro. E.E. Just as founder.
1937	Traveling DR's abolished.
1937	District conferences established constitutionally.
1939	Citizen and Omega Man of the year established.
1940	First history of the Fraternity written and published by Bro. Herman Dreer and dedicated to Bro. Walter H. Mazyck.
1941	Fraternity undergoes redistricting.
1945	Office of 2nd Vice Grand Basileus established.
1945	National Social Action Program adopted.
1946	Resolution outlawing brutality during initiation proposed.
1946	Traveling DR's re-instituted.
1949	Lambda Chapter, Los Angeles, CA, purchases 14-room fraternity house.
1950	36th Grand Conclave resolved to eliminate all brutality and corporal punishment from pledging.
1953	National Talent Hunt Program makes its debut at Cincinnati Conclave.

* - initially located 326 T Street for six weeks

APPENDIX Q

THE ORACLES

The official Organ of Omega Psi Phi Fraternity
(*Stanley Douglas Editor of the first Oracle published Spring 1919)

(Walter T. Richardson, Oracle Editor as of 2008)

The Oracle is a scholarly publication containing literary work intended to ne more insightful and though-provoking than its forerunners. The Oracle features the aristocracy of the Omega Psi Phi intellect. This magazine is published quarterly and is now available on the Internet or mail subscription.[84]

- Summer 1968, VolLVII, No.2, Cover Story – Xi Phi Chapter Hold Achievement Award Luncheon-Articles- Civil Disturbance in America by H. Carl Moultrie/ 52nd Grand Conclave Preparation

- Fall 1969, Vol. LVIII, No. 3, Cover Story – Atlanta Constitution Convention 1968 & Picture of Daniel Thomas who electrifies brothers with Worlds of Challenge-Articles-Lower the Standards? by Grand Basileus Corbett/207 Chapters went Delegates to the Constitutional Convention in Atlanta, Ga. Oct 25-26, 1969

- Summer 1971, Volume 55, No. 1, COVER STORY – Harlem During the New Negro Renaissance Articles- A sick America: Some treatments For Its Cure" by Captain Joseph C. Ramsey, Jr. / Volcanoes… And live Sacrifices by Otto McClarrin/Contenporaries: Profile on W. Montague Cobb, M.D/

- Spring/Summer 1972 Vol. 70, No. 2&3, COVER STORY-Colonial Simon H. Scott, Jr in Command of NATO Air Force Chaplains- Articles-The Law and You by Brother William Bryant/Philosophy of Education And Administration by Patrick H. Walker, Jr.

- Winter 1972, Vo 55, Number 2, COVER STORY-Drugs And The Black commuity by Dr. Lloyd H. Bell/Is Black Racism Better Than White Racism by Judge William H. Hastie /Death in Small Doses by Otto MClarrin/Aticles Sterling Brown, the mentor of thousands… by Hollie I. West. America at the crossroads: " LET US MOUNT UP WITH WINGS AS EAGLES" BY VERNON E. JORDAN JR.

- Summer 1973 Vol 56 No. 2, COVER STORY – Involvement of Blacks in Business & Social Problems by Edward Lewis-Articles- The Involvment of Blacks in the Social Problems/Citizen of the Year: Vernon Jordan

---

[84] The Omega Psi Phi IHQ web site, Publication section

- Spring, 1974, Vol 57 Number 1- COVER STORY - Edgar A. Love, Last of Founding Brothers pa/sses / Matthew Walker MD, 1973 Omega Man by Albert G. Berry//First Olyker Science Graduate/ Raleigh's first Back Mayor/ Articles, Commemorative Stam Honoring Langston Huges

- Fall 1974, Vol59, No. 3,- COVER STORY- Memorial to our Founders-Articles-The Afro Americn MuseumMary McLeod Bethune memorial Dedication by Samuel R. Shepard/Mission To Moscow by Dr. John Marshall Stevenson/Father-Son Atheletes by J.T. Humphrey, Athleics and Sports Editor/New Orleans Site of 1977 Conclave/Pledging From My Perspective by Brother Charles H. Turner,II

- Winter 1976 & Spring 1977 -Volume 61, No. 4 Winter 1976, Vol 62 No.1 Spring 1977, COVER STORY- Memorial Supplement, Judge William H. Hastie Nov 17, 1904-April 14, 1976/ First Black Federal Judge. & Legal Archetect of Civil Rights Reform through Federal Courts/Economic Survival-Everybody's Business by Herbert Simmons, Jr. / Black Students on White Campuses: An Admissions Dilemma by Marvin L. Grant/ from My Perspective By Charles H. Turner,II/ Lest We Forget (Our Four Cardinal principals by Eugene E. Ward – Pi Omega/Amherst College Eulogizes Its Most Distinguished Alumnus by John F. Morrison/ Amherst College Commencement – Charge to the Seniors. By John Willam Ward/President, Amherst college/ Judge William Hastie: Confronting the Social-Military Status of Blacks In the U.S. Army, 1940-1943 by Phillip McGuire

- Winter 1977, Vol 61, No. 4, COVER STORY - Pre-Conclaave Issue, 58th Grand Conclave, New Orleans, La December 26-30, 1977 Articles-Father John Epps by Charles M. Holmes, Sr/ Bringing Our Mainstream Climate Into Our Ghettos by John P. Murchison/Omega and Community Development by Andrew Bell/ A look at the Ghetto Worldwide by Charles H. Turner, II/ The Survival of Omega Psi PhiAn Undergrad Speaks Out On Hazing by Joseph Tubbs, Epsilon Gamma/ Signs Of The Times by Samuel "Chick" Coleman/ The Restitution Service; What ir Means to Victims of Crime by Alan Green/Omega Stomping for Sicle Cell by bro. Robert Pryor, Jr. /"A New Day With A Better Way" by brother Kenneth Wilson/A Love Story That Involves Many by Jeri Harvey? Looking Back After 40 Years by Samel R. Shepard/Psi Chapter Contiues Morehouse's Scholarship and Social Action Tradition by Charles W. Cherry/ 13 Q's on Team That Whipped Michigan 1976 by C. B. Henry/Walter H. "Crow" Riddick (Grand Keeper Of Record and Seal Emeritus by Dr. Edward Braynon, Grand Basileus

- Spring 1978, Vol 62, No. 1, COVER STORY- 58TH Grand Conclave Issue/Judge H. Carl Moultrie, I Honored as A Washingtonian of 1977- Articles-A patriarch's Prophecy by Dr. William C. jason, Jr. /The Saga of Omega/South African Brother's Absence of 43 Years has Mixed

Emotions By Samueo R. Shepard/Benjamin Hooks warns Omega that the Fight is far From Over by Jesse Champions

- Summer 1979, Volume 63, No. 2, COVER STORY- Special Conclave Edition with Panorama of Omega History Supplement by Samuel R. Shepard & Major Frederick Drew Gregory & Ronald Erwin McNAIR, PhD-Articles- Two Astronauts and a Congressman To Be Honored at Grand Conclave/The Honorable Walter E Fauntroy, U.S. House of Representatives/The Spirit Giveth Life by W. Montague Cobb, M.D.You! Your Fraternity by Brother William "Duke" Crawford /To the Class of 79" Welcome To The Real World by Dr. Emerson E. Brown/Let It Be! Let it be! Let It Be! By Arthur B. Williams, Jr./The Silent Minority by Arnold Butler

- Fall 1979 Volume 63, No. 3, COVER STORY-William W. Sutton, Ph.D. Vice-President of Academic Affairs Chicago State University/Omega Pledge $260,000 to United Negro College Fund/Articles-15 Omega Brothers Among Ebony Magazine's 100 Most Influential Black Americans/Trying to Find Yourself?The Census Bureau has an Answer/A Letter To My Three Sons by Moses C. Norman, Ph.D/An Open Letter to the Brothers of Omega Psi Phi by Brother Joseph R.Phillips, M.D./A Call for A New Civil Rights Coalition by Charles H.Turner, II

- Summer 1980 Vol 64 Number 2, COVER STORY - The Decade of The 80s, What Now?/Articles/Grand Basileus and Omega Housing Consultant Discuss Housing Programs With Hud/Urge Senate Action on Gray Appointment/ Dr. Walter Ridley Directs Oral History Project/ 12th District Meets 1980 goal/60th Grnad Conclave program/ Invitation to participate in Exhibits/Job Fair/Why Not Graduate School by Dr. Emerson E. Brown/Thoughts On How To Achieve Job Mobility by S. Gardner Scott/Omega Honor Founder's Widow on 89th Birthday/marathon Up Empire State Building Stairs/ Operation Big Vote Crusade '80/News Coordinator Requests News Photo/Kenneth Norris Now Full Colonel/Rededicate Sundial at Howard University.Dr. Carl H. Carpenter, Vice President at South Carolina/James E. Carter Sr. Marks 50th Year as Dentist/ Jaycees Award to Joseph H. Bell/Three Omegas on Daytona Beach/ Human Relations Officer in Florida Air National Guard/ Special Merit Award to james R. Burress, Fred Rice Candidate for Chicago Police Chief/ Indiana U. Alumni Award to Dr. Tillman/W. Nelso Talbert heads Los Angeles Pan Hellenics/Fighting the Good Figth by Guy Friddel/Jackson Q's and Quettes Annual family Picnic by Alvin Benson.

- Fall 1980, Vol 64 No.3, COVER STORY- Portrait Unveiling Dr. Benjamin E. Mays, South Carolina State House July 12, 1980-ArticlesInfluencing Decisions as Undergraduates By Leon Franks, 2nd Vice Grand Basileus and Lee Grantlin Willis, 2nd Vice-District Representative/Economic Forum by J.P. Murchison and Claude W. Boxborough/Working both Sides of the Street-Clif Moore, Business

Development Executive/EEO Commission Honors Clarence Mitchell, Civil Rights leader/Black Librarianship Endangered-Annette L. Phinasee, Dean of NCCU School of Library Science/Unique Achievement Week Project-Theta Omega and Phi Eta Chapters/Father and Son-Both Omega Men in Same Year/St. Paul's College Honors Husband and Wife PhD. Team/Grand Conclave Program/Scholarship Offered by the hearers and Drew memoriam Funds/Psi Phi Community Services by Rudolph Boone, Sr./Alpha Chapter's Health fair and education Series at Howard University/Doe Grant to Jackson State University/Dedicate Columbia (SC) Omega House/Rust College Honors Gerson Stroud by Harold Shuford. "Nobody Walks Like a Man from Omega" by Donna Johnson and Anthony Willett/"A Purple and Gold Heaven" by J. Aaron Roscoe.

- Winter 1980, Vol. 64, No. 4, COVER STORY-Looking Ahead Into The Decade of the 80's-Articles-Carter G. Woodson Home Proposal- by Robert L. Gill/ The Struggles and Practices of Dr. Martin Luther King, Jr. by Robert Lewis Gills/An Omega man or a First Step Toward Black Economic Growth by John P. Murchison and Claude Roxborough

- Spring 1981, Vol71, No. 2, COVER STORY William "Bill" Cosby, Entertainer, Producer, Activist, Philanthropist-Articles- Col. Charles Young, U.S.A. Second Honorary member of Omega: A Victim of Military Racism By Charles H. Turner II/Some Thoughts For Reclamation and Retention By Brother Junius F. Carter, III/Link To Omega Founders by Brother Mallory K. Millender/Oracle Interviews Charles Bolden by Tony Williams/Crime in the Black Community, Lack of Action by Brother Leroy Adkins

- Fall 1981, Vol. 65, No. 2, COVER STORY- Dr. Wade Wilson, Student, Teacher and President Ends 45 years at Cheyney State College/ (Dr. Luther Burse, Patrick H. Walker, Jr. Interim Vice-President – Top Administrators at Cheyney State University)/Articles "Resurgent Politics and Education Progressivism in the New South" by H.Leon Prather, Sr..,/"Reaffirming Our Beliefs in America" by Charles H. Turner, II/"quality Education-Looking Toward the Future" by William W. Sutton, Ph.D., Chicago State University/ "The Role of Public Relations" by Samuel R. Shepard/Statement of Naturalization Ceremony, by Jude H. Carl Moultrie, I Washington, D.C. Superior Court/Leadership from Conference on Civil Rights letter to Senate leader Urging Extension of Voting Rights Acts/Historical facts on NAACP College Division by Daniel Thomas Jr./ "Carter G. Woodson" by Benjamin E. Mays, PhD,

- Fall 1983, Vol. 67, No. 3, COVERSTORY-U.S. Presidential Candidate, Jesse Jackson Articles- International Chapter Entertains the Grand Basileus by Freeman Holifield/How to Live with Reagonomics by Milt Johnson/

- Spring 1984, Vol 67, No. 4, COVER STORY - U.S. PRESIDENTIAL CANDIDATE, BROTHER REV. JESSE L. JACKSON/ Bro. Capt. Joe D. Howze Sited outstanding Young man Of America For 1983/

- Summer/Fall 1985 Oracle, Vol 68, No. 3&4, COVERSTORY-New Team(Moses C. Norman, Grand Basileus & John S. Epps, National Executive Secretary-ArticlesOmega Grand Conclave Louisville, Kentucky/No Place for the Homeless by Benjamin Foster Jr./ Presidential Ridicule Fails As Communication By Congressman Mickey Leland (D-Texas) /Joltin' Joe Jordan by Mike D'Orso

- Summer/Fall 1986 Vol 69, No.4, COVER STORY Ronald McNair: A Brother Remembered/Washington D.C. 75th Anniversay Observance.Articles-Mayor Barry Welcomes Omega with Excellence by Brother Dewitt H. Evans/Lieutenant Governor Wilder: A Gallant Knight Addresses Omega by Dewitt H. Wvans/ Omega Grand Basileus Dr. Moses Norman Presides at 75th Anniversary Grand Conclave A Heritage Celebration - A Legacy Enhanced by Brother Dewitt H. Evans/ Rev. Dr. Benjamin Hooks Addresses Omega A Tale Of two cities by Brother Dewitt H. Evans/ Liberty and Justice by Brother jesse Jackson

- Winter 1986-87, Vol 70, Number 1, COVER STORY- Farewell Tribute H. Carl Moultrie I, National Executive Secretary 1949-1972

- Fall 1987, Vol 70, No. 2 COVER STORY-Happy Holidays, Ariticles Scholarship Is Point of Pride(Omega Grandmother, Georgia Morgan, Contributes $700.00 to scholarship Fund in memory of her grandshop Bryce Lawrence Morgan.

- Fall 1988, Vol 71, No. 1, COVER STORY –Supreme Council Undergraduate Representatives/Articles- A Footnote On Ernest Everett Just by H. Leon Prather Sr.,Ph.D. /Omega-A Saga of Truth/Raymond Bourgeois-A natural leader/

- Summer/Fall 1991, Vol. 72, No.3, COVER STORY-Brother Charles F. Bolden Jr. Colonel, USMC & Brother Fredrick D. Gregory Colonel, USAF, Articles-At Your Service… Omega-What is our Call? By lloyd J. Jordan/A Changing of the Guard by Brother Michael A. Jefferson/ The Army-It's Tme to Take Another Look by brother/ Confrontation in the Oval Office Brother Grant Reynolds/Omega's Future is In Our Hands by Brother Kenneth M. Morton By Brother Kenneth M. Morton/The National Assault On Illiteracy Program By Leonard Douglas Omega's Purpose By Charles H. Turner, II/

- Winter/Spring 1991, Vol. 72 , No.4, COVER STORY-Warmoth T. Gibbs, Sr. (Gamma "17") & Theodore Randolph (Beta "16")-Articles- Omega Psi Phi Fraternity Gives $100,000.00 to UNCF/The time for Change is Now! A Treatise by John S. Epps/ Omega Psi Phi Fraterntiy Credit Union Notes and Quotes or 20 Pearls of Advice by Brother

James Elam/Economics In Plain English by Brother Milt Johnson/ A Letter to My Sons by Dorsey C. Miller/Omega Psi Phi Fraterntiy, Inc. Statement of PositionAgainst Canine Reference

- Summer/Fall 1992, Vol.73, No. 5, COVER STORY –The Ten Living Grand Basilei: 30 Years of Outstanding Leadership-Articles-67th Grand Conclaave, "The Greatest" by Brother Charles H. Turner II, /BCCLeadeer A Civil Rights Pioneer/Couuthouse Renamed in Honor of Brother H. Carl Moultrie I By Brother Dwayne Brown/Education is the Key By Brother Walter J. Johnson/Charles R. Drew Chair in Surgery Established at Howard University by Brother Isaiah E. Barbwell, Jr./International Headquarters Undergoing Facelift By Brother Bernard S. Little/Gilmore Wants to restore Founders' Grave Sites by Tony Williams.

- Winter/Spring 1993, Vol. 73 No. 5, COVER STORY – "Jim" Clyburn, United States House Of Representatives South Carolina Sixth Congressional District,-Articles-International Intake Chairman Brother Robert W. Fairchild interview/Omega Psi Phi Fraterntiy Federal Credit Union Notes & Quotes by Brother James Elam/Are you making a life Time Investment in Omega by George K. McKinney/Our Image is at Stake by Brother Jeffery A. Shields

- Summer/Fall 1993, Vol 73, No. 7, COVER STORY – Under Graduate members Of The Supreme Council Willie Rock Award , James Edmonds, III, Cedric A. Portis and Clement M. Osimetha (picture)/John Captain, the Intake Chairman, Interview Articles-Thousands of Children Are Waiting by Marty Jones

- Winter/Spring 1994, Vol. 74, No. 8, COVER STORY-c. Tyrone Gilmore, Sr., 34th Grand Basileus,-Articles-The last Word by Brother Herbert E. Tucker, Jr./Omega Grand Men of Leadership of Past Years Come Together and Hammer Out a Solid Document for Future Ceremonies for the Next Decade for Men of Omega by Brother Burnel E. Coulon/ Yesterday, Today and Tommorrow By Brother Adam E. McKee/ Omega In Africa-Somalia Operation Continue Ope by Brother Conrado B. Morgan//The Legacy of the African American Male by Brother Hal Chatman, Jr./Omega Mkes History by Floyd Thomas and Lron Babridege/Seventh District Representative Recommend Chapters/Individual Suspensions and Expulsions by J. B. Carter/ The Struggle to Save Our Young Males by Brother Arthur McLin, Jr

- Summer/Fall 1994, Vol 1994, No. 9, COVER STORY – Elridge McMillian President, Southern Education Foundation /Articles- The Meaning Of Scholarship for an Omega Man by Brother Gordon D. Morgan

- Spring 1995, Volume 75, Number 10, COVER STORY - The New Omega Psi Phi Fraternity World Center-Decatur, Ga. /Articles, Omega Leads the Way by Vernon E. Jordan Jr./The Detroit Omega Foundation

- Support For Nu Omega by leonard Douglas/Executive Director's Message "In Our Forefathers House, There Are Many Mansions by Joh S. Epps, PhD./ A, Farewell At the Omegoing Of Willie A. Smith/ True Legacy, The Omega West Point Story, from Colonel Charles Young to Zededee Freman, Johnell Holly, Troy McHenry, Clayton Nichols, Abel Young, the West Point class of 1995.

- Summer 1995, Vol 75, Number 11, COVER STORY – AFRICA, by Adam E. Mckee, Walter johnson, Wlter Wrenn, Charles Chrstopher/ Aritcles Affirmative Action by Bletcher H. Willey/Executive Director's Message by John S. Epps, " To Whom Much Is Given Much Is Expected"

- Fall 1995, Vol 76, No.12, COVER STORY – Dedication Of Omega World Center/Ariticles-Strenghtening Family Values by David L. Beckley,.

- Winter 1995/96, Vol 76, No. 13, COVER STORY-Omega Brothers Who Are College Presidents or Chancellors/Historical Black Colleges and Universities by brother Walter J. JonhsonArticles-/The Chaplain's Corner by brother Ferrel J. Duncombe/Omegas Dedicated World Center and International Headquarters/Brother Bill Cosby's Visit to Baton Rouge Remembered by Clayton Lewis, Lambda Alpha Chapter/ A Farewell At The Homegoing Of Marion Winston Garnett, 29th Grand Basileus.

- Fall 1995, Vol 76, No. 12, COVER STORY- Dedication of Omega World Center: Master of Ceremony – Bill Cosby, Dedication Speaker- Earl Graves-Articles-Strengthening Family Values by David L. Beckley

- Spring 1996, Vol 76, No. 14, COVER STORY –The Honorable Ernest Everett Just Immortalized Trhough the United States Postal Service Black Heritiage Stamp Series, Articles-What Can one man Do? By Don and Lanetta Lyons & Horace Baldwin/Uplift In Action: The Story of two Stakwart Brothers by James T. Dixon, Sr./Omega participates In The Million man march by brother Walter J. Johnson/Perseverance by Brother marv Dale/"A Rare Species: A Black professional Golfer by Brother martin Roache

- Summer/Fall 1996, Vol 76. No. 15, COVER STORY- "THE RAMIFICATION OF AFFIRMATIVE: can a Nation Divided Against Itself Stand?"/Brother Alonza Bennett-International Omega Man of the Year 1996.-Articles-Crack Cocaine Sentencing: Fair or Foul by Brother Wayne J. Johnson/ The Ramification of Affirmative Action in America By Brother Adam McKee/The Issue of Affirmative Action and Role of the Fraterntiy by Brther Walter J. Johnson/The Contract With America: Prospectus for Unity or Racism by legislation" by Brother Ferrell J. Duncombe.

- Winter/Spring 1997,Vol 76, No.16, COVER STORY – Omega Enter The next Millenium With A Revised Mindset by Sylvester Wilkins/ Brother Leroy Walker President, U.S. Olympic Committee – Brother william Dehart Hubbard (Omega's first Olympic Champion)

- Summer/Fall 1997, Volume 76, Number 18, COVER STORY-Omega Men Reach New Heights: Brother Tony Grant Banker, Brother Thurbert E. Baker Georgia Attorney General-Articles-Omega man at the Top of One of the World's Largest Banks by Fred Monk/Brother Thurbert E. Baker Appointed First Black Attorney General for the State of Georgia by Charles H. Turner/ The Period After Affirmative Action by Brother Russell Mootry Jr.

- Winter/Spring 1998, Vol 76, No. 19, COVER STORY – Brother David Satcher, "America's family Doctor" / Administrative Operations Update by Robert Fairchild/ "The Big Easy" Prepares to Host Omega's 70th Grand conclave/Undergraduates Summit Attracts large Throng And Brothers Vow To Help Omega Move Forward/The Entrepreneurial Renaissance: Rekindling The Spirit Of Enterprise by Brother Carl F. Flipper/My Omega Position Ppaper by brother Dominick Boyce

- Spring/Summer 1999, Vol 76, Number 21 COVER STORY – Brother Edard Lewis Publisher and CEO Essence Communications, Inc. Articles-What You Should Know About Prostate Nodules and Impotence by Brother Charles A. Christopher MD/Colorectal Cancer by brother Walter P. Wrenn/Facts About Open-Angle Glaucoma by Brother Gideon K. Mincy/ Demand Equality For Health Reform by Brother Melvin Pinn, MD

- Summer 2000, COVER STORY –Brother John H. Williams; A Giant Among Men Articles-The Charles Drew Memorial Blood Drive Expands by Brother Allan E. Thomas, PH.D/African American Pioneers in Corporate Sector by Brother James Avery, 28th Grand Basileus/Essential Ingredients to Success: Bonding And Networking by brother Byron Lewis.

- Winter 2000, COVER STORY- Brother Byron Lewis Chairman and CEO Uniworld Group, Inc., Articles-Omega psi Phi launches Hall of fame for African American Business Champions/ "The Best Omega Meeting Ever" by Brother Ed Davis, Upsilon Omega/How About Greek Coalition? By the Rev John M. Burgess/ Addiction and Illness Not a Choice by Brother Fred D. mcQueen, Jr. MD/

- Summer 2001, COVER STORY – Steve Harvey:Above the Laughter, Tau Pi On Line Mentoring, Eta Omega Sat clinic, Rho Gamma Gamma Sponsors Cultural Exhibition-ArticlesOmega psi Phi leaders participate In Roy Wilkins Stamp Unveiling by Brother Edward R. Davis/ The Father is a Brother: national Citizen of the Year: father maurice J. Nutt, D..Min. by Brother Edward R. Davis.

- Summer 2002, COVER STORY-OH! OH! OH! It's Fly Jock, Brother Tom Joyner!, Plus, Eta Omicron Honored At State Workshop/Upsilon Omega 'Rhapsody" Is Scholarship Music/Omega Welcomes First new Chapter of The 21st Century-Articles- The Challenge Of Living The Vision Of Our Founders by Brother James S. Avery, 28th Grand Basleus

- Spring 2003, COVER STORY-"The Legacy and Brotherhood Continues" (Enconomic Empowerment Leading to Social and Political Change) Articles-Education As A Means To An End, by Brother Charles Johnson Jr./ The Successful Principles: Singing Life;s Praises by Michael Jackson/ "Economic Empowerment Leading to Social and Political Change" from a Medical Perspective by Brother Charles A. Chrsitopher/Social Security Important to African Americans by Brother Paul D. Barnes(Social Security Regional Commissioner Atlanta, Georgia/ Omega Psi Phi Fraternity Federal Credit Union-What Is It, and How Does It Serve the membership? By Brother Stafford L. Thompson, Sr., President

- Summer 2003, COVER STORY-A Uniformed Profile Of Leadership (Brothers in the Military)-Article-Message From The Undergraduate Immediate Representative by Brother Wilson White/Message From the Friendship Foundation/2003 Celebrity Weekend-Featured Lee Elders"GolfLegend" by Brother S. Earl Wilson/Rev. Jesse L. Jackson Addresses 2003 Leadership Conference by Dr. isaiah Robinson

- Fall 2003, COVER STORY, "A UNIFIED PROFILE OF LEADERSHIP" Enconomic Empowerment Leading to Social and Political Change" Ariticles The 37th Grand Basilues Speaks " Can't See The Forest For The Trees"/ The former Grand Basilei Speak, (grant Reynolds, Herbert E. Tucker, Jr. James S. Avery, Edward J. Breynon, Burnel E. Coulon, Benjamin Livingston, Moses C. Norman, Sr.C. Tyrone Gilmore, Sr. Dorsey C. Miller, Jr. Lloyd, J. Jordan/ Omega psi Phi fraternity Federal Credit Union-Why does the brotherhood expect for from us?' by Stafford L. Thompson, Sr. President/ Health Initiatives by Brother Charles A. Christopher, MD, / Ques in Sports by Brother Roscoe Nance/spiritual Prospective – essage from the Grand Chaplain by Reverend Dr. Farrell J. Duncombe.

- Spring 2004, Vol 80. No. 6, COVER STORY –Profiels Of Scholarship-Articles-Omega Wealth Building by Carl A. Blunt/Omega Public Policy by Jesse L. Jackson Sr./

- Summer 2004 Vol. 80, No 7, COVER STORY – Honorable Kendrick B. Meek, U.S. Congressman- House of represntative-17th District of Florica; A profile of Political Courage and Leadership-Articles-Omega Wealth Building Through Real Estate by Brother Carl A. Blunt/ Signs Of the Times: The Challenge to Build A More Perfect Union by Brother Jesse L. Jackson Sr./ John E. Jacob Executive Vice president Global Communications Anheuser-Busch Companies "An Uplifter of

Humanity" by Dr. Isaiah Robisnon

- Fall 2004,Vol.80, No.8 COVER STORY – Economic Emporerment Leading to Social And Political Change Picture of Grand Basileus George Grace, Vice Grand Basileus Warrant Lee, Earl Graves, Charles F. Bolden & Louis Anderson Articles- Which Side Is God On by Jesse L. Jackson Sr./Black America: A Cure For What Hurts by Brother Attorney Roy Miller.

- Winter 2004, Vol 80, No. 5, COVER STORY -A Uniformed Profile Of Leadership, Articles- Omega Public Policy by Brother Jesse Jackson, Brotherhood by Richard "Dick" Smith/ HBCU's: Meeting the Challenge in the Twenty-First Centrury Under the leadership Of Omega Brothers by Brother Walter J. Johnson/ Health Initiatives (Erective Dysfunction (ED)/Confronting Impotence by Brother Charles A. Christopher, MD/ The Omega Psi Phi Fraternity Credit Union Still Working For You by Brother Stafford L. Thompson, Sr., President.

- Summer 2005, Vol 80. No.9, COVER STORY –"Ben Crump Spark of Omega Day At The national Capitol-Articles/Omega provide over $100,000 for Katrina and Rita relief/Richard "Dick" Smith Retirement Reception held at HQ o1-21-2005/Omega celebrity Golf Tournament held in Jacksonville Florida/2005 Leadership Conference

- 2005 Winter, Vol. 80 No. 9, COVER STORY –Dr. Andrew Hugins, Jr. "An Omega Building Omega Legacy"-Articles- 2004 Business & Economic Summit by isaiah Robinson/

- Summer 2006, Vol 80. No. 15, COVER STORY – "Three Looks, One Focus: Family, Fraternity , Friends, The Honorable Warren G. Lee, Jr. 38th Grand Basileus. Articles- Brother Melvin B. Tolson 1898-1966 by Brother Isaiah ROBINSON /Omega Psi Phi Fraternity, Inc. /Omega Psi Phi Fraternity, Inc. Youth Leadership Conference by Isaiah Robinson

- Summer 2007, Vol. 80, No.16, COVER STORY-The Spirit of Perseverence, Ambassador Charles R. Stith, Articles- Does Faith Impact Health by Dr. Reuben Warren/ Is There Hope for Black Males by Willie Joe Wright/The Impact of Horizontal & Vertical Dimensions of Faith on Health and Health Care by Brother Brother Reuben C. Warren, DDS/ An Endangered Species at Risk by Brother Willie J. Wright, Ed.D./Omega Continue Legacy in Academic Medicine by Brother Scott Watson.

- Fall/Winter 2008, Vol 85, No. 17, COVER STORY- Uplift for a Falling Generation, Judge Arthur L. Burnett Sr. –Articles- Balck Church and Aids by Brother Byron D'Andra Orey/ Cries in Education by Brother Troy Crayton/Intellective Competence by Brother Edmund W. Gordon/ Life IN AN A.C. World by Brother Joseph

Marshall/Fraternities< A Poem> by Brother Stafford Thompson, Jr. M.A.

- Spring 2008, Vol 80, No.18, COVER STORY-Profiles In Manhood/Conclave Edition The Grand Officers/Moving Toward Theo-Political Incorrectness-ArticlesCriisis In Education by Brother Troy Crayton/Theo-Political Incorrectness by Brother T. Anthony Spearman/Branding In Omega by Brother Charles Johnson

<<>>

APPENDIX R

Omega Bulletins

The first Omega Bulletin, the fraternity's official newsletter, was published in 1928 *SAMPLES DISPLAYED BELOW

VolumeXXXIX, Spring 2008,
Articles-Message to the Districts and Chapters of the Omega Psi Phi Fraternity, Inc. from Charles Bruce, Grand Keeper of Records and Seal/Fending Off Foreclosure by Bro. Carl A. Blunt/Omega Psi Phi Fraternity Internet Policy/Chairman List/ District Meeting Schedule/ 75th Grand Conclave

VolumeXXXVIII, Fall 2007,
Articles-Message to the Districts and Chapters of the Omega Psi Phi Fraternity, Inc. from Charles Bruce, Grand Keeper of Records and Seal/Lock Box Program Enhancements/Message From the 2nd Vice Grand Basileus/2008 District Meeting Information/First Quarter Form 37

VolumeXXXVII, Summer 2007,
Articles-Message to the Districts and Chapters of the Omega Psi Phi Fraternity, Inc. from Charles Bruce, Grand Keeper of Records and Seal/Win Free Registration to the 2008 Grand Conclave/95% of Leadership Conference Registration Accomplished on Line/Proposed amnesty plan aimed at Building Fund Assessments/

VolumeXXXVI, Spring 2007,
Articles-Warren G. Lee-The Grand Basilues Speaks/The Grand KF Announces Change in the way we do business/Customer Service Improvements Coming to IHQ//Memorial Tribute to –Herbert E. Tucker. 2007 District Meeting Schedule/ The John H. Williams Museum Opens at The World Headquarters/One International Committee Needs A Chairman/100th Year Celebration Committee has been Seate/2007 Leadership Conference proposed Agenda

VolumeXXXV, Winter Edition, 2006, Number 7

International Office Efficiency and Effectiveness Initiative/Annual Chapter Assessments/73rd Grand Conclave Minutes/74th Grand Conclave Registration/NAACP Policy/

Volume XXXV, Wnter, 2004 Number 3
Cover Articles–Know one cares about how much you know Until they know how much you care by Warren G. Lee

Volume XXXV, Fall Edition 2004 Number 5
Cover Article-Message from Brother S. earl Wilson Executive Director

Volume XXXV, Conclave (Spring) Editions, No.4
Cover Article-73rd Grand Conclave: America's Center St. Louis, Missouri, July 19-29, 2004.

APPENDIX S

THE CLARION CALL

The official publication of Omega Psi Phi fraternity, Inc.
TROY MOORE EDITOR as of 06/01/08/ *This publication was suspended in July 2008 at the 75th Grand Conclave. It began in Spring 2007

Spring 2007 EDITION, Vol. 1, No. 1, COVER STORY–Former Grand Basileus Herbert E. Tucker 1915-2007-Articles-House of Representative majority Whip, Brother James Clyburn by Brother Glenn Rice/The Essential Role of the Keeper of Records and Seal by Brother Charles A. Bruce/ Black Men Can Fly, The story of Brother George S. Lima/Ret. Col., Brother John Henry Smith by Jeffrey T. Smith/ Rear Admiral Manson K. Brown by Robert L. Woodson.

Summer 2007 EDITION, Vol.1, No.2, COVER STORY-Omega Celebrates Its Undergraduate Scholars, Articles-Lessons Learned From Some of My Favorite Movies by Brother Troy Moore/Corporate Governance Group Training Workshop Held In New Orleans, La./Omega To Test A Bold membership Process by Brother Keith W. Neal/The 2007 Philadelphia Leadership Conferenc/The African-American Civil Rights Movement A Prelude by Brother Carl A. Blunt/One Story Of the Civil Rights Struggle In Litte Rock Arkansas/The Bridge Builder by Brother Richard D. Jones

FALL 2007 EDITION, VOL 1 No. 3, COVER STORY-Brother Charles A. Christopher, Sr., MD, Surgon General to Omega-Articles-The Spigarn Medal by Carl A. Blunt/In The Company Of Great Men: Brother Captain Sean P. Hoggs Named 2007 Outstanidng Young American/ U.S. Census Bureau Appointment: Brother Dorsey C. Miller, Jr. 35th Grand Basileus/Education, Building A Bridge

To The Future by Brother Marc Styles/Meeting Brother General Ward in Ethopia by Brother larry Burks.

Spring 2008 EDITION, Volume 80, No.10, COVER STORY-Profiles in Manhood:Omega's Grand Officers-Articles-Crises in Education byBrother Troy Crayton/Theo-Politica Incorrectness by Brother T. Anthony Spearman/Braanding in Omega by BrotherCharles Johnson/A Poem by Brother Karl J. Coleman

<<>>

Winter 2008, EDITION, Vol 1, No. 4, COVER STORY-Willie Frank Hinchen, Educator and Omega Man of our Time.

<<>>

APPENDIX T

THE SWORD & SHIELD
GRAND BASILEUS NEWSLETTER
Initiated 11-2007

December 03, 2007, Vol. 1, No. 1- Articles/ Staying in Touch with the Brotherhood/Readers Corner/Lest We Stray/Roles Of The Grand Basileus/News For The Ques/Crux Of The Matter/

December 21, 2007. Vol 1, No. 2 – Articles/Season's Greetings/Are We Practicing Excellence?/Omega's Use of Email/OLMF vs OPPF?/Going Forward/Always Remember/Reader's Corner/

February 04, 2008, Vol 1, No. 3 –Articles/The Eyes Of Omega/Reader's Corner/

March 03, 2008, Vol. 1, *No.4 - Articles/Nobody Asked Me....Obama in 08 is Great!/Reader's Corner –Barrack Obama-The Audacity of Hope./Duties of the Supreme Council/*

March 30, 2008, Vol. 1, No. 5 – Articles/To Serve Or be Served/Reader's Corner- John C. Maxwell, "There's No Such Thing As Business Ethics

May 08, 2008, Vol. 1, No. 6 – Articles/What's Your Roy/Reader's Corner Reginald J. Eadie, Jr. – How to Eat and Live Longer

APPENDIX U

FAMOUS OMEGA MEN

Science

- **Dr. Ernest Everett Just** - Internationally known biologist and professor at Howard University. Founder of Omega Psi Phi Fraternity Inc. Initiated in Alpha chapter.
- **Frank Coleman** – Founder of Omega Psi Phi fraternity Inc. and internationally known scientist.
- **Oscar J. Cooper** - Founder of Omega Psi Phi fraternity Inc. and internationally known scientist.
- **Michael DeBaum** – Internationally known Epidemiologist, Neurologist, Biostatistician and Pediatrics. Alpha chapter
- **Major General Charles F. Bolden** - Astronaut, graduate of the United States Naval Academy (pilot) Gamma Nu chapter*UPDATE- 2009, **newly elected president Barack Obama nominate & select Omega man Charlie F. Bolden to head NASA.**
- **Dr. Charles Drew** - Perfected the use of blood plasma; Professor of Surgery at Howard University
- **Dr. Fred Drew Gregory** - Astronaut, graduate of the United States Air Force Academy (pilot) Alpha Omega chapter
- **Langston T. Holly, MD** – Internationally known

preeminent Neurosurgeon. Epsilon Mu chapter.
- **Dr. Percy Julian** - Discovered the use of foam to extinguish fires and discovered a method of producing cortisone synthetically. During his lifetime, he received more than 130 chemical patents. 1st Black chemist inducted into the National Academy of Sciences.
- **Dr. Ronald E. McNair** - Astronaut, graduate of M.I.T., Ph.D. in Physics (civilian) Mu Psi chapter
- **Dr. Hildrus Poindexter** - Bacteriologist who studied the epidemiology of tropical diseases.
- **Dr. Robert E. Lawrence -** was selected as the first Black man in the Astronaut program in 1966. He was killed in a training program early on in the U.S. space program.
- **Mohan Suntharalingam -** Brilliant Scientist and Physician in the field of Cancer. Theta Epsilon chapter
- **Curtis A. Pettaway** – Internationally known MD, in the field of Cancer and Urology. Initiated at Kappa chapter.

Arts

- **William "Count" Base'** - Internationally known pianist, composer, arranger, and band leader. Xi Phi chapter
- **Sterling Brown** - Teacher, poet, writer, Professor Emeritus of Literature at Howard University, has a special foundation for folk culture and jazz music
- **William H. "Bill" Cosby** - Comedian, author, actor, producer. No Zeta chapter
- **Steve Harvey** - Comedian and actor, Tau Tau chapter
- **Roland Hayes** - Internationally known tenor of the 1920s. Hayes sang in five different languages
- **Langston Hughes** - The Black Poet Laureate, excelled as a poet, playwright, novelist, lyrics and humorist. Beta chapter.
- **Matthew Knowles**- Internationally famous music mogul, record Producer and father of Singer, Actor Beyonce'
- **Tom Joyner** - Radio show host. Lambda Epsilon
- **Wanya Morris** – Boyz 2 Men singing group member, Tau Tau chapter
- **Rushion McDonald** –comedian and writer for the Steve H. Show, the Parkers, Ced's new show, and others.)

THE OMEGA PSI PHI FRATERNITY INC. 349

- **Rickey Smiley** - Comedian and actor. Gamma Sigma
- **Tommy Stewart** – Jazz Musician, Producer. Gamma Sigma chapter
- **Lonnie Liston Smith** –Jazz musician-Gamma Gamma chapter
- **Joe Torre** - Comedian and actor. Eta Sigma
- **Gregory Anderson** – Writer, Film Producer & Distributor

Athletics

- **Jerry Ball** - 3 time Pro Bowler and former NFL defensive lineman.
- **Joe Black** - An all-time great Brooklyn Dodger baseball pitcher. In 1952, he had the lowest earned-run average in the Major Leagues. First Black to win a World Series game.
- **Herman Boone** – famous high school football coach the subject of the movie "Remember the Titans" Tau Psi chapter
- **Vince Carter** - 8-time All-Star. 2-time All-NBA guard for the New Jersey Nets. 1999 NBA Rookie of the Year.
- **Mark Duper** - 3 time Pro Bowler and 2-time All-Pro former wide receiver with Miami Dolphins. Theta Delta
- **Clarence E. "Big House" Gaines** - Hall of Fame Basketball coach. Coached at Winston-Salem State University from 1946 - 1993. Also, 4-year All-CIAA lineman in football. Pi chapter
- **Vonta Leach** – NFL football player, Upsilon Zeta
- **Dr. Edwin Bancroft (E.B.) Henderson** - Captain and outstanding player on the Washington 12th Streeters (1906-1910). He is known as the "Father of Black Sport History". First Black male to become certified to teach Physical Education in public schools.
- **William DeHart Hubbart** - A University of Michigan sprinter; was the first Black athlete to win a Gold medal for the United States (1924). His winning long jump in the Paris games was 24' 5".
- **Keith Jackson** - 5 time Pro Bowler and 5 time All Pro former NFL Tight end. He was inducted to the College Football Hall of Fame in 2001. Pi Delta
- **Ed "Too Tall" Jones** - Overall 1st pick of 1974 NFL Draft. Outstanding former player with the Dallas Cowboys football team. Rho Psi

- **Mo Vaugh** – former professional baseball player. Kappa Eta
- **Bo Scott** – professional football player. Iota Psi
- **Michael "His Airness" Jordan** - Outstanding former professional basketball player with the Chicago Bulls and Washington Wizards of the NBA. His accolades and accomplishments include 5 NBA MVPs, 10 All-NBA first teams, 14 NBA All-star appearances, and 6 NBA Final MVPs. Omicron Alpha
- **Cedric "Cornbread" Maxwell** - Outstanding former professional basketball player with the Boston Celtics and other teams. 1981 NBA Finals MVP
- **Steve "Air" McNair** – Three time NFL Pro Bowler. 2003 NFL, MVP. An Outstanding NFL player with the Baltimore Ravens and Tennessee Titans. Initiated in Omega via Eta chapter. *OMEGA CHAPTER-July 4, 2009
- **Matt Snell** – NFL hall of famer - & 1964 AFL rookie of the year. Iota Psi
- **Shaquille O'Neal** - Star center with the Orlando Magic, Los Angeles Lakers and Miami Heat is a 14 time NBA All-star. He is 3 time NBA Final MVP and 2000 NBA MVP.
- **Brice Taylor** - University of Southern California football legend. Guard on mid 1920's team. Schools first All-American.
- Clinton Jones – College All American Football player
- **Sherman Lewis** – NFL coach
- **Terrence Trammell** - 2-time (2000, 2004) Olympic silver medalist in 110m hurdles
- **Charlie Ward** - 1993 Heisman Trophy winner and former NBA guard with the NY Knicks. Chi Theta
- **Ahmad Rashad** – former NFL player and host of <u>NBA Inside Stuff</u> and <u>NBA Access with Ahmad Rashad</u>. Kappa Omicron
- **Gene Washington** – College All American & NFL football player.
- **Robert Mathis** – NFL football player. Nu Epsilon
- **David Justice** - Outstanding MLB baseball player.
- **Jimmy Ray** – All American college quarterback
- **John Salley** – former NBA basketball player. Nu Omega
- **Paul Warfield** – Famous NFL wide

receiver for the Cleveland Browns and Miami Dolphins
- **Herb Adderley** – NFL hall of fame defensive back with the Green Bay Packers
- **Leroy Walker** - A U.S. Olympic coach (sprinters) for many years.
- **Dwight Lee** – Football College All American at Michigan State, halfback
- **Bob Ferguson** - Ohio State All American football player and 1961 Heisman Trophy 2nd runner up

Politics

- **Clifford L. Alexander, Jr.** - Secretary, Department of the Army
- **James E. "Jim" Clyburn** - The House Majority Whip in the 110th Congress. (2nd Black to hold that position).
- **Freeman Bosley Jr.**- First Black Mayor of St. Louis,
- **William Hastie** - First Governor of the U.S. Virgin Islands. Mu Omega chapter
- **Aaron E. Henry** Mississippi State Representative and Head of Mississippi NAACP and civil rights era.
- **Benjamin Hooks** – former Executive Director of NAACP, civil rights and minister. Chi Psi
- **Leonard Haynes** –Executive Director of the White house initiative on HBCUs,
- **Rev. Jesse Jackson** - Founder of both entities that merged to form Rainbow/PUSH. Candidate for the United States Presidency in 1984 and 1988. Served as "Shadow Senator" for DC from 1991 to 1997. Pi Psi chapter
- **Jesse L. Jackson, Jr.** – U.S. Congressman from Illinois. Nu Pi chapter
- **Vernon E. Jordan, Jr.** - 2001 Springarn Medal recipient. Executive Director of United Negro College Fund and a former president of the National Urban League. He also served as a close adviser to President Bill Clinton. Zeta Phi chapter
- **Clarence Lightner** - 1st Black Mayor of Raleigh, NC
- **Kendrick B. Meeks**- U.S. Congressman, House Of Representatives- 17th District Florida.

- **Samuel T**. Mcghee – The Mayor of Hillside New Jersey. Upsilon Phi chapter, Newark NJ
- **Dr. David Satcher** - 16th Surgeon General of the United States. He also held the posts of the Director of the CDC and the Administrator of the Agency for Toxic Substances and Disease Registry from 1993 to 1998. Psi chapter
- **Charles R**. **Stith** – U.S. Ambassador
- **Vernon G. Smith** – Indiana House of Representative
- **Walter E. Washington** - 1st Home-Rule mayor of the District of Columbia. Former Executive Director of the National Capital Housing Authority. Alpha chapter
- **George L.P. Weaver** - Former U.S. Secretary of Labor
- **Robert C. Weaver** - First African American to serve on the Presidential Cabinet when he became Secretary of Housing and Urban Development in 1966 under President Lyndon B. Johnson. Kappa Omicron chapter
- **Togo D. West, Jr.** - 3rd US Secretary of Veterans Affairs. Also served as US Secretary of the Army. Currently, the President of the National Capital Area Council of the Boy Scouts of America.
- **Lawrence Douglas Wilder** - 1st Black to be elected as a governor. He served as Governor of the Commonwealth of Virginia from 1990 to 1994. He is currently the mayor of Richmond, Virginia. He also received the Bronze Star for his military heroics in the Korean War. Zeta chapter.

Civil Rights

- **Wiley Branton** - Attorney of the "Little Rock Nine" and former Dean of Howard University School of Law
- **Arthur Louis Burnett, Sr**. – Judge and Civil rights Attorney for Civil Right Commission and president Jimmy Carter, President Ronald Reagan Judicial appointee 1987. Initiated in Alpha chapter 1954.
- **Oliver Hill** - Civil Rights attorney whose work against racial discrimination helped end the doctrine of "separate but equal". 1999 Presidential Medal of Freedom recipient.
- **Benjamin Hooks** - Succeeded Roy Wilkins as Executive Director of the NAACP, the most effective of all civil rights organizations

THE OMEGA PSI PHI FRATERNITY INC. 353

- **Baynard Ruston** – Civil rights activist who was a key organizer in the March of Washington D.C. in 1963.
- **Khalid Muhammad** - Spokesman for the "Nation of Islam"
- **James Nabrit** - Former Dean of Howard University Law School and former president of Howard University. A leader in the training of the early Civil Rights lawyers
- **Grant Reynolds** - Played a major role in President Truman's 1948 decision to desegregate the United States Armed Forces
- **Roy Wilkins** - Executive Director of the NAACP. Xi chapter.

EDUCATION

- **Edgar A Love** – Founder of Omega Psi Phi Fraternity Inc. and renowned Bishop and educator.
- **Herman Dreer** - Teacher, minister, writer, and author of The History of Omega Psi Phi Fraternity, Inc., 1911-1961
- **Lawrence Jackson** – Director of band at Southern university. Beta Sigma
- **Robert L. Gill** – Author of the Omega Psi Phi Fraternity And The Men Who Made Its History.
- **Benjamin E. Mays** - President Emeritus of Morehouse College, writer and lecturer. Mentor to Dr. Martin L. King, Jr.
- **Melvin B. Tolson** – Famed Wiley College professor who was the subject of the 2008 Movie, "The Great Debate"
- **Dr. Carter G. Woodson** - The earliest and most outspoken proponent for the study of Black History.

MILITARY

- **Charles Young** - Colonel, U.S. ARMY
- **William E. "KIP" Ward** - General, US Army
- **Manson K. Brown** - Rear Admiral, U.S. Coast Guard, Sigma Iota Chapter 1983.

- **Mathew A. Zimmerman** - (Major General, USAArmy ret.) & First Black Chief of Chaplains,
- **Abraham Turner -** (Major General, USA)
- **Charles F. Bolden -** (Major General, USMC ret.) Gamma Nu- Chapter, 1983
- **James W. Monroe-** Brigadier General- Deputy For nation Support US Army Forces Central Command (Desert Shield/Desert Storm)
- **Daniel "Chappie" James** –Four Star General of The Air Force /
- **Major Fred Drew Gregory** - Astronaut, graduate of the United States Air Force Academy (pilot) Alpha Omega Chapter

BUSINESS

- **Nathaniel Bronner** - Co-owner of Bronner Brothers Beauty Supplies
- **Gillard S. Glover** - President, Afro-American Life Insurance Company.
- **EARL GRAVES** - Publisher Black Enterprise Magazine,
- **Jesse Hill** - President of Atlanta Life Insurance Company.
- **BYRON LEWIS** - CEO of Uniworld Group, Inc.
- **JAMES ELAM** - CEO Elam testing Company
- **TONY GRANT** - President professional African-American banking Group-Bank Of America
- **EDWARD LEWIS,** Chairman & CEO Essence Communications
- **Thurman McKenzie** - Co-owner of M and M Products (Sta Soft Fro).
- **William Kennedy III** - President of North Carolina Mutual Insurance Company.
- **Otis M. Smith** - General Counsel, General Motors Corporation.

Omega Men College/University President Past & Present

Name of President	Institution	Location
Bro. Dr. William Harris	Alabama State University	Montgomery, Alabama
Bro. Dr. Billy Black	Albany State College	Albany, Georgia
Bro. Dr. Lawrence A. Davis	University of Arkansas	Pine Bluff, Arkansas
Bro. Dr. Ivory V. Nelson	Central Washington University	Ellensburg, Washington
Bro. Dr. Henry N. Tisdale	Claflin College	Orangeburg, South Carolina
Bro. Dr. Samuel D. Cook	Dillard University	New Orleans, Louisiana
Bro. Dr. Oscar Prater	Fort Valley State College	Fort Valley, Georgia
Bro. Dr. William Harvey	Hampton University	Hampton, Virginia
Bro. H. Patrick Swygert	Howard University	Washington, D.C.
Bro. Dr. James E. Lyons John A. Peoples, Jr.	Jackson State University	Jackson, Mississippi
Bro. Dr. Roy D. Hudson	Livingstone College	Salisbury, North Carolina
Bro. Dr. David Satcher	Meharry Medical College	Nashville, Tennessee
Bro. Dr. Albert Sloan	Miles College	Birmingham, Alabama
Bro. Dr. William W. Sutton	Mississippi Valley State University	
Bro. Dr. Walter E. Massey Bro. Benjamin E. Mays	Morehouse College	Atlanta, Georgia
Bro. Dr. Luns Richardson	Morris College	Sumter, South Carolina
Bro. Dr. Samuel D. Jolley, Jr.	Morris Brown College	Atlanta, Georgia

Bro. Dr. David Beckley	Rust College	
Bro. Dr. William E. Gardner	Savannah State College	Savannah, Georgia
Bro. Dr. James A. Hefner	Tennessee State University	Nashville, Tennessee
Bro. Dr. Haywood Strickland	Texas College	
Bro. Dr. John Rudley	Texas Southern University	Houston Texas
Bro. Dr. Jesse L. Burns	Edward Waters College	
Bro. Dr. Eddie N. Moore, Jr.	Virginia State University	Petersburg, Virginia
Bro. Cleveland Sellars	Voorheers College	Denmark S.C.

APPENDIX V

DISTINGUISHED OMEGA MEN OF OMEGA PSI PHI FRATERNTIY,

1ST DISTRICT

Rudy Arnold, Tau Iota - *Former Deputy Mayor of Hartford, well-known political activist*

Reggie Brothers, Eta Phi - *Successful businessman in the Boston area*

Mike Charles, Alpha Nu - *Director of Non-offset, Sikorsky Aircraft*

DeNorris Crosby, Alpha Nu - *Well-known Retired Educator in the New Haven, CT Public Schools*

Harold Epps, Eta Phi - *Successful businessman, entrepreneur, Marshal-1993 Leadership Conference*

Aaron Garron, Iota Chi - *Successful businessman, former Kansas*

---

[85] From The Omega Men of Distinction Booklet/Carl A. Blunt, Keith Neal...

THE OMEGA PSI PHI FRATERNITY INC. 357

City Chief

Donald Harris, Jr., Tau Iota - *Former Coach of Univ. of Connecticut Women's Basketball, Former D.R.*

Raymond Hilton, Chi Omicron (deceased) - *Former Director of the Conn. Dept. of Children and Family Services, Former D.R.*

Ted Hogan, Chi Omicron - *First Black Executive N.E. Telephone Co., Executive Director of Dixwell Q-House*

Jesse James, Delta Chi - *College Psychology Professor and Writer in Springfield*

Gregory Johnson, Epsilon Iota Iota - *Director of Ansonia Community Center, President/CEO First Priority Productions*

Raymond Jordan, Delta Chi - *Former Massachusetts State Legislator*

Al Maule, Tau Iota - *Retired Brigadier General, U.S. Army, Former D.R.*

Carlton Pickron, Delta Chi - *College Professor & Writer Westfield State, Professional Bowler*

Craig Streeter, Epsilon Iota Iota - *Membership Intake Chairman, International Automation Committee*

Donald Scott, Chi Omicron (deceased) - *Former Chief of Police-University of New Haven*

Stafford Thompson, Jr., Tau Iota - *One of a few Black U.S. Actuaries, Former D.R.*

Herbert E. Tucker, Eta Phi - *Former Grand Basileus, Attorney, Former D.R.*

John Thrner, Eta Phi - *Engineering Consultant, International Social Action Committee*

Robert Wallace, Iota Chi - *Independent Diversity Consultant*

Sylvester Wilkins, Eta Phi - *Former D.R.*

◇◇◇◇

DISTINGUISHED OMEGA MEN OF THE 2ND DISTRICT

Edgar A. Love, Pi Omega, *Founder*

Earl Graves, Pi, *Publisher, Black Enterprise*

George McKinney, Pi, *U.S. Marshall, State of Maryland*

Charles Bolden, Mu Rho, *Astronaut*

William H. Cosby, Jr., Beta Alpha Alpha, *Actor, Comedian, Philanthropist*

Leonard Marshall, Eta Pi, *Professional Football Player*

Mo Vaughn, Kappa Eta, *Professional Baseball Player*

Ahmad Rashad, Grand Chapter, *NBC Sportscaster*

James Usery, Upsilon Alpha, *Mayor, Atlantic City, New Jersey*

Sharpe James, Upsilon Phi, *Mayor, Newark, New Jersey*

Felmon Motley, Psi Iota, *Omega Publicist*

Nathaniel Pollard, Gamma Pi, *President, Bowie State University*

James Avery, Omicron Chi, *28th Grand Basileus*

Maxwell Roach, Grand Chapter, *Jazz Musician*

Langston Hughes, Beta, *Poet, Writer*

Roger K. Williams, Pi Omega, *Psychologist, Scholar*

Joe Black, Pi, *Professional Baseball Player, MLB Rookie of the Year 1952*

Jerome Holland, Mu, *President, Delaware State College*

Eddie P. Hurt, Pi Omega, *Coach, Morgan State College*

A. Leon Higgenbotham, Mu, *Chief Judge, U.S. Court of Appeals*

Robert N.C. Nix, Mu Omega, *U.S. Congressman*

Lonnie Liston Smith, Pi, *Jazz Musician*

George Meares, Kappa Omicron, *26th Grand Basileus*

Walter Amprey, Pi Omega, *Superintendent of PS Instruction.- Baltimore.*

Clarence Mitchell, Jr., Beta, *NAACP-l01st Senator*

Roger Kingdom, Iota Phi - *2 time Olympic Gold Medalist*

William (Bill) Oliver – *Law Enforcement Man of the Year*

DISTINGUISHED OMEGA MEN OF THE 3RD DISTRICT

Leonard L. Haynes, III - *Former Asst. Secretary for Post Secondary Education*

Marion L. Barnwell - Psi Alpha Alpha - *U.S. Army Col. (ret.) Former Operation Branch Chief, Joint Chiefs of Staff, Former 3rd Dist. Rep.*

Henry Reginal Bellinger - Gamma Alpha - *Highly decorated serviceman, including the Bronze Star and Legion of Merit*

Hersey T. Steptoe - Gamma Alpha - *Organizer of Gamma Alpha. Roanoke Virginia, 1932*

Kenneth A. Brown - Kappa Psi - *Former Grand Keeper of Finance and 3rd District Representative*

Dr. William Montague Cobb - Kappa Psi - *Medical writer, scholar, anatomist, anthropologist, research worker, civil rights fighter, former NAACP President and founder of Kappa Psi.*

Martin Mayhew - *National Football League player and supporter of Africare.*

Charles D. Chambliss, Jr. - Phi Psi - *Former Grand Counselor and District Representative*

Brian Lee - Kappa Psi - *Recipient of the Washington D.C. fire department's highest award, the Bronze Bar Medal of Valor*

Robert L. Satcher, Sr. - Omicron Omega - *Professor of Chemistry at St. Paul's College. Highly recognized researcher.*

Preston A. Davis, Sr. - Alpha Omega - *Chairman of the Alpha Omega Social Action and Scholarship Foundation*

Tamer Mokhtar - Eta Lambda - *Undergraduate Intermediate Representative to the Supreme Council, 1996 -1998*

Carlton A. Funn, Sr.-Psi Nu - *Educator and Human Rights Advocate. Developer and director of multicultural exhibit*

Gene R. Carter - Lambda Omega - *Superintendent of Norfolk City Schools and renowned speaker.*

Robert W. Fairchild - Gamma Xi - *Former Grand Keeper of Records & Seal. First Black staff Band Officer in U.S. Army. Former District Representative.*

Turner M. Spencer, Ed.D - Alpha Alpha - *City Councilman for the City of Hampton, VA. Professor and Chairman of Thomas Nelson Community College Biology department.*

H.E. Fauntleroy - Delta Omega - *Former Mayor of Petersburg, Virginia*

Alger B. Harrison - Lambda Nu - *Former Mayor of Franklin, Virginia*

Frank "Frankie P" Byron Patterson - Alpha Omega - *Tireless and Outstanding 3rd District Keeper of Records & Seal*

H. Albion Ferrel, Alpha Omega, *Grand Chaplain Emeritus*

DISTINGUISHED OMEGA MEN OF THE

4ᵀᴴ DISTRICT

Ronald B. Adrine - *Municipal Court Judge*

Russell Adrine - *Attorney, Political Activist in Cleveland, OH*

Douglas Anderson - *Registrar at West Virginia State U, Scholarship named in his honor*

Dr. Samuel Baskerville - *Successful dentist, Scholarship named in his honor*

Flannen Belcher - *Professor at West Virginia State, Fine Arts Theater named in his honor*

LTC Henry Bellinger - *Inducted to the West Virginia State ROTC Hall of Fame*

Horace Belmear - *Inducted to the West Virginia State Sports Hall of Fame*

James Andrew Elam - *President, Belmont Park Laboratories, Philanthropist*

Hal Greer - *Former NBA Basketball Player-Philadelphia 76ers.*

Adolph Hamblin - *Professor at West Virginia State, Science building named in his honor*

Marcel Hodges - *Professor at West Virginia State, Classroom building named in his honor*

Charles P. Lucas, Sr. - *Regional Director of HUD*

Monte Marbley - *Federal District Court Judge*

Dr. James Russell - *President St. Paul's College, Interim President, West Virginia State*

J.L. Scott - *Educator, West Virginia Univ. building named in his honor*

Sam Shepard - *Former Editor of the Oracle*

C. Franklin Spurill - *Attorney, Past Grand Counselor*

LTC Quewnncoii C. Stephens - *Dir. Human Rights Commission-WV*

Dr. Joseph Summerville - *Educator, Prof. Emeritus - Univ. of Toledo*

W. O. Walker - *Founder of Call-In Post*

Charles White - *Judge of Common Pleas Court*

DISTINGUISHED OMEGA MEN OF THE

5ᵀᴴ DISTRICT

Rev. Benjamin L. Hooks - *Past Executive Director of the NAACP, former Criminal Court Judge, President of the National Civil Rights Museum*

Z. Alexander Looby - *17th G and Basileus (1940 - 1945), former Dean of Kent Law School*

Dr. A.A. Branch - *Educator who lead the accreditation of Owen College (now LeMoyne-Owen) Chemistry and Education Departments.*

Lt. George Washington Lee - *Republican Political Pioneer, awarded the French Croix DeGuerre, has a postal station named in his honor.*

Dr. Vasco Smith, Jr. - *First black member of the Shelby County, TN. Commissioner Board*

Dr. James Netters - *Civil Leader and the first black member of the Memphis City Council*

Nat D. Williams - *Editor-in-Chief of the Oracle in* 1944, *and a Disc Jockey at the first black radio station (WLOK) in Memphis.*

Rodney A. Jeffrey - Epsilon Phi - *1993 International Omega Man of the Year*

Robert R. Jefferson - Psi Tau - *1993 International Superior Service Award*

William H. Jones - Kappa Sigma - *1993 International Founders Award*

Mark A. Bishop - Epsilon Phi - *1994 International Omega Man of the Year*

Jerome Ryans - *Executive Director of the Memphis Housing Authority*

Glenn D. Sessoms - *Vice President, Retail Marketing and Operations, FedEx Corporation*

Mark Yates - *Chairman, Shelby Democratic Party*

W. J. Hale - *First President, Tennessee State University*

L. A. Westly - *First Black President of the Memphis Area Association of Realtors in 1996.*

Wilbert Bond, Sr. - *President of the State of Tennessee NAACP*

Ed Temple - *Track Coach, Tennessee State famed Tiger Belles*

Don Q. Pullen - Rho Psi - *Orchestra Leader & Composer of Omega Sweetheart Song*
    Dr. Walter Davis - *President, Tennessee State*

DISTINGUISHED OMEGA MEN OF THE
6ᵀᴴ DISTRICT

James Clyburn - Omicron Phi, Columbia, SC
    U.S. House of Representatives, SC 6th Congressional District
Charles Austin - Omicron Phi, Columbia, SC
    1st Black Chief of Police, City of Columbia, SC
Martin S. Roache - Xi Psi, Orangeburg, SC
    Professional Golfer
C. Tyrone Gilmore - Epsilon Nu, Spartanburg, SC
    District Superintendent, Spartanburg P.S., Past Grand Basileus, S.C. Sports Hall of Fame
Cleveland Sellers - Omicron Phi, Columbia, SC
    1960s Black Activist in SC, Professor University of South Carolina
James Talley - Epsilon Nu, Spartanburg, SC
    1st Black Mayor, City of Spartanburg, SC
Willie Williams - Beta Beta Beta, Wilson, NC
    Chief of Police, City of Wilson, NC
Charles Blackmon - Beta Phi, Durham, NC
    Senior Vice President of N.C. Mutual Insurance Co.
Melvin Pinn - Pi Phi, Charlotte, NC
    Medical Doctor, Past 6th District Representative
Michael Morgan - Iota Iota, Raleigh, NC
    Municipal Judge, City of Raleigh, NC
Herbert U. Fielding - Mu Alpha, Charleston, SC
    Former SC State Senator & SC State House of Representatives
Floyd Breeland - Mu Alpha, Charleston, SC
    Member, SC House of Representatives

Leon Stanback - Beta Phi, Durham, NC
Superior Court Judge in Durham, NC
Luns Richardson - Gamma Iota, Sumter, SC
President, Morris College, Sumter, SC
Henry Tisdale - Epsilon Omega, Orangeburg, SC
President, Claflin University, Orange burg, SC
Clarence Lightner - Iota Iota, Raleigh, NC
Mortician, Former & 1st Black Mayor of Raleigh, NC
Calvin Brown - Pi Phi, Charlotte, NC
Attorney, Former Grand Counselor
Freddy Washington - Mu Alpha, Charleston, SC
Bishop of Roman Catholic Church, 1 of 11 Black Bishops in U.S:
Gregg Austin - Pi Phi, Charlotte, NC
President of National Pan-Hellenic Council
Dr. Leroy Walker - Beta Phi, Durham, NC
President U.S. Olympic Track & Field
Charles Turner III - Lambda Iota Iota, Bennettsville, SC
Editor to the Oracle, Chairman of Marlboro County D.S.S. Board
John H. Moore - Pi Phi, Charlotte, NC
Former Grand Keeper of Finance

DISTINGUISHED OMEGA MEN OF THE 7ᵀᴴ DISTRICT

Dorsey C. Miller Jr.- Zeta Chi - *34th Grand Basileus*

Moses C. Norman - Eta Omega - 32nd *Grand Basileus*

Edward J. Braynon - Sigma Alpha - *30th Grand Basileus*

Carl Von Epps - Alpha Xi - *First Black Legislator elected to the Georgia General Assembly, District 13 Troup County.*

Lee A. Bernard Jr. – *Beta Alpha Chapter – Successful Business man and entrepreneur and 27ᵗʰ @nd District Representative*

George R. Moore - Alpha Xi - *West Georgia youth home named in his honor.*

Thubert E. Baker - Kappa Alpha Alpha - *Appointed 1st Black Attorney General for the State of Georgia*

Floyd Griffin - *Member of the Georgia State Senate and Candidate for Georgia Lt. Governor.*

Clarence E. Anthony - Theta Gamma Gamma - *Mayor of South Bay & 2nd Vice President of the national League of Cities. Former President of the Florida League of Cities.*

James L. Jennings - Chi Tau - *First African American to serve as Deputy Director of the John F. Kennedy Space Center.*

Bobby Johnson - Beta Omicron - *Police Chief of Albany, Georgia*

Hon. Thomas Stringer, Sr. - *Judge & Board Overseer of Stetson University College of Law. First African American to graduate from Stetson Law School.*

Ralph D. Cook - Alpha Phi - *Appointed to Alabama Supreme Court. First African American to hold a State Judgeship in Jefferson County.*

Oscar Adams - *Judge and First African American to serve on Alabama Supreme Court. First African American elected in a statewide race.*

Joseph Hatcher - Chi Omega - *First African American Supreme Court Judge in the State of Florida.*

Ferrell J. Duncombe - Sigma Phi - *Grand Chaplain under Grand Basilei Miller, Grace and Lee*

David Satcher - Psi - *Surgeon General of the United States.*

Alfred Rhodes - Beta Alpha - *President of the Magnolia (Mississippi) Bar Assoc.*

Joseph Dantzler - Alpha Tau - *Superintendent of Gregg County (Alabama) Schools.*

Robert E. James - Mu Phi - *Former Chairman of the National Bankers Assoc. Revived the Savannah Tribune, one of the oldest black-owned newspapers in America, established in 1875.*

Dr. Walter *Massey* - *President of Morehouse College.*

Dr. John H. Peoples – *former president of Jackson State University*

Aaron Henry - Iota Omicron - *President of Mississippi Black Democrats. State President of NAACP. Drug Store and home bombed in the 1950s.*

George Jamison III – BA – Successful Mississippi community advocate, businessman & Basileus

John A. Peoples Jr. – BA - Former President of JSU University and Omega Psi Phi fraternity Inc. Mississippi Hall of Fame.

Sherman E. Jackson – BA – Successful Mississippi businessman and Omega Psi Phi fraternity Inc. Mississippi Hall of Fame.

DISTINGUISHED OMEGA MEN OF THE

8TH DISTRICT

William B. Jason - Eta Alpha - *Interim President and Dean of Men at Lincoln University, Initiated at Alpha Chapter, February 1912.*

Oscar A. Fuller - Eta Alpha - *First Black to earn a Ph.D. in Music from the University of Iowa. Initiated first line at Gamma Chapter 1917.*

James C. McMorries - Eta Alpha - *5th Grand Basileus & President of Lincoln University. Assisted Founder Cooper & George Brannon in initiating 20 men to establish Beta Chapter.*

George Woods -Beta Upsilon - *Active member of the Nebraska Democratic Party for over 50 years. Founder of Beta Upsilon in Omaha.*

Irving Fryar - Beta Upsilon - *NFL Player & Former First Team All-American.*

Samuel Herman Dreer - Upsilon Omega - *Authored first Omega History Book and Fraternity Hymn, awarded the first Omega Man of the Year Award.*

John H. Purnell - Upsilon Omega - *Played key role in establishing first graduate chapter. Two-time Grand Marshall.*

George L. Vaughn - Upsilon Omega- 11th *Grand Basileus. Made history by securing the first Writ of Certiorari from U.S.*

Supreme Court, which ended restrictive housing covenants in St. Louis.

Lynn Beckwith, Ed.D. - Upsilon Omega - *Superintendent of a St. Louis School District. National Social Action Chairman, Former DR.*

Edgar Burnett - Upsilon Omega - *Former Chairman of Omega Life Membership Foundation. '96 Omega Man of the Year.*

Leon Ashford, Ph.D. - Upsilon Omega - *Current President of St. Louis Mental Health Board of Trustees. Director of "Project Manhood", nationally recognized mentoring program.*

Wendell Smith - Gamma Upsilon - *Board of Directors Urban League, NAACP, Black Historical Society, Lions Club. and Metro YMCA, Board of Trustees Southwestern College.*

Hubert H. Hutcherson - Gamma Upsilon - *Charter Member of Gamma Upsilon. Memorial Scholarship named in his honor.*

Harold Holiday, Sr. - Gamma Upsilon - *Attorney, Missouri State Legislature Judge.*

Dr. Carl Peterson - Gamma Upsilon - *Chief MD Truman Medical Center of Kansas.*

Freeman, Bosley Jr. –. First Black Mayor of St. Louis,

Kit Rogue - Gamma Upsilon - *Attorney. Municipal Court Judge, well know child advocate.*

Furman Williams - Gamma Upsilon - *International Educator.*

Rev. John Williams - Gamma Upsilon - *Pastor of the largest Black church in Kansas.*

Lloyd E. Thomas - Xi Pi - *Highly decorated Col. USAF Retired. Former Commander First Aerospace Control Squadron.*

Samuel C. Hunter - Xi Pi – 2007 Congressional Gold Medal recipient, 2004, NAACP Living Legend Recipeint, *Tuskegee Airman, B-25 Bomber pilot and flying instructor at Harlem Airport, Chicago.*

Lloyd J. Jordan, Esq. - Upsilon Omega - *Former DR, Former Grand Counselor, 36th Grand Basileus*
    Clarence F. Holmes-Chi Phi - *6th Grand Basileus*

◇◇◇◇

DISTINGUISHED OMEGA MEN OF THE

9ᵀᴴ DISTRICT

Warren G. Lee Jr .- Grand Basileus of Omega Psi Phi Fraternity, Inc. – *1st Vice Grand Basileus, Grand KF & 2nd Vice Grand Basileus/* Theta Alpha chapter

Willie <Mercenary> Hinchen, - *9th District DR & renown Educator* -Theta Alpha chapter

NELSON ANTHONY – *Architect of the Houston Coalition Concept & successful businessman, Former Vice DR* **/** Rho Beta Beta chapter

Ylysses Simpson (U.S.) Hammond- *Deceased,Theta Alpha Chapter-former 9th District DR, Basileus, Chaplain Omega Psi Phi Fraternity*

Hendricks Cunningham - Epsilon Alpha - *Tireless Texas State Representative* **Robert Hester** - Theta Alpha -*Grand KRS*

C.D. Henry - Pi Tau - *Grand KRS, Former DR*

Clement Osimentha - Mu Beta - *2nd Vice Grand Basileus*

Lee G. Willis - Rho Beta Beta – *27th, 2nd Vice Grand Basileus*

Albert C. Black Jr. - Theta Alpha - *Successful Businessman.*

Vernon Hunt- *Rho Beta Beta chapter-Reknown and highly decorated educator/professor-Texas Southern University*

Ernest Parquet – *of Phi Iota Iota chapter, Founded Omega Kappa chapter in 1978 and Phi Iota Iota in 1992.*

Rev. Ceasar A. W. Clark - Theta Alpha - *Noted Pastor.*

Jack C. Morgan,DDS – *Rho Beta Beta- Lieutenant Colonel, (USAF, Retired) - In 1982 became the fist Black person (male or female) to graduate from The University of Texas Dental School @ San Antonio.*

Thurman White Sr. - Eta Iota - *Noted NAACP Leader*

John Henry Nelson - Psi Upsilon - *Noted Businessman*

James Wise - Pi Omicron - *Noted Educator, Civil Rights Activist, Former DR*

Shelly Steward-*Nu Phi chapter-Former 9th District DR*

Carl E. Steward - Rho Omega - *5th Circuit Court Judge*

Napoleon Lewis - Theta Alpha - *Noted Educator and Principal*

Henry Cooper -*Rho Beta Beta chapter, nationally known Comedian.*

Cal E. Varner - Epsilon Iota - *1st Black Lobbyist in the State of Texas.*

Sam Bisco - Epsilon Iota - *Judge*

Dr. Charles Christopher - Epsilon Iota - *Physician, Fraternity's first Surgeon General, Former DR*

Terrance Duvernay - Rho Phi - *HUD Executive Department Secretary*

Melvin C. Zeno - Gamma Rho - *Judge, 1st Vice Grand Basileus,. Grand Counselor, Grand Chaplain.*

Raymond Bourgeois-Nu Phi - *Businessman*

Samuel Dubose Cook - Rho Phi - *President of Dillard University*

Vernon Steve Weakley – *Rho Beta Beta , nationally known author and publisher.*

Royce West - Mu Beta - *Texas State Senator*

Herman Burroughs - *Rho Beta Beta, CEO, Record Producer and Founder of internationally known Gospel Warehouse Records. Discovered and produced the internationally known gospel group Zie'l.*

Brian S. Gundy – *Gamma Gamma chapter,, 39th, 2nn Vice Grand Basileus.*

Grover Hankins- *Rho Beta Beta, - National General Counsel for the NAACP under the Honorable Benjamin L. Hooks. Also former principal Deputy General Counsel* *for the Department of Health.* Entered Omega chapter April 4th, 2009*

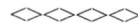

DISTINGUISHED OMEGA MEN OF THE

10ᵀᴴ DISTRICT

Burnel E. Coulon - Zeta Phi - *31st. Grand Basileus & Educator.*

Marion W. Garnett - Sigma Omega - *29th Grand Basileus & Judge*

Cary D. Jacobs - Zeta Phi - *25th Grand Basileus*

Milo C. Murray - Sigma Omega - *20th Grand Basileus*

William E. Baugh - Zeta Phi - *15th Grand Basileus*

William DeHart Hubbard - Phi - *Olympic Champion & the Fist Black to win an individual Gold Medal in the Olympics.*

Michael Parham - Rho Gamma Gamma - *Undergraduate/Intermediate Representative to the Supreme Council.*

Kenny Coles - Iota - *Undergraduate/Intermediate Representative to the Supreme Council.*

J. Cameron Wade - Sigma Omega - *Grand Keeper of Finance.*

Vernon G. Smith - Alpha Chi - *Indiana State Representative & former DR*

Leroy Keyes - Rho Sigma - *Former Heisman Trophy Candidate 1st Team All-American and NFL*

John Salley - Nu Omega - *Former SEC All Conference. NBA player & Sports Announcer.*

Graham Martin - Zeta Phi - *One of the Golden Thirteen, Firs/group of Black Naval Commissioned Officers.*

Coneal Davis - Sigma Omega - *Former Grand Chaplain.*

THE OMEGA PSI PHI FRATERNITY INC. 371

Dean of Illinois State Legislature.

Danny Thomas - Omicron Theta - *First Undergraduate District Representative*

John S. Epps - Tau Upsilon - *Executive Director of Omega Psi Phi Fraternity*

Maj. Gen James G. Monroe - Delta Beta Beta - *Commander General of Rock Island Illinois Arsenal.*

John Williams - *Official Photographer of the Omega Psi Phi Fraternity*

Gene Washington - Sigma- *Former All American & NFL Player*

Clinton Jones - Sigma - *Former All-American & NFL Player*

Elijah Pitts - Kappa Phi - *Former NFL Coach & NFL Player*

Charles E. Harry III - Zeta Phi - *1st Elected District Representative.*

George A. Isabell - Nu Omega - *Grand KRS*

DISTINGUISHED OMEGA MEN OF THE 12ᵀᴴ DISTRICT

Dr. L. Benjamin Livingston - Pi Rho - *32nd Grand Basileus*

Godfrey B. James - Sigma Iota - *Organizer of 12th District. Charter Member of Sigma Iota, oldest graduate chapter in the 12th District, the 16th Twelfth DR*

Verdeese Carter - Sigma Iota -*Educator, Local Park in Oakland named in his honor.*

Carl Earles - Lambda Omicron- *4th Grand Counselor. The 12th District's first Grand Officer.*

H.P. Fitzgerald - Kappa Xi - *Educator, First Black Principal in the State of Nevada, First Black graduate from UNLV. Local School bears his name*

- **Marcus Foster** - Sigma Iota - *Oakland School Superintendent, assassinated by the SLA. Local school and educational foundation named in his honor.*
- **Calvin Goode** -Phi Iota - *Politician, Phoenix Municipal building is named in his honor. Not posthumously.*
- **Philmore Graham** - Theta Pi - *Founder of the Omega Boys Club. the 12th Twelfth District Representative.*
- **Nathan Hare** - Pi Chi - *Nationally acclaimed psychologist.*
- **Joe Marshall** - Theta Pi - *Recipient of the MacArthur & Essence Awards for work with the nationally acclaimed San Francisco Omega Boys Club*
- **Wilson Riles** - Epsilon Xi - *Former California Superintendent of Schools.*
- **Brice L. Taylor** -Lambda - *USC's first All American (Black or White)*
- **Paul Wiliams** - Lambda Omicron - *World renowned architect. Designer of the LAX Tower.*
- **Thomas McPhatter** - Phi Omicron - *One of the Montford Point 40. First group of Black Marines who displayed bravely at the battle of Iwo Iima.*
- **Lincoln Ragsdale** - Phi Iota - *Successful businessman and former Tuskegee Airman. Phoenix Executive Airport bears his name.*
- **Mark A. Illes** - Mu Kappa - *2nd Vice Grand Basileus, 1982 -1984*
- **Larry D. Walls** - Xi Gamma - *Undergraduate/Intermediate Representative 1970 -1974 District Counselor*
- **Joe N. Cole** - Tau Tau - *Grand Chaplain, 1982 -1984*
- **Robert S. Shoffner** - Sigma Iota - *National Omega Man of the Year 1982 awarded at the Louisville Grand Conclave.*
- **Terrance Hamilton** - Sigma Eta - *Undergraduate/Intermediate Representative 1994 -1996, 2nd Vice District Representative*
- **Carl A. Blunt** - Sigma Iota/Phi Iota - *1st Vice Grand Basileus 2006- Present, Grand Keeper of Finance 2002-06, only man elected as DR 2 nonconsecutive terms 1993-95, & 1998-99*
- **H. B. Daniels** - Phi Iota - *Judge, First Black elected to the*

Phoenix Legislature, and First Black admitted to AZ. Bar Association.

<><><><>

DISTINGUISHED OMEGA MEN OF THE

13ᵀᴴ DISTRICT

Richard Smith – International Chapter Rep
Peter L. Mitchell – International Chapter Rep
Edouard T. Delagarde – 13th District Rep
Cipriani A. Phillips, Jr. – 13th District Rep
Jonathan N. Griffin, Sr. – 13th District Rep

APPENDIX W

MANDATED PROGRAMS

INTERNATIONALLY MANDATED PROGRAMS

ACHIEVEMENT WEEK-Originally designed to promote the study of Negro life and history. Achievement Week is observed in November of each year and is designed to seek out and give due recognition to those individuals at the local and international levels who have made a noteworthy contribution toward improving the quality of life for black Americans. A High School Essay Contest is to be held in conjunction with Achievement Week. This contest is open to all college-bound high school seniors. College scholarships are awarded to the winners, each of whom must submit an essay on a theme/topic chosen by the fraternity. This contest is a phase of the International Achievement Week observance.

SCHOLARSHIP - The Scholarship Program is intended to promote academic excellence among the undergraduate members. Graduate chapters are expected to provide financial assistance to student members and non-members. A portion of the fraternity's international budget is allocated to scholarships through the Charles R. Drew Scholarship Commission.

SOCIAL ACTION PROGRAMS - All levels of the fraternity are expected to facilitate, participate and coordinate activities that will uplift their communities. An international committee will coordinate the multifaceted programs of the various chapters. Some of the activities under the umbrella of social action include, but are not limited to: voter registration, education and "getting out the vote"; Assault on Illiteracy; Habitat for Humanity; volunteering time to charities and less fortunate individuals; mentoring; and participation in fundraisers for charities such as American Diabetes Association, United Way, Sickle Cell Anemia, etc.

TALENT HUNT PROGRAM - This program provides exposure, encouragement and financial assistance to talented young people participating in the Performing Arts. Winners of the competition are awarded recognition for their talents. Awards may include college scholarships.

MEMORIAL SERVICE - March 12th of each year has been established as Memorial Day. Chapters are expected to conduct an appropriate service to recall the memory of those members who have entered into Omega Chapter.

RECLAMATION AND RETENTION- A concerted effort at the international, district and local levels to retain active brothers and return inactive brothers to full participatory status so that they may enjoy the full benefits of Omega.

COLLEGE ENDOWMENT FUND- Each year the fraternity gives at least $50,000.00 to Historically Black College Institutions (HBCU) in furtherance of Omega's commitment to provide philanthropic support. Chapters are assessed donations based on chapter size.

HEALTH INITIATIVES- All levels of the fraternity are expected to facilitate, participate and/or coordinate activities that will uplift their communities by promoting good health practices. An international committee will coordinate and facilitate multifaceted programs of the various chapters, districts, etc. It is anticipated that all local chapters will execute the health directives at the local level. Some of the programs under the umbrella of Health Initiatives are the Charles Drew Blood Drive (normally held in June), AIDS/HIV Awareness, and the American Diabetes Association Partnership. This does not prevent the local chapters from performing additional health initiatives under the umbrella of the Health Initiatives mandate.

VOTER REGISTRATION, EDUCATION AND MOBILIZATION- All levels of the fraternity are expected to facilitate, participate and/or coordinate activities that will uplift their communities through the power of the vote. An international committee will coordinate and facilitate multifaceted programs of the various chapters, districts, etc. It is anticipated that all local chapters will execute the directives at the local level. This does not prevent the local chapters from performing additional voter initiatives under the umbrella of the Voter Education, Registration and Mobilization mandate.

NAACP- Every district and chapter of the fraternity is required to maintain a Life Membership at Large in the NAACP. In the event that a chapter or district is not a life member of the NAACP, it must maintain a yearly membership to be in good standing with the fraternity. Furthermore, all members of the fraternity are strongly encouraged to become members of the NAACP.

(All Chapters are required to administer these programs annually.)

<<>>

APPENDIX X

74TH GRAND CONCLAVE MINUTES

Omega Psi Phi Fraternity, Inc. Office of Bro. Charles A. Bruce GRAND KEEPER OF RECORDS AND SEAL 421 Forsheer Drive Chesterfield, MO 63017 Phone: 314/553-3539 E-mail: charles.bruce@emotors.com 74th Grand Conclave July 24 – 27, 2006 Little Rock, Arkansas

Grand Conclave Minutes
Submitted
September 20, 2006
(Approved by the Supreme Council on October 19, 2006)

This document represents a record of the events and actions from the Omega Psi Phi Fraternity, Inc., 74th Grand Conclave that took place in Little Rock, Arkansas in July 2006. This information was extracted and compiled from a variety of sources and is submitted by the Grand Keeper of Records and Seal, Bro. Charles A. Bruce, who was installed as GKRS on Thursday July 27, 2006. A distribution of the detailed transcript of the 74th Grand Conclave will follow when that information becomes available.

Pre-Conclave Events

(Events that took place prior to the Grand Conclave Formal Opening on Monday July 24, 2006)

- (Wednesday July 19, 2006)
    - a. Grand Officers Arrival
    - b. IHQ Staff Arrival
    - c. Omega Life Membership Foundation (OLMF) Board Dinner
- (Thursday July 20, 2006)

a. Youth Leadership Conference Participant Arrival
b. OLMF Board Meeting
c. Supreme Council Meeting
- (Friday July 21, 2006)
    a. Tom Joyner Morning Show
    b. Career Fair
    c. Golf Tournament
    d. Youth Leadership Conference (@ Arkansas Baptist College)
    e. Soul Review Concert (Jerry Butler, Blue Notes, Temptations)
- (Saturday July 22, 2006)
    a. Exhibits Open (Health Fair and Vendors)
    b. OLMF Annual Corporate Meeting
    c. Omega Development Corporation Meeting
    d. Three Undergraduates, Inc. Meeting
    e. OLMF Luncheon
    f. Step Show Competition / Comedy Show
- (Sunday July 23, 2006)
    a. Service Awards Breakfast (40, 50 & 60 Years)
    b. Memorial Service (Rev. Bro. Farrell Duncombe presiding)
    c. Public Program – Welcome from the City of Little Rock, Arkansas
    d. Gospel Show

GKRS COMMUNICATION PAGE 2 74th Grand Conclave Minutes

Grand Conclave

On Monday morning, July 24, 2006, a breakfast event was held to honor the **25 Year** and **70 Year Award** winners.

First Plenary Session

The Grand Conclave began on Monday, July 24, 2006 at 9:15 AM with a call to order,
a procession of Committee Chairmen, Past Grand Basilei, District Representatives and Grand Officers. The Grand Chaplain then gave an opening prayer.
Non-members were excused from the room except for essential audio and video support personnel.

The Grand Basileus, Bro. George H. Grace, performed the Ritualistic Opening. A point of order was raised to question the proposed agenda for the 74th Grand Conclave, indicating a contention that' at the 73rd Grand Conclave in St. Louis, MO the Grand Conclave approved a Recommendation to limit the business proceedings of the Grand Conclave to three (3) days. The Grand Basileus correctly stated the approved Recommendation was for four (4) days and resolved the point of order.

The Grand Keeper of Records and Seal, Bro.Terrell Parris performed the roll call. A quorum was confirmed and announced.

The 74th Grand Conclave agenda was presented and approved following disposition of four motions:

- It was properly moved and second to maintain the standard meeting protocol. The motion passed

The Chairman of the Rules Committee, Bro. Keith Neal, addressed the point and retracted the proposed "Omega Rules" that had been presented at the 2006 District Meetings leading up to the Grand Conclave.

- A motion to move the Recommendations Committee Report to Thursday July 27, 2006 failed for lack of a second. (The initial agenda presentation indicated the Recommendations Committee would report on Thursday July 27th)
- It was properly moved and second to sing the Black National Anthem at the closing ceremony on Thursday. The motion passed.
- A motion to move the run-off election from Thursday to Wednesday was ruled out of order as the agenda as originally presented indicated a run-off as a Wednesday event.

Grand Basileus State of The Fraternity Address

The Grand Basileus, Bro. George H. Grace, presented his State of the Fraternity address to the Grand Conclave indicating:

Membership & Finances

- As of June 30, 2006 the Fraternity has 17,000 financial members.
- The Fraternity's financial situation has made a dramatic turnaround during the period 2002 – 2006. In August 2002, the debt position reported by the Grand Basileus was:

Expense Item Description	Amount
Amount owed in 2002 Conclave Expenses	$X00,000

Amount owed to OLMF	$X00,000
Amount owed to Districts	$X25,000
Amount owed to Friendship Foundation	$X0,000
Amount owed in Back Legal Expenses	$X25,000
Amount owed to Bro. Jim Elam	$X75,000
TOTAL	**$X,XXX,000**

The Grand Basileus went on to say,
• As of May 31, 2006 the fraternity had over $X,XXX,000 in its operating
GKRS COMMUNICATION PAGE 3 74th Grand Conclave Minutes
account with no outstanding long term debt. The Grand Basileus attributed this remarkable improvement to several things such as:

```
1. Administrative operating cost
improvements
2. Refinancing the debt on the IHQ
building in Decatur, Georgia resulting
in lowering the monthly payment from
$25,000/mo to $19,000/mo.
3. Real estate investments at the
University of South Carolina, the Col.
Charles Young property in Ohio and a
future looking housing development
project in Ensley, Alabama.
4. The Rewards Program providing a
revenue stream for the Fraternity and
savings on services to the Brothers who
participate. These opportunities
resulting from collaborations and
partnerships with corporate entities.
5. Direct contributions and sponsoring
assistance from public and private
sources
```

The benefits derived have been retained, maximized and shared with the Membership with savings through:
1. Purchase of a corporate residential property in Atlanta, GA. The property

will be principally used by members of the Supreme Council when they travel to Atlanta, GA for
Fraternity business. The corporate residential property is debt free with no mortgage obligation.

    2. The Fraternity will donate 15 laptop computers to Arkansas Baptist College at the conclusion of the 74th Grand Conclave

    3. The IHQ building and property in Decatur, Georgia has increased in value from \$X.X million dollars (circa 2002) to \$X.5 million dollars per a 2006 appraisal.

    4. The registration fee for the Undergraduate Summit has been eliminated as a classic demonstration of how the Fraternity's success is shared with the Membership.

Infrastructure and Fraternity Operations

• The Grand Basileus commented about several elements responsible for and resulting in improvements in the internal workings of the Fraternity's operations:

    1. The IHQ has improved the bank lock box system, which provides efficiencies in financial processing and yields reduced cost.

    2. A "Track-It" software is in the final phase of testing and will be immediately available to provide tracking capability to Chapters and Districts when problems are experienced when interfacing with the Fraternity's web page and sub-systems. This will enable the IHQ staff to spend more time on special needs and issues and provide a measurable improvement in response time to the Membership.

    3. The Conclave and Leadership Conference "pre" and onsite registration process has been improved. Casual observation indicated the goal to have no registrant wait in line for more than three minutes was realized, for the most part, in Little Rock.

    4. The Oracle:

        • The printing of the Oracle has been "in-sourced" as a result of the activation of previously acquired state-of-the-art printing and duplication equipment.

        • The Oracle is to be published once per quarter.

- Legacy issues with distribution of the Oracle are comprehended and solutions are imminent.

5. Political Action:

- The Fraternity held "Omega Days" at the US Capital in Washington, DC September 26 – 27, 2006. It was noted the presence of the Fraternity and its Leadership was essential in the renewal of the 1965 Voting Rights Act.

<u>Benefit to Grand Conclave Host City</u>

- The Little Rock, Arkansas community benefited from the presence of the Omega's, despite some random, ill-advised and uninformed information distributed by a citizen prior to the arrival of the Omega Nation, in several ways:

1. A yet to be determined financial boon to merchants and retailers
2. Endowment of a Chair at Arkansas Baptist College in Little Rock, in the name of Bro. William H. Cosby, in the amount of $25,000
3. A $150,000 donation to Arkansas Baptist College from the Tom Joyner Foundation, a charity managed principally by Bro. Tom Joyner

<u>Litigation and Liability</u>

- The fraternity has reached disposition on some court cases that were open and/or being litigated.

GKRS COMMUNICATION PAGE 4 74th Grand Conclave Minutes

- There is the potential of a court action being brought against the Fraternity as a result of an incident at a University in the 9th District.

<u>The Friendship Foundation and "Brick and Mortar" Improvements at IHQ</u>

- The Grand Basileus described the Friendship Foundation as being in a sound financial position.

- The Friendship Foundation has an appropriate bank balance.
- Over $500,000 in IHQ building renovations (including painting) have been completed.
- The Bro. John Williams Museum was completed in the IHQ building.

- The Founders Wall and Past Grand Basilei recognition credentials have been placed in a more secure environment.
- Parking lot security has been enhanced.
- A modern video surveillance system, with remote viewing access, has been installed.
- Video monitors are installed in the IHQ Building that provides news via CNN updates.

Undergraduates

Registration at the Undergraduate Summit has improved and increased steadily during the tenure of Bro. Grace as Grand Basileus and his team. Other indicators of the ongoing success of this endeavor are evident:

Year	# of Participants
2003	401
2004	508
2005	601
2006	618

Also, as mentioned above, the Undergraduate Summit registration fee has been eliminated.

It was properly moved and second to accept the Report of the Grand Basileus. The motion passed.

First Plenary Session Continued

Grand Keeper of Finance

The written report of the Grand Keeper of Finance, Bro. Carl A. Blunt, was distributed to all Grand Conclave registrants along with their registration kit. Bro. Blunt provided some additional details concerning the Fraternity finances:

Summary of Additional Balance Sheet Details Provided by GKF

Total Revenues	$X,X18,263
Total Expenses	$482,486
Support	$X,X34,801
Change in Net Assets	$X61,414

Balance Sheet Summary

Total Assets	$X,X31,229
Total Liabilities	$X,X31,229

A review of the **Audit Committee** Report was presented (Power Point wide screen presentation) in conjunction with the report from the **Fiscal Management Committee**. (The intended and expected Fraternity Audit activity was performed however, the timing of the work did not allow it to be printed and available for distribution to the Grand Conclave delegation)
It was properly moved and second to accept the report of the **Fiscal Management Committee** (The Committee written report was distributed to all Grand Conclave registrants in their registration kit). The motion passed.
GKRS COMMUNICATION PAGE 5 74th Grand Conclave Minutes

SECOND PLENARY SESSION

The second plenary session was called to order at 2:30 PM on Monday, 7/24/2006. The second plenary session focus was a presentation on health initiatives, moderated by Bro Charles Christopher (MD). The guest speaker was Dr. Gerald DeVaughn, President of the American Association of Black Cardiologists; a medical association with a mission to decrease the rate of incidence of cardiovascular disease, a leading cause of death among Black Americans.

Also of significance during the Second Plenary Session was the nomination process for the Grand Officer positions. The nomination process was Chaired by Past Grand Basileus, Bro. Moses C. Norman, Sr. (33rd Grand Basileus).

Note: District Caucus sessions were held on Tuesday July 25, 2006 at various locations in the Convention Center. The actual elections were held on Wednesday July 26, 2006 (starting at 7:30 AM) with a run-off for the Offices of 1st Vice Grand Basileus and Grand Keeper of Records and Seal held in the early evening of that same day. The Undergraduate Caucus determined the identification and election of the 2nd Vice Grand Basileus and Undergraduate Representatives to the Supreme Council. Nominations for the Office of Grand Keeper of Finance was closed on one nominee, however, the name of that nominee, Bro. Antonio F. Knox, did still appear on the ballot and received votes. The formal announcement of the election results was read to the Grand Conclave on the morning of Thursday, July 27, 2006. For brevity and clarity, the results of the nomination process, election and election

run-off are indicated together below. (Winners are indicated by all capital letters in bold print.)
Nominees
GRAND BASILEUS Votes Votes
Bro. WARREN G. LEE, JR. 641
Bro. Kenneth A. Brown 498
1ST VICE GRAND BASILEUS RUNOFF
Bro. Carl A. Blunt 454 **Bro. CARL A. BLUNT 571**
Bro. Terrell D. Parris 401 Bro. Terrell D. Parris 310
Bro. Aubrey Nick Pittman 150
Bro. Alcindor R. Rosier 115
Bro. Inaki Bent (on ballot as Inaki Vent) 20
2ND VICE GRAND BASILEUS
Bro. BRIAN GUNDY (Elected by Undergraduate Caucus)
GRAND KEEPER OF RECORDS AND SEAL RUNOFF
Bro. Mandrid N. Williams, Jr. 79
Bro. Edgar L. Mathias, Sr. 335 Bro. Edgar L. Mathias, Sr. 328
Bro. Charles A. Bruce 398 **Bro. CHARLES A. BRUCE 554**
Bro. Marcus W. Shute 326
GRAND KEEPER OF FINANCE
Bro. ANTONIO F. KNOX (Unopposed) 979
GRAND COUNSELOR
Bro. Christopher M. Cooper 560
Bro. MICHAEL R. D. ADAMS 578

GKRS COMMUNICATION PAGE 6

74th Grand Conclave Minutes
The Undergraduate Caucus also elected the Undergraduate Representatives to the Supreme Council. Those new Supreme Council Members are:
Bro. BENJAMIN L. HART (7th District)
Bro. JOSEPH F. BOWERS, Jr. (10th District)
Bro. JAMES McKOY (6th District)
The Grand Conclave activities of Monday, July 24, 2006 ended with the presentation of the International

Talent Hunt Program and the wonderful performances by the District Winners.

THIRD PLENARY SESSION

The third plenary session was called to order on the late afternoon of Tuesday July 25, 2006 following the Undergraduate Luncheon. The delegates and other attendees were directed to several Officer and Committee Reports in the Report booklets distributed to them at registration.

The Grand Conclave went into Recess and the Grand Conclave delegation proceeded to Little Rock Central High School for a ceremony commemorating the "Little Rock Nine" - those brave young high school students who integrated Central High School in 1957. A special presentation was made by one of "the nine" – Bro. Ernest Green – first Black graduate of Little Rock Central High School.

The Front step of Central High School was chosen as the site for the formal Grand Conclave Delegation Photo.

FOURTH and FIFTH PLENARY SESSION

The Fourth Plenary session was called to order on the early afternoon of Wednesday July 26, 2006 following the first round of the election process. This session was the venue for the Economic Empowerment Workshop.

Coincident with that Workshop, Bro. Jesse Jackson, Sr., arrived and held a Press Conference on-site in the Peabody Hotel. Bro. Jackson and other Omega Brothers who are immersed at the City, State and National level of politics, formed a panel for the Fifth Plenary Session/Public Program Workshop on Political Empowerment.

SIXTH PLENARY SESSION

The Sixth Plenary session was called to order at 9:00 AM on Thursday July 27, 2006. There was a formal announcement of the election results as shown on Page 6 of these Minutes above.

The **Recommendations Committee** report was presented. It was properly moved and second to accept the Report of the Recommendations Committee. The motion passed. A summary extract of the presentation and actions taken by the 74th Grand Conclave is presented below:

Summary of 74th Grand Conclave Recommendations Actions
Each recommendation has been assigned an identification number that uniquely identifies the recommendation. The identification number consists of two parts – "XX-YY" – where:

- •
  - XX – represents the Grand Conclave number where the recommendation was presented (e.g. The "73" in

"73-11" represents the 73rd Grand Conclave in St. Louis, MO).
YY – Represents the sequence in which the recommendation was presented at the aforementioned Grand Conclave (e.g. The "11" in "73-11" represents the 11th recommendation that was presented at the 73rd Grand Conclave in St. Louis, MO).

Please note that the first two recommendations were tabled at the 73rd Grand Conclave in St. Louis, MO. It was properly moved and second to remove both Recommendations from the table for consideration at the 74th Grand Conclave. The motion passed.

GKRS COMMUNICATION PAGE 7
74th Grand Conclave Minutes

ID #	Recommendation	Recommendations Committee Preferred Action	74th Grand Conclave Action
73-11	Recommend that all undergraduates should receive two (2) non-dues paying years after both graduation and expiration of his financial card. **AMENDED – All undergraduates who join a graduate chapter after graduation shall pay dues at the undergraduate amount for two years after graduation.**	Referred to Ways & Means Committee. Ways & Means Committee recommended rejection.	Approved (as Amended)
73-43	Creation of undergraduate chapter alumni	Referred to Special Committee of	Rejected

THE OMEGA PSI PHI FRATERNITY INC. 387

	associations.	DR's. Special Committee of DR's recommended rejection.	
74-01	Create Credential Accountability By IHQ – To make IHQ accountable to the brotherhood when credentials are not sent in a timely fashion.	Reject	Rejected
74-02	Creation of an Omega Senate and House of Delegates	Send to Constitution & Bylaws Committee	Sent to Constitution & Bylaws Committee
74-03	Brothers Who Fail to Remain Financial – All members who have allowed a ten year period to pass without paying dues should be dropped from the rolls of Omega.	Send to Membership Committee and the Constitution & Bylaws Committee	Sent to Membership Committee and the Constitution & Bylaws Committee
74-04	Fraternal Restoration Period – Recommend that the fraternity reclaim and restore contrite members and provide barred brothers a chance to pay dues and re-associate with Omega.	Reject	Rejected
74-05	Deadline for Candidates Seeking Office – Candidates for Supreme Council	Reject	Rejected

	should declare candidacy to the GKRS no later than December 15th of the year prior to the Grand Conclave.		
74-06	New Membership Program Review – Recommend that the fraternity establish a comprehensive review (e.g. 2007 Leadership Conference) to review and update the MSP process.	Approve	Approved
74-07	Naming Buildings After Prominent Black Americans – Recommend that Omega Psi Phi Fraternity, Inc. takes on the charge of requesting cities to name buildings after prominent Black Americans.	Reject	Rejected
74-08	Recommend that the Omega Psi Phi Fraternity, Inc. support the Charles H. Wright Museum of African-American History in Detroit, MI. **AMENDED – Delete all supporting bullet points.**	Reject	Approved (As Amended)
74-09	Incorrect Contact Information	Reject	Rejected

ID #	Recommendation	Recommendations Committee 74th Grand Conclave Action	Preferred Action
	Penalty Policy – Recommend that the Omega Psi Phi Fraternity, Inc. implements a financial penalty policy for Brothers, Chapters, and Districts with incorrect contact information.		
74-10	Financial Planning for Scholarship Winners / Undergraduate Representatives – Recommend that each Scholarship winner and Undergraduate Representative shall take a designated financial planning workshop/class before being awarded any funds from the Fraternity.	Reject	Rejected

GKRS COMMUNICATION PAGE 8 74th Grand Conclave Minutes ID # Recommendation Recommendations Committee 74th Grand Conclave Action Preferred Action

ID #	Recommendation	Recommendations Committee 74th Grand Conclave Action	Preferred Action
74-11	Grand Officer Survey – Recommend that the IHQ shall provide the financial Brotherhood with a quarterly web-based Grand Officer's survey	Reject	Rejected

74-12	on the fraternity website. Fraternity Interactive Database For Financial Members – Recommend that the Fraternity/IHQ set up an interactive database as follows for financial members in the fraternity:
	    1. Graduate Brothers enter their respective degree(s) earned, company employed, by, job description, expertise, etc.
	    2. Undergraduate Brothers enter their respective degree(s) being pursued, college/university currently enrolled, major area of study, year in school, anticipated graduation, et cetera.
		Approve	Sent to Budget Committee for review of financial impact to the fraternity

74-13	Various Proposed Constitution & Bylaws Changes	Send to Constitution & Bylaws Committee	Sent to Constitution & Bylaws Committee[1]

The **Constitution and By Laws Committee** presented its report immediately following the Recommendations review. Proposed changes to the Constitution and Bylaws had been submitted to the Constitution and Bylaws Committee. It was properly moved and second to table consideration of the Constitution and Bylaws changes. The motion passed.

The Grand Basileus announced that Bro. Richard "Dick" Smith was appointed as Assistant Executive Director Emeritus.

GKRS COMMUNICATION PAGE 9 74th Grand Conclave Minutes

The **Budget Committee** submitted a budget proposal for FY 2007 and FY 2008. After discussion, it was properly moved and second to approve the budget subject to review and modification by the Supreme Council. The motion passed. That budget proposal is shown below:

PROPOSED GENERAL FUND BUDGET

	Proposed FY 2008	Proposed FY 2007
REVENUES		
Graduate Dues	$ X,060,900	$ X,030,000
Undergraduate Dues	$ X19,351	$ X15,875
Back Dues	$ X3,045	$ X1,500
Life Member Dues	$ X18,270	$ X09,000
Reinstatement and Late Fees	$ X8,644	$ X7,810
Initiations	$ X88,800	$ X71,650
World Headquarters Building Fund Assessment (WHBF)	$ X44,007	$ X36,900
Grand Conclave / Leadership Conference	$ X,750,000	$ X25,000
Merchandising	$ X59,135	$ X54,500
Interest Income	$ -	$ -
Other Revenue	$ -	$ -
License & Royalty Fees	$ X3,045	$ 51,500
Advertising – Oracle	$ 10,609	$ 10,300
Other Conferences & Meetings/Awards	$ 1,061	$ 1,030
Donations and Contributions	$ 2,652	$ 2,575

Golf Tournament	$ 26,523	$ 25,750
Fundraising & Scholarship	$ 10,609	$ 10,300
National Undergraduate Summit	$ 21,218	$ 20,600
Omega Mall	$ 5,305	$ 5,150
Omega Calling Card Program	$ 26,523	$ 25,750
WF - Shared Mtg. Program	$ 1,061	$ 1,030
	$ -	$ -
ISP Program	$ -	$ -
Insurance	$ X27,308	$ X23,600
Total Support Revenue		
Total Revenue	**$ X,608,0665**	**$ X,199,820**
EXPENSES		
Program Services:		
Supreme Council	$ X38,703	$ X31,750
Oracle, Bulletin, and Newsletter	$ X92,023	$ X86,430
Projects & Committees	$ X59,135	$ X54,500
Grand Conclave / Leadership Conferences	$ X,750,000	$ X25,000
Conference & Meetings/B&E/NUS	$ X9,568	$X77,250
Golf Tournament	$ X6,523	$ X5,750
Total Program Services	$ X,445,950	$ X,100,680
Supporting Services:		
Management & General	$ X,389,742	$ X,352,905
Merchandising Costs	$ -	$ -
Rent Expenses	$ X81,924	$ X70,800
Property Expenses	$ -	$ -
Outside Services	$ 132,613	$ 128,750
Scholarships	$ 125,000	$ 125,000
Contingency	$ X32,836	$ X21,685
Total Supporting Services	$ X,162,115	$ X,099,140
Total Expenses	**$ X,608,065**	**$ X,199,820**

GKRS COMMUNICATION PAGE 10 74th Grand Conclave Minutes

Grand Counselor, Bro. A. Nick Pittman, presented three **Resolutions** that were adopted by the Grand Conclave.

I. Resolution for Brother Oliver Hill in recognition of his services rendered and honors received over his long and distinguished career as a Civil Rights attorney.

II. Resolution for all external entities in Little Rock, AR who were responsible for hosting the 74th Grand Conclave.

III. Resolution recognizing Bro. Derek Lewis, Pi Omicron, and all Arkansas chapters for hosting the 74th Grand Conclave.

GRAND MARSHAL REPORT

Brother Derek Lewis, the Grand Marshall of the 74th Grand Conclave, presented his report. The pre-audit registration figures for the 74th Grand Conclave were:

Total Number of Pre-Registered Brothers	1288
Total Number of On-Site Registrations	168
Total Number of Registered Brothers	**1456**

It was properly moved to adjourn the 74th Grand Conclave.
The Formal Grand Conclave Closing Ceremony ended with the singing of the Black National Anthem.

Post Grand Conclave Events

As per normal, after the formal closing of the Grand Conclave, two events followed; The Founder's Banquet (Thursday evening 7/27/06) and a Supreme Council Meeting (Friday morning 7/28/06).

During the Awards Ceremony, the 2004 and 2005 Achievement Awards were announced. A listing of those Awards follows:

Chapter Achievement Awards

Year	Category	Winner
2003-04	Social Action Graduate Chapter of the Year	Psi Alpha Chapter San Antonio, TX (9th District)
2004-05	Social Action Graduate Chapter of the Year	Pi Lambda Lambda Chapter Prince William County, VA (3rd District)
2003-04	Social Action Undergraduate Chapter of the Year	Gamma Gamma Chapter Grambling State University (9th

Year	Award	Winner
		District)
2004-05	Social Action Undergraduate Chapter of the Year	Gamma Gamma Chapter Grambling State University (9th District)
2004	Graduate Chapter of the Year	Tau Gamma Gamma Chapter Fort Bragg, NC (6th District)
2005	Graduate Chapter of the Year	Delta Omega Chapter Petersburg, VA (3rd District)
2004	Undergraduate Chapter of the Year	Alpha Chapter Howard University (3rd District)
2005	Undergraduate Chapter of the Year	Gamma Gamma Chapter Grambling State University (9th District)

GKRS COMMUNICATION PAGE 11 74th Grand Conclave Minutes

Individual Achievement Awards

(Some individual Achievement Awards were announced at the Undergraduate Luncheon Tuesday 7/25/06)

Year	Award	Winner
2004	Omega Citizen of the Year	Mrs. Marylyn J. Ward-Ford (nominated by Alpha Nu Chapter)
2005	Omega Citizen of the Year	Bro. Kenny L. Boyd (nominated by Theta Omega Chapter)
2004	Founders' Award	Bro. Dominic Boyce Xi Phi, Harlem, NY (2nd District)

2005	Founders' Award	Bro. Vic Bruinton Iota Iota, Raleigh, NC (6th District)
2004	Superior Service Award	Bro. Charles Peevy Phi Iota, Phoenix, AZ (12th District)
2005	Superior Service Award	Bro. Walter Glover Xi Pi, Colorado Springs, CO (8th District)
2004	Col. Charles Young Leadership Award	Bro. Lt. Col. Angelo Riddick Lambda Gamma Gamma, Fort Meade, MD (2nd District)
2005	Col. Charles Young Leadership Award	Bro. Col. Lipton Mark Kappa Iota Iota, Fort Houston, VA
2004	Graduate Omega Man of the Year	Bro. Willie Hinchen Theta Alpha, Dallas, TX (9th District)
2005	Graduate Omega Man of the Year	Bro. Eric Fairfax Iota Iota, Raleigh, NC (6th District)
2004	Undergraduate Omega Man of the Year	Bro. Theo Marks (attended NKU 5th District) Initiated Beta Iota Chapter, (4th District)
2005	Undergraduate Omega Man of the Year	Bro. Ricardo Brown Pi Lambda Chapter, Norfolk State University (3rd District)
2005	Scholar of the Year ($10,000)	Bro. Malvern Ngoh (1st District)

Year	Award	Recipient
2005	Founders Scholars ($2500)	Bro. St. Aaron Morris (9th District)
		Bro. Timothy Vaughn (5th District)
		Bro. Chris Ballenger (9th District)
		Bro. Dominic Day (10th District)
2005	Ronald McNair Scholar ($1000)	Bro. St. Aaron Morris (9th District)
2005	Herman Dreer Award ($1000)	Bro. Brandon Vaughn (10th District)
2005	Undergraduate/Graduate Award ($1000)	Bro. Fredrick Powell (1st District)
		Bro. Ali Rashan (10th District)
		Bro. Jevon Burkes (4th District)
		Bro. Tycarri Rogers (9th District)
2005	George E. Mears Award ($1000)	Susan Rowe (Univ. of Texas/Austin)

It was announced, during the banquet, that Bro. William Cosby was recognized with a Lifetime Achievement Award.

The new Grand Officers were installed with their Oath of Office delivered by Past Grand Basileus Bro. Burnel E. Coulon (31st Grand Basileus)

The evening concluded with the singing of the Omega Psi Phi Fraternity, Inc. hymn; Omega Dear.

GKRS COMMUNICATION PAGE 12 74th Grand Conclave Minutes

A **Supreme Council Meeting** was convened on Friday July 28, 2006 at 9:00 AM. A brief extract of the Minutes from that Meeting is inserted below:

The Meeting was called to order at 8:57 AM with Grand Basileus Bro. Warren G. Lee, Jr. presiding.

A prayer was offered by the Grand Chaplain.

The Roll was called by the GKRS.

A Quorum was declared by the Grand Basileus.

    1) The Grand Basileus reappointed Bro. Farrell Duncombe as Grand Chaplain.

    2) Bro. Isaiah Robinson was reappointed as Editor to the Oracle by the Grand Basileus

    3) The Grand Basileus announced a 90-Day transition period (August 1 – November 1, 2006) to provide a smooth transition from the prior administration to that which was installed on the evening of July 27, 2006. For clarity, indeed, the Grand Officers installed on July 27, 2006 are currently empowered.

    4) The District Representatives were asked to submit recommendations for Committee Chairmen to the Grand Basileus by the end of August 2006

    5) The 2nd VGB announced the intention of a 2nd Vice Transition Meeting to take place at IHQ within 30 days of the close of the 74th Grand Conclave.

    6) The Grand Basileus announced a plan for a Strategic Planning Meeting to take place in San Diego, California during the 2006 Labor Day Weekend

        San Diego will be a planning meeting, not a Supreme Council Meeting

            i. No plan to attend the Congressional Black Caucus

            ii. Tentative plan for a Supreme Council Meeting – October 2006 (most likely at IHQ) **Later in the meeting, the meeting date and location was defined as October 13 – 14, 2006 in Atlanta.**

7) The Grand Basileus announced a plan for an Undergraduate Summit to take place Super Bowl weekend (February 2007) with a Supreme Council Meeting to take place on Thursday February 1, 2007. (Site to be determined)
    a. The Fraternity will review bids from cities wishing to host this Undergraduate Summit.
        i. Requirements and specifications for host cities will be issued by August 15, 2006
        ii. Bids are to be received at IHQ (attention Bro. George Smith) by September 15, 2006)
        iii. A decision to be reached by the close of the October 2006 Supreme Council Meeting.
        iv. If no acceptable bids are received, the Summit will take place at IHQ in Atlanta.
    b. Bro. Marvin Dillard asked for a listing of key topics that should be included for a District Undergraduate Summit.

8) Bro. Moses Norman introduced the need to enact a plan for a Grand Conclave to take place in 2011 (as required in the Constitution) in Washington, D.C. Substantial discussion ensued:

GKRS COMMUNICATION PAGE 13 74th Grand Conclave Minutes

    a. Will this be a "regular" Grand Conclave?
        i. Elections?
        ii. Regular Business?
        iii. Etc., etc., etc.
    b. What is the impact of referring to this as a "Celebratory Conclave"?
    c. That the concept of a Conclave in 2011 to be held in Washington, D.C. is not a new discussion topic for the Supreme Council.
    d. Bro. Joseph Williams moved that the 2011 Grand Conclave have a celebratory theme. The Motion passed.

e. The Grand Basileus asked for names to be considered for membership on a 2011 Conclave Planning Committee.

9) Ad Hoc Committees had been formed at the DR Transition meeting held previously. Those Committees requested information and are to report at the October San Diego Meeting:

    a. A DR Transition Committee (Clemons, Jackson, Peevy) will report

    b. A Credit Card Reconciliation Committee (Chase, Smith, Worth) will report

    c. Bro. Rufus Heard has been installed as an Interim Chairman of the Fiscal Management Committee

10) Bids from potential host cities for the 2010 Conclave are being solicited.

11) Discussion was initiated regarding plans for filling the Executive Director position on a permanent basis:

    The Personnel Committee is pursuing candidates for the position:

        i. Consideration is being given to change the position title to something that will avoid confusion, during external contacts, regarding the specific role that is intended for the Executive Director (i.e., that the Executive Director is not the Fraternity's CEO)

        ii. The selection process will be:

            1. Position announcement on webpage by 8/10/06

            2. The Personnel Committee will do a search

            3. Applications will be received

            4. The Committee will identify the top three candidates

>
> 5. The top 3 candidates will be interviewed by the Supreme Council
> 6. Final candidate selection to be accomplished by October 31, 2006
>
> iii. Various means available to the Fraternity (Bulletin, website, DR communications to the Districts, etc.) will be used to alert the Membership of the opportunity.
> iv. Staff positions at IHQ will include:
>> 1. Executive Director (Will report to GKRS)
>> 2. Finance Manager (Will report to GKF)
>> 3. Perhaps an assistant to the Grand Basileus

12) Several DR's asked that IHQ provide a complete set of MSP documents and checklists as was indicated at the 2006 DR Training in Jacksonville, FL .
13) The new 2nd Vice Grand Basileus received his Supreme Council pin from the Grand Basileus
> a. The 2nd Vice Grand Basileus delivered the Supreme Council pins to the three Undergraduate Representatives to the Supreme Council.

GKRS COMMUNICATION PAGE 14 74th Grand Conclave Minutes

> b. Other new Members of the Supreme Council will receive their pins at a later date.

14) The Grand Basileus stated that no pictures would be included in the Oracle without confirmation of the names of all individuals in the pictures.
15) A final Financial Report of the 74th Grand Conclave is planned to be available within 60 days of the close of the Grand Conclave.
16) The Grand Basileus offered each Supreme Council Member an opportunity to offer a closing

remark or comment. Members congratulated the new Grand Officers, pledged their support of the Grand Basileus and the Supreme Council.

Meeting adjourned at 12:00 noon.
Acknowledgements:
The Grand Keeper of Records and Seal wishes to thank those Brothers who assisted with the compilation of these Minutes. Special thanks go to:
Bro. Terrell Parris, Immediate Past GKRS
Bro. Marvin Dillard, 2nd District Representative
Bro. Keith Neal, Rules Committee Chairman
Bro. Andrew Bailey, Nu Chi Chapter 74th Grand Conclave Delegate
Bro. Kendall Franklin, Rho Gamma Gamma Chapter 74th Grand Conclave Delegate

Respectfully submitted,
Bro. Charles A. Bruce
Grand Keeper of Records and Seal

75TH GRAND CONCLAVE MINUTES

Omega Psi Phi Fraternity, Inc. *Office of*
Bro. Charles A. Bruce IMMEDIATE PAST
GRAND KEEPER OF RECORDS AND SEAL Omega Psi Phi Fraternity, Inc. Confidential 421 Forsheer Drive Chesterfield, MO 63017
Phone: 314/553-3539 E-mail: charles.bruce@emotors.com 75th
Grand Conclave Minutes
Meeting Date: July 14 – 17, 2008
Meeting Location: Birmingham, Alabama
Submitted: October 12, 2008

Attendees:
Grand Basileus Bro. Warren G. Lee, Jr. (38th Grand Basileus)

1st Vice Grand Basileus Bro. Carl A. Blunt
2nd Vice Grand Basileus Bro. Brian S. Gundy
Grand KRS Bro. Charles A. Bruce
Grand KF Bro. Antonio F. Knox
Grand Counselor Bro. Michael R. D. Adams
Undergraduate Representative Bro. Joseph F. Bowers, Jr.
Undergraduate Representative Bro. Benjamin L. Hart
Undergraduate Representative Bro. James A. Jamar McKoy
1st District Representative Bro. Carlton Pickron 9/9
2nd District Representative Bro. James W. Jordan 54/56
3rd District Representative Bro. Mark E. Jackson 28/36
4th District Representative Bro. Dewey A. Ortiz, Sr. 13/19
5th District Representative Bro. Edward C. Morant 20/31
6th District Representative Bro. Octavio Miro 61/93
7th District Representative Bro. Keith R. Jackson 91/101
8th District Representative Bro. Glenn E. Rice 20/25
9th District Representative Bro. Willie F. Hinchen 75/80
10th District Representative Bro. Climent J. Edmond, Jr. 36/38
12th District Representative Bro. Charles C. Peevy 31/33
13th District Representative Bro. Jonathan N. Griffin, Sr. 10/13
Grand Marshall Bro. Walter G. Body
Grand Chaplain Bro. Rev. Farrell J. Duncombe
Editor to the Oracle Bro. Walter T. Richardson

Immediate Past Grand Basileus Bro. George H. Grace (37th Grand Basileus)

Past Grand Basileus Bro. Edward J. Braynon, Jr. (30th Grand Basileus)

Past Grand Basileus Bro. Burnel E. Coulon (31st Grand Basileus)

Past Grand Basileus Bro. Moses C. Norman, Sr. (33rd Grand Basileus)

Past Grand Basileus Bro. C. Tyrone Gilmore, (34th Grand Basileus)

Past Grand Basileus Bro. Dorsey C. Miller (35th Grand Basileus)

Past Grand Basileus Bro. Lloyd J. Jordan (36th Grand Basileus)

(The numbers in parenthesis next to the DRs' names indicate their Chapter attendance in this format:
Number of Chapters in Attendance / Number of Financial Chapters in the District)

IPGKRS COMMUNICATION PAGE 2 Grand Conclave Minutes <u>Monday July 14, 2008</u>

1st Plenary Session

The 75th Grand Conclave commenced at 9:30 AM with a processional of the International Committee Chairmen and other dignitaries followed by the Past Grand Basilei and then the Grand Officers.

The 75th Grand Conclave was called to order by the Grand Basileus, Bro. Warren G. Lee, Jr. at approximately 10:00 AM.

There was an Opening Prayer delivered by the Grand Chaplain, Bro. Rev. Farrell J. Duncombe.

The Grand Basileus conducted a formal ritualistic opening and then called upon the Grand Keeper of Records and Seal to call the roll.

The Grand Keeper of Records and Seal, Bro. Charles A. Bruce, called the roll. (Results of that roll call are indicated on page one of these Minutes. (It is important to note that all living Past Grand Basilei were in attendance except one, the 28th Grand Basileus, Bro. James S. Avery, who was unable to attend due to an illness.) The GKRS declared a quorum.

The Grand Basileus asked for a Motion to approve the agenda. There was one change to the agenda. The Honorary Member discussion was removed from the agenda. It was so moved and Second. The Motion passed.

The Grand KRS asked that the Minutes of the 74th Grand Conclave be accepted. It was so moved and second. The Motion passed.

Then came reports from two Committees.

The Chairman of the Ways and Means Committee, Bro. Calvin Zellars gave his report as information. It was moved and Second to accept his report as information. The Motion passed.

The Fiscal Management Committee chairman, Bro Rufus Heard, gave his report. There was much discussion. It was moved and second to accept the report as information only. The Motion passed.

The Grand Keeper of Finance, Bro. Antonio F. Knox, gave his report. A lengthy discussion followed. It was moved and second to accept the report as information. The Motion passed.

It was the consent of the Grand Conclave to reschedule the Budget Committee report to a non-specific time on Tuesday July 15, 2008.

It was moved and second that for Grand Conclaves in the future, all reports will be emailed to the Chapters 30 days in advance. The Motion passed.

Then came the Grand Basileus, Bro. Warren G. Lee, Jr., to give his report. The highlight elements of his report were:
- The Social Action activities planned to occur during the 75th Grand Conclave included:
  o A Feed the Hungry event

IPGKRS COMMUNICATION PAGE 3 Grand Conclave Minutes

  o A home rehab project in the City of Birmingham

- An event where gun safety locks would be given away (this to be coincident with the food giveaway mentioned above)
• The Grand Basileus thanked everyone for their attendance at the Service Award Breakfasts and special thanks to those responsible for the success of the events. The Grand Basileus gave a nod of appreciation to the GKRS, Bro. Charles A. Bruce, for his handling of the Service Awards and in particular for the 75-Year Awardees. Bro. Bruce also acknowledged the assistance he received from Bro. Charles Johnson, Bro. George Smith and the IHQ staff.
• The Grand Basileus praised the Church Service and Memorial Services with special thanks to the Grand Chaplain for an uplifting and timely message and to the GKRS for his reading of the Brothers having passed into Omega Chapter.
• The Grand Basileus gave kudos to the Talent Hunt Program participants and to the chapters who sponsored their attendance. Also special thanks to the Talent Committee were given.
• The Grand Basileus made comments regarding the overwhelming turn-out for the Founder's Banquet that was held for Brothers only the evening of Sunday, July 13, 2008.
• The Grand Basileus asked the Grand Conclave to consider two new programs:
  - A partnership to create a web TV tool to be used for training and communication
  - To contract with an outside firm to do an assessment of the Fraternity's operations and structure. It was moved and second for the 75th Grand Conclave to authorize that Omega Psi Phi undergo an organizational assessment, develop a strategic plan in response to the

findings of that assessment and implement that plan for the betterment of Omega Psi Phi. The Motion passed.
• The Grand Basileus provided commentary on several more topics including:
   o Membership
   o Chapter Operations
   o Communication
   o Accountability
   o Publications
   o The Omega Affiliates
   o The Omega Brand Name
   o The Power of Omega
   o Challenges to the Fraternity
   o The 100 Year Celebration

The Grand Basileus thanked the assembly and closed with the following comment:
OK is not alright
Good won't cut it
Better is not our best
Excellence is our Standard

The Grand Basileus offered a motion to shift the Grand Conclave Schedule from the even years to the odd years. The Motion did receive a second. However, after further discussion, the Grand Basileus withdrew the Motion.

The Grand Basileus reported that the Supreme Council, on July 11, 2008, interviewed 3 candidates for the Executive Director position. And, that the Supreme Council then voted to delay selection of an Executive Director, while in the interim, Bro. George Smith, will provide Executive Director service in addition to his duties as Liaison to the Grand Basileus.

IPGKRS COMMUNICATION PAGE 4 Grand Conclave Minutes The Grand Conclave went into recess at 1:50 PM.

2nd Plenary Session

The Grand Conclave reconvened at 3:45 PM.
First item was a report from the Interim Executive Director (Past Grand Basileus Bro. George H. Grace). His report was delayed momentarily by the introduction of the newly elected President of the Zeta Phi Beta Sorority, Soror Cheryl Underwood. Soror Underwood made a special presentation to the assembly and to the Grand Basileus, Bro. Warren Lee. The Interim Director report detailed some membership statistics, some re-organization plans at the Headquarters and other such details. (Some questions were raised as to why the IED was giving the report rather than the GKRS. The response was that the Constitution requires a report from the Executive Director at each Grand Conclave.) The IED concluded his report by giving thanks to two Brothers who had also volunteered their service at IHQ - Past Grand Basileus, Bro. Burnel E. Coulon and Past Grand Basileus, Bro. Dorsey C. Miller.

Bro. Grace moved for the acceptance of his report. The motion received a second. The Motion passed.

The 1st Vice Grand Basileus, Bro. Carl A. Blunt gave his report. His report was printed in the Grand Conclave documents included in the registration package. It was moved and second to accept the report. The Motion failed. .

The Grand Keeper of Records and Seal, Bro. Charles A. Bruce, gave his report. This report was also in the printed material included in the registration package. The GKRS correctly noted that, as there were no actionable items in his report, there was no need for a motion to accept or receive.

Bro. Vaughn Willis moved to discontinue the publication known as the Omega's Clarion Call. The motion received a second. Based upon a voice vote, the Grand Basileus declared that the Motion failed. There was much discussion and dissension in the assembly. The decision was to treat the imbroglio as a challenge to the ruling of the Chair. It was decided to put the question to the Grand Conclave delegates for a District by District roll call vote on Tuesday morning July 15, 2008. (Ultimately, what did occur was to again present the Motion in whole to the Grand Conclave delegates during the 4th Plenary Session.)

There was a closing prayer by the Grand Chaplain, Bro. Rev. Farrell J. Duncombe.

The Grand Conclave adjourned for the day at 6:00 PM.

Tuesday July 15, 2008

3rd Plenary Session

The Grand Conclave reconvened at 9:10 AM.

There were some short announcements for the good of the order. Then came the Nominating Session for the Grand Officer positions. This Session was chaired by Past Grand Basileus, Bro. C. Tyrone Gilmore.

IPGKRS COMMUNICATION PAGE 5 Grand Conclave Minutes The nominating slate, after passage of motions to cast one unanimous ballot for uncontested positions was :

Grand Basileus:
Bro. Kenneth A. Brown (520)
Bro. Warren G. Lee, Jr. (593)
Bro. Melvin M. Slater, Sr (33)
1st Vice Grand Basileus (Unopposed)
Bro. Carl A. Blunt
2nd Vice Grand Basileus (Unanimous from the Undergraduate Caucus)
Bro. Jamin Powell
Grand Keeper of Records and Seal
Bro. Lewis Anderson (650)
Bro. Charles A. Bruce (510)
Grand Keeper of Finance
Bro. Lee Bernard, Jr. (135)
Bro. Antonio F. Knox (1018)
Grand Counselor (Unopposed)
Bro. Michael R. D. Adams
Undergraduate Representative to the Supreme Council (Unanimous from Undergraduate Caucus)
Bro. Alexander Gibson

Bro. Phillip Merchant
Bro. James Swinson
(The elected Brothers are shown above in bold font. These results were announced on Wednesday July 16, 2008 by the Credentials Chairman, Bro. Greg Epps.)
The Membership Chairman, Bro. Keith Neal, presented the updated and revised New Member Program.
The Grand Conclave recessed for lunch at 12:30 PM.

4th Plenary Session
The Grand Conclave reconvened at 1:30 PM.

IPGKRS COMMUNICATION PAGE 6 Grand Conclave Minutes Bro. John Ball was installed as the Parliamentarian for the 75th Grand Conclave. A set of standing rules was presented by the Grand Basileus to the Grand Conclave. It was moved and second to adopt these rules for the 75th Grand Conclave. The Motion passed. Those rules are shown below:

75th GRAND CONCLAVE
PROPOSED STANDING RULES
July 14, 2008

RULE #1, CHAPTERS MUST PROVIDE PROOF OF PAYMENT OF INSURANCE, AND CEF DUES IN ORDER TO VOTE.

RULE #2, THE DRESS CODE FOR THE CONCLAVE IS BUSINESS.

RULE #3, DURING DEBATE, EACH BROTHER IS ALLOWED A TOTAL OF TWO MINUTES, WHICH INCLUDES ONE FOLLOW-UP QUESTION. YOU CAN ONLY SPEAK ONE TIME ON THE PENDING QUESTIONS UNTIL EVERYONE HAS HAD AN OPPORTUNITY TO SPEAK.

RULE #4, ALL SPEAKERS SHOULD LINE UP AT THE MICROPHONES TO SPEAK ON THE PENDING QUESTION WHEN DIRECTED BY THE CHAIR. IT IS UP TO THE CHAIR TO RECOGNIZE YOU AFTER BROTHERS ARE LINED UP AND READY TO SPEAK.

RULE #5, DURING OFFICER NOMINATIONS THERE WILL BE ONE NOMINATING SPEECH AND UPTO TWO SECONDING SPEECHES WITH A ONE MINUTE TIME LIMIT FOR EACH SPEAKER PER CADIDATE.

RULE #6, THE USE OF PROFANITY OR INFLAMMATORY REMARKS WILL NOT BE ALLOWED WHEN ADDRESSING THE CHAIR OR ANOTHER BROTHER.

RULE #7, ALL QUESTIONS SHOULD BE DIRECTED TO THE CHAIR.

RULE #8, DURING THE MEETINGS, CELL PHONES SHOULD BE TURNED OFF OR ON VIBRATE.

RULE #9, ANY BROTHER WHO IS LATE FOR THE START OF ANY PLENARY SESSION SHALL BE ASSESSED ONE DOLLAR AND 00/100 ($1.00) PAYABLE TO THE KEEPER OF PEACE AT THE ENTRY POINT OF THE SESSION.

ROBERT'S RULES OF ORDER NEWLY REVISED 10TH EDITION

IPGKRS COMMUNICATION PAGE 7 Grand Conclave Minutes Bro. John Ball clarified the process to declare a "Division of the House" when the ruling by the Chair on a Motion or some other action is disputed by a member of the assembly.

The assembly was then segregated such that voting delegates were clearly evident by their placement at the front of their District delegation.

The Recommendations Chairman, Bro. Dylan Bess, gave his Committee report and presented several Recommendations to the Grand Conclave for disposition. Four Recommendations were brought forward from the 74th Grand Conclave for disposition. (This resulting from the seamless transition between Bro. Bess and the Recommendations Chairman who preceded him.)

{Please note: one Recommendation was received after the cut-off date imposed by the Recommendations Process on the Fraternity's web site. (These rules had been posted there for over two years). As such, that Recommendation was mentioned but not presented for disposition.} A tally of the entire list of Recommendations and the disposition reached by the Grand Conclave is shown below:

Recommendation Number	TITLE	Grand Conclave Disposition
74 - 02	Creation of an Omega Senate and House of Delegates	Rejected
74 - 03	Brothers Who Fail To Remain Financial	Rejected
74 - 12	Fraternity Interactive Database	Rejected

<<>>

74 - 13	Various Proposed Constitution and By Laws Changes	Referenced as 75 - 25 (a - o) See Below
75 - 01	Annual Worship Service	Rejected
75 - 02	Changing the Conclave Experience	Rejected
75 - 03	Common Sense Conclave Agenda Template	Accepted
75 - 04	Conclave Registration Attached Membership Fees	Rejected
75 - 05	Conditional Amnesty Period	Rejected
75 - 06	Contracting for Certain Administrative Functions	Rejected
75 - 07	Financial Status For Non - Distributed Frat Cards	Rejected

75 - 08	Founder's Day Recognition	Rejected
75 - 09	Mobility of the National Undergraduate Summitt	Rejected
75 - 10	No Compensation For Supreme Council Members	Rejected
75 - 11	Providing Gill History Book to new Initiates	Accepted
75 - 12	Reclamation / Retention Graduate Moratorium	Rejected
75 - 13	Undergraduate Chapter Advisor Award	Accepted
75 - 14	Uniform Sanction Matrix	Rejected

75 - 15	Waiving Fees for 60-year Brothers	Accepted
75 - 25e	Article VI Fiscal Affairs Section 2 - Bonding of Officers	Accepted

75 - 16	Grandfathering Housing Assessment Fee	Accepted
75 - 17	Omega Employment Network	Accepted
75 - 18	District Counselor Duties - Contract Review	Rejected
75 - 19	District Counselor Duties - Chapter House Loans	Rejected
75 - 20	District Representative's Term of Office	Rejected
75 - 21	Due Process Clarification Regarding Expulsion	Accepted
75 - 22	Revision to Article IV (a) of the Constitution	Rejected
75 - 23	Raise (New Member) GPA to 2.7	Rejected
75 - 24	Revision of (New Member) Initiation Criteria	Rejected
75 - 25a	Composition of the Supreme Council	Rejected
75 - 25b	Grand Basileus Assessment	Rejected
75 - 25c	Supreme Council Authorization of Property Purchase	Rejected
75 - 25d	Redistricting	Rejected

IPGKRS COMMUNICATION PAGE 9 Grand Conclave Minutes

75 - 25f	Article VI Fiscal Affairs Section 3 - Budget Distribution before Conclave	Accepted
75 - 25g	Article VI Fiscal Affairs Section 4 - GKF Report Distribution Before Conclave	Accepted
75 - 25h	Article VI Fiscal Affairs - Section 5 - Budget Restriction	Tabled
75 - 25i	Article VI Fiscal Affairs - Section 6 - Grand Basileus Stipend	Rejected
75 - 25j	Article VI Fiscal Affairs Section 7 - Grand Officer Budget	Accepted
75 - 25k	Chapter II Article I Section 2 (a - e)	Rejected
75 - 25l	Article VI Fiscal Affairs	Rejected
75 - 25m	Chapter II Article I Section 1	Rejected
75 - 25n	Chapter II Article I Section 4	Rejected
75 - 25o	Chapter II Article I Section 6	Accepted
	One Man One Vote	Not Presented

Recommendation number is interpreted as:
"Sequential Number of Grand Conclave – Sequential Number of Recommendation" such that
Recommendation #74 – 03 was the #3 Recommendation presented at the 74th Grand Conclave.

IPGKRS COMMUNICATION PAGE 10
Grand Conclave Minutes

Then the question regarding the discontinuation of publication of the Omega's Clarion Call {from the day before (Monday July 14, 2008)} was put to the Grand Conclave delegates for disposition. (Not a question to challenge the previous ruling of the Chair) The question:

That the Fraternity discontinues publication of The Omega's Clarion Call. Moved and second. The results of the Roll Call vote were:

District	Yea	Nay
1	11	0
2	126	2
3	119	0
4	22	2
5	22	3
6	4	141
7	101	30
8	27	0
9	30	145
10	110	4
12	30	2
13	13	0
Total	615	329

The Motion Passed. (Omega's Clarion Call publication will cease)

The Grand Conclave adjourned for the day at 5:45 PM.

Wednesday July 16, 2008
5th Plenary Session

The Grand Conclave reconvened at 3:30 PM on Wednesday July 16, 2008. (The morning was consumed by delegate voting for Grand Officers and training in breakout sessions conducted by the GKRS, Bro. Charles A. Bruce, on the My Page function of the web page, KRS duties, KRS Best Practices and the Lock Box protocol.)

The Credentials Chairman, Bro. Greg Epps, gave the election results. (Previously reported in these Minutes.)

IPGKRS COMMUNICATION PAGE 11

Grand Conclave Minutes

The Membership Chairman, Bro. Keith Neal, gave the final version of the New Membership plan and moved:

That this body accept the Lampados Club as its membership program with the current eligibility requirements, effective September 2009. The Motion received a second.

The roll call tally of the votes on this Motion is shown below:

District	Yea	Nay
1	3	8
2	44	59
3	0	49
4	21	3
5	16	0
6	20	47
7	92	18
8	8	19
9	68	44
10	28	4
12	29	4
13	8	2
Total	337	257

The Motion passed.

While the votes were being tallied for the above Motion, the Grand Basileus took the opportunity to introduce the new Chairman of the Omega Life Membership Foundation, Bro. Ted Greer. Bro. Greer made a few comments to the assembly, including:

"I want to announce to the Life Members that, when you buy your life membership, 60 percent of that is kept by the National; 40 percent goes to the Life

Membership Foundation, which is invested so that we can do the things like we did at the Undergraduate Luncheon and Undergraduate Summit.

It was about 419 Brothers who have paid since the last transaction, so about $334,000 that the organization is supposed to give the foundation. We are going to exchange that today."

IPGKRS COMMUNICATION PAGE 12
Grand Conclave Minutes

The Budget Committee Chairman (Bro. Donnie Bowser) and Co-Chair (Bro. Vic Bruinton) gave their Committee Report. It was moved and second to accept their report. The Motion passed.

The 2_{nd} Vice Grand Basileus, Bro. Brian S. Gundy, gave his report and farewell remarks.

The Grand Marshal of the 75_{th} Grand Conclave, Bro. Walter G. Body gave an interim report. He gave some preliminary (unaudited) numbers for registration:

Preregistration was 1,684 Brothers.

1,448 graduate Brothers picked up their packets.

107 Brothers or 6.4 percent did not pick up packets.

98 undergraduates picked up packets.

31 Brothers or 1.8 percent did not.

On-site registration was 210 Brothers

(155 Graduate; 55 Undergraduate)

Total registration for the 2008 Grand Conclave in Birmingham, Alabama - 1,894 Brothers.

His report included one suggestion for future Grand Conclaves; that a private, independent manager be hired to regulate the meetings.

The Grand Counselor, Bro. Michael R. D. Adams, then provided the Grand Conclave Resolutions over his name and that of the Grand Keeper of Records and Seal, Bro. Charles A. Bruce. The statement of resolution:

Be it known to all that the Omega Psi Phi Fraternity celebrated the 75th Grand Conclave in the City of Birmingham, Alabama, July 11 through 17, 2008. Let it be known to all that the Conclave was hosted
by Alpha Phi, Kappa Delta, and Eta Epsilon.
Be it also known that there were 1,894 registered delegates in attendance, 195 Quettes, and 15 Que kids.
Be it also known that the City of Birmingham rolled out the red carpet through its food, hospitality, and courtesy.
Be it known that Mayor Larry Langford and the City Council of Birmingham welcomed the Fraternity through their support as well as the support of the Civil Rights Institute,
Alabama Power & Light, Coca-Cola of Birmingham, State Farm, Kelly Construction, Jefferson County
Commission and Ken Owens, Omega, the State of Alabama and 7th District.

IPGKRS COMMUNICATION PAGE 13

Grand Conclave Minutes

Be it known that the Conclave was supported by over 40 vendors selling licensed Omega products controlled by Omega's brand.
Be it known that the Conclave experienced a spiritual high through its religious services and recognized outstanding talent during the Talent Program.
Be it known that the Conclave was opened by a heartfelt experience of Brothers rededicating
themselves to our four Cardinal Principles of Manhood, Scholarship, Perseverance and Uplift.
Be it known that the Conclave was opened by the 38th Grand Basileus, Brother Warren G. Lee, who
presented the Conclave with the adoption of a comprehensive assessment plan, a new partnership with General Electric, the Omega Online Que Nation TV, and fundraising partnerships with the NFL
Alumni.

Be it known that at the Ronald McNair Undergraduate Luncheon that Brother Bob Holmes chastised
and challenged the Brotherhood to control and determine our brand and that we strive as Omega's for
greatness and that we should not worry about the future but be in it.

Be it known that the Brothers were entertained through the majestic melody of Brother Tapscott, Bro.
Richardson and Brother Porter at the Brothers' Rededication and at the Undergraduate Luncheon.

Be it known that the Scholarship Commission presented $96,000 through the Omega Life
Membership Foundation to Omega scholars.

Be it also known that Omega Psi Phi made a lasting impact on the City of Birmingham on Social
Action Day through the Omega food giveaway, the gun rack giveaway, and the home refurbishing project.

Be it known that Omega Psi Phi made a difference in the lives 131 young people through the Youth Leadership Conference held at Miles College during the Conclave.

Be it also known that the Omega Psi Phi Fraternity remembered the past and will celebrate our great
future through a historical tour and a march through downtown -- through a march from Selma to Birmingham as well as a review of the Omega members in the Civil Rights Institute.

Be it known that Omega Psi Phi has taken the lead among black college organizations and adopted and returned to the Lampados program as the official membership process of entering the Fraternity.

Now, therefore, be it resolved that the Omega Psi Phi Fraternity hereby extends great heartfelt thanks
and appreciation to the City of Birmingham, the Mayor, its corporate sponsors, and the local host
chapters for all of their hard work.

Be it also resolved that as a result of the 75th Grand Conclave, the City of Birmingham would never be the same

because of the positive impact of the Omega Psi Phi Fraternity and all that we have done
in this community.

Be it further resolved that all in attendance participated in spirited debate, serious decision making, and fundamental review of the future of this great Fraternity.

IPGKRS COMMUNICATION PAGE 14

Grand Conclave Minutes

And now the 75th Grand Conclave be declared a success. Done and signed this 16th day of July 2008,

Bro. Michael R. D. Adams, Grand Counselor,

Bro. Charles A. Bruce, Grand Keeper of Records and Seal.

The Grand Basileus informed the assembly of a web site where they could go to learn about and support the candidacy of Bro. George H. Grace for a legislative position in the State of Florida.

Bro. Ron Adrine came forward to report on an anti-violence program he is managing for the Fraternity
along with Bro. Peter Harvey.

The room was cleared of all non-Members.

The Grand Basileus closed the 75th Grand Conclave via the formal ritualistic closing ceremony. The
Grand Conclave was adjourned at 5:10 PM.

The assembly joined in the singing, in customary fashion, of the Omega hymn.

Thursday July 17, 2008

Early Thursday morning, a strong contingent of the Grand Conclave assembly participated in a
recreation of the Famous Selma March and a historic Civil Rights tour.

The Formal Closing Banquet took place on the evening of Thursday July 17, 2008. The new officers
were installed and certain awards were presented.

<◇>

APPENDIX Y

THE YOUTH LEADERSHIP CONFERENCE
OF
OMEGA PSI PHI FRATERNITY, INC.

THE BEGINNING. The first Youth Leadership Conference (YLC) was held in Dallas, Texas in 1988 under the leadership of Brother Arnold Butler who was the Chairman of the International Social Action Committee. Brother Moses C. Norman was the Grand Basileus at that time. In 1988 there were a vast number of programs for "at risk kids." It was the general feeling of the Fraternity's leadership that there were not enough programs designed to recognize young black males who were exhibiting positive academic and leadership abilities. Thus, the YLC was formed and adopted by Omega Psi Phi Fraternity. It is important to emphasize here that the YLC is not an "at risk" Conference!

ABOUT THE YLC. One of primary purposes of the activities of the YLC is to make sure that young participants are aware of the problems and conditions existing in the communities in which they live and how they can use their leadership skills and abilities to help improve these conditions. A relevant theme is chosen for each YLC. The format for the first YLC and the second YLC was primarily a lecture format. The presenter in each workshop would lecture from a stage to the young participants who would be seated in a theater type setting. However, the format for the workshops changed starting with the third YLC held in Atlanta in 1992 and is has been used for each YLC held since.

PAST YOUTH LEADERSHIP CONFERENCES.

The following is a list of all of the Youth Leadership Conferences held to date.

1988 – Dallas, Texas (Hotel)
1990 - Detroit, Michigan (Housed in hotel – YLC on campus of Wayne State University)
1992 – Atlanta, Georgia (Hotel)
1994 – Cleveland, Ohio (Case Western Reserve University)
1996 – Los Angeles, California (University of Southern California)
1998 – New Orleans, Louisiana (Dillard University)
2000 – Indianapolis, Indiana (University of Indianapolis)
2002 – Charlotte, North Carolina (Johnson C. Smith College)
2004 – Saint Louis, Missouri (Washington University)
*2005 –Atlanta, Georgia (Morris Brown College)
2006 – Little Rock, Arkansas (Baptist College)
*2008- Birmingham, Alabama (Miles College)

the first time held in conjunction with the Fraternity's Leadership Conference

QUALIFICATIONS. In order for the young black male to participate, he had to be a junior or senior in high school during the school year immediately following the end of the YLC. The primary reasons for this requirement is that each participant must first be mature enough to deal with the format of the YLC and, secondly, he will be charged with the responsibility of sharing with other young black males in his high school the experiences he gained during the YLC – multiplying the effectiveness of the YLC! Each participant must also have a minimum cumulative GPA of 2.5. Initially, sons of Omega men were prohibited from participating. However, this restriction was eliminated prior to the second YLC held in Detroit, Michigan in 1990 and sons of Omega men could participate.

EXPENSES. The young participants are not required to pay for any of the expenses related to the YLC . Local districts and/or chapters are responsible for paying the travel expenses of the participants to and from the city where the YLC is held (the YLC is always held in the city hosting the Fraternity's Grand Conclave or National Leadership Conference and is held in conjunction with these events). Omega Psi Phi Fraternity, Inc. pays for all of the other expenses related to the YLC.

HOUSING. For the first YLC held in Dallas, the second YLC held in Detroit, and the third YLC held in Atlanta; the participants were housed in hotels in the cities hosting the Grand Conclave. However, starting with the fourth YLC, the participants were housed on the campus of a college located in the city hosting the Fraternity's Grand Conclave. This has proven to be much more effective in the process of providing a safer and securer environment for all the participants – surely safer and more secure than the environment present in a busy hotel!

PRESENT FORMAT. At some point after the participants would have arrived at the site of the YLC, they are organized into groups. At the beginning of each workshop for each YLC, a presenter will introduce the theme of the workshop to all of the participants assembled, give them limited information related to the theme of workshop, and then instruct the participants to break up into their groups and then work on solutions to problems given to them relating to the theme of the workshop. After working in groups, the participants will reassemble and then each group will report its findings. Each group is encouraged to use its imagination in determining how it will report its findings to the assembled group (for example "role playing" may be used).

This format has proven to be much more effective than the lecture format. The participants are much more actively involved in each workshop and are given increased opportunities to utilize their academic and leadership abilities they are require to possess in order for them to be qualified to participate in the YLC.

ORGANIZING A YLC. Well in advance of the time each YLC is held, the members of the YLC Committee meet to select a general theme for the YLC, a theme for each workshop, and then plan all activities for the Conference. Once this is done and the dates for the YLC are set, each District Representative is provided with vital information concerning the YLC and requested to share this information with the chapters in his district. Application and Medical Release forms are also sent to the District Representative to be given to the participants from his district so that they may be completed and returned to the YLC Committee by an established deadline date. The District Representative is the key person in helping to identify chapters in his district willing to sponsor youths from the district and pay their travel expenses. Once a possible site for the YLC is selected, the Chairman of the YLC Committee makes at least one (1) site visit (preferable a college campus) to make sure that the site is suitable for the activities of the YLC. If the site is suitable, then arrangements are finalized for the YLC to be held at the site.

COMMUNICATING WITH THE PARTICIPANTS. Once a completed application form and medical release form is received from a participant and checked by the designated member of the YLC Committee assuring that the participant qualifies, a letter will be sent to the participant indicating that he has been accepted as a participant in the YLC. The letter will also contain information indicating how he will be transported to the site of the YLC from the airport or other terminals. The letter will further indicate what items to bring and what the acceptable dress code will be (it is the responsibility of the chapter/brother to make sure that each potential participant chosen meets the requirements stated above – if not the application should not be forwarded)

LOCAL CHAPTERS ROLE. The YLC is an International Program of Omega Psi Phi Fraternity, Inc. Therefore, the YLC Committee has the responsibility of overseeing the activities of the Conference. However, the brothers in the local chapter(s) have played important roles in connection with the YLC. A local brother is chosen to serve as the liaison between the local chapter(s) and the YLC Committee and is utilized to communicate with the local brothers how they can best assist in insuring that the YLC is successful. Local brothers have historically been involved in assisting in transporting the participants between the airport, or other terminals, and the site if the YLC.

A TYPICAL YLC. The following is a general sketch of the YLC as it is presently
conducted.

The First Day – The first day includes check-in and room assignments (in addition to the participants, members of the YLC Committee
are also assigned rooms). Usually one meal is served (dinner).
An orientation session is held during which time the rules and
regulations of the YLC are discussed and the participants are
divided, usually, into eight groups (Gold Manhood, Gold

Scholarship, Gold Perseverance, Gold Uplift, Purple Manhood, Purple Scholarship, Purple Perseverance, and Purple Uplift).

The Second Day – Three meals are served (breakfast, lunch, and dinner). A morning workshop is held and an afternoon workshop is held (the morning workshop always has a theme relating to Black History).

The Third Day – Generally the same as the second day.

The Fourth Day – Breakfast is served. Participants check out of rooms and Are transported to airport.

Tours and recreational activities are also scheduled and included in the activities of the YLC. [86]

<<>>

---

[86] The Omega Psi Phi Fraternity, Inc. IHQweb site

APPENDIX Z

The History of Omega Psi Phi Fraternity by Founder, Bishop Amos Love as taken word for word from a recording made just prior to his death.

As I make the recording for the fraternity, it gives me great pleasure to do it. Omega Psi Phi fraternity was born out of a dream; that three young men, who were freshman at Howard University, were drawn together, and an abiding friendship developed. There was already on the campus at Howard University a fraternity, which was born **not on the campus itself,** but was a part of a fraternity that came into Howard. We had watched it for two years, but it did not represent what we thought a fraternity ought to represent. It seemed to us, the three young men, that they were a bigoted group, who were status conscience; who believed that only men who had money to spend, or who had great family backings, or even color conscience; so that we were not interested in becoming a part of it at that time.

Early in our college career, we begin thinking in terms of establishing a fraternity that would be a fraternity in reality, as well as in name. But when we began to get ourselves in position to request recognition of the university, we were opposed by the administration. Time after time we asked for a hearing before the faculty committee indicating what was our objective and each time we were rebuffed. The Dean of our college, Kelly Miller, a gray-haired character, a man whom I admired greatly; as a matter of fact, I came to

Howard University because Kelly Miller was one of its professors.

He asked us, why don't you join the fraternity that's already here? We're not responsible at Howard University for its being. But this fraternity you project will be spawned on our campus and we will be the mother chapter and we will be more or less responsible for what it may become. This also was voiced by Dean George Cook; both of whom were members of the fore-said fraternity.

Seeing that we were making no headway with the administration after the three of us had formed our organization and had brought into being, fourteen other members of the Alpha Chapter, original members, one evening we struck upon a bold move that we would make in order to get ourselves recognized. So that there were printed many number of flyers and placards with the names of seventeen Omega Men attached declaring our presence on the campus of Howard University.

That very day at Chapel, the president of the university, Dr. Thirkeil very angrily declared that there is no such organization on the campus of Howard University and that "I want all those young men whose names are attached to the announcement on the campus and on our trees to come into my office, immediately, at the close of the chapel." And so we went to present ourselves in the president's office. He told us that we had made ourselves liable not only to suspension but possible expulsion, because of the high-handed way in which we had announced our existence when no such organization had been recognized by the university. We did not feel he would expel or even suspend these seventeen young men who stood high in the scholastic record of the university and were members of its debating teams and heads of its several auxiliary organizations

Finally he declared he would give us a hearing but that we must take down all the placards and cards that were attached to trees on the campus, which we agreed to do.

Then he agreed to give us a hearing before the faculty committee. When we were brought before this committee which Dean Kelly Miller was the chairman, he talked about the spawning of a new fraternity on the campus of Howard University.

He said there is a great deal of opposition to fraternities on college campuses and how do we know that this fraternity will continue to be the kind of fraternity that you men represent here. "You are gentlemen," he said. He gave us that distinction. Well, we answered, we can only guarantee that as we have, the Founders, selected fourteen other men who were like-minded to ourselves, with the same ideals and aspirations and with the same scholarship, that they in turn would select other men like themselves; then when ever the fraternity might be established that would be the order and men of high ideals and scholastic standing would be selected or infinitum.

So, and with that, we were accepted on the campus but only with the understanding that for the time being we would be a local fraternity. We had already three young men, Oscar J. Cooper, Frank Coleman and myself, together with Associate Professor Ernest Everett Just established what would be our motto and our name. The motto chosen was Philia Ophelema Psukis, Greek words meaning, "Friendship is Essential to the Soul" and we translate the "soul" freely to say "life." "Friendship is Essential to Life," and the letters of our fraternity of these three young men and this Associate Professor, Dr. Ernest Everett Just; and we believe that friendship is the strongest attachment that can exist between individuals or groups of individuals.

We oft time hear people say that, blood is stronger than water. It may or may not be true because we know that blood brothers often are antagonistic to each other and the Bible even records where one brother who ascended a throne had all his other brothers put to death that they might not contest his right to the throne in order. The same Bible also records the existence of a friend who gave up his right to the throne in order that his friend might succeed his father as King of Israel. Jonathan protected the life of David when he knew that it would mean that he himself would never be King. So that, friendship, you see, is really a stronger tie than blood relationships might be.

Then we adopted our Cardinal Principals, Manhood, Scholarship, Perseverance and Uplift. To us Manhood means character; one who dares to do all that doth become a man, and who does more is none. We put Manhood first because we think that character is more essential as we look for prospects in Omega than any other one thing. Secondly we put Scholarship, there is a place for mediocrity in our society but, not in Omega.

We want men whose minds are at least above the average, that they can make a contribution to the life of an institution and to the world. Then Perseverance; we want men who will realize that they have a responsibility to stand by any project that they may begin and see it through. And finally, Uplift; which puts man in connection with the community in which he lives and lets him realize he has a responsibility to those who are less fortunate than himself; that he must also do what he does with the idea of service to the community and to the nation. **Bring all these together, we have the true Omega man.**

Omega doesn't want men simply because they are popular on a campus. Omega doesn't want men simply because they have money to spend. Omega doesn't want men simply because they have a splendid family background. All this is good, if they have at the same time, sterling character and the scholarship that will make them leaders among men rather than followers.

Omega men in every community, as I have gone around our world, and in 48 of the 50 states of the Union, stand out in every community; and the roll call of men in our graduate chapters sounds like, Who's Who in the Negro Community in that particular chapter. I'm not going to elucidate on these to any great extent, but let me say that the first two men to receive the Spingarn Medal were Negroes; were Omega Men. That the 'perfector' of blood plasma was an Omega man; Dr. Brother Charles Drew, and I can go on and on. Name the present situation in our American life, but you know that as well perhaps as I.

Omega Psi Phi Fraternity is not a status club but a fraternity; a brotherhood of high minded, serious thinking, noble living men. Leaders not followers, makers of policy and molders of opinion. Let us never forget that we're developed out of the friendship of three young men and a young college professor. That friendship is essential to life; pick no man for Omega unless you know that he is a friendly man. For he who would have a friend, must be one. We do not want men who live within themselves but men who are outgoing so that they can express themselves in terms of friendship.

I said before in this recording that friendship is the strongest tie that binds men together. You have to accept your relatives, blood relatives, whether you want them or not' they're wished upon you. But you choose your friends and friendship is always motivated by love; and love always thinks not in terms of itself but in terms of those whom the individual may love.

So let me say in concluding that let's keep the ideals high. It's easy to go along with the crowd but the man or the woman who carries civilization afar is the individuals who take leadership and go against the public opinion if it is not in harmony with the highest ideals of the individual. Prove yourself to be a man. **Prove yourself to be a true Omega man.**

Let me say a word regarding the Founders, each one of whom went to the top of his profession. Dr. Ernest Everett Just was one of the greatest Biologist that America has ever produced, Dr. Frank Coleman retired as the head of the Department of Physics at Howard University, Dr. Oscar J. Cooper is an eminent and successful Physician in Philadelphia and your speaker is a Bishop in the Methodist church, the highest office within the gift of the church. **Let me also say just a word regarding my hopes for the future.** I want that we shall not lose the ideals; and a man ought always have his ideals so high; for a man's reach ought to exceed his grasp, for what's ahead of him. The idea is to lift us, as we look towards them and try to make them real in our community. **I don't want Omega to lose the ideals established by the Founders and carried on through more than 50 years to date.**

An Interview with A Founder of Omega Psi Phi Fraternity, Inc.
Founder Bishop Edgar A. Love
Conducted & Taped By Brother Joshua Mark Hyman
October 3, 1973
Transcribed By Brother Henry C. Skrine Jr.

Mark Hyman: What was the single most difficult obstacle that you had to overcome in attempting to establish Omega other than obtaining administration acceptance at Howard?

Founder Edgar A. Love: Of course that was the big obstacle we had to overcome, ran the risk there of being suspended or even expelled from the school for breaking the laws and forming an organization without the consent of the university body committee on student affairs......you wouldn't believe it but the next, as far as I'm concerned we had no real pressures in Omega until we came to the Charlotte Conclave, when this man.....I don't recall his name had turned.....came with a group of young turks we called them to change the whole program of the Fraternity to retransform the Fraternity into a social action committee or organization when the Fraternity is not meant for that, and I said and so many people since that time, I hope every man in Omega is an activist but the organization is not an activist organization.....I said you can do anything you want to do under three of the four cardinal principles.....in Uplift you can go out and do anything you want to help the poor and the less fortunate than yourself and Perseverance means when you want to start on something hard and difficult you do it outside the Fraternity.....stand by till you see it through.....we had in existence a Constitutional Committee for two years to draft a new constitution with sixteen of the best minds in the Fraternity on that.....we had three or four lawyers on there I know we had three I think four.. and Presidents of schools and men of high intellectual ability on that program on that constitutional revision committee.....and we spent two years and nearly $30,000 dollars making that new constitution and a new ritual.....because all the men were scattered all over the United States the world way out in California, we had you had to pay their expenses and it cost us a whole lot to have.....

Mark Hyman: Bishop another question, if you had it all to do over again what aspect of the entire Omega founding would you change?

Founder Edgar A. Love: Nothing in the founding would change, nothing, I think we started off with a constitution that wasn't tampered with for maybe forty or fifty years and nobody has ever questioned the preamble except at the Conclave in Charlotte and nobody has ever questioned the four principles of our organization.....nobody has ever questioned them so we got off to a good start and we were men of high ideals and we organized on the basis of friendship and that's what a Fraternity ought to be.....I said there was another Fraternity in existence at the time but it was a caste, you had to be fair or you had to have money to get in there.

Mark Hyman: There wasn't too much of the latter around at that time though was there?

Founder Edgar A. Love: Two or three boys know from the south whose parents were sending them 50 dollars a month.....

Mark Hyman: This is 191

Founder Edgar A. Love: 19 and 1 ....Jimmy McPenlin from Jacksonville, I know his father sent him 50 dollars a month, I got 50 dollars for four years from home and two of us were approached for the organization we never though went to join because.......turned it down flat and when we organized we went to a hearing before the faculty committee on student affairs so we just went on and initiated fourteen other men and put their names on flyers and on placards and tacked them up all up on the trees on the hill around Howard University and all that naming the fact we would be born and when we were born.....that day at chapel President Thirkield a very nervous man anyhow......I want everyone who's here whose name appears on those placards to get in my office directly after chapel.....so we went into his office after chapel and he stressed Gentlemen do you don't you know that you have made yourself liable to expulsion from the University.....suspension maybe expulsion from the University.....yes sir we know that.....we were willing to run that risk.....to be men to be heard.....you wouldn't hear us.....Why don't you join the Fraternity already on the campus.....we said we don't want to join because its a social club but call it a Fraternity.....and that's what it was.....it was only a social club.....we wanted our Friendship.....I nominated Frank Coleman for president of the Freshman Class the first time we met.....the first time we three met we became friends and through all four years we were on the hill we were inseparable.....Friendship we put it on there and that's why we have Friendship and Fraternity on our shield

Mark Hyman: Which founder gave Omega its name, its motto and its color?

Founder Edgar A. Love: Its difficult to say, its difficult to say, its difficult to say, we all discussed it and Earnest Just, Professor Just he was, gave us a lot of good help, because he knew more about Fraternity's then we did and he helped us really to get our name and motto because he knew greek and he got a book in which there was listed all the known incorporated fraternities in America so we wouldn't take a name which was already incorporated and he was the one who helped us to choose our motto in greek.....Ophelema Philia Psukis.....Friendship is Essential to the Soul and we translate it freely saying Friendship is Essential to Life and it is because we were born as a Fraternity of brothers and friends always love each other and Friendship is the closest affinity that people can have on earth.....closer that blood relationships because brothers will fight, sisters will fight but friends never.....you got to take your relatives whether or not they're wished on you.....but you choose your friends and you usually choose them because they're like minded with yourself and your ideals and your aspirations and that's how the Fraternity was born.....and another thing too......they demanded that we take out of our constitution a national Fraternity and put in a local Fraternity.....well we compromised on that.....and had written into the constitution, to the Grand Basileus in Atlanta Georgia 1936, Frank Coleman had written it.....but the very next year we set up a chapter in Lincoln Beta chapter and the next year Gamma and we began moving on we haven't heard a word from them since to be a local chapter.....we told some of our friends, we didn't believe that they would expel from Howard University from the School of Liberal Arts, College of Liberal Arts and the Teachers College, fourteen men who all had "B" averages and three of nine, six debaters of the nine came among that group.....we had the president of the German Club.....we had the President of the Se Frances French Club.....we had the Presidents of the Student Organizations on the campus among those men....we didn't believe that they would throw them off.

Mark Hyman: What void did you think Omega would fill when the four of you organized it?

Founder Edgar A. Love: We never expected it.....we never dreamed of it being as large as it has become and really as influential as it has become but we wanted to have a group of young people in every.....in those days.....every black college in the United States.....we had the kind of leadership that men like the founders had been or were and the President of Howard University asked us how would we know that you were going to have an organization patterned after the men who founded it.....I said the only guarantee we could give you is the guarantee that the men that we three have chosen and they'd go on establishing an organization and start off with men pledged to the same high ideals and they'd carry on through on into finitum.

Mark Hyman: Did you consider how it would improve the life of brothers after their graduation from Howard or other colleges?.....Did you have anything in mind about how Omega would improve the lifestyle, the quality of life for its members once they were out of college?

Founder Edgar A. Love: Oh yes, oh yes we thought they would improve the life of their communities in which they might separately go because they had been inspired by the idealism of the Fraternity that they would influence the life of their communities and that they would enjoin to make themselves relevant to the community and not to be an exclusive club and lose contact with people of the community.

Mark Hyman: You already answered part of the next question.....But how does it feel to have spawned an organization that now has 378 chapters and 10,000 active men?

Founder Edgar A. Love: You don't know how happy I feel I got plaques in there on my wall.....150 of them and I'm proud as I can be to think that three humble students in three different fields, one in physics, one in medicine and one in the ministry, would get together and form an organization that would be as large and as influential in the life of America and the communities in which they reside as we find today.

Mark Hyman: What would you consider your prediction for the future of the Fraternity, its done 61 years what about the next 60?

Founder Edgar A. Love: I think you have to make very little change, just as our own American Constitution has stood with very little change, its 150 or more years, I think it will remain with very little change in what it expresses.

Mark Hyman: What do you consider the essential role that any Black Fraternity should play in social structure now in America?

Founder Edgar A. Love: I think they should participate in the Social Action.....We are.....the social end of our life is an important part of our life and one of the areas we need to cultivate

THE OMEGA PSI PHI FRATERNITY INC.

but we must keep our social life on a decent level.

Mark Hyman: Social Action, lets get into that. Is the Fraternity as you see it today growing closer to the ideals of the Fraternity envisioned by you and the other founders at the inception?

Founder Edgar A. Love: No, I can't say that I do see it growing closer to it, yet I find some outstanding men in the Fraternity who are outspoken and who I think are just as strong in sustaining and upholding the honor of the Fraternity through its four cardinal principals as we were envisioning in my day.

Mark Hyman: This may a duplicate situation here but, Do you think Omega Men are living up to your initial inception by way of the four cardinal principles?

Founder Edgar A. Love: Not all of them, not all of them are, I'm sorry to say the master made a mistake he only chose twelve disciples and among them a traitor, you can't expect Omega to have 30,000 in there without making some mistakes, you get men who once in a while who don't belong in there but are in there and stay in there unless he does something to be put out I don't say that so often.....sometimes we made mistakes, we got to be very careful we don't want men just because they're great athletes without any character or because they're outstanding in some phase of school life with no character, we don't want them.....we don't care how popular they may be or how big their name may be, they're not big enough for us.....a man whose mind is not capable of making at least the average that the Fraternity requires.....there's a place for mediocre men but not in Omega.

Mark Hyman: You just mentioned that we have some outstanding men who are not particularly active with the Fraternity but they are outstanding in there fields, How do you suggest we reclaim these men back to Omega for active work?

Founder Edgar A. Love: That's a hard question, how we get them back.....I wrote to Moultrie some years ago to send me the names of all the men of prominence who were not active members.....I never received it, I was going to write them a personal letter and ask them if they would take out a life membership because I know some of them spend as much as a life membership would cost on one night's entertainment.....on one night's entertainment.....and one man I won't call his name we gave him a scholarship to help him to get through school and now he's a millionaire and he's never given back to the Fraternity one penny and I don't believe he's even financial with the Fraternity.

Mark Hyman: Do you think we have a weakness an identifiable weakness today as an organization?

Founder Edgar A. Love: That's kind of hard.

Mark Hyman: Alright.....we don't have to have.....that was just a question that one brother wrote to us and I can think of the strengths that we've got but that was just a question

Founder Edgar A. Love: If we have a weakness it is in having some men in there who don't belong in there who carry the name of the Fraternity and like to boast of their Fraternity but at the same time are not living up to the ideals of the Fraternity.....it gives the Fraternity a bad name.....we do have a few of them.

Mark Hyman: You touched on something a while ago, maybe you would elaborate, what do you think Omega has done to shape the present society in which we live, I know we've had some impact on our communities?

Founder Edgar A. Love: Oh we have.....we have so many Omega Men in high places.....we had the first Federal Judge who was an Omega Man and should have been on the Supreme Bench......if the President had had guts enough at that time to name a man of color to the Supreme Court.....that's a.....Hastie.....Bill Hastie, we have a man Lawrence Oxley in Washington who is the only negro I know of who has had a direct wire to the White House, very few people know that he had a direct wire to the White House, he was the Assistant of Labor and then he came out of the cabinet.....subcabinet.....he was so well thought of and done so much for Washington and for Congress through his influence so that they gave him the privilege of calling direct and I don't know of any other negro who has been so honored.

Mark Hyman: This was during the Roosevelt Administration?

Founder Edgar A. Love: Yeah but, He had it ever since as far as know.

Mark Hyman: Oh. How many of the men did you know in the Black cabinet, I understand that all of them when Ms. Bethune was the top person in Washington, that all the men were Omega Men?

Founder Edgar A. Love: All But one, Evans, I forget his first name.

Mark Hyman: Oh Leonard Evans, Not Leonard.. James Evans from Miami.

Founder Edgar A. Love: He was in there.....he blamed Oxley for that.....you got in there first and you brought all Omega Men in and Oxley said No.....I didn't bring them in.....their training.....their character.....their so forth.....when they wanted a good man and looked around for him they picked him..... he just happened to be an Omega Man

Mark Hyman: Some of those men, do you remember their names, Trent, Weaver, Horne.....Frank Horn I think he's the housing man.

Founder Edgar A. Love: You caught me at a bad time, I don't remember so many.

Mark Hyman: That's a no no, that's alright.....we'll just talk ..we're just talking off the top about some of the things, just go on and just talk about Omega, Bishop my questions have expired here, we had about twenty and some of them were duplications.....but whatever you would like to say about the future of Omega, about the past of Omega, about Omega today anything that you would like to say you go right ahead.

Founder Edgar A. Love: We have got to some how or another put an end to too much politicking at our Grand Conclaves.....its natural in any organization to try to use influence but we've got to be.....we must not carry it too far because after a while you have a little trick here.....a trick there.....one trick younger than the other trick.....to defeat somebody else for some office in the Fraternity.....he wanted to be Grand Chancellor so bad that he was ready to disrupt the Fraternity to get himself elected and he defeated the reporting of the Constitutional Committee by calling for a role call vote on every portion put before the house and took forty five minutes for a role call.....well see how much time himself that so we couldn't get anywhere with the constitution and then on saturday when I made my final report I.....someone had been prompted to make a motion.....that we call our next Conclave a Conclave and Conventional Meeting and the first whole day would be given to the handling of the constitution and nothing else and we completed it at that time but he was there with his young turks and the.....championship football game but you see and they wanted to vote us down and voted for a constitutional convention to meet within the year and appropriated 15,000 dollars for this committee that the Conclave national organization would pay the way and expenses of all the undergraduates delegates to this Conclave all the delegates were invited to come but the graduate chapters would have to pay the expenses of their own delegates.....partners of young delegates in there and gave the constitution the way he wanted it.....I was ill at the time I couldn't go.....but I sent a two hundred word telegram black letter and I wish I had copy of it to read to you and they say when they read the telegram the house got up and cheered they say that took the house.....they weren't going to change anything.

Mark Hyman: What have been some of your personal triumphs within Omega over the 61 years?

Founder Edgar A. Love: I wouldn't call them triumphs, but highlights.

Mark Hyman: Alright highlights, we'll use highlights.

Founder Edgar A. Love: Have been the entertainment that have been held for me in the various cities to which I have gone and the lovely entertainment given to me and my wife and the plaques that the men have given me made me feel good some of them so heavy I can hardly lift them

THE OMEGA PSI PHI FRATERNITY INC.

INDEX SECTION

A

Abel's Fabulous 27(1967)-53
Adams, Michael-202, 210,224
Adams, Oscar W.-110, 146
Alpha Chapter- Howard University-d,11,16,
Alpha Kappa Alpha-4,16
Alexander, Clifford-91
Amprey, Walter G.-109,120,121,
Anderson, Floydel H.-72
Anderson, Gregory-230,
Anderson, Lewis-167,224
Anti Hazing Public Service Announcements-178
Atkins, Alston J.-17,146,
Argonne Forest-22
Armstead, Ray-135
Avery, James S.-c, 57,*65,71,71,72,76,85,215

B

Babridge, Leon-151,165
Baker, Thurbert T.-154,185
Bamiduro, Ademuyiwa-189,192
Barnwell, Marion-150, 174
Basie, William "Count"-136,145
Baylor, Curtis A.189,192
Beckley, David-109
Beckwith, Lynn-96
Beta Chapter- 16,58
Bell, Darryl L.150
Benjamin, Christopher E.-172,174
Bennett, Alonza-182
Bent, Inaki-199,
Bernard Jr. Lee A.., ii,, 178,217
Bernard, Gilliam-108
Berry, Albert G.72,156
Berry, Warren M.-81
Bess, Dylan-189,219
Birth, Frederick-72
Bishop, Mark A.-150
Blayton, Jesse B-48,51,56,104,107,119,124
Blunt, Carl A., 1,189,184,192,206,210,217,219,221, 222,
Bohannon, Otto-16
Bolden, Charles F. e,147,164,172,186,204, 217
Bowden, Steve R.167,174,178
Bowden, Frank W. Jr.-96

Bowers, Jr., Joseph F.-210,226
Boswell, Carrol G.-70
Body, Walter-199,210,21,2255
Boswell, Carroll G.-72
Boyd, Larry B.-80,168
Brassfiield, William C.-168, 174
Braynon, Edward,J.- 72,78,*94,101,109,110,208,
Brazeale, Anthony-136
Bridges, Edgar-109
Brooks, Charles-81
Brown, Chapel,A.M.E. Church227
Brown, Calvin L.160,168
Brown David A.-121
Brown, Henry-148
Brown Kenneth A.-110,145,150,201
Brown, larry A.-104,109
Brown, Manson-207
Brown, William E. Jr.-92
Bruce, Charles-174,192, 200,210
Bryant, Otis-90
Burks, Larry-192
Burnett, Edgar A.-71,80
Burton,Gerald L-97
Butler, Arnold-140
Butler, Ronald J.-168, 174
Burnett, Edgar A.-72,81
Byers, Charles R.-96

C

"Can't See The Forest For the Tree" -196
Campbell, William "Bill"-172
Carnegie Library, Howard university, 5
Capehart, Jr., Lymus D.189,192
Carrauthers, Michael-139
Carter, Alonzo Jr,139
Carter, Vince-209
Cashin, John L-71.
Challenger, Space Disaster, 1986, vi,138, 145,172
Chambliss, Jr. Charles D.-92,96,100,102,109
Chase,Horace W.-210
Cherry, Kevin-134,139, 182
Chicago University-28
Childers, Curt-219
Christ, Jesus - 3,
Christopher, Charles A.-150,166,205

Cipriani, Phillip A. Jr.-189.192
Clark, Gary-161
Clark Hall, Howard University, 5,16
Clarion Call-208,348
Clements, Edwrd-135
Clemons, Todd S.- 210
Clyburn, James E,-g,237
Coaches VS. Cancer Initiative-212
Cobb, William Montaque,181
Cole, Joe N. Sr.-121
Coleman, Frank- iv, xi, 2,7,9,10,16,2,41,59,72,123,213
Collins, Tony-161
Comeaux,William-184
Compulsory Grand Conclave Attendance-44
Cook, Harld J. -72,80,96
Cook, Sameul Dubois-99
Cook, Mercer W.-145
Cooper, Christopher M.-164, 168
Cooper, Oscar J.- iv xi, , 2,5, 6,9,10,16,21,44,72,86,213
Cooper, Willie May-235
Comer Darrel G.-121
Cornell University in Ithaca, New York.
Conclave Meeting Format Revision-113
Corbett, Ellis F. 42, 48,55,*57,72
Cosby, William (Bill)-g,59,61,219
Coulon, Burnel E.-174-iv,81,91,95,100,103,106,, 107,108,121,136,152,170,216
Council of Presidents National Pan-Hellenic Council Joint Position Statement on Hazing-182
Cromwell, John W. Jr.-80
Custom Converse Shoe Initiatve-221

D

Daniels, Robert-53
Dancy, Larry-227
Darmouth College-44
Davis, Arthur P
Davis, Corneal-78,80,96,100
Davis, Donald-189,92
Delta Chapter, 16
Dent, Thomas-207
Delagarde, Edouard-,174
DeVaugh, Gerald-201
Diabetes Testing-58
Dillard, Marvin-210
Douglass, Joseph R.-144
Dirden, Benjamin G-174.
District of Columbia-11

Dixon, Christopher-80
Dixon, Herbert B.-148
Drew, Charles R.-182
Dreer, Herman- v, xii, 4, 5,146,218
Drew, Charles R.-g, 1,187,175
Stanley Douglas-16
Alexander Dumas – 7, 9
Dubois, Samuel-99
Dubois, W.E.B., -b
Douglass, Joseph R.-147
Douglass, Stanley M.-91
Duncombe, Ferrel J.-160,168,189,192,210,224,227

E

Earles, Carl A. -42
"Economic Empowerment Bringing About Political and Social Change"-190,
Economic Summits-169
Edmond, Jr. Climent J.-223,*248
Edmonds, James III-153
Edouard, Delagarde T.-171
Elam, James- A.-g,165,171,182
Elam, James A. Auditoruim--180
Evers, Medgar-38
Epps, Gregory D.-189
Epps, John S. –c,121,134150,158, 165,171
Eyeball to Eyeball Test-69
Executive Secretary changed to Executive Director-153

F

Fairchild, Robert W.-134,157,163, 168,
Felder, James L. -42,79,80
Ferguson, Bob-207
Ferrell, H. Albiob-56,66,71
Fields, Charles-102,107,
Fisk University-16
Funn, Carlton A.-99
Ferguson, Earl K.-95
Franklin, Floyd-53
Franks, Leon-103,109
Fraternal Evangelism-130,
Freeman, Michael-168
Founders' Resting Places(location)-33
Fortune, Thierry-121

G

Gasden, Mithchell E.-96

Gadsden, Robert Washington-105
Gallman, James-176
Gaines, Clarence "Big House"-214
Garnett, Marion W. - 41,56,66,70,*80,81,83,96,111,119,176,205
Gibson, Raymond-150
Gill, Robert L. -v, xii, 4, 5
Gilmore, Sr. Tyrone C-136,*149,*149,153,160,168,157,208
Gipson, Alexander-224
Glaspie, Jr,, Henry W.-161
Glover, Nathaniel Jr.-183
Graham, Filmore-122
Grady, Marshal-96
Graves, Earl G.-g,62, 174,177,186,193
Grace, George H.-161,170,179,181,*189,192,210,2224
Grady, James A.-121
Grand Basileus Avery's Most Powerful Emotional Memory-74
Grand Basilei Comprehensive Review Committee(origin)-153,156,
Grand Basilei Rings * lapel pins (origin)- 153
Grand Basilei Video Interviews-218
Grand Basileus Sword & Shiel Publication-208,349
Grant, James-81
Tony Grant—g, 182, 191
Graves, Earl G.-61,87
Green, Jarvis-205
Greenup, Jeff-48
Gregory, Frederick D.-e,101,102,147
Greer, Theodore N.-96
Griffin, Andrew-166
Griffin, Sr. Jonathan N.-210,224,*249
Griffin, Ronald-168
Gundy, Brian S.-210,222,

H

Hall, George E -16
Hale,Kenneth L.-232
Hargrove, Jesse J.- ii.
Hargrave, Zoel, Jr.-72
Harris, Rayfield L170.
Harvey, Steve-179,217
Hamilton, Terrance L.-161
Hampton, Willa Mae Cooper
Harper, Joseph W.-121
Harry, Charles E,-89
Harris, Donald F.-137

Hart,, Benjamin L.-193,199,210,213
Hatcher, John-176
Hatchett, Joseph Woodrow-90,96
Hastie, Willie 17
Hastie, William H.- vii,90,91,97
Hayes, Roland,91
Health-O-Rama-73
Henry, Charles D-66,70,71,78,80,87
Hester, Robert H.-95,100
High, Jesse L.-120,121
Higginbotham, Leon Aloyisus-99,177,186
Hill, Oliver-97,120
Hill, Jesse Jr.-146
Hinchen, Willie F.-212,223,*249
Hoffler, William H.-137
Hoggs, Sean P.-236
Holliday, Harold Sr.-121
Holmes, Charles-168
Holmes, Clarence F.-16,87,92,
Holmes, Robert-216, 227
Hood, Stafford- ii
Hooks, Benjamin- vii,91,93, 97131,
Hornbuckle, Donald R. – 1,
Horner, Ulysses W.-109
Howard University -6
Howze, Joe D.-147
H.Rap Brown-38
Hughes, Langston-59,60m
Hughes, Ronald J.161
Hurricane Katrina-197
Hurrican Rita-200
Hunley, Maurice T.-96,100,103,109,110
Hunter, William L.-81

I

Iles, Mark A.-120,121
Industrial School State College-23

J

Jackson, Sr. Jesse L. – vii-42,120,127,,131, 143, 146
Jackson, Henry, F.-167,170
Jackson, Keith R.-223,*249
Jackson, Mark E.-161,210, 224,248
Cary D. Jacobs-42,48,49,51,*80
Jacobs, John-120,146,
Jackson State College 1969 Lamps-63
James A. Elam Auditorium-171
Jarvis, Green-217
Jefferson, Robert J.-81
Jenkins, Melvin L.-174

Jenkins, Richard E.-109
Jeffers, Benjamin-189,192
Jesus Christ,-3
Jewell, Tommy-175
John H. Williams Museum-194,217
Jordan, Albert L.-174
Jordan, James "Scappy"-224,*248
Jordan, Lloyd J.,-96, 101,103,109,150, 153,166,167,169,*173, 208
Jordan, Michael-140,144,150, 177,185,219,
Jordan, Vernon L.-76,137,146
Johnson, Charles- 212
Johnson, Lyndon B. -53
Johnson Milton-72,165
Johnson, Milt-150
Johnson, Ralph E.-157
Johnson, Samuel W. -72
Johnson, Vernon- 121, 127
Johnson, Walter-162
Jones, Ed "Too Tall" -91,207
Jones, Richard-181
Jones, William "Parlez Vous"
Julian, Dr. Percy-87
Charles FraserJust-23
Just, Earnest E.- iv, xi, b,7,9,8,17, 21,23,158,183,,213
Mary Mathews Just-24
Julian, Percy-89,214
Junius, Jesse-210

K

Kappa Alpha Psi Fraternity Inc- 4
Kennedy, John F.-38
Kennedy, Robert-40
King, Martin Luther-38,40,41,42
Knox, Antonio F.-189,192, 201, 210,225
Knox, Kurmmel W.-150,192

L

Lane, James C.-150, 1535148,
lambda Xi Chapter-91
Lambda Epsilon Chapter-102
Lampados Club Initiative-208
Leverette, Emory Lewis-105
Lawrence, Clarence-166
Lawrence, Curtis-217
Lawrence, Robert H.-e,f, 60,100
Leadership Conference,2007-214

Lee, Warren G.-a,80, 161,164,168,182,53,189,192,198,203,* 207,210,223,228
Lewis, Byron-182
Lewis, Edward-182
Lewis, Derek-193
Lewis, Ricky L.-160,168
Lightner, Clarence E. -76
Life Memebership Program-76
Lincoln Memorial Cemetery -32
Lincoln University, 6,16
Littlejohn, Walter-109
Livingston, Benjamin L.-96, 103,109,110,111,116, 119,120,134,136,194,204
Lee, Warren G., v, - 5,79,80,157,162,202,210
Leverette, Emory Lewis-104
Long,Ralph Sr., -80
Love, Edgar A.- iv, xi,1,2, 6,9,10,20,21,22,45,72,82,84,86,101,2 13
Julius Love- 20
Susie C. Love-20
Looby, Alexander Z.-59,76
Lyles, Michael- 1,219

M

Mack, Astrid K.-137
Mack, Rayford-227
Malcolm X-37
Omega's Leadership Summit for Male Undergraduates-215
Mandated Programs-375
Mann, Thomas J.-127,147
Martin, William D.-42
Mathews, Glenn A.-210
Mathis, Edgar L.181,192
Maule, Albert-81
Mays, Benjamin E.-62,97
McCain, Will III-71
McClain, Julius Scotland-90
McClarrin, Otto-72
McDaniel, Norman A. Lt. Col-59
McDaniels, Robert-53
*McKee,Adam 2,153,148,161*167*
McKinney, George K.-150
McKoy-James-210,222
McMorris, Jr,, Bennie M.- 101,103,107
McMillian William A.-83,104,116
McMorries, James C -16
McMorris, Bennie-100
McNair, Ronald E. vi,e,100,101,141, 144,172

THE OMEGA PSI PHI FRATERNITY INC. 441

McNair, Steve-21,46,219
McPhatter, Thomas-72
Meeks, Kenrick B.-203
Meares, George E.-48, 50,*52,54,55,56,89
Meharry University-16
Merchant, Phillip-224
Membership Selection & Education Program(1985)-132
Methodist Epicopal Church-20
Mitchell, Peter L.-159,174
Miller, Jr. Dorsey C. .-51,120,126, 150,151,155,*159,160167,175,170,208,225,236
Miller, Dorsey C. III-172
Stewart, Pelton-120
Miller, Gregory-80
Miner, the Hall of 249Manual Arts,
Miro Octavio-224,
Mitchell, Peter L.-161,168
Mokhtar, Tamer Ahmed-168
Montgomery, Thomas-165
Moore Clifton,-71,80,96,100
Moore, Darryl, G-157
Moore, John H.-66,72,79
Morgan College-22, 38
Morant, Edward C.-224,*249
Morris Clearthur-137
Morris, Thomas D.-55
Moses, Henry-73
Mosley, William E.-204
Mt Auburn Cemetery, Baltimore, MD-32
Moultrie, Carl H-g. 18,42,48,51,56,71,72,76,80,92,100,109,121,121,137,170,
Mourning,, Alonzo-219
Mullins, James-103
Murray, Milo Cravath-90
Mu Phi Chapter-104

N

NAACP-38, 53, 172, 176
Napper, James W.-170
Nabrit, James-96
Nasty Q Dog Image-124
National Urban league-120
Neal, Delvert T. 159
Neal, Keith K.-b, 174,215
Neal, Keath W.-171
Nelson, Sr. Herbert J.-62
Newman, TC-197
Newton, I. Gregory-*42,43
Norman, Conrad M.-136

Norman, Moses C.-h,81,96,103,109, ,110,119,120,*129,131,135,138,141, 148, 150,208,
Nu Omicron-148
Nuesom, Daniel B.-99

O

Obama, Barack-237, 238,239
Omega's Census Bureau Partnership-181
Omega Charity Honors-219
Omega's Communication Czar-212
Omega's Comprehensive Review Committee-156
Omega's Co-Sponsoring of Mid-eastern Athletic Conference Basketball Tournament-215
Omega Dear Hymn-17
Omega Development Corp.170
Omega's First Economic Summit,(1997)-169
Omega's First Academic Chair Endowment-116
Omega's First Surgeon General-205
Omega's First Undergraduate Summit,(1998)-170
Omega Friendship Foundation-170,188
Omega Life Membership Foundation-123,-134
Omega Men in the Civil Rights Struggle 2008 Birmingham Exhibit-225
Omega Political Summit-190
Omega Psi Phi Fraternity Federal Credit Union-135, 159
Omega's 75th Grand Conclave-135
Omega's Supportof UNCF Schools-113
Omega World Center-150, 164
Omega's Youth Economic Summit-193
Omega's Youth leadership Conference-146
O'Neal, Shaquille-219,
Operation Big Vote-93
Ortiz, Dewey-223,*249
Owens, James-170
Osimetha, Clement M.-155,150,

P

Palmer, Zeldrix Jason-168,
Parnham, Michael-96
Parris, Terrel D. 174,,189,192,

Patterson, Kenneth-189
Payton, Fred B.-122
Pearson, Colone-230
Peevy, Charles C.-210,224,*249
Penn, Harry T.-90
Pennsylvania University -28
Peterson, James A.-168
Pettaway, Collin-227
Pettrie, Harry L. 48
Pi Chapter-164
Pickerron, Carlton-214,224,*248
Pinn, Melvin-167,178
Pittman, Aubrey "Nick"189,192
Pi Xi Chapter-91
Phillip Jr., Cipriani-189,192
Pullen, Don J.-17
Poindexter, Hildrus-214
Pointer, Dwight E.-189,192
Portis, Cedric A.-155
Powell, Jamin-224
Priest, James Alfred-102
Price, Aaron E.-172, 174
Prince, Samuel-96
Project Aspiration-73
Project for the Perpetuation of the Black Male-164
Project Uplift-69
Pruitt, Audrey-51
Psi Psi Chapter's 1971 Lampados Club-72
Pullen, Don Q.-18, 131
Purnell, John Henry-92

Q

R

Rankin Memorial Chapel, 6
Rashad, Ahmad-219
Ratcliff, Billy-139, 155
Ray, Andrew-137
Reeder, Robert "Pete"-1032,103,109,115
Reynolds, Al-110
Reynolds, Grant-iv
Rice, Fred, Jr.-127
Rice, Glenn E.-214,*249
Rice, Melvin-79
Riddick, Walter H. -42,48,51,56,75,77
Ridley, Walter N.-99
Roach, Louis Charles-83,87
Roach, Max-233
Rolle, Kevin- ii,219
Robinson, Isaiah-189
Robinson, Lenord A.-174,177

Robinson, Howard-227
Robinson, Raymond G. -16
Robinson, Robert L.-174
Robinson, Virgil-164, 168,
Rockwell, Willie-148,155
Rosier, Alcindor R.-166, 172,174,192
Russel, Rodney J.-157
Rustin, Baynard-39,40,121
Rutherfore, Jerry, W.-178

S

Salley, John-219
Sanders, Joseph C.-177,185
Sciene Hall, Howard University, 5
Scott, John H.-160,177,
Scott, Lincoln C. -56
Sears,Lewis J.-137
Sears, Thomas-136
Sellars, Cleveland-62
Selma to Montogmery Voting Rights March and 2008 Tour-226
Senior Citizen Highrises-58
Shaq-209
Shedd, Nevil-214
Shelton, Charles B.B.-181,184
Shepard, Samuel R.-80, 82,84,96,99,109
Shoffner, Robert S.-122
Shute, Marcus W.-172,192
Sickle Cell Anemia-80
Smiley, Ricky-220,225
Smith Darnell 100
Richard (Dick) Smith iv,150,155,170,189,192,229
Smith, George A.-203
Smith, Jeffrey T.-210
Smith, Patrick B. ii
Smith, Richard-148,
Smith, Richard (Dick-157,219,
Smith, Vernon G.-150
Smith, Wendel V.-174
Smith, Willie A.-109,121,135,139
Spears, Henry A.-150,176
Spiller, Owseley G-96
Spottswood, Robinson-97
Spruill, J. Franklin-66,70
Stewart, Pelton-122
Stomp The Yard Movie-230
Stomp Out Dope Initiative-69
Stop The Violence Initiative-214
Stroud, , Gerson L. -56
Stafford,Thomas jr.-189,192
Strawbridge, Joseph-150,165
Stevens, Mark E.-157,

Streeter, Hayves-81
South Carolina Partnering Project-188, 215
Swinson, James-224
Suggs, Joseph "Jake"-203
Sutton, Will Jr.-122

T

Taylor, Brice-214
Taylor, Eddie H., iii, 233
Taylor, Richarl L.-66,68,76,80
Taylon, Kenneth M.-103,109,108,121,132,136
Theta Rho chapter, Frankfurt Germany-58
The Life Membership Story/Origin-77
The Supreme Basileus Of the Universe Speaks-35
Thirkield, Wilbur P. - 8, 9,11,13,14, 15
Tilford, Walter J.-80
Tillery, Raymond-150
The African Project-165
The 74th Grand Conclave-210
The 75th Grand Conclave-225
The Great Debaters-232
The First Undergraduate Summit-176
The History Book Committee-ii, iv,211,
Thomas, Jarrett A.-137
Thompson, Harold D.-53
Thompson, Stafford-192
Three Looks, One Focus: Family/Fraternity/Friends-208
Thurman, Howard,-75
Tilford, Walter J.-79
Tolson, Melvin-232
Torre, Joe-220
Trammel, Terrence-220
Trent, John Spencer-87
Tucker Jr, Herbert E., iii, 49, 80, 231
Tucker, Erin-172
Tucker, Robert H.-74
Turner, Oscar-78
The Supreme Basileus of Universe ,13

U

Usry, James L.-147

V

Vance, Reginald E.- 1,219,444
Vaughn, Maurice "Mo"-220
Vick, William-176
Vosges Mountai-, 22

W

Wade, Cameron-81,121,132,139
Walker, Leroy T.-89,176,
Walker, Mathew Sr.-75 100
Walker, William O.-59
Walls, Larry D.-70
Walton, Elbert A. Jr.-110,120
Ward, William E. "Kip"-169,194,204, 217,235
Washington, Anthony-189
Washington DC Headquarters—39,166
Washington, Johnnie D.-137
Washington, Melvin-71,79,96
Weakley, Vernon Steve - a, b, 5,d,73,87,214,217,219
Weaver, Frederick Sr.-114
Weaver, Robert C.-44,60,61
Weaver. L.P. George-44
West Alvin,-66,70
Westley, L.A.-176
Wilder, Douglas l.-141,150,182
Wilkins, Roy-130, 146,
Willis, Lee Grantlin-109
Willis, Vaughn M.-200
Wilson, S. Earl-175,182,186,189,203
Wilson, S.M. "Chucky"-164,177
Woodson, Carter G,-98
WRECKING-162
Wrenn, Walter F, III-121
Wright, Carl-136
Wright, Willie J.-99
White Marsh Memorial Park, Ambler, PA,-32
White, Wilson-189,192
Wilder, L. Douglas vii, 146
Wilkins, George-150
Wilkins, Roy vii,58
Williams, Frank C.-121,155
Williams, John H.-194, 215,216,215
Williams, Joseph T.-210
Williams, Leroy C.-121
William & Mary, College of- 3
Williams, Mandrid N.-192
Williams, Robert C.-150
Winkler, Finus L-56
Woodard, S.P.-109
Woodson, Carter G. 98,128, 133,
Worth, Charles-202,210

Wrenn, Walter F.-121,165, 166
Wright, Andy-157
Wright,Carl-136
Wright, Jeremiah A.-236
Wright, Willie J.-98

X

Xi Pi,-96

Y

Young, Col. Charles-121,136,141,155,214
Youth Leadership Conference-143, 146, 226, 423

Z

Zellars, Calvin C.-160
Zeno, Melvin C.-121,135,139,174,178,
Zeta Omega Chapte142, r-170

THE END
<><><><>

OMEGA PSI PHI FRATERNITY INC.

MANHOOD<>SCHOLARSHIP<>PERSEVERANCE<>UPLIFT

THE HISTORY OF
OMEGA PSI PHI FRATERNITY INC.

AN UPDATE
FROM 1960 TO 2008

BY
VERNON (BOP SWALOS) WEAKLEY
PROJECT CHAIRMAN & CHIEF AUTHOR
****

LONG LIVE OMEGA PSI PHI FRATERNITY INC.
AND THE DREAM OF ITS BELOVED FOUNDERS!!!

MAY GOD SAVE, PROTECT AND MAINTAIN THIS
GREAT ORGANIZATION THAT IS MAKING A POSITIVE
DIFFERENCE IN THE LIVES OF
BLACK PEOPLE!

ABOUT THE CHIEF AUTHOR

Vernon (Bop Swalos) Weakley was initiated into Omega Psi Phi Fraternity at Jackson State University, Upsilon Epsilon (YE) Chapter December 05, 1969.

Vernon Steve Weakley is also the author of the nationally acclaimed books," Standing At The Edge Of Madness" and "Fear No Evil." These books are published by ZWORLDNET PUBLISHING and can be found at book stores all across America and internet book providers such as Amazon.com, Books a Million.com, and Barnes & Noble.com. They can also be found on www.zworldnet.com.

Vernon Steve Weakley has written several successful books and numerous short stories that have brought him acclaim throughout America. He has had major book signings in Washington DC, New York, New Jersey, Atlanta, Indiana, Arkansas, North Carolina, Virginia, Texas, Mississippi and all across the South.

Vernon Steve Weakley has received many awards and recognitions for his outstanding literary work as well as his many other life accomplishments. Among Mr. Weakley's many accomplishments is the fact that he is officially recognized by the CONGRESSIONAL BLACK CAUCUS as an OUTSTANDING author with a powerful, positive message for the world. As a result of his tremendous meritorious accomplishments in the literary field, Mr. Weakley has been a featured author at several CONGRESSIONAL BLACK CAUCUS Expos in Washington DC.

Vernon Steve Weakley is often asked to do book signings and is also an excellent motivational speaker. He can be reached at 281 589 9178 or by email at Zworldnet@aol.com.

" When my life is over Lord. When this old life is through! I want to be satisfied that FOR YOU, I have done the best that I can do. My most powerful life question is, "Is the Master satisfied with me?" And then deep in my soul, God smiled, Jesus nodded yes in agreement and the Holy Spirit chuckled knowingly that he had done his job. (Comforting, guiding, protecting and representing me) before the Heavenly Father.
A poem by Vernon (Bop Swalos) Weakley

THE OMEGA PSI PHI FRATERNITY INC. 447

THIS SECTION IS FOR MEMBERS OF OMEGA PSI PHI FRATERNITY INC. ONLY

THIS BOOK IS THE PROPERTY OF OMEGA MAN

Print Name: _____
Signature: _____

I was officially initiated into Omega Psi Phi Fraternity Inc. on:
Date_____ Hour_____ Minute_____ Second_____ in
Chapter_____ at
Location_____
My Omega sponsor was_____
My mentor is_____
My line had _____ brothers on it. Our line name was_____
I was number_____ on my line. My line brothers were:

The chief officiating Omega man for my line ceremony was_____, his
title was_____

AUTOGRAPHS_____
_____
_____
_____

ALL PRAISE BE TO THE SUPREME BASILEUS OF THE UNIVERSE FOR BLESSING ME AND GIVING ME THE GIFT OF BEING A GOOD OMEGA MAN!

THE HISTORY
OF THE
OMEGA PSI PHI
FRATERNITY INC.

A BROTHERHOOD OF EXCEPTIONAL MEN OF LIKE ATTAINMENT

AN UPDATE
1960 TO 2008

THIS UPDATE WAS WRITTEN AND ORGANIZED
BY
VERNON STEVE WEAKLEY

THIS REVISION IS PUBLISHED BY
ZWORLDNET PUBLISHING INC.

~ THE END ~

CPSIA information can be obtained
at www.ICGtesting.com
Printed in the USA
LVHW051142070321
680781LV00001B/3